Book 1

Literature & Comprehension

Writing Skills

Language Arts

Lesson Guide

Book Staff and Contributors

Beth Zemble   *Director, Alternative Learning Strategies; Director, English Language Arts*
Marianne Murphy   *Senior Content Specialist*
Amy Rauen   *Senior Instructional Designer*
Miriam Greenwald, Mariana Holliday, Lenna King, David Shireman, Sandra Smith   *Instructional Designers*
Mary Beck Desmond   *Senior Text Editor*
Anne Vogel   *Text Editor*
Suzanne Montazer   *Creative Director, Print and ePublishing*
Sasha Blanton   *Art Director, Print and ePublishing*
Carol Leigh   *Print Visual Designer*
Stephanie Shaw Williams   *Cover Designer*
Anna Day   *Director, Instructional Design for Language Arts and Humanities*
Joshua Briggs, Tim Mansfield, Lisa Moran   *Writers*
Amy Eward   *Senior Manager, Writers*
Susan Raley   *Senior Manager, Editors*
Alden Davidson   *Senior Project Manager*
David Johnson   *Director, Program Management Grades K–8*

Maria Szalay   *Executive Vice President, Product Development*
John Holdren   *Senior Vice President, Content and Curriculum*
David Pelizzari   *Vice President, K¹² Content*
Kim Barcas   *Vice President, Creative*
Laura Seuschek   *Vice President, Assessment and Research*
Christopher Frescholtz   *Senior Director, Program Management*

Lisa Dimaio Iekel   *Director, Print Production and Manufacturing*
Ray Traugott   *Production Manager*

Credits

All illustrations © K12 Inc. unless otherwise noted
Red fox. © Vladimir Chernyanskiy/Bigstock.com

About K12 Inc.

K12 Inc., a technology-based education company, is the nation's leading provider of proprietary curriculum and online education programs to students in grades K–12. K¹² provides its curriculum and academic services to online schools, traditional classrooms, blended school programs, and directly to families. K12 Inc. also operates the K¹² International Academy, an accredited, diploma-granting online private school serving students worldwide. K¹²'s mission is to provide any child the curriculum and tools to maximize success in life, regardless of geographic, financial, or demographic circumstances. K12 Inc. is accredited by CITA. More information can be found at www.K12.com.

978-1-60153-301-2
Printed by RR Donnelley & Sons, Roanoke, VA, USA, May, 2015

Contents

Literature & Comprehension

Writing Skills

K¹² Language Arts Purple

General Overview

K¹² Language Arts Purple lays a strong foundation for readers and writers. A well-balanced Language Arts program provides instruction on understanding the meaning of the words on the page (comprehension) as well as putting words on the page (writing). According to the National Reading Panel, a comprehensive reading program includes fluency, text comprehension, spelling, vocabulary, and writing skills. K¹² Language Arts Purple provides this instruction through five separate-yet-related programs.

You will spend about two hours a day working with Language Arts Purple. The tables describe the programs, the time you can expect to spend on them, and the overarching big ideas that are covered.

Program	Daily Lesson Time (approximate)	Online/Offline
K¹² Language Arts Purple Literature & Comprehension	50 minutes	Lessons may be all online, all offline, or a combination, moving from online to offline.

Big Ideas

- *Fluency*   The ability to decode text quickly, smoothly, and automatically allows readers to focus on comprehension.

- *Comprehension*   Comprehension is the reason why we read. Reading strategies are conscious plans that readers apply and adapt to make sense of text. Comprehension requires readers to actively think, ask themselves questions, and synthesize information to make meaning from their reading. There are a variety of strategies that proficient readers employ to make sense of text, and these strategies should be actively practiced, self-evaluated, and reinforced.

- *Analysis and Interpretation*   Comprehension is a prerequisite to analysis. Following comprehension of literal meaning, readers must read "between the lines" to understand how an author creates meaning. Readers must pay careful attention to organizational structure, language, and literary elements to appreciate the underlying meaning or message of an author's work.

- *Application and Evaluation*   The ability to apply and evaluate what one has read demonstrates not only comprehension, but also the ability to think critically about ideas. Readers need to synthesize, draw conclusions about, evaluate, and interpret what they have read. Readers must be able to make connections between and among the texts that they have read and relate what they read to the world around them.

- *Enjoyment*   To develop a lifelong love of reading, readers should independently read for their own enjoyment.

Program	Daily Lesson Time (approximate)	Online/Offline
K[12] Language Arts Purple Spelling	15 minutes	Each unit: 4 offline lessons, 1 online review
Big Ideas		

- Spelling represents sounds, syllables, and meaningful parts called *morphemes*.
- The spelling of all English words can be explained by rules or patterns related to word origins.

Program	Daily Lesson Time (approximate)	Online/Offline
K[12] Language Arts Purple Vocabulary	10 minutes	All online
Big Ideas		

- Vocabulary words are words we need to know to communicate and understand.
- A *speaking vocabulary* includes the words we know and can use when speaking.
- A *reading vocabulary* includes the words we know and can read with understanding.
- A *listening vocabulary* includes the words we know and understand when we hear them.
- A *writing vocabulary* includes the words we know and understand when we write.
- The more we read, the more our vocabulary grows.
- Early learners acquire vocabulary through active exposure (by talking and listening, being read to, and receiving explicit instruction).

Program	Daily Lesson Time (approximate)	Online/Offline
K¹² Language Arts Purple Writing Skills	35 minutes (Days 1–90) 45 minutes (Days 91–180)	Lessons may be all online, all offline, or a combination, moving from online to offline.

Big Ideas

Composition

- Developing writers should study models of good writing.
- The study of writing models provides students with opportunities to read, analyze, and emulate good models.
- Writing can be broken out into a series of steps, or a process, that will help developing writers become more proficient.
- Teaching the writing process encourages students to organize their ideas before they write and to revise their work after they write.
- Writing varies by purpose and audience. The specific reason for writing and the writer's intended readers (audience) determine the correct form and language to use.
- Following a specific organizational structure is a useful tool for novice writers; however, writers require the freedom and flexibility to follow their ideas to completion.
- Writing requires thought and planning.
- Writers must be able to articulate a main idea and support it with appropriate details.
- All writers revise, and revision is best performed in discrete tasks.
- Good writers carefully check their work for errors.
- To improve, writers require frequent practice.

Grammar, Usage, and Mechanics (GUM)

- To be effective communicators, writers and speakers should recognize and use complete sentences.
- Sentence combining—teaching students to construct complex, sophisticated sentences—is an effective instructional strategy and an important element in learning to write well.
- Using different kinds of sentences helps writers and speakers express their ideas accurately.
- A noun is a basic part of speech. Understanding nouns gives students a basic vocabulary for building sentences and understanding how language works.
- Recognizing and using action verbs helps writers make their work specific and interesting to readers.
- Using pronouns to take the place of some nouns helps writers avoid repetition.
- The use of descriptive adjectives can turn an ordinary piece of writing into one that enables the audience to form clear mental pictures of a scene.
- Using a wide range of adverbs allows a writer to convey specific information about how, when, where, or why an action occurs.

Program	Daily Lesson Time (approximate)	Online/Offline
K[12] Language Arts Purple Cursive Handwriting	10 minutes	All offline
Big Ideas		

- Instruction in posture, pencil grip, and letter formation improves students' handwriting skills.
- Proper modeling of letter formation is imperative for developing handwriting skills.
- Students who have formal instruction in handwriting are more engaged in composition writing.

Structure

Literature & Comprehension, Spelling, Vocabulary, Writing Skills, and Cursive Handwriting are independent programs that work together to give students a complete, well-balanced education in Language Arts.

1. **Literature & Comprehension** Students read independently in a variety of genres—fiction, poetry, drama, and nonfiction—to suit diverse tastes. Students are expected to apply comprehension strategies before and during their reading. Activities emphasize literal and inferential comprehension, analysis, evaluation, and application. There is a balance among oral, written, and project work. Students work on literal and inferential comprehension lessons, as well as those lessons that are designed to emulate standardized test-taking formats.

2. **Spelling** Students learn to focus on spelling patterns that are necessary to be fluent, proficient readers, writers, and spellers.

3. **Vocabulary** Students increase their vocabulary by learning the meanings of groups of conceptually related words. Vocabulary skills help students read and compose written material.

4. **Writing Skills** Students study writing models and then use the writing process to write a variety of compositions. They learn about grammar, usage, and mechanics skills and apply those skills as they revise and proofread their work. In addition, students work on language, vocabulary, spelling, and writing-strategy skills in lessons that are designed to emulate standardized test-taking formats.

5. **Cursive Handwriting** For the first half of the year, students practice cursive handwriting at a pace that meets their needs. For the second part of the year, students may continue to practice handwriting skills as they complete written work in other programs.

Flexible Lesson Planning

A key aspect of K[12] is the flexibility we offer students. Doing things that work best for them is vital to students' mastery. The structure of K[12] Language Arts Purple, with the separate programs, allows you to work on one skill at a time, which gives you flexibility. You will be able to

▸ **Find content more easily.** The descriptive titles, both in the lesson lists online and in the Lesson Guide, allow you to find lessons and activities quickly.

▸ **Manage progress more easily.** You can track progress, mastery, and attendance by program so you can see at a glance how a student is progressing in each. This tracking will allow you to better customize your schedule to meet students' needs.

▸ **Pace work appropriately for students.** The focused lessons enable you to identify skills that students need to spend more or less time on and make adjustments. You can decide the pace that works best for students in each program. For example, a student may work through two Vocabulary lessons at a time but need to spend some extra time on Writing Skills.

▸ **Control your own schedule.** You can arrange lessons to meet your needs.

TIP Get to know the different lesson types and then set up your lesson schedule in the best way for you and your students.

How to Work Through a Lesson

Preview and Prepare

1. **Prepare in advance** by scheduling time to plan at the beginning of each week and before each school day. You may want to look ahead at any assessments or writing assignments so you know what students are working toward in each unit.

2. **Check the Lesson Guide or the online lesson** to see the lesson plan and read any instructions for completing the lesson.

3. **Complete Advance Preparation** before you begin a lesson. Look for Advance Preparation in the Lesson Guide or the online lesson.

4. **Preview the Lesson Guide** so that you are prepared to provide support during the offline activities. You may also want to preview the online lesson and the word lists for Vocabulary.

5. **Gather the materials** listed in the Lesson Guide or the online lesson before you begin. You should always have paper and pencil available in addition to any other materials that are listed.

6. **Set up the workspace** for offline activities or move students to the computer to complete online activities.

TIP You might want to check the materials and Advance Preparation for the week in addition to reviewing them before each lesson so you know of any materials or tasks that may require some extra time or planning. For example, you may need to plan a trip to the library to get a book or go to the craft store for special materials.

Where to Begin?

For programs with both online and offline components, there is more than one way to begin a lesson. Either way will get you where you need to go.

Beginning Online If you begin from the online lesson, the lesson screens will walk you through what you need to do, including gathering materials and moving offline if necessary.

- ▸ If the lesson begins with online activities, students will need to come to the computer to complete them.
- ▸ If the lesson begins with offline activities, gather the materials listed and begin the activities described in the lesson plan with students when you're ready.

Beginning Offline You may choose to begin a lesson by first checking the lesson plan for the day in the Lesson Guide. The table on the first page of the lesson plan will indicate whether the lesson begins with online or offline activities.

- ▸ If the lesson begins with online activities, students will need to move to the computer to complete them.
- ▸ If the lesson begins with offline activities, gather the materials listed and begin the activities described in the lesson plan with students when you're ready.

Complete Activities with Students

Offline Activities During offline activities, you will work closely with students away from the computer. Follow the instructions in the Lesson Guide for completing these activities.

Online Activities Online activities take place at the computer. At first, you may need to help students learn how to navigate and use the online activities. You may also need to provide support when activities cover new or challenging content. Eventually, students will complete online activities with minimal support from you.

Work with Students to Complete Assessments

Offline Assessments   Students will complete offline assessments in Literature & Comprehension, Writing Skills, and Spelling. After students complete the assessments offline, you will need to enter assessment scores in the Online School.

Online Assessments   Students will complete online assessments in Literature & Comprehension, Writing Skills, and Vocabulary. Because these assessments are online, the computer will score them for you. You do not need to enter these assessment scores in the Online School.

Track Progress in Portfolios

K[12] recommends keeping students' work samples in a portfolio as a record of their progress. A simple folder, large envelope, or three-ring binder would work. Place offline assessments, unit project pages, compositions, Activity Book pages, and handwriting samples in the portfolio. Look back through the portfolio monthly and at the end of the year with students. Celebrate their progress and achievements.

How to Use This Book

K[12] *Language Arts Lesson Guide* contains information that will be helpful to you as you begin K[12] Language Arts Purple and on a daily basis as you work through the programs. Here is what the Lesson Guide contains and how to use it:

Lesson Guide Contents	What To Do with It
Overviews of each of the programs included in K[12] Language Arts Purple, including instructional philosophies, materials, and unit and lesson structure for the programs	• **Read the overviews** of the programs as you begin K[12] Language Arts Purple. • **Refer to the overview** information if you have questions as you work through the programs.
Glossary of key terms used in Literature & Comprehension and Writing Skills	• **Use the keywords list** in the back of the book any time you need to look up a keyword used in Literature & Comprehension or Writing Skills.
Lesson plans for teaching • Literature & Comprehension lessons • Writing Skills lessons	• **Scan the unit and lesson overviews** for the lessons you will be working on each day. • **Follow the instructions** in the lesson plans to complete the activities with students. • **Use the answer keys** to check students' work on Activity Book pages and offline assessments.

Following are examples of the unit overview, lesson overview, and activity instructions that you will see in the lesson plans for teaching a Literature & Comprehension or Writing Skills lesson.

Unit Overview

There is one unit overview page per unit.

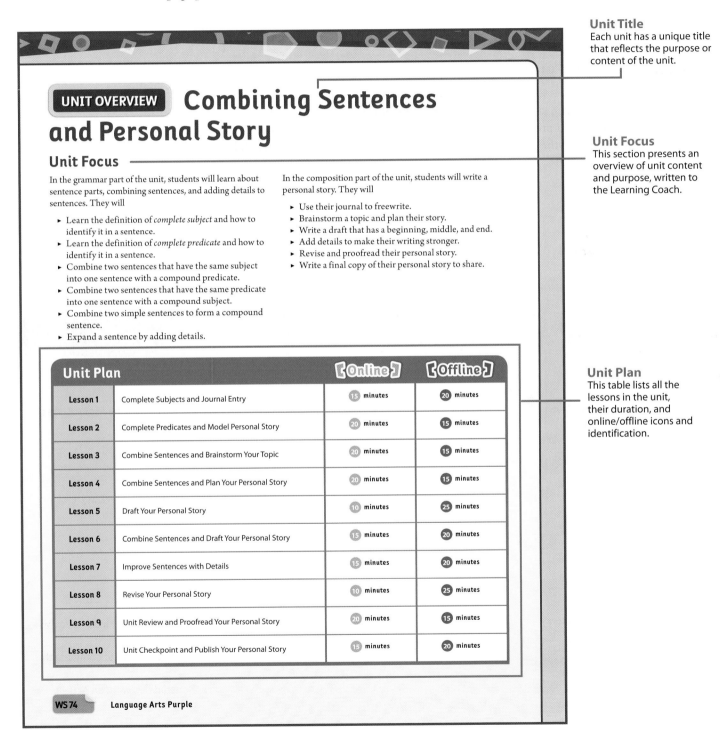

UNIT OVERVIEW **Combining Sentences and Personal Story**

Unit Title
Each unit has a unique title that reflects the purpose or content of the unit.

Unit Focus

In the grammar part of the unit, students will learn about sentence parts, combining sentences, and adding details to sentences. They will

- Learn the definition of *complete subject* and how to identify it in a sentence.
- Learn the definition of *complete predicate* and how to identify it in a sentence.
- Combine two sentences that have the same subject into one sentence with a compound predicate.
- Combine two sentences that have the same predicate into one sentence with a compound subject.
- Combine two simple sentences to form a compound sentence.
- Expand a sentence by adding details.

In the composition part of the unit, students will write a personal story. They will

- Use their journal to freewrite.
- Brainstorm a topic and plan their story.
- Write a draft that has a beginning, middle, and end.
- Add details to make their writing stronger.
- Revise and proofread their personal story.
- Write a final copy of their personal story to share.

Unit Focus
This section presents an overview of unit content and purpose, written to the Learning Coach.

Unit Plan		Online	Offline
Lesson 1	Complete Subjects and Journal Entry	15 minutes	20 minutes
Lesson 2	Complete Predicates and Model Personal Story	20 minutes	15 minutes
Lesson 3	Combine Sentences and Brainstorm Your Topic	20 minutes	15 minutes
Lesson 4	Combine Sentences and Plan Your Personal Story	20 minutes	15 minutes
Lesson 5	Draft Your Personal Story	10 minutes	25 minutes
Lesson 6	Combine Sentences and Draft Your Personal Story	15 minutes	20 minutes
Lesson 7	Improve Sentences with Details	15 minutes	20 minutes
Lesson 8	Revise Your Personal Story	10 minutes	25 minutes
Lesson 9	Unit Review and Proofread Your Personal Story	20 minutes	15 minutes
Lesson 10	Unit Checkpoint and Publish Your Personal Story	15 minutes	20 minutes

Unit Plan
This table lists all the lessons in the unit, their duration, and online/offline icons and identification.

WS 74   Language Arts Purple

Lesson Overview

Each Literature & Comprehension and Writing Skills lesson has a lesson overview page.

Lesson Title
The title indicates the lesson topic.

Lesson Overview Table
This table has an overview of the lesson's activities, their approximate times, and whether they take place offline or online.

This section of the lesson overview page includes Advance Preparation, Big Ideas, and Content Background, if any, that you need to know.

Advance Preparation
This information is what you need to prepare before beginning the lesson.

Big Ideas
Students will work toward these major organizing ideas in Language Arts.

Content Background
You might need this information to help you better understand the content you will be teaching.

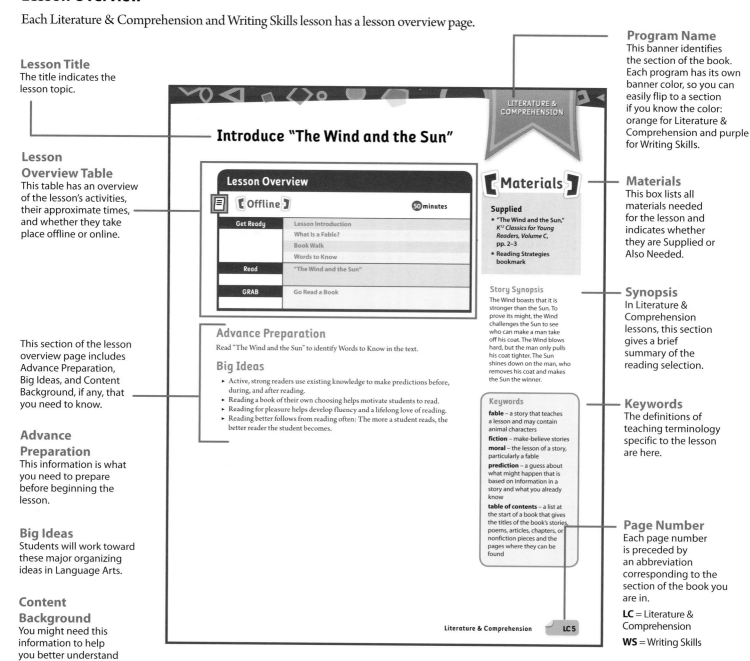

Introduce "The Wind and the Sun"

Lesson Overview

📋 🕐 Offline 🕐   50 minutes

Get Ready	Lesson Introduction
	What Is a Fable?
	Book Walk
	Words to Know
Read	"The Wind and the Sun"
GRAB	Go Read a Book

Advance Preparation
Read "The Wind and the Sun" to identify Words to Know in the text.

Big Ideas
- Active, strong readers use existing knowledge to make predictions before, during, and after reading.
- Reading a book of their own choosing helps motivate students to read.
- Reading for pleasure helps develop fluency and a lifelong love of reading.
- Reading better follows from reading often: The more a student reads, the better reader the student becomes.

LITERATURE & COMPREHENSION

Materials

Supplied
- "The Wind and the Sun," *K¹² Classics for Young Readers, Volume C,* pp. 2–3
- Reading Strategies bookmark

Story Synopsis
The Wind boasts that it is stronger than the Sun. To prove its might, the Wind challenges the Sun to see who can make a man take off his coat. The Wind blows hard, but the man only pulls his coat tighter. The Sun shines down on the man, who removes his coat and makes the Sun the winner.

Keywords
fable – a story that teaches a lesson and may contain animal characters
fiction – make-believe stories
moral – the lesson of a story, particularly a fable
prediction – a guess about what might happen that is based on information in a story and what you already know
table of contents – a list at the start of a book that gives the titles of the book's stories, poems, articles, chapters, or nonfiction pieces and the pages where they can be found

Literature & Comprehension   **LC 5**

Program Name
This banner identifies the section of the book. Each program has its own banner color, so you can easily flip to a section if you know the color: orange for Literature & Comprehension and purple for Writing Skills.

Materials
This box lists all materials needed for the lesson and indicates whether they are Supplied or Also Needed.

Synopsis
In Literature & Comprehension lessons, this section gives a brief summary of the reading selection.

Keywords
The definitions of teaching terminology specific to the lesson are here.

Page Number
Each page number is preceded by an abbreviation corresponding to the section of the book you are in.

LC = Literature & Comprehension

WS = Writing Skills

Activity Instructions

Lesson plans in the Literature & Comprehension and Writing Skills sections of the
Lesson Guide include detailed instructions for each activity.

Program Name
This banner identifies the section of the book. Literature & Comprehension has an orange banner and Writing Skills has a purple banner.

Activity Type
This label tells you what kind of activity you are working on.

Activity Description
This text describes what will happen in the activity. For offline activities, it provides step-by-step instructions. Answers are in magenta text.

Objectives
These learning goals indicate what students should be able to do as a result of the lesson.

Activity Book Page Answer Key
A miniature version of the Activity Book page is included in the Lesson Guide, with answers to help you check students' work.

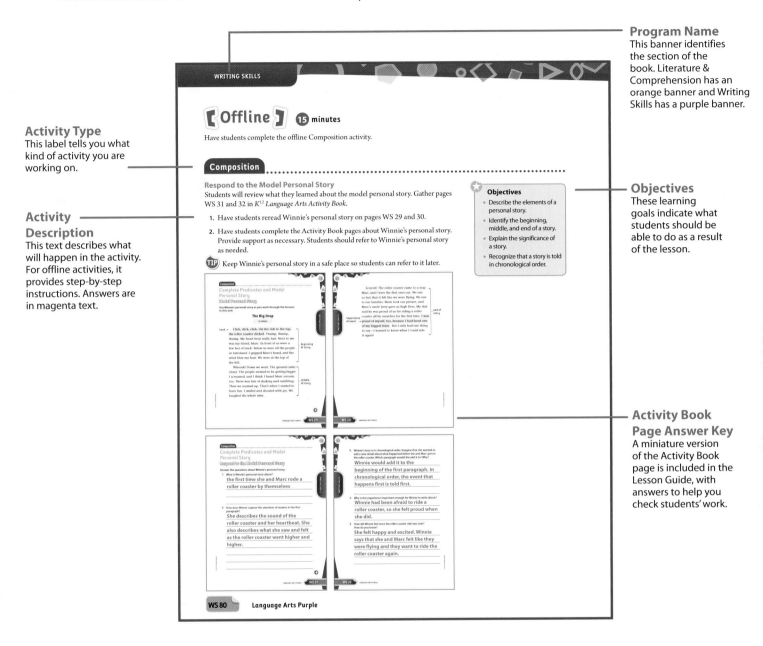

Look for Icons

The lesson plans contain icons to help you quickly see key elements as you work through the lesson. Look for these icons as you use the lesson plans.

Icon	Description
🖥 [Online]	Shows that an activity is online.
▤ [Offline]	Shows that an activity is offline.
(TIP)	Offers additional advice to help you explain the content.
✏	Appears next to activities that provide students with the opportunity to practice their handwriting.
🏵	Indicates that students have reached a milestone that should be rewarded, usually by adding a sticker to the My Accomplishments chart.
➕ OPTIONAL:	Indicates that an activity is optional.
⮌ Learning Coach Check-In	Indicates an opportunity for you to check in on students' work or progress before they continue.

(TIP) Use a bookmark or a sticky note to mark the lesson that you are working on in Literature & Comprehension and in Writing Skills. These markers will help you quickly find the page you need each day.

My Accomplishments Chart

Research shows that rewarding students for quality work can increase their motivation. To help you reward students, you will receive a My Accomplishments chart and sticker sheet for use throughout K[12] Language Arts Purple. This chart gives students a tangible record of their progress and accomplishments throughout Literature & Comprehension, Spelling, Vocabulary, and Writing Skills. There is also extra space that you can use to track progress for other accomplishments, such as reading additional books, if you wish.

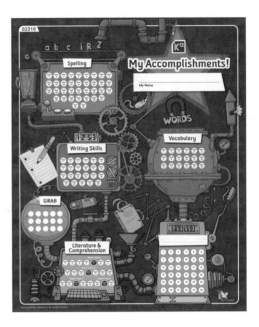

Help students proudly display and share their accomplishments with others by placing the chart somewhere visible, such as on the refrigerator or wall. Throughout the lessons, look for the reward icon 🎖, which indicates when and where students should place a sticker on the chart. Encourage students to set goals and watch their stickers accumulate. Praise students to help them understand the connection between their own growing skill set and the My Accomplishments chart. (For specific information about how to use the chart in each program, see the My Accomplishments Chart section in the individual program overviews.)

K[12] My Journal

Research demonstrates that emerging writers are more motivated and become more confident when writing about self-selected topics. Journal writing allows young writers to explore and express themselves in a nonthreatening environment and make connections to their present knowledge. You will receive K[12] My Journal for use throughout K[12] Language Arts Purple. Students will use the journal as they complete some lessons in Writing Skills, but they can also use the journal to write on their own. The journal has three sections that students will use as they work through lessons or on their own.

- ▶ **Writing Skills** has prompts that students will use to freewrite and make connections to the things that they learn as they complete the lessons in Writing Skills. When appropriate, students may use their freewriting as the basis for their assigned composition.
- ▶ **Thoughts and Experiences** has prompts to help students start writing. Students can use the pages in this section at any time.
- ▶ **Ideas** has blank pages, without prompts, on which students can write freely on topics of their choice. Students can use the pages in this section at any time.

K¹² Language Arts Purple Literature & Comprehension Overview

Program	Daily Lesson Time (approximate)	Online/Offline
K¹² Language Arts Purple Literature & Comprehension	50 minutes	Lessons may be all online, all offline, or a combination, moving from online to offline.

Structure and Materials	
22 units that vary in length and structure, depending on the number and length of literary selections • 11 units of fiction, nonfiction, and poetry • 4 Reader's Choice units • 5 Critical Skills Practice units • 2 Semester Review and Checkpoint units	**Materials** • *K¹² Language Arts Lesson Guide* • *K¹² Language Arts Activity Book* • *K¹² Language Arts Assessments* • *K¹² Classics for Young Readers, Volume C* • *K¹² World: Weather or Not* • *George Washington: Soldier, Hero, President* • *The Glory of Greece* • Reading Strategies bookmark

Philosophy

K¹² Language Arts Purple Literature & Comprehension engages students in classic works of literature from various genres. Works are grouped thematically to help students see the connections among texts or genres. The program requires students to read often, think critically about what they have read, and evaluate the ideas and apply the skills they have learned.

The scaffolded approach to each reading selection requires students to prepare for reading by activating prior knowledge, read independently, comprehend what they have read, analyze the language or structure of the text to find its meaning, evaluate the ideas in selections and form substantiated analyses about them, and apply the ideas or skills they have learned to other texts or to the broader world. This consistent pattern—from inward knowledge to outward application—is developed through the lesson activity structure, which is designed to help students model the habits of mind to make them proficient and critical readers, writers, and communicators. The pyramid represents the skills—from lower- to higher-order thinking skills—that students encounter in each lesson and unit in Literature & Comprehension. With each lesson and reading experience, students begin at the foundation of the pyramid and work their way through the lessons and unit, tackling increasingly complex questions and assignments that require them to use higher-order thinking skills.

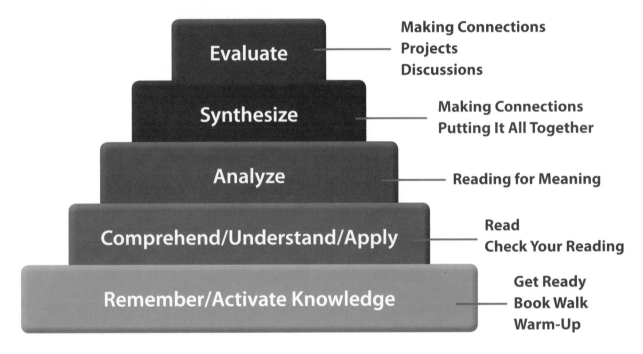

Evaluate
- Making Connections
- Projects
- Discussions

Synthesize
- Making Connections
- Putting It All Together

Analyze
- Reading for Meaning

Comprehend/Understand/Apply
- Read
- Check Your Reading

Remember/Activate Knowledge
- Get Ready
- Book Walk
- Warm-Up

TIP Look in the first lesson of the first unit of this program for more information about the different approaches to reading in K[12] Language Arts Purple.

Overview of Literature & Comprehension Lessons

Materials

The following materials are supplied for Literature & Comprehension:

K¹² Language Arts Lesson Guide

K¹² Language Arts Activity Book

K¹² Language Arts Assessments

K¹² Classics for Young Readers, Volume C

K¹² World: Weather or Not

The following trade books are also supplied:

▶ *George Washington: Soldier, Hero, President* by Justine and Ron Fontes
▶ *The Glory of Greece* by Beth Zemble and John Holdren

Also included in your materials is a GRAB (Go Read a Book) bag where students can store their reading materials. Encourage them to keep a list of all the works they complete and praise their efforts.

You should always have paper and pencils available. You will also need the following general materials to complete Activity Book pages:

- ► crayons or coloring pencils
- ► glue
- ► scissors (Safety note: When students are working with scissors, please supervise them to make sure they use their scissors safely and stay seated.)

Additional materials, ranging from index cards to library books, may be needed for certain lessons.

Using the Activity Book

Keep in mind that students will write in and tear out pages from the Activity Book; you may want to store loose Activity Book pages in a three-ring binder. Remember to build students' portfolios with completed Activity Book pages.

(TIP) Look for instructions in Advance Preparation and tips within activities for saving and gathering materials that get used in more than one lesson.

Unit Structure

Literature & Comprehension consists of 22 units: 17 Literature & Comprehension units and 5 Critical Skills Practice units. Each lesson within each unit should take about 50 minutes to complete.

- ► **Literature & Comprehension units**   In these units, students focus on reading selections from *K¹² Classics for Young Readers, Volume C*, an anthology; *K¹² World: Weather or Not*, a nonfiction magazine; the trade books *George Washington: Soldier, Hero, President* and *The Glory of Greece*; and the Reader's Choice book list. The number of lessons in a unit varies and the lessons themselves have different combinations of activities, but the activities include prereading, reading, and postreading instruction.

- ► **Critical Skills Practice units**   In these units, students read a variety of passages and practice answering questions similar to those found on standardized assessments, including multiple choice and extended response (writing to a prompt) items. Students read and answer questions about fiction, nonfiction, forms, instructions, poetry, and paired passages. Each unit contains five lessons, with four instructional lessons and one Unit Checkpoint lesson.

Lesson Activities

Lesson plans in the Literature & Comprehension section of this Lesson Guide include detailed instructions for each activity. Literature & Comprehension activity types include the following:

- **Get Ready (Offline or Online)**   The Get Ready activities prepare students for that day's reading selection and lesson. They include a brief overview of the lesson, instructions to help students build background knowledge, and strategies needed for comprehension or to activate their own prior knowledge or experience. Prereading activities include discussions and becoming familiar with the text through the Book Walk and review of Words to Know, words from the selection with which students should become familiar.

- **Warm-Up (Online)**   Students listen to a model of a text being read aloud and then record themselves reading that same text aloud. The text usually is one they have read in the previous lesson. The purpose of this activity is for students to demonstrate their reading fluency—their pace and ability to read text fluidly and with proper expression. Fluency is a prerequisite to comprehension. This activity is a regular feature of the first semester. By the end of the first semester, proficient readers will not require a model of fluent reading.

- **Read (Offline)**   Students read the selection using the comprehension strategies they have reviewed in the Get Ready. **Note:** Watch for **Learning Coach Check-In** opportunities in these activities. You check in with students after they read and ask a few basic questions (which are provided) to ensure that students comprehend the reading selection.

- **Read (Online)**   A second type of **Read** activity appears in Days 91–180. In this activity, students record themselves reading aloud a text they have not seen previously. The purpose of this activity is for students to demonstrate their reading fluency. Unlike the Warm-Up activity in the first semester, this activity does not include a model of fluent reading.

- **GRAB (Offline)**   GRAB stands for Go Read a Book. Research indicates that dedicated, daily reading (of works of one's own choosing) helps develop reading fluency skills and a lifelong habit of reading.

- **Check Your Reading (Online)**   Students answer online multiple choice questions to demonstrate literal and inferential comprehension of the reading selection. In most cases, these questions require students to know what happened in the selection or to identify elements of the selection. These questions become more difficult as the year progresses, requiring students to apply terms and ideas learned in earlier units to later selections.

- **Reading for Meaning (Online)**   Students develop a deeper understanding of the reading selection through application of comprehension strategies and analysis of the selection. These activities have both instruction and practice components. Students may be asked to refer to the reading selection as they go through these activities.

- **Making Connections (Offline)**   Students apply the reading selection information and strategies learned from lessons. They also evaluate the selection and communicate their ideas using textual evidence in support of statements. This activity often involves students' making a connection between and among texts or between the text and themselves or the larger world. This activity may or may not have an Activity Book page.

- **OPTIONAL Beyond the Lesson (Offline)**   This activity is for students who have extra time and interest in exploring the reading selection further. Beyond the Lesson activities are not required and can be skipped.

- **OPTIONAL Peer Interaction (Offline)**   You lead a discussion with students about the reading selection. Ideally, students should discuss their reading with their peers. Peer Interaction activities are not required.

- **Putting It All Together (Offline)**   Students apply information, skills, and strategies learned during the unit. This activity often involves students making a connection among the texts read in the unit. This activity may or may not have an Activity Book page. You score students' work using a checklist and enter the results online.

- **Performance Review (Online)**   You listen to the recordings that students have made during the Warm-Up or Read activities and score students' reading fluency using a checklist. This activity is optional in the first semester but is required in the second semester.

- **Semester Review (Online and Offline)**   Students review skills to prepare for the Semester Checkpoint.

- **Unit and Semester Checkpoints (Online and Offline)**   Students apply the skills learned in the program as they read fiction, nonfiction, and poetry selections. Critical Skills Practice units include a Unit Checkpoint, which tests the skills students have learned in the unit. A Semester Checkpoint covers the concepts learned in the entire semester.

- **More Practice (Online)**   After each Checkpoint, activities are provided to aid review and to practice areas where students may need extra work.

- **Learn (Online)**   In Critical Skills Practice units, students learn strategies for analyzing and responding to various types of questions similar to those found on standardized tests, including answering objective multiple choice questions and responding to a writing prompt. Though students learn the strategies as they particularly relate to the testing formats, the reading, writing, and comprehension skills are taught elsewhere in the course.

- **Try It (Online)**   In Critical Skills Practice units, students practice using skills by completing online exercises. These questions give students experience answering the kinds of items found on common standardized assessments.

My Accomplishments Chart

Rewards in Literature & Comprehension are tied to completing units. When students complete a unit, have them add a sticker for that unit to the My Accomplishments chart.

Reader's Choice Units

Throughout K[12] Language Arts Purple Literature & Comprehension, Planning and Progress in the Online School will alert you to an approaching Reader's Choice unit. These units are designed to give students an opportunity to choose books to read while fine-tuning their comprehension skills. Research indicates that providing opportunities for choice enhances performance and motivates early readers.

In each of the Reader's Choice units, you and your students will select a work from a bank of possible texts. K[12] suggests that you discuss the possible texts with students to guarantee that they will read the texts that interest them. Reader's Choice units are 11 lessons each. There are three important differences from other units in the program.

1. **You will need to acquire these texts on your own, through a library or bookstore.** To help you choose a text for a Reader's Choice unit, K[12] includes a brief synopsis of the story and information about grade and interest level. If you have difficulty locating a work, try your local library. The older works are time-honored classics. Newer works should be readily available online.

2. When you have selected the text, you will be prompted to *print* the accompanying lesson guide and activity pages. **You must print these pages because they are not provided in this Lesson Guide or the Activity Book.**

3. To keep students engaged, deepen comprehension, and develop public speaking capabilities, they are required to complete a unit project as part of each Reader's Choice unit. There are eight possible unit projects that students can choose to complete. Detailed instructions for creating, grading, and presenting each unit project can be found in the online support materials for each Reader's Choice unit. **Once students have chosen which project they will complete, you must print the applicable unit project pages because they are not provided in this Lesson Guide or the Activity Book.**

K¹² Language Arts Purple Spelling Overview

Program	Daily Lesson Time (approximate)	Online/Offline
K¹² Language Arts Purple Spelling	15 minutes	Each unit: 4 offline lessons, 1 online review
Structure and Materials		
36 units with 5 lessons each	**Materials** • *K¹² Spelling Handbook*	

The Spelling materials are separate from the K¹² Language Arts Purple materials, so you will not find Spelling lesson plans in *K¹² Language Arts Lesson Guide* or activity pages in *K¹² Language Arts Activity Book*. Please refer to *K¹² Spelling Handbook* for all materials related to the program.

K¹² Language Arts Purple Vocabulary Overview

Program	Daily Lesson Time (approximate)	Online/Offline
K¹² Language Arts Purple Vocabulary	10 minutes	All online
Structure and Materials		
18 units with 10 lessons each	**Materials** • *K¹² Language Arts Vocabulary Word Lists* Online Book	

Vocabulary is entirely online. Students will work through the online lessons with your supervision. You can access the word lists for all the units from the online lessons.

K¹² Language Arts Purple Writing Skills Overview

Program	Daily Lesson Time (approximate)	Online/Offline
K¹² Language Arts Purple Writing Skills	35 minutes (Days 1–90) 45 minutes (Days 91–180)	Lessons may be all online, all offline, or a combination, moving from online to offline.

Structure and Materials	
23 units that vary in length and structure • 17 Writing Skills units • 4 Critical Skills Practice units • 2 Semester Review and Checkpoint units	**Materials** • *K¹² Language Arts Lesson Guide* • *K¹² Language Arts Activity Book* • *K¹² Language Arts Assessments* • *K¹² My Journal*

Philosophy

Learning to express one's ideas in writing is a fundamental requirement of an educated person. K¹² Language Arts Purple Writing Skills prepares students to express themselves as educated people in the twenty-first century. Grammar, Usage, and Mechanics (GUM) lessons teach students the nuts and bolts of communicating in standard written English. Knowing how to form strong sentences, use verbs and subjects that work together correctly, and capitalize and punctuate their writing without distracting errors helps students communicate their ideas in an understandable way. Composition lessons teach students how to put their ideas together in a form that is appropriate for their purpose and audience. Students will learn how to plan, write, revise, and proofread their writing so that their ideas are presented effectively for their readers. Most Writing Skills units encompass both GUM and Composition.

Grammar, Usage, and Mechanics (GUM)

What Is It?   The grammar, usage, and mechanics lessons give students practice as they learn about sentences and the parts of sentences, including the subject and predicate. They learn about using the eight parts of speech—nouns, verbs, pronouns, adjectives, adverbs, conjunctions, prepositions, and interjections—in sentences. They learn how to use verb tense so that they can express their thoughts in a logical manner, and they discover how capitalization and punctuation marks aid in conveying the message of sentences.

Why We Do It   While it is true that knowing grammar does not make someone a good writer, understanding how grammar works makes writing easier. When students understand basic grammar skills such as how to write a complete sentence, what kind of punctuation is used within a sentence and at the end of a sentence, and which words need capital letters, they can spend their time focusing on ideas. When the focus is on ideas, not on mechanics, writing becomes more fluent and expressive.

Composition

What Is It?   In composition lessons, students do a great deal of writing to practice presenting their ideas fluently and expressively. To help students' writing become more fluent and expressive, each Writing Skills unit begins with a lesson that includes journal writing. Journal writing allows students to freewrite—to write what they want and as much as they want with the knowledge that journal writing is ungraded. Journal writing also helps students warm up for the rest of the composition unit, where they will explore a model that presents the form of writing they will be doing. It might be a narrative, an informational piece, an opinion, a letter, or a research report. During the rest of the unit, students see how one student brainstorms ideas, chooses a topic, makes a plan for writing, drafts, revises, proofreads, and finally publishes the writing as they then do the same with their own writing. In addition, some units end with an oral presentation, where students can hone their speaking skills and choose media to enhance their presentation.

Why We Do It   Research shows that daily writing practice is essential for the developing writer. The lessons are based on a process-writing model of instruction. Research demonstrates that engaging in a variety of prewriting techniques (such as freewriting in a journal or brainstorming) and planning activities (using graphic organizers or outlines) helps novice writers learn to transform their ideas into organized writing. Throughout each unit, students practice skills in discrete stages, and they ultimately write a polished piece of writing that is ready to be "published" or shared. Students learn that the writing process is not a straight line forward and that writing always means rewriting for improvement. As you help students through these lessons, encourage them to express their thoughts and ideas. Student writing is not adult writing. Expect errors in sentence structure and mechanics, but encourage students to express their thoughts in written form.

Overview of Writing Skills Lessons

Materials

The following materials are supplied for Writing Skills:

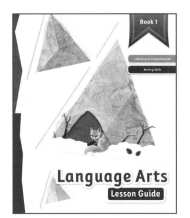

K¹² Language Arts Lesson Guide

K¹² Language Arts Activity Book

K¹² Language Arts Assessments

K¹² My Journal

You should always have paper and pencils available for students. You will also need the following general materials to complete some assignments:

▶ craft materials (crayons or coloring pencils, glue, scissors, and so forth) (Safety note: When students are working with scissors, please supervise them to make sure they use their scissors safely and stay seated.)

▶ 3½ x 5-inch index cards

Using the Activity Book

Students write in and tear out pages of the Activity Book, so periodically place the Activity Book pages in a student writing portfolio. In addition, save students' graphic organizers, drafts, and published compositions in the portfolio to keep track of their growth as writers. Consult the portfolio regularly and keep it as a record to share with teachers. Also, share the work with students so that they can see the progress they have made and celebrate it. Remember that student writing is not adult writing. Do not expect perfection, but rather look for progress over time and clarity of thought and intent.

The Activity Book contains pages with examples of different types of writing or other kinds of materials that students refer to over the course of a unit. Look for tips in the Lesson Guide alerting you to store these materials for further use. Be sure to keep these pages in a safe place so you can easily find and refer to them.

TIP Look for instructions in Advance Preparation and tips within activities for saving and gathering materials that get used in more than one lesson.

Using the Journal

As students complete Writing Skills lessons, they freewrite about topics and ideas in *K¹² My Journal.* Specific instructions in the Lesson Guide help students get started and encourage their writing. Students may use the Thoughts and Experiences and Ideas sections of the journal to write on their own.

TIP You can print additional copies of the journal pages used in the Writing Skills lessons from the online lessons.

Unit Structure

Writing Skills consists of 23 units: 19 Writing Skills units and 4 Critical Skills Practice units. For Days 1–90, lessons should take about 35 minutes to complete. For Days 91–180, lessons should take about 45 minutes to complete.

▶ **Writing Skills units**   In these units, students learn grammar, usage, and mechanics (GUM) skills, write compositions, and complete related projects or presentations. The number of lessons in a unit varies and the lessons themselves have different combinations of activities, but the activities generally include both GUM and composition instruction.

▶ **Critical Skills Practice units**   In these units, students review a variety of writing strategies and language, vocabulary, and spelling skills. They practice answering questions similar to those found on standardized assessments, including multiple choice and extended response (writing to a prompt) items. Students read and answer questions about such topics as main idea and supporting details, purpose and audience for writing, sentences and parts of sentences, subject and verb agreement, prefixes and suffixes, synonyms and antonyms, homophones, and spelling vowel suffixes. Each unit contains five lessons, with four instructional lessons and one Unit Checkpoint lesson.

Lesson Activities

Lesson plans in the Writing Skills section of this Lesson Guide include detailed descriptions or instructions for each activity. Writing Skills activity types include the following:

- **GUM (Online/Offline)** Online GUM activities provide instruction and practice in grammar, usage, and mechanics concepts. Offline GUM activities, found on Activity Book pages, provide additional practice.

- **Composition (Online/Offline)** Online composition activities introduce the composition assignments and model the steps needed to complete them. Offline Composition activities allow students to apply what they've learned by taking writing assignments through the entire writing process, from prewriting to publishing. Students also complete freewriting activities by responding to prompts in their journal during some offline Composition activities. **Note:** Watch for **Learning Coach Check-In** opportunities in some of the Composition activities. After students have finished a first draft of their composition, you have the opportunity to print a feedback sheet from the online lesson and use it offline to share with students the strengths and weaknesses of their writing. Each feedback sheet is customized for the particular type of composition students are writing. By sharing your responses to students' writing, you not only provide ways that students can improve their writing, you also give students confidence through the positive feedback you include.

- **OPTIONAL Beyond the Lesson (Offline)** Students with extra time have an opportunity to complete additional entries in *K¹² My Journal*. Beyond the Lesson activities are not required and can be skipped.

- **Skills Update (Online)** Students complete a few short exercises to check the GUM skills covered in the previous lesson. If students struggle with the exercises, suggestions for review activities are provided. Completion of these activities is strongly encouraged before continuing with new concepts.

- **OPTIONAL Peer Interaction (Offline)** Most composition assignments include a Peer Interaction activity, in which students share their writing with a peer or anyone else willing to give feedback. Students can benefit from this interaction by using the feedback to revise their work, as appropriate. Peer Interaction activities are not required.

- **Unit and Semester Review (Online)** Units with GUM content include an online activity as an opportunity to review and practice the GUM skills students have learned in preparation for the Unit Checkpoint. A Semester Review covers the GUM and Critical Skills Practice concepts learned in preparation for the Semester Checkpoint.

- **Unit and Semester Checkpoints (Online)** Units with GUM content and Critical Skills Practice units include a Unit Checkpoint, which tests the skills that students have learned in the unit. A Semester Checkpoint covers the GUM and Critical Skills Practice concepts learned in the entire semester.

- **Write Now (Offline)** Composition assignments end with students completing the assignment that they have been planning, drafting, and revising throughout the unit or over multiple units. You evaluate students' writing on a three-point scale for purpose and content, structure and organization, and grammar and mechanics. Sample papers (available online) help evaluate the strength of the writing and areas in which students can improve.

- **More Practice (Online/Offline)** After Unit Review, Semester Review, Unit Checkpoint, Semester Checkpoint, and Write Now, activities are usually provided to aid review and to practice areas where students may need extra work, along with links to access these materials.

- **Get Ready (Online)** In Critical Skills Practice units, the Get Ready is a short activity to prepare students for the skills that they will learn in the lesson. Often the Get Ready draws on students' previous knowledge or builds background knowledge in preparation for the skill.

- **Learn (Online)** In Critical Skills Practice units, students learn strategies for analyzing and responding to various types of test questions, including answering multiple choice questions and responding to a writing prompt.

- **Try It (Online)** Students practice using the skills that they have learned by completing online exercises.

My Accomplishments Chart

Rewards in Writing Skills are tied to completing both Unit Checkpoints and Write Now assignments satisfactorily. When students score 80 percent or higher on a Unit Checkpoint and/or when students' writing achieves "meets objectives" in all three categories on the grading rubric, have them add a sticker for that unit to the My Accomplishments chart.

If students score lower than 80 percent on a Unit Checkpoint, review each Checkpoint exercise with them and work with them to correct any exercises they missed. If students' composition work scores "does not meet objectives" in any category, help them review and revise their work to achieve "meets objectives."

K¹² Language Arts Purple
Cursive Handwriting Overview

Program	Daily Lesson Time (approximate)	Online/Offline
K¹² Language Arts Purple Cursive Handwriting	10 minutes	All offline
Structure and Materials		
18 units with 5 lessons each	**Materials** • *Cursive Handwriting* • *3rd Grade Cursive Teacher's Guide* • lined paper	

Philosophy

K¹² supplies the proven Handwriting Without Tears® program for students in kindergarten through grade 3. This gentle, multisensory approach focuses on careful practice at a pace that suits students' fine motor skills development.

The Handwriting Without Tears website (www.hwtears.com) is full of helpful tips, demonstration videos, and other resources. **Use the passcode found on the cover of the *3rd Grade Cursive Teacher's Guide*** to create an account and gain access to A Click Away. There you will be able to use the Digital Teaching Tools, A+ Worksheet Maker, and Screener of Handwriting Proficiency. In addition, visit www.hwtears.com/k12 for information on ordering supplemental materials and teaching aids.

Overview of Cursive Handwriting Lessons

Materials

The following books and materials are supplied for Cursive Handwriting:

► *Cursive Handwriting*
► *3rd Grade Cursive Teacher's Guide*
► one package of specially lined writing paper for Handwriting Without Tears
  If you need more of this paper, the following options are available:

  ► Online lesson openers provide a handwriting sheet that you can print and photocopy.
  ► You can order more wide double-lined notebook paper directly from Handwriting Without Tears at http://www.hwtears.com/.

These materials are separate from *K¹² Language Arts Lesson Guide* and *K¹² Language Arts Activity Book*.

Lesson Structure

K[12] Cursive Handwriting is entirely offline and uses the supplied Handwriting Without Tears materials. Before beginning the program, become familiar with *3rd Grade Cursive Teacher's Guide*. The guide includes a Teaching Guidelines chart to help you plan students' handwriting lessons.

In each lesson, you work with students for 10 minutes. (You may want to set a timer for 10 minutes; most students enjoy the Cursive Handwriting program, so it's easy to lose track of time and do too much in one day.)

Students should complete as many workbook pages as they can, picking up where they left off during the previous Cursive Handwriting lesson and continuing from there. They are not expected to complete a set number of pages during the 10-minute lessons. Be sure to monitor students' writing time so you can help them develop good letter formation habits.

Depending on students' pace, the workbook should provide about eight weeks of instruction. Move as quickly or as slowly as students need. When students have completed the workbook, have them use the packaged lined writing paper from Handwriting Without Tears to practice their handwriting. Also look for the Handwriting icon throughout the Lesson Guide. This icon indicates that the associated activity provides a perfect opportunity to practice proper handwriting, and if students pay careful attention to their handwriting, this time can also count as Cursive Handwriting time.

Literature & Comprehension

Lessons Learned

Unit Focus

In this unit, students will have an introduction to Language Arts Purple: Literature & Comprehension. They will then get started in their studies by reading three fables and considering how the events in the fables teach readers a lesson. In the course introduction, students will learn about

- The books used in the course
- The kinds of lessons
- The structure of the course, including both offline and online lessons
- The kinds of activities they will do, such as reading, writing, and projects

Unit Plan		[Online]	[Offline]
Lesson 1	Introduction to Literature & Comprehension	20 minutes	30 minutes
Lesson 2	Introduce "The Wind and the Sun"		50 minutes
Lesson 3	Explore "The Wind and the Sun"	40 minutes	10 minutes
Lesson 4	Introduce "The Bundle of Sticks"		50 minutes
Lesson 5	Explore "The Bundle of Sticks"	40 minutes	10 minutes
Lesson 6	Introduce "Why the Larks Flew Away"		50 minutes
Lesson 7	Explore "Why the Larks Flew Away"	40 minutes	10 minutes
Lesson 8	Reflections on Lessons Learned	varies	50 minutes
Lesson 9	Your Choice		50 minutes

Introduction to Literature & Comprehension

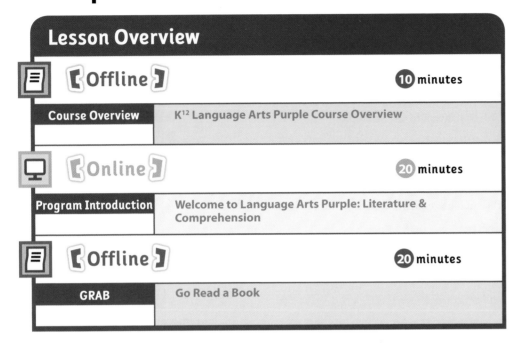

Lesson Overview

[Offline]   ⏱ **10** minutes

Course Overview	K¹² Language Arts Purple Course Overview

[Online]   ⏱ **20** minutes

Program Introduction	Welcome to Language Arts Purple: Literature & Comprehension

[Offline]   ⏱ **20** minutes

GRAB	Go Read a Book

Materials

Supplied
- Reading Strategies bookmark

 **minutes**

Review the K[12] Language Arts Purple Course.

Course Overview

K[12] Language Arts Purple Course Overview
Read the information on pages x–xxi and xxii–xxviii in *K[12] Language Arts Lesson Guide* if you have not already done so. Go to page xx to get started.

Objectives
- Understand the general course overview and structure in K[12] Language Arts Purple.

Online **20** **minutes**

Work **together** with students to complete the online introduction to Language Arts Purple: Literature & Comprehension.

Program Introduction

Welcome to Language Arts Purple: Literature & Comprehension
Go online to view with students the introduction to Literature & Comprehension to learn how to navigate through the program and help students successfully complete their learning journey.

Objectives
- Navigate the K[12] Language Arts Purple Literature & Comprehension program online.

 **20** **minutes**

Students will read a book or magazine of their own choosing.

GRAB

Go Read a Book
Have students read a book or magazine of their own choosing for at least 20 minutes. Remind them to use the strategies on their Reading Strategies bookmark before and during reading to help them understand the text.

Research demonstrates that extensive and regular reading is critical to the development of reading proficiency. Students who read more gain more general language skills, such as vocabulary development and familiarity with more complex syntactic structures. These skills, in turn, help them become even better readers. Simply stated: The more students read, the better readers they become.

Objectives
- Read literature independently and proficiently.
- Read a variety of texts for information and pleasure.
- Evaluate reading strategies.
- Use before-reading strategies.

Introduce "The Wind and the Sun"

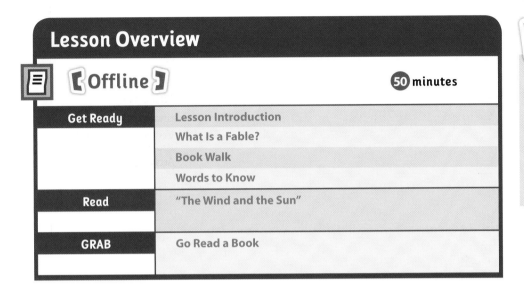

Lesson Overview

[Offline]   50 minutes

Get Ready	Lesson Introduction
	What Is a Fable?
	Book Walk
	Words to Know
Read	"The Wind and the Sun"
GRAB	Go Read a Book

Advance Preparation

Read "The Wind and the Sun" to identify Words to Know in the text.

Big Ideas

- ▶ Active, strong readers use existing knowledge to make predictions before, during, and after reading.
- ▶ Reading a book of their own choosing helps motivate students to read.
- ▶ Reading for pleasure helps develop fluency and a lifelong love of reading.
- ▶ Reading better follows from reading often: The more a student reads, the better reader the student becomes.

[Materials]

Supplied

- "The Wind and the Sun," *K¹² Classics for Young Readers, Volume C,* pp. 2–3
- Reading Strategies bookmark

Story Synopsis

The Wind boasts that it is stronger than the Sun. To prove its might, the Wind challenges the Sun to see who can make a man take off his coat. The Wind blows hard, but the man only pulls his coat tighter. The Sun shines down on the man, who removes his coat and makes the Sun the winner.

Keywords

fable – a story that teaches a lesson and may contain animal characters

fiction – make-believe stories

moral – the lesson of a story, particularly a fable

prediction – a guess about what might happen that is based on information in a story and what you already know

table of contents – a list at the start of a book that gives the titles of the book's stories, poems, articles, chapters, or nonfiction pieces and the pages where they can be found

[Offline] 50 minutes

Work **together** with students to complete offline Get Ready, Read, and GRAB activities.

Get Ready

Lesson Introduction

Prepare students to read "The Wind and the Sun."

1. Explain to students that before they read "The Wind and the Sun," they will discuss with you

   ► What fiction is
   ► What fables are
   ► What a moral or lesson is

2. Tell students that they will read independently, but you will check in on them to make sure they understand what they are reading.

3. Tell students that after they read, they will answer questions about the story.

> **Objectives**
> - Differentiate among various literary genres.
> - Define *fiction*.
> - Define a *fable* as a story with a moral or lesson.
> - Define *moral* or *lesson learned*.
> - Use text organizational features to locate and comprehend information (table of contents).
> - Use text features to make a prediction (illustrations, title).
> - Increase concept and content vocabulary.

What Is a Fable?

Review what fiction, fables, and morals are.

1. Tell students that they are going to be reading some short stories that are **fiction**. Have them tell what fiction is. make-believe stories

2. Explain that students are going to read a special kind of fiction called a **fable**. Have them tell what a fable is, or define it for them. a story that teaches a lesson and may contain animal characters who behave like humans

3. Remind students that the lesson in a fable is called a **moral**.

4. Refresh student's memory of the fable "The Tortoise and the Hare." Have students retell what happens in the story, or retell the story for them.

5. Explain that sometimes a fable has the moral written at the end of the story. Tell students that they should look for the moral of the fable they are going to read today.

TIP If students are unfamiliar with the fable "The Tortoise and the Hare," have them retell another fable they might know, such as "The Grasshopper and the Ants."

Book Walk

Have students lead you through a Book Walk of "The Wind and the Sun."

1. Show students the cover of *K¹² Classics for Young Readers, Volume C*. Explain that the book is a collection of stories, plays, and poems.

2. Have students find the selection in the book's **table of contents**.

3. Have students read the **title** and turn to that page in the book.

4. Remind students how to take a Book Walk. Tell them to read the title, look at the **illustrations**, and ask themselves questions based on what they read and see. Give examples of questions they might ask themselves.

   ▸ Who might the characters be?
   ▸ What do I think will happen in this story?

5. Introduce the term **prediction** by telling students what it is (a guess about what might happen that is based on information in a story and what you already know). Explain that good readers make predictions so they are prepared for what might happen in a story and know what kind of text they're going to read.

6. Have students make predictions about "The Wind and the Sun" based on the story's title and **illustrations**.

Words to Know

Before reading "The Wind and the Sun," go over Words to Know with students.

1. Have students find the Words to Know at the bottom of the selection's pages. Tell them that these words will appear in the text in purple.

2. Have students read aloud each word and definition.

3. Ask them if they know what each word means.

   ▸ If students know a word's meaning, have them use it in a sentence.
   ▸ If they don't know a word's meaning, discuss it with them.

4. Tell students they should use the definitions as they read so that they can understand the story.

Read

"The Wind and the Sun"

Have students read "The Wind and the Sun." Give them the Reading Strategies bookmark and remind them to use the strategies while they read. For example, they may want to reread any part of the story that they find confusing, or they should ask themselves questions as they read.

⮌ **Learning Coach Check-In** This reading assignment should take about 10 minutes. Check in with students after they finish reading to assess their comprehension of the selection by asking the following questions:

▸ Who is in this story? the Wind and the Sun

▸ What happens in the story? The Wind says it's stronger than the Sun and the Sun asks the Wind to prove it. The Wind says the first one to make a man take off his coat is stronger. The Wind blows hard, but the man doesn't take off his coat. The Sun shines on the man, and the man takes off his coat because he's hot. So the Sun is stronger.

▸ Were any of your predictions correct? Students should tell which predictions they made about the story that were correct.

If students have trouble answering these questions, ask them what reading strategies they used and suggest they reread the selection.

Objectives
- Read literature independently and proficiently.
- Apply information read to answer questions.
- Evaluate reading strategies.
- Compare a prediction about an action or event to what actually occurred within a text.

GRAB

Go Read a Book

Have students read a book or magazine of their own choosing for at least 20 minutes. Remind them to use the strategies on their Reading Strategies bookmark before and during reading to help them understand the text.

Objectives
- Read literature independently and proficiently.
- Read a variety of texts for information and pleasure.
- Evaluate reading strategies.
- Use before-reading strategies.

Explore "The Wind and the Sun"

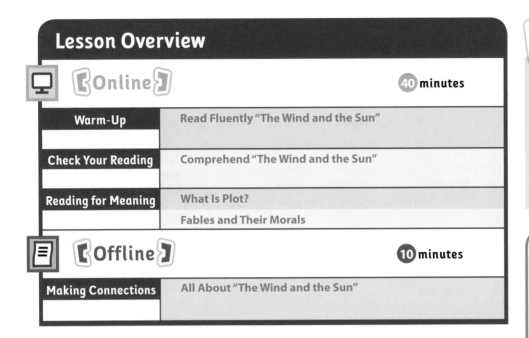

Lesson Overview

Online — 40 minutes

Warm-Up	Read Fluently "The Wind and the Sun"
Check Your Reading	Comprehend "The Wind and the Sun"
Reading for Meaning	What Is Plot?
	Fables and Their Morals

Offline — 10 minutes

Making Connections	All About "The Wind and the Sun"

Big Ideas

▶ Active, strong readers employ reading strategies such as drawing inferences during and after reading, and synthesizing information as they read and after they read.

▶ Fluency is the ability to decode text quickly, smoothly, and automatically.

▶ Interpretation occurs between reader and text as the reader attempts to discover the unstated and communicate about the text's meaning.

Materials

Supplied

● "The Wind and the Sun," *K¹² Classics for Young Readers, Volume C*, pp. 2–3
● *K¹² Language Arts Activity Book*, p. LC 1

Keywords

fable – a story that teaches a lesson and may contain animal characters

moral – the lesson of a story, particularly a fable

plot – what happens in a story; the sequence of events

sequence – the order in which things happen

 **40 minutes**

Students will work **independently** to complete online Warm-Up, Check Your Reading, and Reading for Meaning activities.

Warm-Up

Read Fluently "The Wind and the Sun"
Students will read aloud and record a passage from "The Wind and the Sun." The purpose of this activity is to improve students' oral reading and fluency. Remind students to listen to the model on each screen before they begin their recording.

Objectives
- Read poetry and prose aloud.
- Read aloud grade-level text with appropriate automaticity, prosody, accuracy, and rate.

Check Your Reading

Comprehend "The Wind and the Sun"
Students will answer questions about "The Wind and the Sun" to demonstrate their literal and inferential comprehension of the story.

Objectives
- Identify concrete answers to questions.
- Apply information read to answer questions.

Reading for Meaning

What Is Plot?
Students will learn that every story has a plot, which occurs in a specific sequence with a beginning, middle, and end. They will practice identifying the order, or sequence, of events in "The Wind and the Sun" and using the words *first*, *next*, *then*, and *finally* to show the sequence.

Objectives
- Define *plot* as what happens in a story.
- Define *sequence*.
- Sequence events in a story.
- Differentiate among various literary genres.
- Identify fable.
- Identify a story in this unit as a fable.
- Identify the moral or lesson in a fable.

Fables and Their Morals
Students will examine the behavior of the characters in "The Wind and the Sun" to determine the moral of the fable. They will identify the sentence in the fable that states the moral.

 **10 minutes**

Work **together** with students to complete the offline Making Connections activity.

Making Connections ....

All About "The Wind and the Sun"
Have students put the events of the story in order and explain the moral of the story in their own words. Turn to page LC 1 in *K¹² Language Arts Activity Book*.

Objectives
- Sequence events in a story.
- Explain the moral or lesson in a fable.

1. Direct students' attention to the Activity Book page and have them read the directions.

2. Have students complete the Activity Book page.

TIP Keep the Activity Book page in a safe place so students can refer to it later.

Introduce "The Bundle of Sticks"

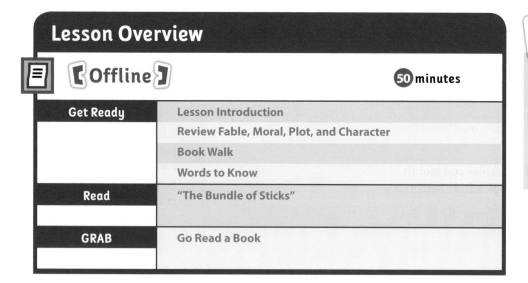

Lesson Overview

[Offline]   50 minutes

Get Ready	Lesson Introduction
	Review Fable, Moral, Plot, and Character
	Book Walk
	Words to Know
Read	"The Bundle of Sticks"
GRAB	Go Read a Book

Advance Preparation

Read "The Bundle of Sticks" to identify Words to Know in the text.

Big Ideas

- ► Active, strong readers use existing knowledge to make predictions before, during, and after reading.
- ► Reading a book of their own choosing helps motivate students to read.
- ► Reading for pleasure helps develop fluency and a lifelong love of reading.
- ► Reading better follows from reading often: The more a student reads, the better reader the student becomes.

[Materials]

Supplied

- "The Bundle of Sticks," *K¹² Classics for Young Readers, Volume C*, pp. 4–5
- Reading Strategies bookmark

Story Synopsis

A man cannot stop his sons from arguing. To teach them a lesson, he ties together a bundle of sticks. He asks each son to break the bundle, but none can. Then he separates the sticks and asks his sons to break them, which they do easily. The man says his sons are like the sticks: strong when they stick together, weak when they separate and quarrel.

Keywords

character – a person or animal in a story

fable – a story that teaches a lesson and may contain animal characters

moral – the lesson of a story, particularly a fable

plot – what happens in a story; the sequence of events

 **50 minutes**

Work **together** with students to complete offline Get Ready, Read, and GRAB activities.

Get Ready

Lesson Introduction
Prepare students to read "The Bundle of Sticks."

1. Explain to students that before they read "The Bundle of Sticks," they will discuss with you

   ▶ What they remember about fables and morals
   ▶ What they remember about plot and characters

2. Tell students that while they read, you will check in on them to make sure they understand what they are reading.

3. Tell students that after they read, they will answer questions about the story.

 Objectives
- Define a *fable* as a story with a moral or lesson.
- Define *moral* or *lesson learned*.
- Define *plot* as what happens in a story.
- Define *character*.
- Use text organizational features to locate and comprehend information (table of contents).
- Use text features to make a prediction (title, illustration).
- Increase concept and content vocabulary.

Review Fable, Moral, Plot, and Character
Review what fables, morals, plot, and character are.

1. Tell students that they are going to read another fable. Then have them define the following terms:

   ▶ **fable** a story that teaches a lesson and may contain animal characters
   ▶ **moral** the lesson of a story, particularly a fable
   ▶ **plot** what happens in a story

2. Tell students that all stories have **characters**. Have students tell what a character is and identify the characters in a fable they have read. a person or animal in a story; the Wind and the Sun in "The Wind and the Sun," for example

Book Walk
Have students lead you through a Book Walk of "The Bundle of Sticks."

1. Have students use the **table of contents** to find the selection in *K¹² Classics for Young Readers, Volume C.*

2. Have them read the **title** and turn to that page in the book.

3. Remind students how to take a Book Walk. Have them read the title, look at the **illustrations**, and make predictions about the characters and plot of "The Bundle of Sticks."

Words to Know

Before reading "The Bundle of Sticks," go over Words to Know with students.

1. Have students find the Words to Know at the bottom of the selection's pages. Tell them that these words will appear in the text in purple.

2. Have students read aloud each word and definition.

3. Ask them if they know what each word means.

   ▸ If students know a word's meaning, have them use it in a sentence.
   ▸ If they don't know a word's meaning, discuss it with them.

4. Tell students they should use the definitions as they read so that they can understand the story.

Read

"The Bundle of Sticks"

Have students read "The Bundle of Sticks." Give them the Reading Strategies bookmark and remind them to use the strategies while they read. For example, they may want to ask themselves questions about the story as they read.

 Learning Coach Check-In This reading assignment should take about 10 minutes. Check in with students after they finish reading to assess their comprehension of the selection by asking the following questions:

▸ Who are the characters in the story? a father and his sons
▸ What happens in the story? The father is upset because the sons are always fighting. He ties together a bundle of sticks and asks each son to try to break the bundle. They can't. Then the father separates the bundle into individual sticks, and the sons can break them easily. The father says the sons should be like the sticks. They're strong when they stick together and weak when they're alone.
▸ Were any of your predictions correct? Which ones? Students should tell which predictions they made that were correct about the story.

If students have trouble answering these questions, ask them what reading strategies they used and suggest they reread the selection.

Objectives
- Read literature independently and proficiently.
- Apply information read to answer questions.
- Evaluate reading strategies.
- Compare a prediction about an action or event to what actually occurred within a text.

GRAB

Go Read a Book

Have students read a book or magazine of their own choosing for at least 20 minutes. Remind students to use the strategies on their Reading Strategies bookmark before and during reading to help them understand the text.

Objectives
- Read literature independently and proficiently.
- Read a variety of texts for information and pleasure.
- Evaluate reading strategies.
- Use before-reading strategies.

Explore "The Bundle of Sticks"

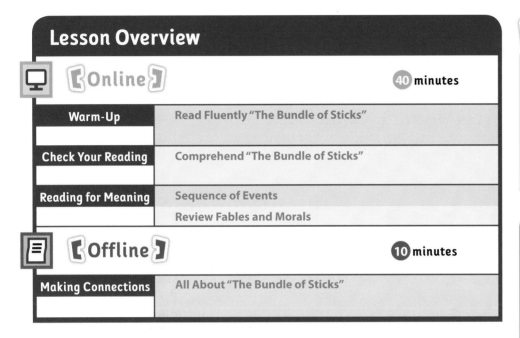

Lesson Overview

🖥 〔Online〕 ④⓪ minutes

Warm-Up	Read Fluently "The Bundle of Sticks"
Check Your Reading	Comprehend "The Bundle of Sticks"
Reading for Meaning	Sequence of Events
	Review Fables and Morals

📄 〔Offline〕 ①⓪ minutes

Making Connections	All About "The Bundle of Sticks"

〔Materials〕

Supplied
- "The Bundle of Sticks," *K¹² Classics for Young Readers, Volume C*, pp. 4–5
- *K¹² Language Arts Activity Book*, pp. LC 2

Keywords

fable – a story that teaches a lesson and may contain animal characters

moral – the lesson of a story, particularly a fable

plot – what happens in a story; the sequence of events

sequence – the order in which things happen

Big Ideas

▸ Active, strong readers employ reading strategies such as drawing inferences during and after reading, and synthesizing information as they read and after they read.

▸ Fluency is the ability to decode text quickly, smoothly, and automatically.

▸ Interpretation occurs between reader and text as the reader attempts to discover the unstated and communicate about the text's meaning.

 **minutes**

Students will work **independently** to complete online Warm-Up, Check Your Reading, and Reading for Meaning activities.

Warm-Up

Read Fluently "The Bundle of Sticks"

Students will read aloud and record a passage from "The Bundle of Sticks." The purpose of this activity is to improve students' oral reading and fluency. Remind students to listen to the model on each screen before they begin their recording.

Objectives

- Read poetry and prose aloud.
- Read aloud grade-level text with appropriate automaticity, prosody, accuracy, and rate.

Check Your Reading

Comprehend "The Bundle of Sticks"

Students will answer questions about "The Bundle of Sticks" to demonstrate their literal and inferential comprehension of the story.

Objectives

- Identify concrete answers to questions.
- Apply information read to answer questions.

Reading for Meaning

Sequence of Events

Students will review signal words that signify the sequence of events, such as *first*, *next*, *then*, and *finally*.

Objectives

- Define *plot* as what happens in a story.
- Sequence events in a story.
- Identify fable.
- Identify the moral or lesson in a fable.

Review Fables and Morals

Students will recognize that "The Bundle of Sticks" is a fable and identify the moral of the story.

 **minutes**

Work **together** with students to complete the offline Making Connections activity.

Making Connections

All About "The Bundle of Sticks"

Have students use signal words to sequence the plot events and explain the moral of the story in their own words. Turn to page LC 2 in *K¹² Language Arts Activity Book*.

1. Direct students' attention to the Activity Book pages and have them read the directions.

2. Have students complete the Activity Book pages. They may put some of the events in different boxes than the sample answer shows. The important thing is that they get all the events in the correct sequence. They may state the moral in their own words, but it should convey the same meaning as the answer.

TIP Keep the Activity Book page in a safe place so students can refer to it later.

Objectives
- Sequence events in a story.
- Explain the moral or lesson in a fable.
- Use transition words to signal order.

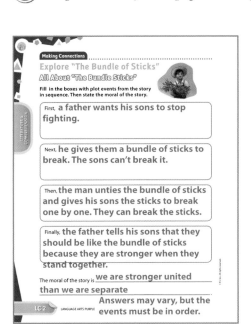

Introduce "Why the Larks Flew Away"

Lesson Overview

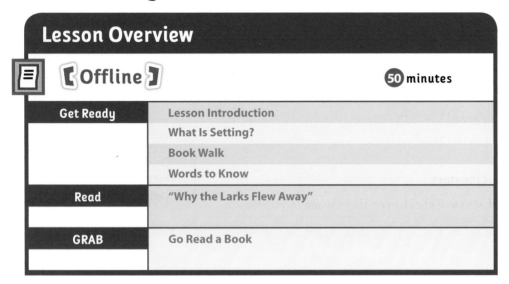

Offline **50 minutes**

Get Ready	Lesson Introduction
	What Is Setting?
	Book Walk
	Words to Know
Read	"Why the Larks Flew Away"
GRAB	Go Read a Book

Advance Preparation

Read "Why the Larks Flew Away" to identify Words to Know in the text.

Big Ideas

- ▶ Active, strong readers use existing knowledge to make predictions before, during, and after reading.
- ▶ Reading a book of their own choosing helps motivate students to read.
- ▶ Reading for pleasure helps develop fluency and a lifelong love of reading.
- ▶ Reading better follows from reading often: The more a student reads, the better reader the student becomes.

[Materials]

Supplied

- "Why the Larks Flew Away," *K¹² Classics for Young Readers, Volume C,* pp. 6–11
- Reading Strategies bookmark

Story Synopsis

A mother lark and her babies live in a wheat field, but they must leave as soon as the farmer comes to cut down the grain. For two mornings, the mother lark says it isn't time to leave, because the farmer has asked others to help cut the wheat. When the baby larks finally hear the farmer say he and his son must do the work themselves, the mother lark says it is truly time to leave.

Keywords

setting – when and where a story takes place

 **50 minutes**

Work **together** with students to complete offline Get Ready, Read, and GRAB activities.

Get Ready

Lesson Introduction

Prepare students to read "Why the Larks Flew Away."

1. Explain to students that before they read "Why the Larks Flew Away," they will discuss with you

   ▸ What a setting is
   ▸ What their predictions are for the story

2. Tell students that while they read, you will check in on them to make sure they understand what they are reading.

3. Tell students that after they read, they will answer questions about the story.

What Is Setting?

Discuss with students what the setting of a story is.

1. Have students think of a favorite story.

2. Ask them to tell when and where the story takes place. Answers will vary, but students should include a time period for the story if they know one and the place where the action takes place.

3. Define **setting** as when and where a story takes place.

4. Tell students that sometimes the setting gives a lot of details about both when and where a story takes place, sometimes only a few, and sometimes only one or the other.

Book Walk

Have students lead you through a Book Walk of "Why the Larks Flew Away."

1. Have students use the **table of contents** to find the selection in *K¹² Classics for Young Readers, Volume C*.

2. Have them read the **title** and turn to that page in the book.

3. Remind students how to take a Book Walk. Have them read the title, look at the **illustrations**, and make predictions about the characters and plot of "Why the Larks Flew Away."

Words to Know

As students read "Why the Larks Flew Away," remind them to refer to the Words to Know as they appear at the bottom of the pages of the story.

Objectives

- Define *setting*.
- Define a *fable* as a story with a moral or lesson.
- Define *moral* or *lesson learned*.
- Define *plot* as what happens in a story.
- Define *character*.
- Use text organizational features to locate and comprehend information (table of contents).
- Use text features to make a prediction (illustrations, title).
- Increase concept and content vocabulary.

Read

"Why the Larks Flew Away"

Have students read "Why the Larks Flew Away." Give them the Reading Strategies bookmark and remind them to use the strategies while they read. For example, they may want to ask themselves questions about the story as they read.

⮏ **Learning Coach Check-In** This reading assignment should take about 10 minutes. Check in with students after they finish reading to assess their comprehension of the selection by asking the following questions:

▸ Who are the characters in the story? a family of larks, a farmer, and his son

▸ What happens in the story? The larks live in a wheat field, and the mother lark has to go away to find food. She tells her babies to listen to what the farmer says when he comes through the field, so she will know when it is time to leave. The babies hear the farmer tell his son to get a neighbor and then his cousins to help cut the wheat. The mother lark says it isn't time to leave. Then the farmer says he and his son have to cut the wheat themselves, so the larks move away.

▸ Were any of your predictions correct? Which ones? Students should tell which predictions they made that were correct about the story.

If students have trouble answering these questions, ask them what reading strategies they used and suggest they reread the selection.

Objectives
- Read literature independently and proficiently.
- Apply information read to answer questions.
- Evaluate reading strategies.
- Compare a prediction about an action or event to what actually occurred within a text.

GRAB

Go Read a Book

Have students read a book or magazine of their own choosing for at least 20 minutes. Remind them to use the strategies on their Reading Strategies bookmark before and during reading to help them understand the text.

Objectives
- Read literature independently and proficiently.
- Read a variety of texts for information and pleasure.
- Evaluate reading strategies.
- Use before-reading strategies.

Explore "Why the Larks Flew Away"

Lesson Overview

💻 [Online]   ⓸⓪ minutes

Warm-Up	Read Fluently "Why the Larks Flew Away"
Check Your Reading	Comprehend "Why the Larks Flew Away"
Reading for Meaning	Sequence of Events
	The Moral of the Story
	Summarize a Story

📄 [Offline]   ⑩ minutes

Making Connections	All About "Why the Larks Flew Away"

Big Ideas

- Active, strong readers employ reading strategies such as drawing inferences during and after reading, and synthesizing information as they read and after they read.
- Fluency is the ability to decode text quickly, smoothly, and automatically.
- Interpretation occurs between reader and text as the reader attempts to discover the unstated and communicate about the text's meaning.
- Readers should be able to retell the story (or information) in their own words, not repeat what was written.
- Explicit instruction in how to summarize a text is an important element in learning how to write well.
- Writing requires organization and structure.

Materials

Supplied

- "Why the Larks Flew Away," *K¹² Classics for Young Readers, Volume C,* pp. 6–11
- *K¹² Language Arts Activity Book,* p. LC 3

Keywords

fable – a story that teaches a lesson and may contain animal characters

moral – the lesson of a story, particularly a fable

plot – what happens in a story; the sequence of events

sequence – the order in which things happen

summarize – to tell in order the most important ideas or events of a text

summary – a short retelling that includes only the most important ideas or events of a text

 **40 minutes**

Students will work **independently** to complete online Warm-Up, Check Your Reading, and Reading for Meaning activities.

Warm-Up

Read Fluently "Why the Larks Flew Away"

Students will read aloud and record a passage from "Why the Larks Flew Away." The purpose of this activity is to improve students' oral reading and fluency. Remind students to listen to the model on each screen before they begin their recording.

 Objectives
- Read poetry and prose aloud.
- Read aloud grade-level text with appropriate automaticity, prosody, accuracy, and rate.

Check Your Reading

Comprehend "Why the Larks Flew Away"

Students will answer questions about "Why the Larks Flew Away" to demonstrate their literal and inferential comprehension of the story.

 Objectives
- Identify concrete answers to questions.
- Apply information read to answer questions.

Reading for Meaning

Sequence of Events

Students will correctly sequence the plot events of "Why the Larks Flew Away" and order them with signal words such as *first, next, then,* and *finally.*

 Objectives
- Define *plot* as what happens in a story.
- Sequence events in a story.
- Identify a story in this unit as a fable.
- Identify the moral or lesson in a fable.
- Define *summary.*
- Define *summarize.*
- Summarize a work of literature and maintain accurate sequence.

The Moral of the Story

Students will identify the moral of the fable "Why the Larks Flew Away."

Summarize a Story

Students will learn how to write a summary of the fable: introducing its title and setting, including its characters, sequencing plot events, and stating the moral of the story.

 **Offline** **10** minutes

Work **together** with students to complete the offline Making Connections activity.

Making Connections

All About "Why the Larks Flew Away"

Have students put the events of the story in order and explain the moral of the story in their own words. Turn to page LC 3 in *K¹² Language Arts Activity Book*.

1. Direct students' attention to the Activity Book page and have them read the directions.

2. Have them complete the Activity Book page. They may put different events in the boxes from what the sample answer shows. The important thing is that main events from the story are in the correct sequence on the activity page. They may state the moral in words different from the sample answer, but they should convey the same lesson.

Objectives
- Sequence events in a story.
- Explain the moral or lesson in a fable.

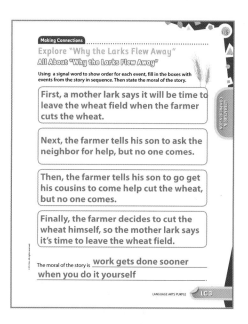

Reflections on Lessons Learned

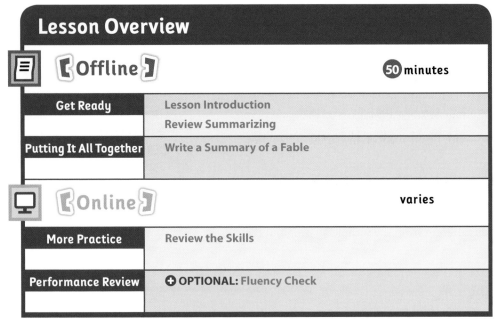

Lesson Overview

Offline — 50 minutes

Get Ready	Lesson Introduction
	Review Summarizing
Putting It All Together	Write a Summary of a Fable

Online — varies

| More Practice | Review the Skills |
| Performance Review | ⊕ OPTIONAL: Fluency Check |

Materials

Supplied

- "The Wind and the Sun," "The Bundle of Sticks," "Why the Larks Flew Away," *K¹² Classics for Young Readers, Volume C,* pp. 2–11
- *K¹² Language Arts Activity Book,* pp. LC 1, 2, 5–6
- Putting It All Together Assessment Checklist (printout)
- Fluency Performance Checklist (optional printout)

Advance Preparation

Have students gather completed pages LC 1 (All About "The Wind and the Sun") and 2 (All About "The Bundle of Sticks") in *K¹² Language Arts Activity Book.*

Big Ideas

- ▸ Readers should be able to retell the story (or information) in their own words, not repeat what was written.
- ▸ Explicit instruction in how to summarize a text is an important element in learning how to write well.
- ▸ Writing requires organization and structure.

Keywords

fable – a story that teaches a lesson and may contain animal characters

moral – the lesson of a story, particularly a fable

plot – what happens in a story; the sequence of events

sequence – the order in which things happen

summarize – to tell in order the most important ideas or events of a text

summary – a short retelling that includes only the most important ideas or events of a text

 50 **minutes**

Work **together** with students to complete the offline Get Ready and Putting It All Together activities.

Get Ready

Lesson Introduction

Prepare students for writing a summary about one of the fables from this unit.

1. Tell students that they are going to write a summary of one of the fables they read in this unit.

2. Explain that before students write their summary, they will get ready by reviewing with you
   ▶ What a summary is
   ▶ What goes into a summary

Objectives
• Define *summary*.
• Define *summarize*.

Review Summarizing

Review the parts of a summary to prepare students for writing a summary about one of the fables in the unit.

1. Have students tell what a **summary** is or define it for them. a short retelling that includes only the most important ideas or events of a text

2. Review what goes into a summary.
   ▶ A first part that tells the title, the author if there is one, the setting, and the main characters
   ▶ A middle part that describes at least three main events from the plot in sequence
   ▶ A conclusion

3. Remind students that a conclusion about a fable should tell the moral of the story.

Putting It All Together

....

✏ **Write a Summary of a Fable**

Students will write a summary of one of the fables in the unit. Turn to pages LC 5 and 6 and gather either completed page LC 1 or 2 in *K¹² Language Arts Activity Book*.

1. Have students find "The Wind and the Sun" and "The Bundle of Sticks" in *K¹² Classics for Young Readers, Volume C*.

2. Have them choose either the "Wind and the Sun" or "The Bundle of Sticks" for their summary.

3. Have students take out their completed Activity Book page for the story they choose, which will help them organize their summary.

4. Have students complete the Activity Book pages by writing their summary in the space provided, using their best cursive handwriting.

5. When students have completed their summary, use the materials and instructions in the online lesson to evaluate students' work.

6. Enter the answers (Yes or No) for each line of the assessment checklist online.

   ➲ **Learning Coach Check-in** Check in with students after about 40 minutes to see if they have completed the assignment.

> ### Objectives
> - Summarize a work of literature and maintain accurate sequence.
> - Sequence events in a story.
> - Write a summary.

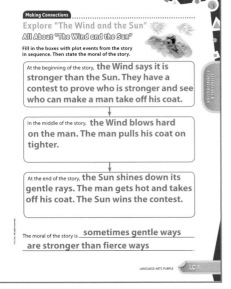

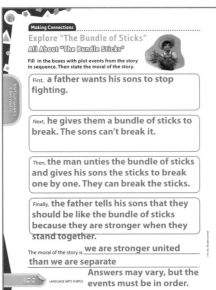

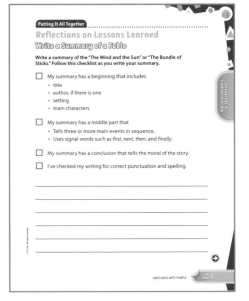

 **varies**

Students will work **independently** to complete the online More Practice activity.

More Practice

Review the Skills

If students scored less than 80 percent or had difficulty meeting the objectives of the Putting It All Together activity, have them go online for more practice.

 Reward: If students score 80 percent or more on the Putting It All Together activity, add a sticker for this unit on the My Accomplishments chart. If students did not score 80 percent or more, work with them to revise their writing until they do score 80 percent and then add a sticker to the My Accomplishments chart.

 Objectives
- Describe setting.
- Sequence events in a story.
- Explain the moral or lesson in a fable.
- Summarize a work of literature and maintain accurate sequence.
- Write a summary.

Performance Review

⊕ **OPTIONAL: Fluency Check**

Listen to students' recordings and use the Fluency Performance Checklist to review fluency and track performance. Keep the completed checklist so you can review students' progress over time.

 Objectives
- Read aloud grade-level text with appropriate automaticity, prosody, accuracy, and rate.

 **Animal Tales**

Unit Focus

In this unit, students will read folktales and think about the problems the characters face and how they solve their problems. Students will read these selections:

- ► "Chipmunk and Bear"
- ► "The Tiger, the Brahman, and the Jackal"
- ► "Squirrel and Spider"

Unit Plan		Online	Offline
Lesson 1	Introduce "Chipmunk and Bear"		50 minutes
Lesson 2	Explore "Chipmunk and Bear"	40 minutes	10 minutes
Lesson 3	Introduce "The Tiger, the Brahman, and the Jackal"		50 minutes
Lesson 4	Explore "The Tiger, the Brahman, and the Jackal"	40 minutes	10 minutes
Lesson 5	Introduce "Squirrel and Spider"		50 minutes
Lesson 6	Explore "Squirrel and Spider"	40 minutes	10 minutes
Lesson 7	Reflections on Animal Tales	varies	50 minutes
Lesson 8	Your Choice		50 minutes

Introduce "Chipmunk and Bear"

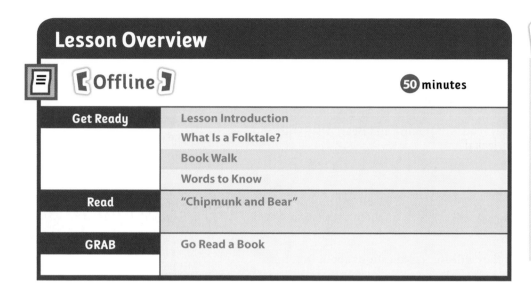

Lesson Overview

[Offline]   **50** minutes

Get Ready	Lesson Introduction
	What Is a Folktale?
	Book Walk
	Words to Know
Read	"Chipmunk and Bear"
GRAB	Go Read a Book

Big Ideas

► Active, strong readers use existing knowledge to make predictions before, during, and after reading.
► Active, strong readers employ reading strategies such as asking questions before, during, and after reading and monitoring their comprehension (for example, self-check) as they read.
► Reading a book of their own choosing helps motivate students to read.

[Materials]

Supplied
• "Chipmunk and Bear," *K¹² Classics for Young Readers, Volume C,* pp. 12–17
• Reading Strategies bookmark

Also Needed
• whiteboard (optional)

Story Synopsis

Bear boasts that he is the strongest of all the animals, so Chipmunk challenges Bear to stop the sun from rising. When Bear fails, Chipmunk laughs at him. Bear catches Chipmunk and plans to kill him, but Chipmunk tricks Bear into freeing him. As Chipmunk escapes, Bear's claws make the three white stripes on Chipmunk's back, which are found on all chipmunks today.

Keywords

folktale – a story, which usually teaches a lesson important to a culture, that is passed down through many generations

 **50 minutes**

Work **together** with students to complete offline Get Ready, Read, and GRAB activities.

Get Ready

Lesson Introduction
Prepare students to read "Chipmunk and Bear."

1. Explain to students that before they read "Chipmunk and Bear," they will discuss with you
   - ▸ What a folktale is
   - ▸ What is the purpose of folktales

2. Tell students that while they read, you will check in on them to make sure they understand what they are reading.

3. Tell students that after they read, they will answer questions about the story.

What Is a Folktale?
Discuss what folktales are.

1. Have students think of a family story that everyone likes to tell and briefly retell it.

2. Tell students that a story passed from person to person through a family or another group of people is called a **folktale**.

3. Write the word *folktale* on a whiteboard or sheet of paper. Explain that the word *folk* means a group of people. A *tale* is a story.

4. Explain that folktales used to be told, not written down. They were told by older people to younger people, and so on from one generation to the next. They also were used to teach important ideas or lessons and explain things. Folktales often included animals that could talk.

Book Walk
Have students lead you through a Book Walk of "Chipmunk and Bear."

1. Have students find the selection in the **table of contents** of *K¹² Classics for Young Readers, Volume C*, and turn to that page.

2. Have students read the **title** of the story and take you on a Book Walk. Remind them to use the title and **illustrations** to make predictions about what will happen in the story.

Objectives
- Differentiate among various literary genres.
- Define *folktale*.
- Understand a variety of literature representing different cultures and traditions.
- Use text features to make a prediction (illustrations, title).
- Use text organizational features to locate and comprehend information (table of contents).
- Use before-reading strategies.
- Increase concept and content vocabulary.

Words to Know

As students read "Chipmunk and Bear," remind them to refer to the Words to Know as they appear at the bottom of the pages of the story.

Read

"Chipmunk and Bear"

Have students read "Chipmunk and Bear." Remind them to use the strategies on their Reading Strategies bookmark. For example, they should reread when they find something in the story they don't understand.

 Learning Coach Check-In This reading assignment should take about 15 minutes. Check in with students after they finish reading to assess their comprehension of the selection by asking the following questions:

- ▶ Who are the two characters in this story? Bear and Chipmunk
- ▶ What does Bear try to do in the story? stop the sun from rising
- ▶ Why does Bear want to hurt Chipmunk? Chipmunk makes fun of Bear.

If students have trouble answering these questions, ask them what reading strategies they used and suggest they reread the selection.

Objectives
- Read literature independently and proficiently.
- Apply information read to answer questions.
- Evaluate reading strategies.
- Compare a prediction about an action or event to what actually occurred within a text.

GRAB

Go Read a Book

Have students read a book or magazine of their own choosing for at least 20 minutes. Remind them to use the strategies on their Reading Strategies bookmark before and during reading to help them understand the text.

 Remember: The more students read, the better readers they become.

Objectives
- Read literature independently and proficiently.
- Read a variety of texts for information and pleasure.
- Evaluate reading strategies.
- Use before-reading strategies.

Explore "Chipmunk and Bear"

Lesson Overview

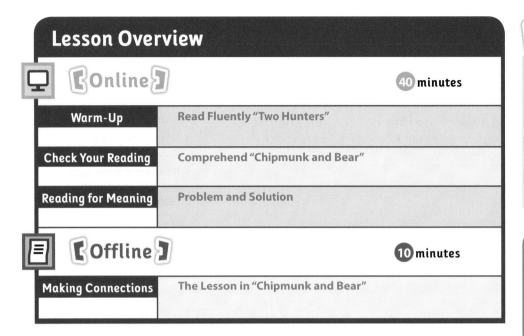

Online — 40 minutes

Warm-Up	Read Fluently "Two Hunters"
Check Your Reading	Comprehend "Chipmunk and Bear"
Reading for Meaning	Problem and Solution

Offline — 10 minutes

Making Connections	The Lesson in "Chipmunk and Bear"

Materials

Supplied

- "Chipmunk and Bear," *K¹² Classics for Young Readers, Volume C*, pp. 12–17
- *K¹² Language Arts Activity Book*, pp. LC 7–8

Keywords

character – a person or animal in a story

folktale – a story, which usually teaches a lesson important to a culture, that is passed down through many generations

problem – an issue a character must solve in a story

solution – how a character solves a problem in a story

Big Ideas

► Active, strong readers employ reading strategies such as drawing inferences during and after reading, and synthesizing information as they read and after they read.
► Fluency is the ability to decode text quickly, smoothly, and automatically.
► Readers need to synthesize, draw conclusions about, and interpret what they have read.

 **40 minutes**

Students will work **independently** to complete online Warm-Up, Check Your Reading, and Reading for Meaning activities.

Warm-Up

Read Fluently "Two Hunters"

Students will read aloud and record the passage "Two Hunters." The purpose of this activity is to improve students' oral reading and fluency. Remind students to listen to the model on each screen before they begin their recording.

Objectives
- Read poetry and prose aloud.
- Read aloud grade-level text with appropriate automaticity, prosody, accuracy, and rate.

Check Your Reading

Comprehend "Chipmunk and Bear"

Students will answer questions about "Chipmunk and Bear" to demonstrate their literal and inferential comprehension of the story.

Objectives
- Identify concrete answers to questions.
- Apply information read to answer questions.
- Infer answers to questions.

Reading for Meaning

Problem and Solution

Students will learn that in most stories, the characters face problems they must solve. They will explore the problems the characters face in "Chipmunk and Bear," examine the solutions the characters find, and analyze the manner in which these solutions can become new problems. Students will also characterize the kinds of solutions that these characters find to determine whether they exemplify strength or intelligence. Understanding how characters solve problems will help them find the lesson or theme of the folktale.

Objectives
- Define *problem*.
- Define the problem in a story.
- Define the *solution* to the problem a character faces.
- Identify problems and solutions in a story.
- Describe the characters in the story using evidence from the text.
- Describe how the solution to a problem demonstrates a character's traits.

 **Offline** **10** minutes

Work **together** with students to complete the offline Making Connections activity.

Making Connections

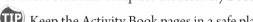

The Lesson in "Chipmunk and Bear"

Have students review some of the problems and solutions in the story and identify the lesson of the folktale. Turn to pages LC 7 and 8 in *K¹² Language Arts Activity Book*.

1. Direct students' attention to the Activity Book pages and have them read the directions.

2. Have students complete the Activity Book pages.

TIP Keep the Activity Book pages in a safe place so students can refer to them later.

 Objectives

- Identify problems and solutions in a story.
- Determine the theme, moral, or lesson of a work of literature.
- Summarize text and maintain accurate sequence.

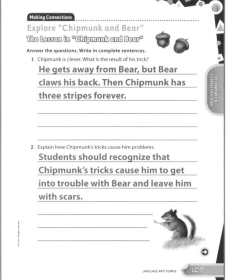

Making Connections

Explore "Chipmunk and Bear"
The Lesson in "Chipmunk and Bear"

Answer the questions. Write in complete sentences.

1. Chipmunk is clever. What is the result of his trick?

   He gets away from Bear, but Bear claws his back. Then Chipmunk has three stripes forever.

2. Explain how Chipmunk's tricks cause him problems.

   Students should recognize that Chipmunk's tricks cause him to get into trouble with Bear and leave him with scars.

LANGUAGE ARTS PURPLE **LC 7**

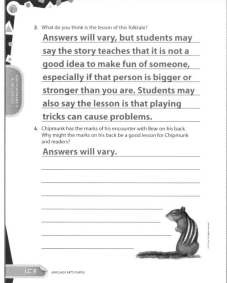

LC 8 LANGUAGE ARTS PURPLE

3. What do you think is the lesson of this folktale?

   Answers will vary, but students may say the story teaches that it is not a good idea to make fun of someone, especially if that person is bigger or stronger than you are. Students may also say the lesson is that playing tricks can cause problems.

4. Chipmunk has the marks of his encounter with Bear on his back. Why might the marks on his back be a good lesson for Chipmunk and readers?

   Answers will vary.

Introduce "The Tiger, the Brahman, and the Jackal"

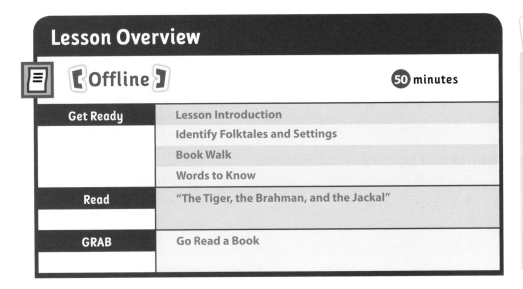

Lesson Overview

[Offline]   50 minutes

Get Ready	Lesson Introduction
	Identify Folktales and Settings
	Book Walk
	Words to Know
Read	"The Tiger, the Brahman, and the Jackal"
GRAB	Go Read a Book

Big Ideas

▶ Active, strong readers use existing knowledge to make predictions before, during, and after reading.
▶ Reading a book of their own choosing helps motivate students to read.

[Materials]

Supplied

- "The Tiger, the Brahman, and the Jackal," *K¹² Classics for Young Readers, Volume C*, pp. 18–25
- Reading Strategies bookmark

Also Needed

- household objects – world map

Story Synopsis

A Brahman in India comes upon a tiger trapped in a cage. The tiger begs to be freed and promises not to eat the Brahman. When the Brahman frees the tiger, the tiger breaks his promise and prepares to eat the Brahman. When it seems no one will help the man, a jackal comes along and pretends to be confused about what has happened. The tiger, in an attempt to demonstrate the events, steps into the cage, and the jackal closes the door on him.

Keywords

folktale – a story, which usually teaches a lesson important to a culture, that is passed down through many generations

setting – when and where a story takes place

 **50** minutes

Work **together** with students to complete offline Get Ready, Read, and GRAB activities.

Get Ready

Lesson Introduction

Prepare students to read "The Tiger, the Brahman, and the Jackal."

1. Explain to students that before they read "The Tiger, the Brahman, and the Jackal," they will discuss with you

   ▶ What they remember about folktales
   ▶ How to identify the setting of a story

2. Tell students that while they read, you will check in on them to make sure they understand what they are reading.

3. Tell students that after they read, they will answer questions about the story.

Objectives

- Define *folktale*.
- Define *setting*.
- Identify setting(s).
- Understand a variety of literature representing different cultures and traditions.
- Use text organizational features to locate and comprehend information (table of contents).
- Use before-reading strategies.
- Increase concept and content vocabulary.
- Use text features to make a prediction (illustrations, title).

Identify Folktales and Settings

Discuss the characteristics of folktales and how to identify the setting of a story. Gather the world map.

1. Tell students that they are going to read another **folktale**. Have them tell what they remember about folktales. A folktale is a story told from one generation to the next, which usually teaches a lesson important to a culture.

2. Ask students if they know what a **setting** is. If necessary, tell them setting is when and where a story takes place.

3. Have students describe the setting of a favorite story or movie. Remind them to include both the time and place.

4. Have students find "The Tiger, the Brahman, and the Jackal" in the **table of contents** of *K¹² Classics for Young Readers, Volume C*, and turn to that page.

5. Have students read the opening phrase in the story, "Once upon a time in India." Ask students to tell the setting of this story. India once upon a time, which likely means long ago

6. Ask students if they think this story takes place now or in the past and tell why they think this. in the past, because of the phrase "once upon a time"

7. Have students find India on a world map and tell what they know or think they know about the country.

Book Walk

Have students lead you through a Book Walk of "The Tiger, the Brahman, and the Jackal." Remind them to use the **title** and **illustrations** to make predictions about what will happen in the story.

Words to Know

As students read "The Tiger, The Brahman, and the Jackal," remind them to refer to the Words to Know as they appear at the bottom of the pages of the story.

Read

"The Tiger, the Brahman, and the Jackal"

Have students read "The Tiger, the Brahman, and the Jackal." Remind them to use the strategies on their Reading Strategies bookmark. For example, they may want to read more slowly when they find they are having trouble understanding something.

 Learning Coach Check-In This reading assignment should take about 20 minutes. Check in with students after they finish reading to assess their comprehension of the selection by asking the following questions:

- ► Who are the characters in the story? a tiger, a Brahman, and a jackal; Students may also mention a tree, a water buffalo, and a road.
- ► What happens after the Brahman lets the tiger out of the cage? The tiger says he's going to eat the Brahman anyway. The Brahman asks others to tell the tiger he should keep his promise, but he doesn't. A jackal comes along and tricks the tiger into getting back into the cage.
- ► Were any of your predictions correct? Which ones? Students should tell which predictions they made about the story that were correct, if any.

If students have trouble answering these questions, ask them what reading strategies they used and suggest they reread the selection.

Objectives

- Read literature independently and proficiently.
- Apply information read to answer questions.
- Evaluate reading strategies.
- Compare a prediction about an action or event to what actually occurred within a text.

GRAB

Go Read a Book

Have students read a book or magazine of their own choosing for at least 20 minutes. Remind students to use the strategies on their Reading Strategies bookmark before and during reading to help them understand the text.

Objectives

- Read literature independently and proficiently.
- Read a variety of texts for information and pleasure.
- Evaluate reading strategies.
- Use before-reading strategies.

Explore "The Tiger, the Brahman, and the Jackal"

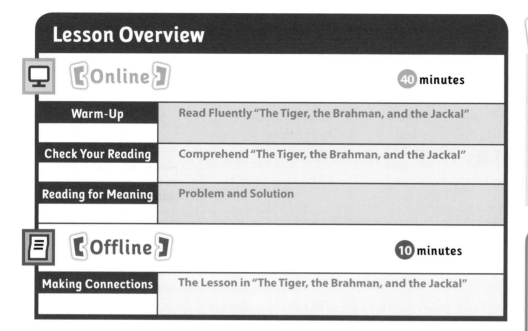

Lesson Overview

Online — 40 minutes

Warm-Up	Read Fluently "The Tiger, the Brahman, and the Jackal"
Check Your Reading	Comprehend "The Tiger, the Brahman, and the Jackal"
Reading for Meaning	Problem and Solution

Offline — 10 minutes

Making Connections	The Lesson in "The Tiger, the Brahman, and the Jackal"

Materials

Supplied

- "The Tiger, the Brahman, and the Jackal," *K¹² Classics for Young Readers, Volume C*, pp. 18–25
- *K¹² Language Arts Activity Book*, pp. LC 9–10

Keywords

character – a person or animal in a story

folktale – a story, which usually teaches a lesson important to a culture, that is passed down through many generations

problem – an issue a character must solve in a story

solution – how a character solves a problem in a story

Big Ideas

▸ Active, strong readers employ reading strategies such as drawing inferences during and after reading, and synthesizing information as they read and after they read.

▸ Fluency is the ability to decode text quickly, smoothly, and automatically.

▸ Readers need to synthesize, draw conclusions about, and interpret what they have read.

 **40 minutes**

Students will work **independently** to complete online Warm-Up, Check Your Reading, and Reading for Meaning activities.

Warm-Up

Read Fluently "The Tiger, the Brahman, and the Jackal"
Students will read aloud and record a passage from "The Tiger, the Brahman, and the Jackal." The purpose of this activity is to improve students' oral reading and fluency. Remind students to listen to the model on each screen before they begin their recording.

Objectives
- Read poetry and prose aloud.
- Read aloud grade-level text with appropriate automaticity, prosody, accuracy, and rate.

Check Your Reading

Comprehend "The Tiger, the Brahman, and the Jackal"
Students will answer questions about "The Tiger, the Brahman, and the Jackal" to demonstrate their literal and inferential comprehension of the story.

Objectives
- Identify concrete answers to questions.
- Apply information read to answer questions.
- Infer answers to questions.

Reading for Meaning

Problem and Solution
Students will explore the problems the characters face in "The Tiger, the Brahman, and the Jackal," and they will examine the solutions the characters find. They will see how solutions can become new problems, and they will also evaluate the kinds of solutions that are most effective (those that require cleverness).

Objectives
- Define the problem in a story.
- Define the solution to the problem a character faces.
- Identify problems and solutions in a story.
- Describe the characters in the story using evidence from the text.
- Describe how the solution to a problem demonstrates a character's traits.

[Offline] ⏱ 10 minutes

Work **together** with students to complete the offline Making Connections activity.

Making Connections ···

The Lesson in "The Tiger, the Brahman, and the Jackal"
Have students review some of the problems and solutions in the story and identify the lesson of the folktale. Turn to pages LC 9 and 10 in *K¹² Language Arts Activity Book*.

1. Direct students' attention to the Activity Book pages and have them read the directions.

2. Have students complete the Activity Book pages.

TIP Keep the Activity Book pages in a safe place so students can refer to them later.

Objectives
- Identify problems and solutions in a story.
- Determine the theme, moral, or lesson of a work of literature.
- Generate plausible alternative endings to plot.
- Make connections between text and self, text and world, and text to text.

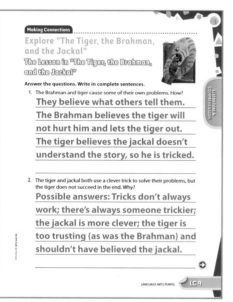

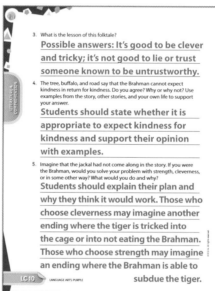

Introduce "Squirrel and Spider"

Lesson Overview

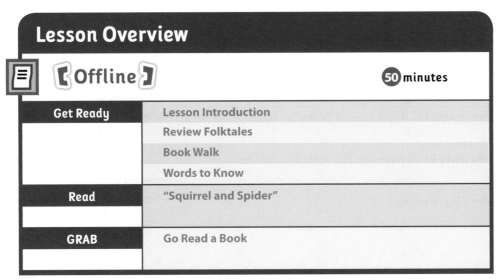

Offline   **50 minutes**

Get Ready	Lesson Introduction
	Review Folktales
	Book Walk
	Words to Know
Read	"Squirrel and Spider"
GRAB	Go Read a Book

Big Ideas

- ▶ Active, strong readers use existing knowledge to make predictions before, during, and after reading.
- ▶ Reading a book of their own choosing helps motivate students to read.
- ▶ To understand and interpret a story, readers need to understand and describe characters and what they do.

Materials

Supplied
- "Squirrel and Spider," *K¹² Classics for Young Readers, Volume C,* pp. 26–31
- Reading Strategies bookmark

Also Needed
- household objects – world map

Story Synopsis

Squirrel has grown a crop of grain on his farm. Spider wants the grain for himself, so he builds a road to the farm and acts like the grain is his. When Squirrel goes to a judge, the judge believes Spider and gives the grain to him. One day, when Spider and his family are harvesting the grain, a storm forces them to leave the grain by the roadside and take cover. Crow finds the grain, says it's his, and takes it, leaving Spider with none.

Keywords

character – a person or animal in a story

folktale – a story, which usually teaches a lesson important to a culture, that is passed down through many generations

 **Offline** 50 minutes

Work **together** with students to complete offline Get Ready, Read, and GRAB activities.

Get Ready

Lesson Introduction
Prepare students to read "Squirrel and Spider."

1. Explain to students that before they read "Squirrel and Spider," they will discuss with you

   ▸ What they remember about folktales
   ▸ Where this folktale is from
   ▸ What characters are in the tale

2. Tell students that while they read, you will check in on them to make sure they understand what they are reading.

3. Tell students that after they read, they will answer questions about the story.

Review Folktales
Review the characteristics of folktales and discuss where this folktale is from.

1. Tell students that they are going to read another **folktale** and have them tell what they remember about folktales. Folktales are stories that teach lessons important to a culture and are told from one person to another in families and communities

2. Tell students the folktale they will read comes from Africa. Have students find Africa on a world map.

3. Explain that many African folktales have animal characters, and spiders are one of the most common types of animals. In African folktales, spiders often use tricks to try to get what they want.

Book Walk
Have students use the **table of contents** to locate the story "Squirrel and Spider" and lead you through a Book Walk. Remind them to use the title and **illustrations** to make predictions about what will happen in the story.

Words to Know
As students read "Squirrel and Spider," remind them to refer to the Words to Know as they appear at the bottom of the pages of the story.

> **Objectives**
> - Understand a variety of literature representing different cultures and traditions.
> - Use text organizational features to locate and comprehend information (table of contents).
> - Use text features to make a prediction (illustrations, title).
> - Use before-reading strategies.
> - Increase concept and content vocabulary.

Read

"Squirrel and Spider"

Have students read "Squirrel and Spider." Remind them to use the strategies on their Reading Strategies bookmark. For example, they may want to reread when they don't understand something.

 Learning Coach Check-In This reading assignment should take about 15–20 minutes. Check in with students after they finish reading to assess their comprehension of the selection by asking the following questions:

- ► How does Squirrel get to his farm? He jumps from one tree to another.
- ► Who says Spider can keep Squirrel's grain? a judge
- ► Who ends up with the grain in this story? Crow

If students have trouble answering these questions, ask them what reading strategies they used and suggest they reread the selection.

Objectives

- Read literature independently and proficiently.
- Apply information read to answer questions.
- Evaluate reading strategies.
- Compare a prediction about an action or event to what actually occurred within a text.

GRAB

Go Read a Book

Have students read a book or magazine of their own choosing for at least 20 minutes. Remind students to use the strategies on their Reading Strategies bookmark before and during reading to help them understand the text.

Objectives

- Read literature independently and proficiently.
- Read a variety of texts for information and pleasure.
- Evaluate reading strategies.
- Use before-reading strategies.

Explore "Squirrel and Spider"

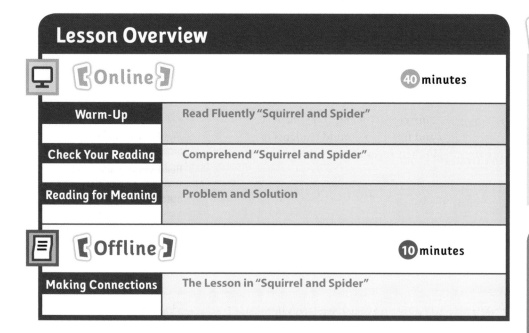

Lesson Overview

🖥 Online   40 minutes

Warm-Up	Read Fluently "Squirrel and Spider"
Check Your Reading	Comprehend "Squirrel and Spider"
Reading for Meaning	Problem and Solution

📄 Offline   10 minutes

Making Connections	The Lesson in "Squirrel and Spider"

Big Ideas

▸ Active, strong readers employ reading strategies such as drawing inferences during and after reading, and synthesizing information as they read and after they read.

▸ Fluency is the ability to decode text quickly, smoothly, and automatically.

▸ Readers need to synthesize, draw conclusions about, and interpret what they have read.

▸ To understand and interpret a story, readers need to understand and describe characters and what they do.

〖 Materials 〗

Supplied

- "Squirrel and Spider," *K¹² Classics for Young Readers, Volume C*, pp. 26–31
- *K¹² Language Arts Activity Book*, pp. LC 11–12

Keywords

character – a person or animal in a story

folktale – a story, which usually teaches a lesson important to a culture, that is passed down through many generations

problem – an issue a character must solve in a story

solution – how a character solves a problem in a story

 **minutes**

Students will work **independently** to complete online Warm-Up, Check Your Reading, and Reading for Meaning activities.

Warm-Up

Read Fluently "Squirrel and Spider"
Students will read aloud and record the passage "Squirrel and Spider." The purpose of this activity is to improve students' oral reading and fluency. Remind students to listen to the model on each screen before they begin their recording.

 Objectives
- Read poetry and prose aloud.
- Read aloud grade-level text with appropriate automaticity, prosody, accuracy, and rate.

Check Your Reading

Comprehend "Squirrel and Spider"
Students will answer questions about "Squirrel and Spider" to demonstrate their literal and inferential comprehension of the story.

 Objectives
- Identify concrete answers to questions.
- Apply information read to answer questions.
- Infer answers to questions.

Reading for Meaning

Problem and Solution
Students will review problem and solution and sequencing events using order words. Then they will focus on the characters in "Squirrel and Spider" and closely examine the problems those characters face, and the consequences of some of the solutions the characters attempt. Students will evaluate the characteristics of the various solutions in preparation for considering the lesson that the folktale teaches.

 Students may be frustrated that honesty and hard work are not rewarded in this story. You may wish to discuss this issue with them. Just as Spider is not ultimately rewarded for his trickery, it is possible that Crow might lose the grain, too.

Objectives
- Identify problems and solutions in a story.
- Describe the characters in the story using evidence from the text.
- Sequence events in a text.
- Describe how the solution to a problem demonstrates a character's traits.

 **Offline** ⏱ **10 minutes**

Work **together** with students to complete the offline Making Connections activity.

Making Connections •

The Lesson in "Squirrel and Spider"
Have students review some of the problems and solutions in the story and identify the lesson of the folktale. Turn to pages LC 11 and 12 in *K¹² Language Arts Activity Book*.

1. Direct students' attention to the Activity Book pages and have them read the directions.

2. Have students complete the Activity Book pages.

TIP Keep the Activity Book pages in a safe place so students can refer to them later.

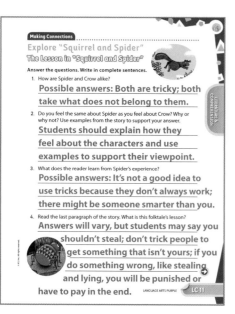

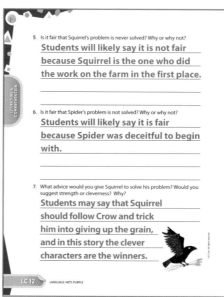

> ⭐ **Objectives**
> - Indentify problems and solutions in a story.
> - Determine the theme, moral, or lesson of a work of literature.
> - Compare and contrast using evidence from the text.
> - Distinguish own opinion from that of the narrator or those of the characters.
> - Describe the characters in the story using evidence from the text.
> - Generate plausible alternative endings to plot.

Reflections on Animal Tales

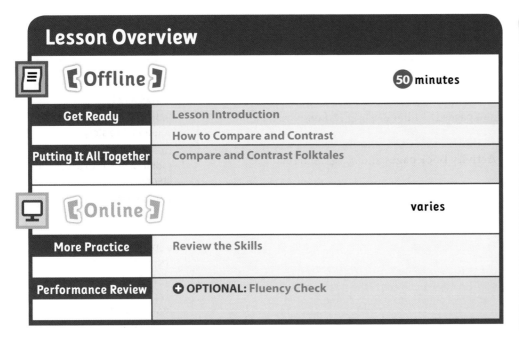

Lesson Overview

[Offline]　　　　　　　　　　　　　　**50** minutes

Get Ready	Lesson Introduction
	How to Compare and Contrast
Putting It All Together	Compare and Contrast Folktales

[Online]　　　　　　　　　　　　　　**varies**

More Practice	Review the Skills
Performance Review	✚ OPTIONAL: Fluency Check

[Materials]

Supplied

- "Chipmunk and Bear," "The Tiger, the Brahman, and the Jackal," "Squirrel and Spider," *K¹² Classics for Young Readers, Volume C,* pp. 12–31
- *K¹² Language Arts Activity Book,* pp. LC 7–15
- Putting It All Together Assessment Checklist (printout)
- Fluency Performance Checklist (optional printout)

Advance Preparation

Have students gather completed pages LC 7–12 (The Lesson in "Chipmunk and Bear," The Lesson in "The Tiger, the Brahman, and the Jackal," and The Lesson in "Squirrel and Spider") in *K¹² Language Arts Activity Book.*

Big Ideas

- ▶ To understand and interpret a story, readers need to understand and describe characters and what they do.
- ▶ Signal words—such as *before, consequently, compare/contrast, therefore*—are a guide to understanding the relationship between and among ideas.
- ▶ Writing requires organization and structure.

Keywords

compare – to explain how two or more things are alike

contrast – to explain how two or more things are different

folktale – a story, which usually teaches a lesson important to a culture, that is passed down through many generations

problem – an issue a character must solve in a story

solution – how a character solves a problem in a story

 **50 minutes**

Work **together** with students to complete the offline Get Ready and Putting It All Together activities.

Get Ready

Lesson Introduction

Prepare students for comparing and contrasting the folktales in this unit.

1. Tell students that they are going to think and write about the folktales they read in this unit.

2. Explain that before students write about the folktales, they will get ready by reviewing and discussing with you what the words *compare* and *contrast* mean.

> **Objectives**
> - Define *compare* and *contrast*.
> - Use a graphic organizer to organize information related to this unit's readings.

How to Compare and Contrast

Review with students how to compare and contrast characters in a story using a Venn diagram.

1. Tell students that they are going to **compare** and **contrast** the characters and their problems in the folktales they read.

2. Ask students if they know what *compare* and *contrast* mean. Define the words if they don't know them. *Compare* is to explain how two or more things are alike; *contrast* is to explain how two or more things are different.

3. Explain that students will compare and contrast the characters in folktales.

Putting It All Together

 Compare and Contrast Folktales

Students will compare and contrast characters from the folktales in the unit, as a way to understand the lessons in the stories. Turn to pages LC 13–15 and gather completed pages LC 7–12 in *K¹² Language Arts Activity Book*.

1. Have students find "Chipmunk and Bear," "The Tiger, the Brahman, and the Jackal," and "Squirrel and Spider" in *K¹² Classics for Young Readers, Volume C*.

2. Have students complete the Venn diagram portion of the Activity Book pages, using their completed pages to help them. If necessary, help students complete the Venn diagram.

3. Check students' Venn diagram before they begin to write their paragraph. Be sure they have described the characters. Then have students complete the remainder of the Activity Book pages, using their best cursive handwriting and leaving spaces between words so that others can read what they wrote.

> **Objectives**
> - Compare and contrast characters from different stories.
> - Compare texts from different cultures and time periods.
> - Compare and contrast literary elements in two or more literary selections.
> - Write an introductory statement.
> - Identify the solution to the problem a character faces.

4. When students have completed the Activity Book pages, use the materials and instructions in the online lesson to evaluate students' work.

5. Enter the answers (Yes or No) for each line of the assessment checklist online.

➲ **Learning Coach Check-In** Check in with students after about 40 minutes to see if they have completed the assignment.

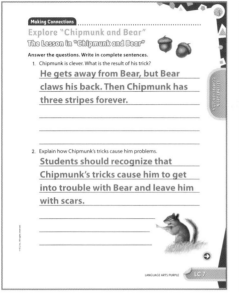

Making Connections

Explore "Chipmunk and Bear"
The Lesson in "Chipmunk and Bear"

Answer the questions. Write in complete sentences.

1. Chipmunk is clever. What is the result of his trick?

He gets away from Bear, but Bear claws his back. Then Chipmunk has three stripes forever.

2. Explain how Chipmunk's tricks cause him problems.

Students should recognize that Chipmunk's tricks cause him to get into trouble with Bear and leave him with scars.

LANGUAGE ARTS PURPLE   LC 7

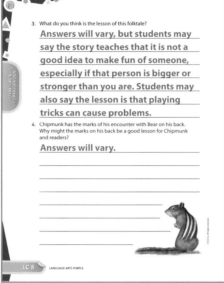

3. What do you think is the lesson of this folktale?

Answers will vary, but students may say the story teaches that it is not a good idea to make fun of someone, especially if that person is bigger or stronger than you are. Students may also say the lesson is that playing tricks can cause problems.

4. Chipmunk has the marks of his encounter with Bear on his back. Why might the marks on his back be a good lesson for Chipmunk and readers?

Answers will vary.

LC 8   LANGUAGE ARTS PURPLE

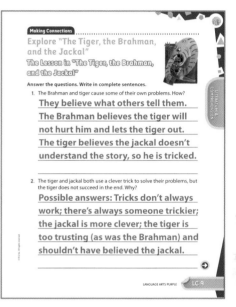

Making Connections

Explore "The Tiger, the Brahman, and the Jackal"
The Lesson in "The Tiger, the Brahman, and the Jackal"

Answer the questions. Write in complete sentences.

1. The Brahman and tiger cause some of their own problems. How?

They believe what others tell them. The Brahman believes the tiger will not hurt him and lets the tiger out. The tiger believes the jackal doesn't understand the story, so he is tricked.

2. The tiger and jackal both use a clever trick to solve their problems, but the tiger does not succeed in the end. Why?

Possible answers: Tricks don't always work; there's always someone trickier; the jackal is more clever; the tiger is too trusting (as was the Brahman) and shouldn't have believed the jackal.

LANGUAGE ARTS PURPLE   LC 9

3. What is the lesson of this folktale?

Possible answers: It's good to be clever and tricky; it's not good to lie or trust someone known to be untrustworthy.

4. The tree, buffalo, and road say that the Brahman cannot expect kindness in return for kindness. Do you agree? Why or why not? Use examples from the story, other stories, and your own life to support your answer.

Students should state whether it is appropriate to expect kindness for kindness and support their opinion with examples.

5. Imagine that the jackal had not come along in the story. If you were the Brahman, would you solve your problem with strength, cleverness, or in some other way? What would you do and why?

Students should explain their plan and why they think it would work. Those who choose cleverness may imagine another ending where the tiger is tricked into the cage or into not eating the Brahman. Those who choose strength may imagine an ending where the Brahman is able to subdue the tiger.

LC 10   LANGUAGE ARTS PURPLE

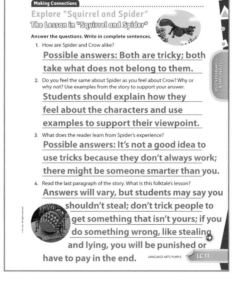

Making Connections

Explore "Squirrel and Spider"
The Lesson in "Squirrel and Spider"

Answer the questions. Write in complete sentences.

1. How are Spider and Crow alike?

Possible answers: Both are tricky; both take what does not belong to them.

2. Do you feel the same about Spider as you feel about Crow? Why or why not? Use examples from the story to support your answer.

Students should explain how they feel about the characters and use examples to support their viewpoint.

3. What does the reader learn from Spider's experience?

Possible answers: It's not a good idea to use tricks because they don't always work; there might be someone smarter than you.

4. Read the last paragraph of the story. What is this folktale's lesson?

Answers will vary, but students may say you shouldn't steal; don't trick people to get something that isn't yours; if you do something wrong, like stealing and lying, you will be punished or have to pay in the end.

LC 11   LANGUAGE ARTS PURPLE

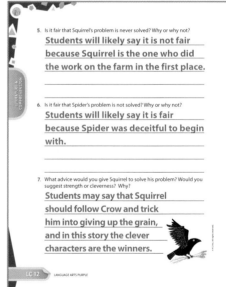

5. Is it fair that Squirrel's problem is never solved? Why or why not?

Students will likely say it is not fair because Squirrel is the one who did the work on the farm in the first place.

6. Is it fair that Spider's problem is not solved? Why or why not?

Students will likely say it is fair because Spider was deceitful to begin with.

7. What advice would you give Squirrel to solve his problem? Would you suggest strength or cleverness? Why?

Students may say that Squirrel should follow Crow and trick him into giving up the grain, and in this story the clever characters are the winners.

LC 12   LANGUAGE ARTS PURPLE

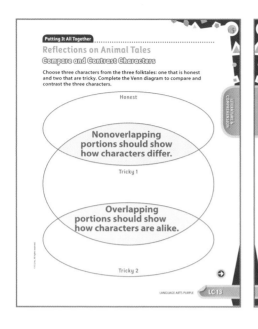

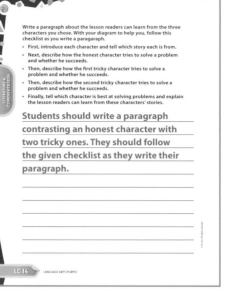

Online varies

Students will work **independently** to complete the online More Practice activity.

More Practice

Review the Skills

If students scored less than 80 percent or had difficulty meeting the objectives of the Putting It All Together activity, have them go online for more practice.

Reward: If students score 66 percent or more on the Putting It All Together activity, add a sticker for this unit on the My Accomplishments chart. If students did not score 66 percent or more, work with them to revise their writing until they do score 66 percent and then add a sticker to the My Accomplishments chart.

Objectives
- Identify problems and solutions in a story.
- Describe the characters in the story using evidence from the text.

Performance Review

⊕ OPTIONAL: Fluency Check

Listen to students' recordings and use the Fluency Performance Checklist to review fluency and track performance. Keep the completed checklist so you can review students' progress over time.

Objectives

- Read aloud grade-level text with appropriate automaticity, prosody, accuracy, and rate.

Animals and Their People

Unit Focus

In this unit, students will learn about characters in fiction and discover how to find the clues to characters' traits in a literary text. They will explore the literary device of point of view and discover the effect that the narrator has on a story. They will read and explore these selections:

► "Charlie and Topsy"
► "Moufflu"
► "Black Beauty" (a short adaptation of the novel)

Unit Plan		[Online]	[Offline]
Lesson 1	Introduce "Charlie and Topsy"		50 minutes
Lesson 2	Explore "Charlie and Topsy"	40 minutes	10 minutes
Lesson 3	Introduce "Moufflu"		50 minutes
Lesson 4	Explore "Moufflu"	40 minutes	10 minutes
Lesson 5	Introduce "Black Beauty"		50 minutes
Lesson 6	Explore "Black Beauty"	40 minutes	10 minutes
Lesson 7	Reflections on Animals and Their People	varies	50 minutes
Lesson 8	Your Choice		50 minutes

Introduce "Charlie and Topsy"

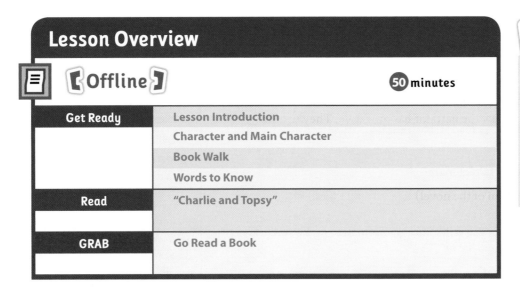

Lesson Overview

[Offline] **50 minutes**

Get Ready	Lesson Introduction
	Character and Main Character
	Book Walk
	Words to Know
Read	"Charlie and Topsy"
GRAB	Go Read a Book

Big Ideas

▸ Active, strong readers employ reading strategies such as monitoring their comprehension (for example, self-check) as they read.

▸ To understand and interpret a story, readers need to understand and describe characters and what they do.

▸ Reading better follows from reading often: The more a student reads, the better reader the student becomes.

[Materials]

Supplied

- "Charlie and Topsy," *K¹² Classics for Young Readers, Volume C,* pp. 32–41
- Reading Strategies bookmark

Story Synopsis

Charlie loves his cat Jane and especially his kitten Topsy. Unfortunately, Charlie is overly zealous and bothers his cats with unwanted attention, so they avoid him. After Charlie is captured by a giant girl who is rough with her affection, Charlie learns to be gentle with his cats and earns their love.

Keywords

author – a writer

character – a person or animal in a story

main character – an important person, animal, or other being who is central to the plot

Offline · 50 minutes

Work **together** with students to complete offline Get Ready, Read, and GRAB activities.

Get Ready

Lesson Introduction

Prepare students to read "Charlie and Topsy."

1. Explain to students that before they read "Charlie and Topsy," they will discuss with you

   ▶ What a character and main character are

   ▶ Their predictions about the text

   ▶ Important words to know in the text

2. Tell students that while they read, you will check in on them to make sure they understand what they are reading.

3. Tell students that after they read, they will answer questions about the story.

Objectives

- Define *character*.
- Define *main character*.
- Identify a character.
- Use text organizational features to locate and comprehend information (table of contents).
- Use text features to make a prediction (illustrations, title).
- Use before-reading strategies.
- Increase concept and content vocabulary.

Character and Main Character

Review character and main character in fiction.

1. Ask students what a **character** is, or provide the definition for them. a person or animal in a story

2. Have students tell what a **main character** is, or define it for them. an important person, animal, or other being who is central to the plot

3. Tell students that we must be able to understand characters, particularly main characters, if we are to understand stories. We need to read carefully and look for clues about characters.

4. Have students name one of their favorite characters from a story they've read and describe the character.

Book Walk

Have students lead you through a Book Walk of "Charlie and Topsy." Remind them to use the **title** and **illustrations** to make predictions about what will happen in the story.

Words to Know

As students read "Charlie and Topsy," remind them to refer to the Words to Know as they appear at the bottom of the pages of the story.

Read

"Charlie and Topsy"

Have students read "Charlie and Topsy." Remind them to use the strategies on their Reading Strategies bookmark.

⮌ **Learning Coach Check-In** This reading assignment should take about 15 minutes. Check in with students after they finish reading to assess their comprehension of the selection by asking the following questions:

▶ Who are Charlie and Topsy? a boy and a kitten that the boy loves
▶ Were your predictions about the story correct? What did you predict that was true, and what surprised you about the story? Students should tell which predictions they made about the story were correct, if any, and what surprised them about the story.

If students have trouble answering these questions, ask them what reading strategies they used and suggest they reread the selection.

Objectives

- Read literature independently and proficiently.
- Apply information read to answer questions.
- Evaluate reading strategies.
- Compare a prediction about an action or event to what actually occurred within a text.

GRAB

Go Read a Book

Have students read a book or magazine of their own choosing for at least 20 minutes. Remind them to use the strategies on their Reading Strategies bookmark before and during reading to help them understand the text.

TIP Remember: The more students read, the better readers they become.

Objectives

- Read literature independently and proficiently.
- Read a variety of texts for information and pleasure.
- Evaluate reading strategies.
- Use before-reading strategies.

Explore "Charlie and Topsy"

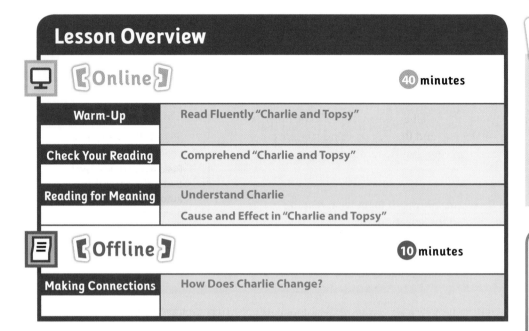

Lesson Overview

🖥 Online — 40 minutes

Warm-Up	Read Fluently "Charlie and Topsy"
Check Your Reading	Comprehend "Charlie and Topsy"
Reading for Meaning	Understand Charlie
	Cause and Effect in "Charlie and Topsy"

📄 Offline — 10 minutes

Making Connections	How Does Charlie Change?

Big Ideas

To understand and interpret a story, readers need to understand and describe characters and what they do.

Materials

Supplied
- "Charlie and Topsy," *K¹² Classics for Young Readers, Volume C*, pp. 32–41
- *K¹² Language Arts Activity Book*, pp. LC 17–18

Keywords

cause – the reason something happens

character – a person or animal in a story

effect – the result of a cause

main character – an important person, animal, or other being who is central to the plot

theme – the author's message or big idea

[Online] ⏱ minutes

Students will work **independently** to complete online Warm-Up, Check Your Reading, and Reading for Meaning activities.

Warm-Up ··

Read Fluently "Charlie and Topsy"
Students will read aloud and record a passage from "Charlie and Topsy." The purpose of this activity is to improve students' oral reading and fluency. Remind students to listen to the model on each screen before they begin their recording.

Objectives
- Read poetry and prose aloud.
- Read aloud grade-level text with appropriate automaticity, prosody, accuracy, and rate.

Check Your Reading ··

Comprehend "Charlie and Topsy"
Students will answer questions about "Charlie and Topsy" to demonstrate their literal and inferential comprehension of the story.

Objectives
- Identify concrete answers to questions.
- Infer answers to questions.
- Apply information read to answer questions.
- Explain how specific aspects of a text's illustrations contribute to the meaning of the text.

Reading for Meaning ··

Understand Charlie
Students will explore the main character, Charlie. They will learn to read text closely to look for clues about characters, including what they say, what they do, and what others say about them. Students will also learn that characters can change over time.

Objectives
- Identify characters in a story.
- Identify main character.
- Describe characters by what they do, what they say, or what others say about them.
- Define *cause and effect*.
- Identify cause and effect.
- Make inferences using evidence from the text.
- Apply information read to answer questions.

Cause and Effect in "Charlie and Topsy"
Students will learn how examining causes and their effects in a story can help them understand how and why a character changes. They will look specifically at the causes that bring about a change in Charlie's behavior toward the cats. Understanding cause and effect and the changes in characters will help students ascertain the theme of a story.

Offline ⑩ minutes

Work **together** with students to complete the offline Making Connections activity.

Making Connections

✏️ **How Does Charlie Change?**

Help students understand how Charlie's change leads readers to the theme of the story. Turn pages LC 17 and 18 in *K¹² Language Arts Activity Book*.

1. Remind students that characters in stories can change.

2. Explain that when we understand how and why characters change, we can understand what the author is trying to tell us about life.

3. Review the definition of **theme**: the author's message or big idea in a story. Tell students that a theme is a statement about life that we can learn from the characters and their experiences in a story.

4. Have students complete the Activity Book pages.

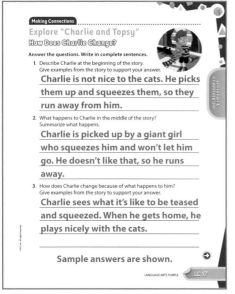

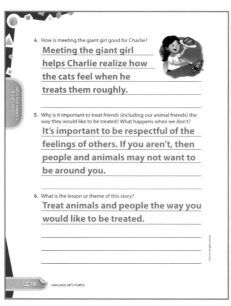

Introduce "Moufflu"

Lesson Overview

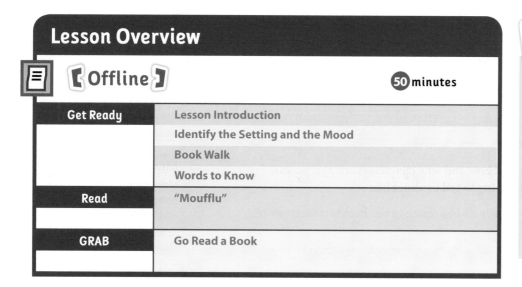

[Offline]   **50** minutes

Get Ready	Lesson Introduction
	Identify the Setting and the Mood
	Book Walk
	Words to Know
Read	"Moufflu"
GRAB	Go Read a Book

Big Ideas

▶ Active, strong readers employ reading strategies such as monitoring their comprehension (for example, self-check) as they read.

▶ To understand and interpret a story, readers need to understand and describe characters and what they do.

▶ Readers should pay close attention to the visual elements (for example, illustrations) that accompany a story to help create and describe the meaning of a text.

▶ Reading better follows from reading often: The more a student reads, the better reader the student becomes.

[Materials]

Supplied

• "Moufflu," *K¹² Classics for Young Readers, Volume C*, pp. 42–51
• Reading Strategies bookmark

Also Needed

• household objects – world map

Story Synopsis

A lame little boy named Lolo lives with his beloved dog Moufflu in Florence, Italy. The talented and lively dog Moufflu performs tricks for passersby. One day, a man buys Moufflu for a sick little boy. Lolo becomes so ill over Moufflu's disappearance that it seems he will die. Then Moufflu comes back to Lolo on his own. The man agrees to let Lolo keep Moufflu and train another dog for the boy.

Keywords

character – a person or animal in a story
mood – the emotions or feelings conveyed in a literary work
setting – when and where a story takes place

[Offline] 50 minutes

Work **together** with students to complete offline Get Ready, Read, and GRAB activities.

Get Ready ....

Lesson Introduction

Prepare students to read "Moufflu."

1. Explain to students that before they read "Moufflu," they will discuss with you

   ▶ The setting of the story
   ▶ Their predictions about the text
   ▶ Important words to know in the text

2. Tell students that while they read, you will check in on them to make sure they understand what they are reading.

3. Tell students that after they read, they will answer questions about the story.

Identify the Setting and the Mood

Have students identify the setting of "Moufflu." Gather the world map.

1. Have students tell what the **setting** of a story is, or define it for them. when and where a story takes place

2. Have students find "Moufflu" in *K¹² Classics for Young Readers, Volume C,* using the **table of contents**. Have them read the first paragraph of the story aloud.

3. Tell students that Florence is a city in Italy. Have them find Italy and Florence on a world map. Then have students identify Rome, the capital of Italy, on the map. Tell students that these two places are mentioned in the story.

   ▶ Is Rome near Florence or far from it? far from it

4. Explain that one of the important places in Florence is a large cathedral in the center of the city—the one in the picture on page 43. Review the meaning of the word *cathedral* using the definition at the bottom of the page.

5. Tell students that the **mood** of the story is the emotions or feelings that are conveyed. Just like a person's mood can change depending on what is going on and how she or he is feeling, so can the mood of a story. The illustrations and the words in a story both help readers understand the mood.

6. Tell students to look at the illustration on page 43. Ask them what the picture tells them about the setting and the mood of this part of the story. Possible answers: The story takes place a long time ago; the building looks old; this is a happy part of the story; I can tell by the blue skies and the birds.

Objectives

- Define *setting*.
- Identify setting(s).
- Use text organizational features to locate and comprehend information (table of contents).
- Use text features to make a prediction (illustrations, title).
- Use before-reading strategies.
- Increase concept and content vocabulary.
- Define *mood*.
- Identify the mood of a literary selection.
- Use information gained from illustration to demonstrate understanding.

Book Walk

Have students lead you through a Book Walk of "Moufflu." Remind them to use the **title** and **illustrations** to make predictions about what will happen in the story. Ask them to think about the mood of the story: Does it change? What do the illustrations show?

Words to Know

As students read "Moufflu," remind them to refer to the Words to Know as they appear at the bottom of the pages of the story.

Read

"Moufflu"

Have students read "Moufflu." Remind them to use the strategies on their Reading Strategies bookmark.

⊃ **Learning Coach Check-In** This reading assignment should take about 15 minutes. Check in with students after they finish reading to assess their comprehension of the selection by asking the following questions:

▸ Who are Lolo and Moufflu? a boy and his dog who live in Florence
▸ Why is Moufflu special? The dog is smart, can do a lot of tricks, and loves Lolo so much he finds his way back to Florence all the way from Rome.

If students have trouble answering these questions, ask them what reading strategies they used and suggest they reread the selection.

Objectives
- Read literature independently and proficiently.
- Apply information read to answer questions.
- Evaluate reading strategies.
- Compare a prediction about an action or event to what actually occurred within a text.

GRAB

Go Read a Book

Have students read a book or magazine of their own choosing for at least 20 minutes. Remind students to use the strategies on their Reading Strategies bookmark before and during reading to help them understand the text.

Objectives
- Read literature independently and proficiently.
- Read a variety of texts for information and pleasure.

Explore "Moufflu"

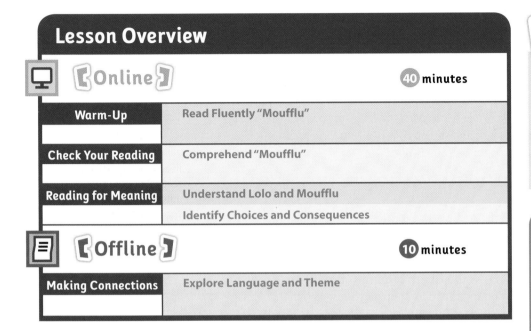

Lesson Overview

🖥 〖Online〗 **40** minutes

Warm-Up	Read Fluently "Moufflu"
Check Your Reading	Comprehend "Moufflu"
Reading for Meaning	Understand Lolo and Moufflu
	Identify Choices and Consequences

📄 〖Offline〗 **10** minutes

Making Connections	Explore Language and Theme

〖Materials〗

Supplied
- "Moufflu," *K¹² Classics for Young Readers, Volume C,* pp. 42–51
- *K¹² Language Arts Activity Book,* pp. LC 19–20

Keywords

character – a person or animal in a story

consequence – what happens because of an action or event

main character – an important person, animal, or other being who is central to the plot

theme – the author's message or big idea

Big Ideas

▸ To understand and interpret a story, readers need to understand and describe characters and what they do.

▸ Identifying choices and consequences helps readers understand characters and the central message in a story.

 **40** **minutes**

Students will work **independently** to complete online Warm-Up, Check Your Reading, and Reading for Meaning activities.

Warm-Up

Read Flulently "Moufflu"

Students will read aloud and record a passage from "Moufflu." The purpose of this activity is to improve students' oral reading and fluency. Remind students to listen to the model on each screen before they begin their recording.

Objectives
- Read poetry and prose aloud.
- Read aloud grade-level text with appropriate automaticity, prosody, accuracy, and rate.

Check Your Reading

Comprehend "Moufflu"

Students will answer questions about "Moufflu" to demonstrate their literal and inferential comprehension of the story.

Objectives
- Identify concrete answers to questions.
- Infer answers to questions.
- Apply information read to answer questions.

Reading for Meaning

Understand Lolo and Moufflu

Students will examine the main character, Lolo. They will learn to read text closely and also explore illustrations to look for clues about Lolo's feelings for his dog, Moufflu. They will also examine Moufflu's behavior to determine what his actions tell us about his character.

Objectives
- Identify main character.
- Describe characters by what they do, what they say, or what others say about them.
- Describe the main character in a story using evidence from the text.
- Identify choices that a character makes and their consequences.

Identify Choices and Consequences

Students will look at the choices some of the peripheral characters in the story make and analyze the consequences of those choices. This will help students learn more about the characters and recognize their importance to the plot and theme of the story.

 **Offline** ⑩ **minutes**

Work **together** with students to complete the offline Making Connections activity.

Making Connections

✏️ **Explore Language and Theme**

Help students understand how the language the author uses influences the readers' feelings and helps readers understand the theme of the story. Turn to pages LC 19 and 20 in *K¹² Language Arts Activity Book.*

1. Explain that authors sometimes tell us how a character feels. An author might write, "He is sad." Other times authors just show us a character's feelings by using words that describe something that happens. An author might write, "He wept an ocean of tears." Ask students which is more descriptive or tells more about how sad the person is. "He wept an ocean of tears" is more descriptive.

2. Tell students that showing language creates an image in the readers' mind, so readers can see what a character is feeling and experiencing.

3. Tell students that the words the author chooses help readers know more about many elements of a story, including the story's **theme.** Have students define theme. the author's message or big idea

4. Have students complete the Activity Book pages.

🛑 **TIP** Keep the Activity Book pages in a safe place so students can refer to them later.

> ### Objectives
> - Identify descriptions that support comprehension.
> - Describe methods the authors use to influence readers' feelings.
> - Identify theme.
> - Identify language that shows, not tells.

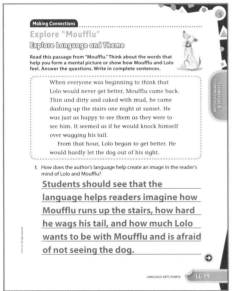

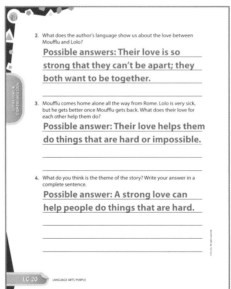

Introduce "Black Beauty"

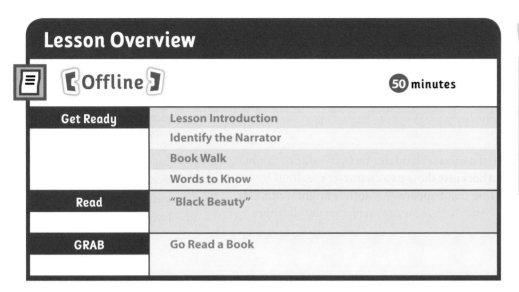

Lesson Overview

[Offline]   **50** minutes

Get Ready	Lesson Introduction
	Identify the Narrator
	Book Walk
	Words to Know
Read	"Black Beauty"
GRAB	Go Read a Book

Big Ideas

► Active, strong readers employ reading strategies such as monitoring their comprehension (for example, self-check) as they read.

► To understand and interpret a story, readers need to understand and describe characters and what they do.

► The point of view that a story is told from determines how much information readers have about plot events and characters' feelings.

► Written words have a voice, or a sense that someone has written them.

► Reading better follows from reading often: The more a student reads, the better reader the student becomes.

Materials

Supplied

• "Black Beauty," *K¹² Classics for Young Readers, Volume C*, pp. 52–65
• Reading Strategies bookmark

Story Synopsis

Black Beauty is a young horse who tells about his experiences from the first-person point of view. He describes his life on a farm learning how to carry riders and pull carriages. Then he tells about his sale to a new master and how he must ride until he nearly drops to save the master's wife.

Keywords

author – a writer

character – a person or animal in a story

first-person point of view – the telling of a story by a character in that story, using pronouns such as *I*, *me*, and *we*

narrator – the teller of a story

point of view – the perspective a story is told from

[Offline] 50 minutes

Work **together** with students to complete offline Get Ready, Read, and GRAB activities.

Get Ready

Lesson Introduction

Prepare students to read "Black Beauty.

1. Explain to students that before they read "Black Beauty," they will discuss with you

   ► The narrator of the story
   ► Their predictions about the text
   ► Important words to know in the text

2. Tell students that while they read, you will check in on them to make sure they understand what they are reading.

3. Tell students that after they read, they will answer questions about the story.

Objectives

- Define *narrator*.
- Distinguish between author and narrator.
- Use text features to make a prediction (illustrations, title).
- Use before-reading strategies.
- Increase concept and content vocabulary.

Identify the Narrator

Help students identify the narrator of "Black Beauty."

1. Have students tell what an **author** is. a writer; a person who writes a story

2. Have them tell if they know what a **narrator** is. If not, define it for them. the teller of a story

3. Explain that the author and the narrator of a fictional story are different.

4. Explain that sometimes the narrator is a character that takes part in the story, but sometimes not. Sometimes the narrator is another person who is not part of the story.

5. Tell students that the narrator in "Black Beauty" is the main character of the story. He will tell his own story.

Book Walk

Have students lead you through a Book Walk of "Black Beauty." Remind them to use the **title** and **illustrations** to make predictions about what will happen in the story.

Words to Know

As students read "Black Beauty," remind them to refer to the Words to Know as they appear at the bottom of the pages of the story.

Read

"Black Beauty"

Have students read "Black Beauty." Remind them to use the strategies on their Reading Strategies bookmark.

⟳ **Learning Coach Check-In** This reading assignment should take about 15 minutes. Check in with students after they finish reading to assess their comprehension of the selection by asking the following questions:

▸ Who is Black Beauty? a horse
▸ Who tells the story? Black Beauty
▸ What are some of the things that Black Beauty learns before he is sold to Squire Gordon? Possible answers: how to wear a saddle, bridle, and horseshoes; how to carry a rider and pull a carriage; how to be unafraid near trains

If students have trouble answering these questions, ask them what reading strategies they used and suggest they reread the selection.

Objectives

- Read literature independently and proficiently.
- Apply information read to answer questions.
- Evaluate reading strategies.
- Compare a prediction about an action or event to what actually occurred within a text.

GRAB

Go Read a Book

Have students read a book or magazine of their own choosing for at least 20 minutes. Remind them to use the strategies on their Reading Strategies bookmark before and during reading to help them understand the text.

Objectives

- Read literature independently and proficiently.
- Read a variety of texts for information and pleasure.

Explore "Black Beauty"

Lesson Overview

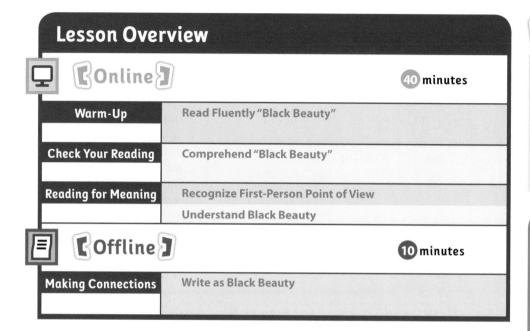

Online — 40 minutes

Warm-Up	Read Fluently "Black Beauty"
Check Your Reading	Comprehend "Black Beauty"
Reading for Meaning	Recognize First-Person Point of View
	Understand Black Beauty

Offline — 10 minutes

Making Connections	Write as Black Beauty

Big Ideas

▸ To understand and interpret a story, readers need to understand and describe characters and what they do.
▸ The point of view that a story is told from determines how much information readers have about plot events and characters' feelings.
▸ Written words have a voice, or a sense that someone has written them.

Materials

Supplied

● "Black Beauty," *K¹² Classics for Young Readers, Volume C,* pp. 52–65
● *K¹² Language Arts Activity Book,* pp. LC 21–22

Keywords

character – a person or animal in a story

first-person point of view – the telling of a story by a character in that story, using pronouns such as *I, me,* and *we*

narrator – the teller of a story

point of view – the perspective a story is told from

theme – the author's message or big idea

trait – a quality of a person or character

 **Online** 🔟 **minutes**

Students will work **independently** to complete online Warm-Up, Check Your Reading, and Reading for Meaning activities.

Warm-Up ···

Read Fluently "Black Beauty"
Students will read aloud and record a passage from "Black Beauty." The purpose of this activity is to improve students' oral reading and fluency. Remind students to listen to the model on each screen before they begin their recording.

 Objectives
- Read poetry and prose aloud.
- Read aloud grade-level text with appropriate automaticity, prosody, accuracy, and rate.

Check Your Reading ·······························

Comprehend "Black Beauty"
Students will answer questions about "Black Beauty" to demonstrate their literal and inferential comprehension of the story.

 Objectives
- Identify concrete answers to questions.
- Infer answers to questions.
- Apply information read to answer questions.
- Distinguish between author and narrator.

Reading for Meaning ·····························

Recognize First-Person Point of View
Students will work through the concept of literary point of view (which is different from opinion) to understand how the point of view of the narrator in a story determines what readers learn about events and characters. They will also learn to recognize the first-person point of view and explore how this technique provides readers with a window into the narrator's experiences and perspective.

Understand Black Beauty
Students will think about the character of Black Beauty and identify his character traits by looking at what he does, what he says, and what he reports that others say about him in the story. Students will identify some of his most prominent character traits.

 Objectives
- Define *first-person point of view*.
- Define *third-person point of view*.
- Identify point of view.
- Identify first-person narrator.
- Describe the effect point of view has on a story.
- Describe characters by what they do, what they say, or what others say about them.
- Describe the main character in a story using evidence from the text.

 **Offline** ⏱ **10 minutes**

Work **together** with students to complete the offline Making Connections activity.

Making Connections

 Write as Black Beauty

Have students write a passage that reflects the point of view of Black Beauty. Turn to pages LC 21 and 22 in *K¹² Language Arts Activity Book*.

1. Have students define **narrator** and **first-person point of view**. the teller of a story; the telling of a story by a character in that story, using pronouns such as *I, me,* and *we*

2. Review that when a story is told in the first person, the narrator describes what he or she sees, experiences, thinks, and feels.

3. Have students tell what a character **trait** is and tell what some of Black Beauty's traits are. a quality of a person or character; Black Beauty's traits include pride, bravery, caring, and a willingness to work hard.

4. Explain that when a character is the first-person narrator of a story, much of what that narrator describes shows readers something about that character's traits. We have the best understanding of the narrator.

5. Have students complete the Activity Book pages.

TIP If students are hesitant to make up a story, tell them to use the content that is on the page and start telling it as if they were Black Beauty. You may wish to allow them to dictate to you first. If they are still struggling, start them off. Say, "Once I was sold to an unkind master . . . ." Ask, "And then what happened?"

 Objectives
- Describe story action from a different perspective.
- Identify descriptions that support comprehension.
- Makes connections between text and self, text and world, and text to text.

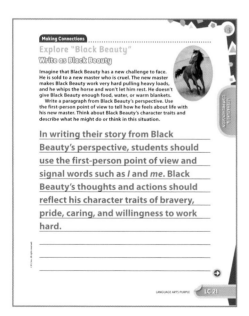

Reflections on Animals and Their People

Lesson Overview

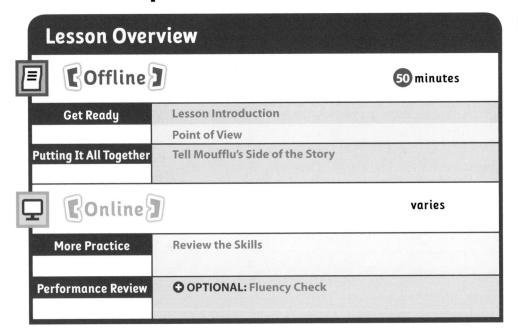

Offline		**50** minutes
Get Ready	Lesson Introduction	
	Point of View	
Putting It All Together	Tell Moufflu's Side of the Story	

Online		varies
More Practice	Review the Skills	
Performance Review	**⊕ OPTIONAL:** Fluency Check	

Advance Preparation

Have students gather completed pages LC 19 and 20 (Explore Language and Theme) in *K¹² Language Arts Activity Book*.

Big Ideas

▸ Written words have a voice, or a sense that someone has written them.
▸ Writing requires organization and structure.
▸ Readers should be able to retell the story (or information) in their own words, not repeat what was written.
▸ The point of view that a story is told from determines how much information readers have about plot events and characters' feelings.

[Offline] 50 minutes

Work **together** with students to complete the offline Get Ready and Putting it All Together activities.

Get Ready

Lesson Introduction
Prepare students for retelling "Moufflu."

1. Tell students that they are going to retell the story "Moufflu."

2. Have students use the **table of contents** to find the story in *K¹² Classics for Young Readers, Volume C.*

3. Have them retell what happens in the story. If they have trouble remembering, suggest that students take a Book Walk through the story to refresh their memory.

Objectives

- Use text organizational features to locate and comprehend information (table of contents).
- Summarize the plot of a story.
- Define *character*.
- Define *narrator*.
- Define *point of view*.
- Identify third-person narrator.
- Identify point of view in a selection.
- Describe the effect point of view has on a story.

Point of View
Review the point of view in "Moufflu" to prepare students to retell the story from a different point of view.

1. Review the definitions of **character, narrator,** and **point of view.** A *character* is a person or animal in a story; a *narrator* is the teller of a story; *point of view* is the perspective a story is told from.

2. Have students identify whether the narrator in "Moufflu" is a **first-person narrator** or **third-person narrator** and explain why. The narrator is a third-person narrator because he or she is not a character in the story.

3. Have students explain how the narrator's point of view affects what we know about the events in the story and how we feel about them. Possible answers: The narrator tells us a little bit about how Lolo feels, but mostly just about what happens; the narrator does not know what happens to Moufflu after he is sold to the gentleman or how he gets back to Lolo; we don't know how Moufflu or anyone else feels.

4. Tell students that they're going to think about how the story might be different if Moufflu were the narrator and told the story from his point of view.

Putting It All Together

 Tell Moufflu's Side of the Story

Have students write a summary to demonstrate their understanding of "Moufflu" and the narrative device of point of view. Turn to pages LC 23–25 and gather completed pages LC 19 and 20 in *K¹² Language Arts Activity Book*.

1. Give students the Activity Book pages. Their completed pages will help them write the draft and final copy of their summary.

2. Tell them that they are going to retell the story from Moufflu's point of view. Remind students that changing the narrator of a story will change what the reader learns and feels about events in the story.

3. Have students complete the Activity Book pages. Guide them to summarize what occurs in the story, but they may embellish their retelling. Remind students how dirty and tired Moufflu is when he returns to Lolo. Remind them to complete their summary on the Activity Book pages using their best cursive handwriting and leaving spaces between words so that others can read what they wrote.

4. When students have completed their summary, use the materials and instructions in the online lesson to evaluate students' work.

5. Enter the answers (Yes or No) for each line of the assessment checklist online.

    ⟳ **Learning Coach Check-In** Check in with students after about 40 minutes to see if they have completed the assignment.

Objectives

- Describe characters by what they do, what they say, or what others say about them.
- Identify descriptions that support comprehension.
- Write a summary.
- Distinguish one's own opinion from that of the narrator or those of the characters.
- Organize ideas.
- Use the first-person point of view.
- Use descriptive details in writing.
- Identify details that explain characters' actions and feelings.
- Use vivid images that relate to the main idea.

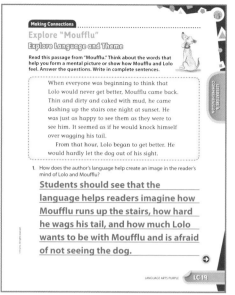

Explore "Moufflu"
Explore Language and Theme

Read this passage from "Moufflu." Think about the words that help you form a mental picture or show how Moufflu and Lolo feel. Answer the questions. Write in complete sentences.

> When everyone was beginning to think that Lolo would never get better, Moufflu came back. Thin and dirty and caked with mud, he came dashing up the stairs one night at sunset. He was just as happy to see them as they were to see him. It seemed as if he would knock himself over wagging his tail.
>
> From that hour, Lolo began to get better. He would hardly let the dog out of his sight.

1. How does the author's language help create an image in the reader's mind of Lolo and Moufflu?

Students should see that the language helps readers imagine how Moufflu runs up the stairs, how hard he wags his tail, and how much Lolo wants to be with Moufflu and is afraid of not seeing the dog.

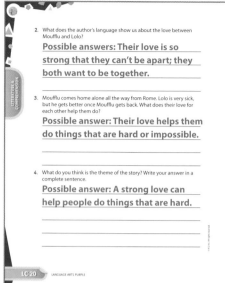

2. What does the author's language show us about the love between Moufflu and Lolo?

Possible answers: Their love is so strong that they can't be apart; they both want to be together.

3. Moufflu comes home alone all the way from Rome. Lolo is very sick, but he gets better once Moufflu gets back. What does their love for each other help them do?

Possible answer: Their love helps them do things that are hard or impossible.

4. What do you think is the theme of the story? Write your answer in a complete sentence.

Possible answer: A strong love can help people do things that are hard.

Reflections on Animals and Their People
Tell Moufflu's Side of the Story

Pretend that you are Moufflu, and retell the story from Moufflu's point of view. Organize your story this way:

- First, tell who you are and where you live. Be sure to explain how you feel about Lolo.
- Then, summarize what happens from the point at which the gentleman buys you until you return to Lolo. Use language that shows, rather than tells, when you say what happens to you and how you feel.
- Finally, end your story by telling how you feel about being home.

When you have finished your first draft, use this checklist to review your work. After you revise your story, write a neat final copy ready to publish and share.

☐ Tell the story with Moufflu as the first-person narrator. Use the words *I, me,* and *mine.*

☐ Describe events the way Moufflu would see them and feel about them. Stay true to his character traits.

☐ Be creative when describing Moufflu's journey home. Add details about new settings and what might have happened to him.

☐ Use showing language and vivid words to describe settings, events, characters, and Moufflu's feelings.

☐ Use order words and transition words to connect your sentences, ideas, and events.

☐ Tell what Moufflu says or thinks, what he does, and what others say about him to help readers understand Moufflu's character.

Write your neat final copy on this page.

Students should include in their summary all of the items in the checklist.

 **varies**

Students will work **independently** to complete the online More Practice activity.

More Practice ···

Review the Skills

If students scored less than 80 percent or had difficulty meeting the objectives of the Putting It All Together activity, have them go online for more practice.

 Reward: If students score 80 percent or more on the Putting It All Together activity, add a sticker for this unit on the My Accomplishments chart. If students did not score 80 percent or more, work with them to revise their writing until they do score 80 percent and then add a sticker to the My Accomplishments chart.

 Objectives
- Describe characters by what they do, what they say, or what others say about them.
- Describe the effect point of view has on a story.
- Write a summary.

Performance Review ··

⊕ OPTIONAL: Fluency Check

Listen to students' recordings and use the Fluency Performance Checklist to review fluency and track performance. Keep the completed checklist so you can review students' progress over time.

 Objectives
- Read aloud grade-level text with appropriate automaticity, prosody, accuracy, and rate.

Critical Skills Practice 1

Unit Focus

This is the first Critical Skills Practice unit of the Literature & Comprehension program. Be sure to watch the Introduction to Critical Skills Practice in the online lesson.

In this unit, students will focus on reading fiction, directions, and forms, and on answering multiple choice questions about those readings in a test format. In this unit, students will focus on reading fiction, directions, and forms, and on answering multiple choice questions about those readings in a test format.

Unit Plan		[Offline]	[Online]
Lesson 1	Fiction Passages (A)		50 minutes
Lesson 2	Fiction Passages (B)		50 minutes
Lesson 3	Directions (A)		50 minutes
Lesson 4	Practical Reading: Forms		50 minutes
Lesson 5	Unit Checkpoint	50 minutes	varies

Fiction Passages (A)

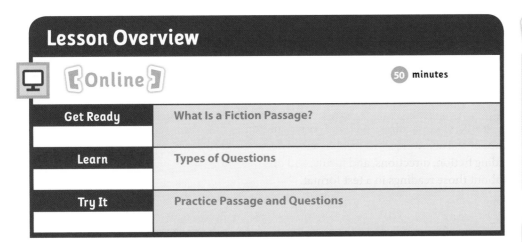

Lesson Overview

Online — 50 minutes

Get Ready	What Is a Fiction Passage?
Learn	Types of Questions
Try It	Practice Passage and Questions

Advance Preparation

Watch the Introduction to Critical Skills Practice with students before beginning the lesson.

Big Ideas

- ▸ Comprehension entails asking and answering questions about the text.
- ▸ Comprehension strategies can be taught through explicit instruction.
- ▸ Reading strategies are conscious plans that readers apply and adapt to make sense of text.
- ▸ Comprehension requires an understanding of story structure.

Materials

Supplied

- Types of Questions (optional printout)
- Practice Passage and Questions (optional printout)

Keywords

character – a person or animal in a story

fable – a story that teaches a lesson and may contain animal characters

fiction – make-believe stories

folktale – a story, which usually teaches a lesson important to a culture, that is passed down through many generations

plot – what happens in a story; the sequence of events

prediction – a guess about what might happen that is based on information in a story and what you already know

setting – when and where a story takes place

theme – the author's message or big idea

 **minutes**

Students will work online to complete Get Ready, Learn, and Try It activities.

Get Ready

What Is a Fiction Passage?
Students will review what a fiction passage is. Before they begin, ask students what fiction is and then have them do the activity to see if they were correct.

Objectives
- Identify examples of fiction and nonfiction.
- Identify genre.

Learn

Types of Questions
Students will learn about different types of multiple choice questions. The questions will be about predictions, setting, plot elements, character traits, and theme in a fictional passage.

- ► The **setting** is when or where the story takes place.
- ► The **plot** is what happens in the story.
- ► The **characters** are who the story is about.
- ► The **theme** is the message or lesson of the story.
- ► To make a **prediction** is to guess what might happen next in a story.

 TIP If students are not comfortable reading the passage for this activity online, print Types of Questions and have students read the printout.

Objectives
- Identify setting(s).
- Identify plot elements.
- Identify character traits.
- Identify the theme of a third-grade passage.
- Use information from the text to make predictions.

Try It ....

Practice Passage and Questions

Students will practice answering multiple choice questions about a fiction passage.

TIP If students are not comfortable reading the passages for this activity online, print Practice Passage and Questions and have students read the printout.

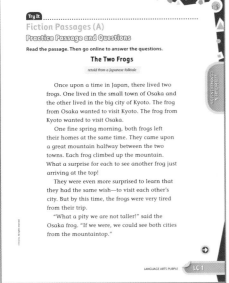

Fiction Passages (B)

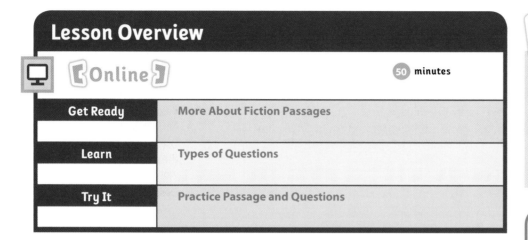

Lesson Overview

Online   **50 minutes**

Get Ready	More About Fiction Passages
Learn	Types of Questions
Try It	Practice Passage and Questions

Big Ideas

▶ Comprehension entails asking and answering questions about the text.
▶ Comprehension strategies can be taught through explicit instruction.
▶ Reading strategies are conscious plans that readers apply and adapt to make sense of text.
▶ To understand and interpret a story, readers need to understand and describe characters and what they do.
▶ Knowing how to use context clues to extract meaning from unfamiliar words is critical to determining what is important in text.

Materials

Supplied
- Types of Questions (optional printout)
- Practice Passage and Questions (optional printout)

Keywords

biography – the story of someone's life written by another person

character – a person or animal in a story

context clue – a word or phrase in a text that helps you figure out the meaning of an unknown word

fiction – make-believe stories

nonfiction – writings about true things

purpose – the reason for writing

Online 🕐50 minutes

Students will work online to complete Get Ready, Learn, and Try It activities.

Get Ready ●●●

More About Fiction Passages

Students will review skills they need to answer questions about **fiction** passages, including being able to identify a passage as a work of fiction, recognizing how a **character** changes over the course of a story, and using **context clues** to determine the meaning of an unfamiliar word.

Objectives

- Identify examples of fiction and nonfiction.
- Use context to determine the meaning of unfamiliar words.
- Describe how characters change.
- Describe characters by what they say, what they do, or how others feel about them.

Learn ●●

Types of Questions

Students will analyze different types of multiple choice questions that are commonly asked about fiction passages. They will review how to identify a passage as a work of fiction, focus on using context clues to determine the meanings of unfamiliar words, and describe how a character changes over time. They will also be asked to recall specific events in the passage and respond to questions that ensure their overall comprehension.

TIP If students are not comfortable reading the passage for this activity online, print Types of Questions and have students read the printout.

Objectives

- Identify examples of fiction and nonfiction.
- Use context to determine the meaning of unfamiliar words.
- Demonstrate comprehension of text.
- Answer literal comprehension questions about a third-grade passage.
- Describe how characters change.
- Describe characters by what they say, what they do, or how others feel about them.
- Make inferences and draw conclusions from a third-grade passage.
- Make inferences using evidence from text.

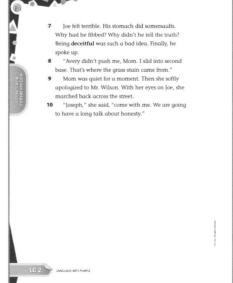

Try It

Practice Passage and Questions

Students will practice answering multiple choice questions about a fiction passage.

TIP If students are not comfortable reading the passages for this activity online, print Practice Passage and Questions and have students read the printout.

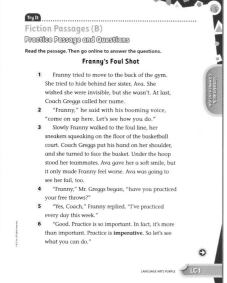

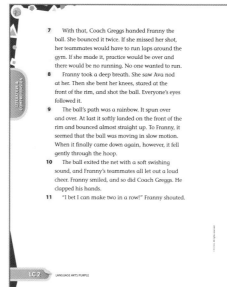

Objectives

- Identify examples of fiction and nonfiction.
- Use context to determine the meaning of unfamiliar words.
- Demonstrate comprehension of text.
- Answer literal comprehension questions about a third-grade passage.
- Describe how characters change.
- Describe characters by what they say, what they do, or how others feel about them.
- Use context to confirm or self-correct word recognition and understanding, rereading as necessary.

Directions (A)

Lesson Overview

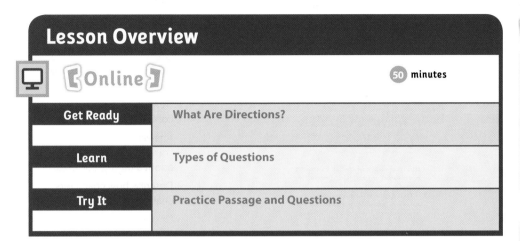

Online — 50 minutes

Get Ready	What Are Directions?
Learn	Types of Questions
Try It	Practice Passage and Questions

Big Ideas

▸ Comprehension entails asking and answering questions about the text.

▸ Comprehension strategies can be taught through explicit instruction.

▸ Reading strategies are conscious plans that readers apply and adapt to make sense of text.

▸ Readers analyze a text to determine more about how the text's parts work as a whole, and how its parts contribute to meaning.

▸ A set of written steps is also known as a how-to piece of writing. Think of a process of steps as a recipe or set of instructions for learning how to do something.

Materials

Supplied

• Types of Questions (optional printout)

• Practice Passage and Questions (optional printout)

Keywords

process – a series of steps that explains how to do something

sequence – the order in which things happen

[Online] 50 minutes

Students will work online to complete Get Ready, Learn, and Try It activities.

Get Ready

What Are Directions?

Students will review what directions are, why **sequence** matters in a **process**, and the importance of details in directions. Before they begin, you may want to ask students what directions are and then have them do the activity to see if they were correct.

Objectives
- Follow the directions in a process.
- Use context to determine the meaning of unfamiliar words.

Learn

Types of Questions

Students will learn about different types of multiple choice questions associated with directions. The questions will be about what the directions say, details included in the directions, the sequence of the directions, and how to follow the steps of the directions.

The **sequence** of the directions is the order of the steps in the **process**.

TIP If students are not comfortable reading the passage for this activity online, print Types of Questions and have students read the printout.

Objectives
- Follow third grade-level multistep instructions.
- Identify directions as a way to organize ideas through sequencing.
- Read instructional-level text with 90 percent accuracy.
- Infer literal information from text.
- Identify the organizational pattern of a recipe.
- Identify sequencing as critical to a recipe.
- Acquire grade-appropriate words and phrases from various subject-matter areas and use them accurately, including terms having to do with space and time relationships.

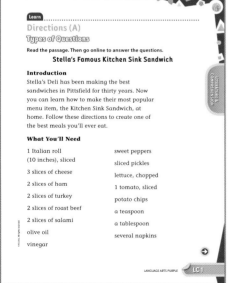

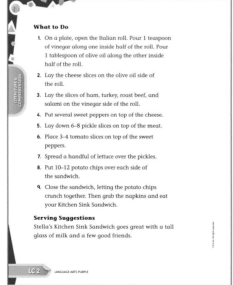

Try It

Practice Passage and Questions

Students will practice answering multiple choice questions associated with directions.

TIP If students are not comfortable reading the passage for this activity online, print Practice Passage and Questions and have students read the printout.

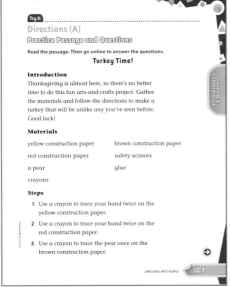

Try It

Directions (A)

Practice Passage and Questions

Read the passage. Then go online to answer the questions.

Turkey Time!

Introduction

Thanksgiving is almost here, so there's no better time to do this fun arts-and-crafts project. Gather the materials and follow the directions to make a turkey that will be unlike any you've seen before. Good luck!

Materials

yellow construction paper   brown construction paper

red construction paper   safety scissors

a pear   glue

crayons

Steps

1. Use a crayon to trace your hand twice on the yellow construction paper.
2. Use a crayon to trace your hand twice on the red construction paper.
3. Use a crayon to trace the pear once on the brown construction paper.

LANGUAGE ARTS PURPLE   LC 1

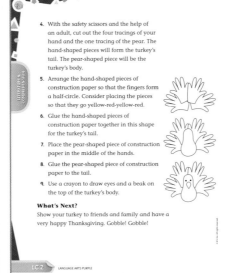

LC 2   LANGUAGE ARTS PURPLE

4. With the safety scissors and the help of an adult, cut out the four tracings of your hand and the one tracing of the pear. The hand-shaped pieces will form the turkey's tail. The pear-shaped piece will be the turkey's body.
5. Arrange the hand-shaped pieces of construction paper so that the fingers form a half-circle. Consider placing the pieces so that they go yellow-red-yellow-red.
6. Glue the hand-shaped pieces of construction paper together in this shape for the turkey's tail.
7. Place the pear-shaped piece of construction paper in the middle of the hands.
8. Glue the pear-shaped piece of construction paper to the tail.
9. Use a crayon to draw eyes and a beak on the top of the turkey's body.

What's Next?

Show your turkey to friends and family and have a very happy Thanksgiving. Gobble! Gobble!

Objectives

- Follow third grade-level multistep instructions.
- Identify directions as a way to organize ideas through sequencing.
- Read instructional-level text with 90 percent accuracy.
- Infer literal information from text.
- Identify the organizational pattern of a recipe.
- Identify sequencing as critical to a recipe.
- Acquire grade-appropriate words and phrases from various subject-matter areas and use them accurately, including terms having to do with space and time relationships.

Practical Reading: Forms

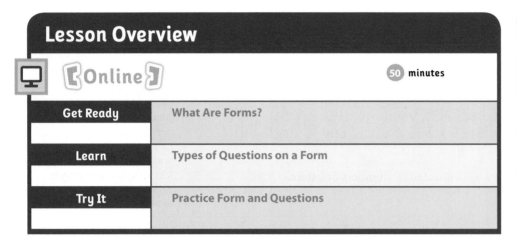

Lesson Overview

Online — 50 minutes

Get Ready	What Are Forms?
Learn	Types of Questions on a Form
Try It	Practice Form and Questions

Big Ideas

- Comprehension strategies can be taught through explicit instruction.
- Reading strategies are conscious plans that readers apply and adapt to make sense of text.
- Readers analyze a text to determine more about how the text's parts work as a whole, and how its parts contribute to meaning.

 **Online** **50 minutes**

Students will work online to complete Get Ready, Learn, and Try It activities.

Get Ready

What Are Forms?

Students will review what forms are and what purpose forms serve. Before they begin, ask students what a form is and whether they've ever filled out one. If so, encourage them to discuss what they remember about filling out a form. Then have students complete the activity.

 TIP Tell students that form fields may be delineated by numbers or letters.

Objectives

- Acquire grade-appropriate words and phrases from various subject-matter areas and use them accurately, including terms having to do with space and time relationships.
- Understand multistep-applications that contain instructions (for example, for a bank account, job, or club membership).
- Recall how to fill out forms correctly.

Learn

Types of Questions on a Form

Students will learn about different types of multiple choice questions associated with forms. The questions will be about identifying where to put information in a form, what information does or does not belong in a form, and following a form's directions.

 TIP If students are not comfortable reading the passage for this activity online, print Types of Questions on a Form and have students read the printout.

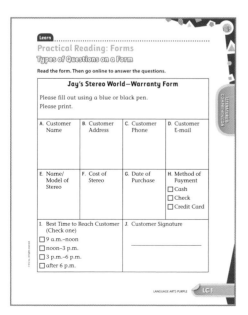

Objectives

- Use text organizational features to locate and comprehend information.
- Follow multiple-step application instructions (for example, for a bank account, job, or club membership).
- Infer literal information from text.
- Read instructional-level text with 90 percent accuracy.
- Use graphics and visuals to comprehend meaning and answer questions (diagrams, charts, captions).

Try It

Practice Form and Questions

Students will practice answering multiple choice questions associated with forms.

TIP If students are not comfortable reading the passage for this activity online, print Practice Form and Questions and have students read the printout.

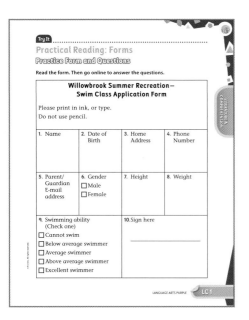

Objectives

- Use text organizational features to locate and comprehend information.
- Follow multiple-step application instructions (for example, for a bank account, job, or club membership).
- Infer literal information from text.
- Read instructional-level text with 90 percent accuracy.
- Use graphics and visuals to comprehend meaning and answer questions (diagrams, charts, captions).

Unit Checkpoint

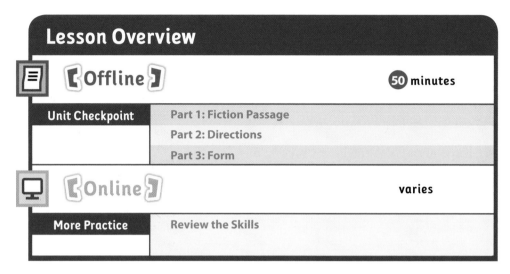

Big Ideas

► Comprehension entails asking and answering questions about the text.
► Comprehension strategies can be taught through explicit instruction.
► Reading strategies are conscious plans that readers apply and adapt to make sense of text.

Objectives

- Identify setting(s).
- Identify plot elements.
- Identify character traits.
- Identify the theme of a third-grade passage.
- Use information from the text to make predictions.
- Identify genre.
- Demonstrate comprehension of text.
- Answer literal comprehension questions about a third-grade passage.
- Describe how characters change.
- Describe characters by what they say, what they do, or how others feel about them.

- Follow third grade-level multistep instructions.
- Identify directions as a way to organize ideas through sequencing.
- Read instructional-level text with 90 percent accuracy.
- Infer literal information from text.
- Identify the organizational pattern of a recipe.
- Identify sequencing as critical to a recipe.
- Use text organizational features to locate and comprehend information.
- Follow multiple-step application instructions (for example, for a bank account, job, or club membership).

Offline 50 minutes

Unit Checkpoint

Explain that students are going to show what they have learned about reading and answering questions about fiction passages, directions, and forms.

1. Give students the Unit Checkpoint pages.

2. Read the directions together.

3. Use the Answer Key to score the Checkpoint and then enter the results online.

4. Review each exercise with students. Work with students to correct any exercise that they missed.

Part 1: Fiction Passage
Have students read "All Wet" and answer the questions.

Part 2: Directions
Have students read the directions on how to build a birdfeeder and answer the questions.

Part 3: Form
Explain to students that they do not need to fill in the form, but that they are to use the form to answer the questions.

Panel 1 (LC 1)

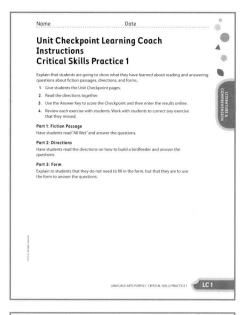

Name _____ Date _____

Unit Checkpoint Learning Coach Instructions
Critical Skills Practice 1

Explain that students are going to show what they have learned about reading and answering questions about fiction passages, directions, and forms.

1. Give students the Unit Checkpoint pages.
2. Read the directions together.
3. Use the Answer Key to score the Checkpoint and then enter the results online.
4. Review each exercise with students. Work with students to correct any exercise that they missed.

Part 1: Fiction Passage
Have students read "All Wet" and answer the questions.

Part 2: Directions
Have students read the directions on how to build a birdfeeder and answer the questions.

Part 3: Form
Explain to students that they do not need to fill in the form, but that they are to use the form to answer the questions.

LANGUAGE ARTS PURPLE | CRITICAL SKILLS PRACTICE 1   **LC 1**

Panel 2 (LC 2)

Name _____ Date _____

Unit Checkpoint Answer Key
Critical Skills Practice 1

Part 1. Fiction Passage
Read the passage and answer the questions.

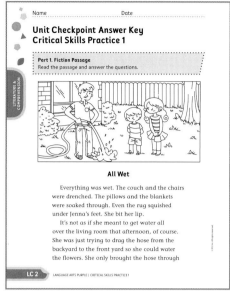

All Wet

Everything was wet. The couch and the chairs were drenched. The pillows and the blankets were soaked through. Even the rug squished under Jenna's feet. She bit her lip.

It's not as if she meant to get water all over the living room that afternoon, of course. She was just trying to drag the hose from the backyard to the front yard so she could water the flowers. She only brought the hose through

LC 2   LANGUAGE ARTS PURPLE | CRITICAL SKILLS PRACTICE 1

Panel 3 (LC 3)

Name _____ Date _____

the house because it was quicker than walking around the house.

She didn't realize that the hose was still attached to the outdoor faucet. She didn't know her brother David was going to accidentally kick his soccer ball into the faucet. She didn't think the water would suddenly start shooting out of the hose in the living room. When she heard Dad call down from the bedroom and ask what was going on downstairs, Jenna panicked.

She ran to the backyard with the hose. Then she went to kick the soccer ball with David, who still didn't realize his part in the accident. A moment later, she heard Dad shout. She kicked the ball to David and acted as if nothing were wrong. Then Dad was standing at the backdoor.

"How did the living room get all wet?" he demanded. "Jenna? David? Does anyone want to tell me what happened?"

"I don't know," Jenna lied.

"Me, neither," said David.

Yet David was standing next to the hose, which still had water pouring out of it. Dad thought David wasn't telling the truth. His face grew red.

"David, how many times have we talked about honesty?" Dad asked. "I am tired of your

LANGUAGE ARTS PURPLE | CRITICAL SKILLS PRACTICE 1   **LC 3**

Panel 4 (LC 4)

Name _____ Date _____

fibbing, young man. I don't know how you expect me to trust you if—"

"Stop!" Jenna interrupted, which made Dad turn to her. "David isn't the one who just fibbed. I am. I didn't mean to get the living room wet, Dad. I was just trying to bring the hose to the front yard when it turned on. It was an accident. But David had nothing to do with it."

Now Jenna waited. Dad looked from her to her brother and back to her again. His face seemed a little less red. He sighed.

"Thank you for telling me the truth, Jenna," Dad said. "I think we both owe your brother an apology."

Jenna and Dad both apologized. Then Dad continued, "I also think we all need to figure out how to dry the living room before Mom gets home from work."

1. What is the setting of this passage?
   A. the flowers in front of Jenna's house
   B. Jenna's house and backyard one afternoon
   C. the hose, the living room, and Jenna's father
   D. Jenna's brother David and the soccer ball

2. How does everything in the living room get wet?
   A. Jenna forgets that she left the water running in the kitchen.
   B. Jenna sprays water in through an open window.
   C. David turns on the water to help Jenna water flowers.
   D. David accidentally hits the outside faucet with the soccer ball.

LC 4   LANGUAGE ARTS PURPLE | CRITICAL SKILLS PRACTICE 1

Panel 5 (LC 5)

Name _____ Date _____

3. Which best describes Jenna?
   A. She makes some bad choices but owns up to her mistakes.
   B. She is a liar who never feels bad about not telling the truth.
   C. She loves to play pranks on her dad and brother.
   D. She is a bully who picks on others rather than be kind to them.

4. What is David doing when Jenna has the hose in the house?
   A. helping her by turning on the water
   B. talking upstairs with Dad
   C. kicking the soccer ball in the backyard
   D. shopping with Mom

5. Which is this passage an example of?
   A. a poem   C. a newspaper article
   B. a short story   D. a journal entry

6. Why does Dad's face grow red when he first talks to Jenna and David?
   A. He's angry because he thinks David isn't telling him the truth.
   B. He's upset because he realizes that his furniture is ruined.
   C. It is hot outside and his face is getting sunburned.
   D. He is trying not to laugh at what his children have done.

7. Where is Jenna's mom when the events of this passage take place?
   A. room   C. yard
   B. upstairs   D. work

LANGUAGE ARTS PURPLE | CRITICAL SKILLS PRACTICE 1   **LC 5**

Panel 6 (LC 6)

Name _____ Date _____

8. How does Jenna change in this passage?
   A. She gets less honest.
   B. She gets more honest.
   C. She gets more afraid.
   D. She gets less brave.

9. What is Jenna likely to do the next time she wants to water the flowers in the front yard?
   A. put plastic covers on all the furniture so things won't get too wet
   B. buy a new hose to make sure it does not leak
   C. carry the hose around the house rather than through the house
   D. blame whatever happens on David

10. Which lesson do the events of this passage teach Jenna and readers?
   A. Honesty is the best policy.
   B. Money can't buy happiness.
   C. Slow and steady wins the race.
   D. Never talk behind someone else's back.

LC 6   LANGUAGE ARTS PURPLE | CRITICAL SKILLS PRACTICE 1

Page LC 7

Name _____ Date _____

Part 2. Directions
Read the directions about how to build a birdfeeder and answer the questions.

Build Your Own Birdfeeder

Introduction
Many people like the sounds of birds tweeting and singing. If you do, why not build your own birdfeeder? It's quick and easy, and it will bring birds right to your backyard to sing all the time. Here are directions for building your own birdfeeder.

Materials
- a clean cardboard milk carton
- a 10-inch wooden dowel
- scissors
- craft sticks
- glue
- paint
- paintbrush
- birdseed
- yarn or thin rope

What to Do

Step 1 With an adult's help, cut two openings in opposite sides of the milk carton. These holes will be the entrances to the birdfeeder.

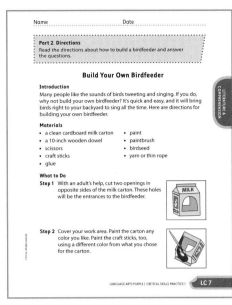

Step 2 Cover your work area. Paint the carton any color you like. Paint the craft sticks, too, using a different color from what you chose for the carton.

LC 7 | LANGUAGE ARTS PURPLE | CRITICAL SKILLS PRACTICE 1

Page LC 8

Name _____ Date _____

Step 3 When the paint is dry, with an adult's help, poke a small ½-inch slit under each opening. Slide the wooden dowel through the slits so that it sticks out evenly on each side of the carton. The dowel will be the perch that birds sit on as they eat.

Step 4 Use glue to attach the craft sticks horizontally to the top of the carton. The craft sticks will look like shingles on the roof of the birdfeeder.

Step 5 With an adult's help, poke two small holes in the top of the carton. Thread the yarn or thin rope through the holes, and leave the ends loose.

Step 6 Fill the bottom of the carton with birdseed.

Step 7 Hang the birdfeeder by tying the ends of the yarn or rope to make a closed loop around the branch of a nearby tree.

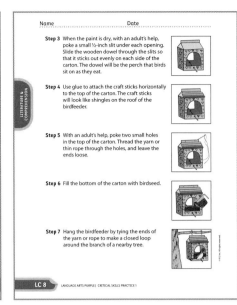

LC 8 | LANGUAGE ARTS PURPLE | CRITICAL SKILLS PRACTICE 1

Page LC 9

Name _____ Date _____

11. Where in these directions would you look to find out what you need to begin this project?
   A. Introduction
   B. Materials
   C. What to Do
   D. When You're Finished

12. Why would it be foolish to do Step 6 before Step 2?
   A. You would not be able to get the birdseed into the carton.
   B. You would not know what color birdseed to use.
   C. You could accidentally get paint on the birdseed.
   D. You might not have a place to hang the birdfeeder.

13. If you wanted to place the birdfeeder on your windowsill rather than hang it from a tree branch, which of these instructions could you skip?
   A. Paint the carton.
   B. Fill the carton with birdseed.
   C. Glue the craft sticks to the carton.
   D. Poke two small holes in the top of the carton.

14. What does the Introduction explain?
   A. why you might want to build your own birdfeeder
   B. how to build your own birdfeeder
   C. where to get the supplies for your birdfeeder
   D. what time of year is best to feed the birds

15. When do the directions say to attach the craft sticks to the carton?
   A. before you paint the carton and craft sticks
   B. after you hang the birdfeeder from a tree branch
   C. at the same time that you cut holes in the carton
   D. after you slide the dowel through the slits in the carton

LANGUAGE ARTS PURPLE | CRITICAL SKILLS PRACTICE 1 | LC 9

Page LC 10

Name _____ Date _____

Part 3. Form
Review this form for applying for a library card and answer the questions.

Public Library Card Application Form
(PLEASE USE PEN AND WRITE NEATLY)

1. NAME	2. MALE ☐ FEMALE ☐

3. ADDRESS	

4. CITY	5. STATE

6. ZIP CODE	7. AGE	8. PHONE NUMBER	9. E-MAIL ADDRESS

10. HOW DID YOU HEAR ABOUT THE PUBLIC LIBRARY?
(CIRLCE ALL THAT APPLY)
FRIEND/FAMILY   NEWSPAPER   RADIO/TV
INTERNET   VISIT/ALREADY KNEW   OTHER

11. PLEASE READ
I understand that I am responsible for all materials borrowed with this card. I also understand that I may face fines if I return borrowed materials late or if I damage borrowed materials.

I promise to obey all library rules and to treat the library and its staff with respect. I realize that failure to do so may result in the cancelation of my library membership.

12. SIGNATURE	13. DATE

LC 10 | LANGUAGE ARTS PURPLE | CRITICAL SKILLS PRACTICE 1

Page LC 11

Name _____ Date _____

16. What information belongs in Box 9?
   A. phone number
   B. signature
   C. age
   D. e-mail address

17. How should a person complete this form?
   A. type in the information
   B. write the information in pencil
   C. write the information in pen
   D. tell the information to a librarian

18. Which piece of information does a person **not** have to include on this form?
   A. the city she lives in
   B. her favorite books
   C. her age
   D. how she learned of the library

19. If a person's brother told her about the library and she saw an ad for the library on the Internet, which choices should she circle in Box 10?
   A. FRIEND/FAMILY and INTERNET
   B. FRIEND/FAMILY
   C. INTERNET
   D. INTERNET and OTHER

20. Where should a person sign this form?
   A. Box 2
   B. Box 5
   C. Box 11
   D. Box 12

LANGUAGE ARTS PURPLE | CRITICAL SKILLS PRACTICE 1 | LC 11

 **varies**

Students will work **independently** to complete the online More Practice activity.

More Practice

Review the Skills

If students scored less than 80 percent or had difficulty meeting the objectives of the Unit Checkpoint, have them go online for more practice.

 Reward: If students score 80 percent or more on the Unit Checkpoint, add a sticker for this unit on the My Accomplishments chart. If students did not score 80 percent or more, work with them to revise their work until they do score 80 percent, and then add a sticker to the My Accomplishments chart.

 Objectives
- Evaluate Unit Checkpoint results and choose activities for more practice.

Weather or Not

Unit Focus

In this unit, students will read five nonfiction articles about weather. They will learn skills necessary for reading and understanding nonfiction texts, including

- ▶ Identifying the author's purpose, main idea, and supporting details
- ▶ Recognizing cause-and-effect relationships
- ▶ Comparing and contrasting texts
- ▶ Summarizing texts
- ▶ Using context clues to determine the meanings of unfamiliar words
- ▶ Identifying and using features of nonfiction texts, such as headings, captions, sidebars, and glossaries

Unit Plan		[Online]	[Offline]
Lesson 1	Introduce "Forecasting the Weather"		50 minutes
Lesson 2	Explore "Forecasting the Weather"	40 minutes	10 minutes
Lesson 3	Introduce "Let It Rain"		50 minutes
Lesson 4	Explore "Let It Rain"	40 minutes	10 minutes
Lesson 5	Introduce "Winter Storms"		50 minutes
Lesson 6	Explore "Winter Storms"	40 minutes	10 minutes
Lesson 7	Introduce "Wind"		50 minutes
Lesson 8	Explore "Wind"	40 minutes	10 minutes
Lesson 9	Introduce "Storm Chasers"		50 minutes
Lesson 10	Explore "Storm Chasers"	40 minutes	10 minutes
Lesson 11	Reflections on *Weather or Not*	varies	50 minutes
Lesson 12	Your Choice		50 minutes

Introduce "Forecasting the Weather"

Lesson Overview

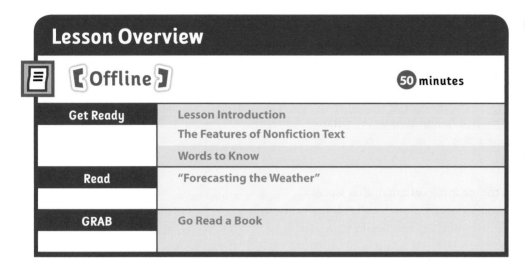

Offline		50 minutes
Get Ready	Lesson Introduction	
	The Features of Nonfiction Text	
	Words to Know	
Read	"Forecasting the Weather"	
GRAB	Go Read a Book	

Big Ideas

► Active, strong readers employ reading strategies such as using existing knowledge to make sense of texts.
► Nonfiction texts differ from fiction texts in that they describe real or true things in life, rather than things made up by the author.
► Comprehension is facilitated by an understanding of physical presentation (headings, subheads, graphics, and other features).

Materials

Supplied
- "Forecasting the Weather," *K¹² World: Weather or Not*, pp. 2–13
- Reading Strategies bookmark

Article Synopsis
This article is about how meteorologists forecast the weather and the tools they use to track it.

Keywords

caption – writing printed with a picture that describes or explains the picture

glossary – a list of important terms and their meanings that is usually found in the back of a book

graphic – a picture, photograph, map, diagram or other image.

heading – a title within the body of a text that tells the reader something important about a section of the text

index – an alphabetical list at the end of a book or magazine that tells the pages where a subject or name can be found

nonfiction – writings about true things

opinion – something that a person thinks or believes, but which cannot be proven to be true

sidebar – a short text within a larger text that tells something related but not necessary to the main story

topic – the subject of a text

[Offline] 50 minutes

Work **together** with students to complete offline Get Ready, Read, and GRAB activities.

Get Ready

Lesson Introduction
Prepare students to read "Forecasting the Weather."

1. Explain to students that before they read "Forecasting the Weather," they will discuss with you

   ▸ What they will find in nonfiction magazine articles
   ▸ Their predictions about the text
   ▸ Important words to know in the text

2. Tell students that while they read, you will check in to make sure they understand what they are reading.

3. Tell students that after they read, they will answer questions about the article.

The Features of Nonfiction Text
Discuss with students what they can expect to find in nonfiction magazine articles.

1. Ask students about the qualities of **nonfiction**. Provide answers when students do not know an answer.

   ▸ What is nonfiction? writing about true things
   ▸ How is **nonfiction** different from **fiction**? Nonfiction is writing about true or real things; fiction is writing about make-believe things.

2. Tell students that nonfiction writing contains **facts**. Ask students to define what a fact is, or tell them. A fact is something that can be proven true. This means you can find it in a reference source, like a dictionary, encyclopedia, or reference website.

3. Explain the difference between a fact and an **opinion** and give examples.
   A fact is something that is true and can be proven by using a reference source. An opinion is something that a person believes but cannot be proven true. For example, it is a fact that the surface of the sun is much hotter than the surface of the earth. An opinion would be that it is much better to live in a warm climate than a cold one.

Objectives
- Define *glossary*.
- Define *index*.
- Define *title*.
- Define *caption*.
- Define *heading*.
- Define *sidebar*.
- Define *topic*.
- State the topic directly.
- Identify table of contents.
- Identify glossary.
- Identify chapters.
- Identify index.
- Identify title.
- Identify caption.
- Identify heading.
- Use before-reading strategies.
- Increase concept and content vocabulary.

4. Show students the magazine *K¹² World: Weather or Not*. Define **topic** or ask students what a topic is. Have them tell what they think the topic of the magazine is. A topic is the subject of a text; the topic of the magazine is weather.

5. Guide students on a Book Walk of the magazine and the article "Forecasting the Weather." Introduce the following key nonfiction terms and point to examples in the magazine.

   ▸ **Title of the magazine**
   ▸ **Table of contents** – point out that there are five articles in the magazine
   ▸ **Article titles** – point out that there are no authors' names listed for the articles, but articles in other magazines might list authors' names
   ▸ **Headings** – the titles of sections of the articles, printed in bold type
   ▸ **Graphics** – things like illustrations, photographs, diagrams, charts, graphs, and maps that show information
   ▸ **Captions** – writing printed with pictures that describes or explains them
   ▸ **Sidebars** – a short section of writing, set off from the main text, that tells something related to the main text but is not essential
   ▸ **Words in bold and italic type** – explain that boldfaced words are found in the glossary, while italicized words may be important or unfamiliar terms
   ▸ **Glossary** – an alphabetical listing of important terms and their meanings found at the back of the magazine
   ▸ **Index** – an alphabetical list at the end of the magazine that tells the pages where a subject or name can be found

Words to Know

Before reading "Forecasting the Weather," explain that the Words to Know are the boldfaced words in the article that can be found in the glossary.

1. Have students locate a boldfaced word in the article, find it in the glossary, and read its definition.

2. Ask them if they understand what the word means.

   ▸ If students understand a word's meaning, have them use it in a sentence.
   ▸ If they don't understand a word's meaning, discuss it with them.

3. Tell students that as they read, they should turn to the glossary when they don't know the meaning of boldfaced words. They should use the definitions they find in the glossary to help them understand the article.

Read

"Forecasting the Weather"

Have students read "Forecasting the Weather." Remind them to use the strategies on their Reading Strategies bookmark. For example, they may want to stop at the end of each page of the article and ask themselves questions about what they just read.

 Learning Coach Check-In This reading assignment should take about 15 minutes. After students finish reading, ask the following questions to assess their comprehension of the selection:

▶ What is a meteorologist? A meteorologist is a person who studies the earth's atmosphere and weather conditions.

▶ What is one tool that a meteorologist uses to forecast the weather? Possible answers: satellites; radar; weather balloons; weather computers; weather models

If students have trouble answering these questions, ask them what reading strategies they used and suggest they reread the selection.

Objectives
- Read literature independently and proficiently.
- Apply information read to answer questions.
- Evaluate reading strategies.

GRAB

Go Read a Book

Have students read a book or magazine of their own choosing for at least 20 minutes. Remind students to use the strategies on their Reading Strategies bookmark before and during reading to help them understand the text.

TIP Remember: The more students read, the better readers they become.

Objectives
- Read literature independently and proficiently.
- Read a variety of texts for information and pleasure.

Explore "Forecasting the Weather"

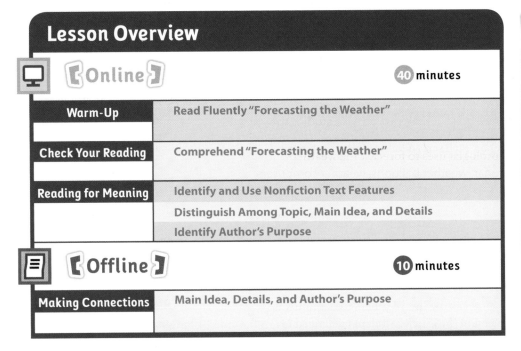

Lesson Overview

🖥 【Online】   40 minutes

Warm-Up	Read Fluently "Forecasting the Weather"
Check Your Reading	Comprehend "Forecasting the Weather"
Reading for Meaning	Identify and Use Nonfiction Text Features
	Distinguish Among Topic, Main Idea, and Details
	Identify Author's Purpose

📄 【Offline】   10 minutes

Making Connections	Main Idea, Details, and Author's Purpose

Big Ideas

▸ Comprehension is facilitated by an understanding of physical presentation (headings, subheads, graphics, and other features).

▸ Narrative and expository text differ significantly, for example, in structure, content, and purpose.

▸ Readers must understand the relationship between main idea and supporting details.

【Materials】

Supplied
- "Forecasting the Weather," *K¹² World: Weather or Not*, pp. 2–13
- *K¹² Language Arts Activity Book*, pp. LC 27–30

Keywords

author's purpose – the reason the author wrote a text: to entertain, to inform, to express an opinion, or to persuade

caption – writing printed with a picture that describes or explains the picture

heading – a title within the body of a text that tells the reader something important about a section of the text

index – an alphabetical list at the end of a book or magazine that tells the pages where a subject or name can be found

main idea – the most important point the author makes; it may be stated or unstated

sidebar – a short text within a larger text that tells something related but not necessary to the main story

supporting details – the sentences that give information about the main idea or topic sentence

topic – the subject of a text

 **40 minutes**

Students will work **independently** to complete online Warm-Up, Check Your Reading, and Reading for Meaning activities.

Warm-Up

Read Fluently "Forecasting the Weather"
Students will read aloud and record a passage from "Forecasting the Weather." The purpose of this activity is to improve students' oral reading and fluency. Remind students to listen to the model on each screen before they begin their recording.

Objectives
- Read poetry and prose aloud.
- Read grade-level text with purpose and understanding.

Check Your Reading

Comprehend "Forecasting the Weather"
Students will answer questions about "Forecasting the Weather" to demonstrate their literal and inferential comprehension of the article. Students will need to understand the text features of this article, including the key to the weather map, the purpose of a sidebar, and the location and purpose of captions, to answer these questions.

Objectives
- Identify concrete answers to questions.
- Infer answers to questions.
- Apply information read to answer questions.
- Explain how specific aspects of a text's illustrations contribute to the meaning of the text.
- Use text features to comprehend text meaning (bold, italic, headers, etc.).

Reading for Meaning

Identify and Use Nonfiction Text Features
Students will recognize the importance and uses of nonfiction text features, including headings, captions, maps, sidebars, and indexes.

Distinguish Among Topic, Main Idea, and Details
Students will learn how to find the topic of an article and distinguish it from the main idea, or what the author's main point about the topic is. They will also use supporting details to help them identify the main idea.

Identify Author's Purpose
Students will learn about the four reasons authors write nonfiction texts: to inform, to entertain, to persuade, or to describe. They will identify this author's purpose (to inform) and learn that knowing an author's purpose can help decide how to read a text.

Objectives

- Identify caption.
- Identify heading.
- Identify index.
- Determine the meanings and pronunciations of unknown words by using dictionaries, glossaries, technology, and textual features, such as definitional footnotes or sidebars.
- Use text features to comprehend text meaning (bold, italic, headers, etc.).
- Use graphics and visuals to comprehend meaning and answer questions (diagrams, charts, captions).
- Distinguish between main idea and details.
- Define *main idea* and *supporting details*.
- Identify main idea.
- Define *author's purpose*.
- Identify author's purpose.

 **minutes**

Work **together** with students to complete the offline Making Connections activity.

Making Connections

Main Idea, Details, and Author's Purpose
Students will practice identifying main ideas, supporting details, and author's purpose. Turn to pages LC 27–30 in *K¹² Language Arts Activity Book*.

1. Make sure students have their copy of *K¹² World: Weather or Not*. Tell them they will need to refer to the article "Forecasting the Weather" to answer the questions on the Activity Book pages.

Objectives

- Identify the main ideas and supporting details of a text read aloud or information presented in a variety of media and formats.
- Identify author's purpose.
- Make inferences using evidence from the text.

2. Direct students' attention to the Activity Book pages and have them read the directions.

3. Have students complete the Activity Book pages.

TIP Keep the Activity Book pages in a safe place so students can refer to them later.

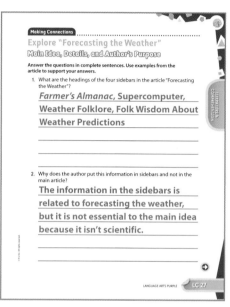

Making Connections

Explore "Forecasting the Weather"
Main Idea, Details, and Author's Purpose

Answer the questions in complete sentences. Use examples from the article to support your answers.

1. What are the headings of the four sidebars in the article "Forecasting the Weather"?

   Farmer's Almanac, Supercomputer, Weather Folklore, Folk Wisdom About Weather Predictions

2. Why does the author put this information in sidebars and not in the main article?

   The information in the sidebars is related to forecasting the weather, but it is not essential to the main idea because it isn't scientific.

LANGUAGE ARTS PURPLE — LC 27

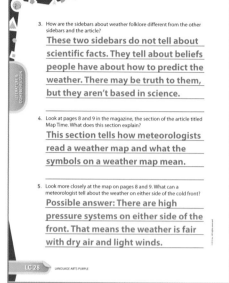

3. How are the sidebars about weather folklore different from the other sidebars and the article?

   These two sidebars do not tell about scientific facts. They tell about beliefs people have about how to predict the weather. There may be truth to them, but they aren't based in science.

4. Look at pages 8 and 9 in the magazine, the section of the article titled Map Time. What does this section explain?

   This section tells how meteorologists read a weather map and what the symbols on a weather map mean.

5. Look more closely at the map on pages 8 and 9. What can a meteorologist tell about the weather on either side of the cold front?

   Possible answer: There are high pressure systems on either side of the front. That means the weather is fair with dry air and light winds.

LC 28 — LANGUAGE ARTS PURPLE

6. How does the section titled Map Time support the main idea of this article?

   Possible answer: The main idea is that meteorologists use many tools to predict the weather. Weather maps are one of the tools they use. This section explains what the weather maps show.

7. How do the pictures and captions on pages 5 and 6 help you understand the text? What other graphics could the author have included?

   Possible answer: The pictures help by showing the reader what some of the weather forecasting tools look like. The author could have included pictures of other tools, like a weather balloon or a Doppler radar.

8. What are four reasons authors write nonfiction?

   to inform, to entertain, to express an opinion, or to persuade

LANGUAGE ARTS PURPLE — LC 29

9. The author's main purpose for writing "Forecasting the Weather" is to inform. Reread the last page of the article. What other purpose might the author have for writing? Why do you think this?

   Possible answers: The author may be trying to persuade readers that predicting the weather is hard, but we need to do it. The author says this in the last paragraphs of the article. The author may also be trying to entertain readers with the sidebars on folklore. These sidebars are interesting, but they do not really inform readers about true or factual things.

10. Do you think the author does a good job in this article of explaining how weather forecasting works? Why or why not?

    Students should give an opinion about how informative the article is and explain their answer with reasons drawn from the text.

LC 30 — LANGUAGE ARTS PURPLE

Introduce "Let It Rain"

Lesson Overview

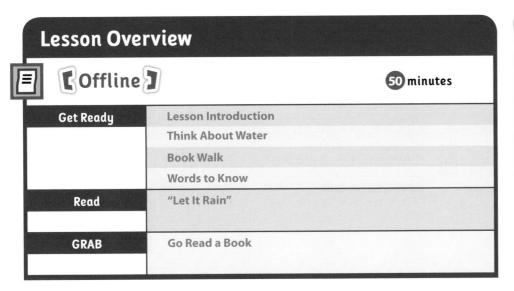

[Offline]	**50** minutes

Get Ready	Lesson Introduction
	Think About Water
	Book Walk
	Words to Know
Read	"Let It Rain"
GRAB	Go Read a Book

Big Ideas

▸ Active, strong readers employ reading strategies such as using existing knowledge to make sense of texts.

▸ Nonfiction texts differ from fiction texts in that they describe real or true things in life, rather than things made up by the author.

▸ Reading better follows from reading often: The more a student reads, the better reader the student becomes.

[Materials]

Supplied

- "Let It Rain," *K¹² World: Weather or Not*, pp. 14–25
- Reading Strategies bookmark

Article Synopsis

This article explains what rain is and where it comes from. It describes the water cycle and explains other phenomena related to rain, such as clouds, thunder, and lightning. The article also highlights the importance of freshwater from rain and the problems when there is too much rain or not enough.

Keywords

fact – something that can be proven true

graphic – a picture, photograph, map, diagram, or other image

nonfiction – writings about true things

topic – the subject of a text

 **Offline** (50) **minutes**

Work **together** with students to complete offline Get Ready, Read, and GRAB activities.

Get Ready

Lesson Introduction

Prepare students to read "Let It Rain."

1. Explain to students that before they read "Let It Rain," they will discuss with you

   ▸ What they know about water and rain
   ▸ Their predictions about the text
   ▸ Important words to know in the text

2. Tell students that while they read, you will check in to make sure they understand what they are reading.

3. Tell students that after they read, they will answer questions about the article.

> **Objectives**
> - Make connections between text and self, text and world, and text to text.
> - Connect text to prior knowledge.
> - Use before-reading strategies.
> - Increase concept and content vocabulary.

Think About Water

Discuss with students what facts they know about water and rain.

▸ **What are the three forms that water can take?** Students may know that water comes in three forms: liquid, which is water; solid, which is ice; and gas, which is steam or water vapor.

▸ **What is the difference between freshwater and saltwater? Where would you find each one?** Students may know that freshwater does not have salt in it. Saltwater does have salt. Freshwater is found in lakes, ponds, rivers, streams, and rain. Saltwater is found in the seas and oceans.

▸ **What are some of the uses for water?** Possible answers: drinking; bathing; washing; watering plants; giving water to animals

▸ **Where do you think we get the water we need?** Possible answers: rain; lakes and rivers; the pipes in our homes

Book Walk

Have students lead you through a Book Walk of "Let It Rain." Remind them to use the **title** and **graphics** to make predictions about what the article is about.

Words to Know

Before reading "Let It Rain," remind students that the Words to Know are the words in boldfaced type within the article. They can find the definitions of these words in the glossary at the back of the magazine.

Read

"Let It Rain"

Have students read "Let It Rain." Remind them to use the strategies on their Reading Strategies bookmark. For example, they may want to stop at the end of each page of the article and summarize what they just read. Tell students that they may want to do the word find puzzle on page 21 as they read.

 Learning Coach Check-In This reading assignment should take about 15 minutes. After students finish reading, ask the following questions to assess their comprehension of the selection:

► Why is rain important? Possible answers: Rain is a source of freshwater; rain gives us drinking and bathing water; rain waters crops.

► What is it called when there is not enough rain? drought

If students have trouble answering these questions, ask them what reading strategies they used and suggest they reread the selection.

Objectives
- Read literature independently and proficiently.
- Apply information read to answer questions.
- Evaluate reading strategies.

GRAB

Go Read a Book

Have students read a book or magazine of their own choosing for at least 20 minutes. Remind students to use the strategies on their Reading Strategies bookmark before and during reading to help them understand the text.

Objectives
- Read literature independently and proficiently.
- Read a variety of texts for information and pleasure.

Explore "Let It Rain"

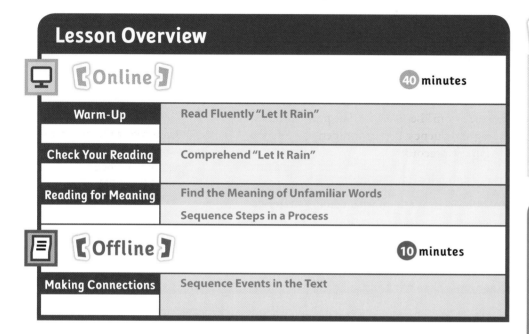

Lesson Overview

💻 [Online]   40 minutes

Warm-Up	Read Fluently "Let It Rain"
Check Your Reading	Comprehend "Let It Rain"
Reading for Meaning	Find the Meaning of Unfamiliar Words
	Sequence Steps in a Process

📄 [Offline]   10 minutes

Making Connections	Sequence Events in the Text

Big Ideas

▸ Knowing how to use context clues to extract meaning from unfamiliar words is critical to determining what is important in text.
▸ Readers need to be able to sequence, summarize, and articulate the main idea.

[Materials]

Supplied

- "Let It Rain," *K¹² World: Weather or Not*, pp. 14–25
- *K¹² Language Arts Activity Book*, pp. LC 31–34

Keywords

context clue – a word or phrase in a text that helps you figure out the meaning of an unknown word

diagram – a drawing or design that shows how pieces of information are related

glossary – a list of important terms and their meanings that is usually found in the back of a book

sequence – the order in which things happen

summarize – to tell in order the most important ideas or events of a text

summary – a short retelling that includes only the most important ideas or events of a text

 **40 minutes**

Students will work **independently** to complete online Warm-Up, Check Your Reading, and Reading for Meaning activities.

Warm-Up

Read Fluently "Let It Rain"
Students will read aloud and record a passage from "Let It Rain." The purpose of this activity is to improve students' oral reading and fluency. Remind students to listen to the model on each screen before they begin their recording.

Objectives
- Read poetry and prose aloud.
- Read aloud grade-level text with appropriate automaticity, prosody, accuracy, and rate.

Check Your Reading

Comprehend "Let It Rain"
Students will answer questions about "Let It Rain" to demonstrate their literal and inferential comprehension of the article.

Objectives
- Apply information read to answer questions.
- Use context clues to determine word meanings.
- Identify main idea.
- Identify author's purpose.

Reading for Meaning

Find the Meaning of Unfamiliar Words
Students will learn how to use various kinds of context clues, such as definition, explanation, and example, to determine the meaning of unfamiliar words in a text. They will also review the use of the glossary.

Sequence Steps in a Process
Students will learn that one way authors organize information in a nonfiction text is by sequence of events. They will identify sequence in the article "Let It Rain" by recognizing the steps in the process that makes thunder.

Objectives

- Use context clues to determine word meanings.
- Use resources or other tools to determine the meaning of a word (glossary).
- Determine the meaning of general academic and domain-specific words and phrases in a text.
- Define *sequence*.
- Identify a process as a series of steps.
- Sequence events in a text.
- Describe the logical connection between particular sentences and paragraphs in a text (for example, comparison, cause-effect, first-second-third in a sequence).

 **10** minutes

Work **together** with students to complete the offline Making Connections activity.

Making Connections

Sequence Events in the Text
Students will sequence and summarize important events in the text. Turn to pages LC 31–32 (The Water Cycle) and 33–34 (Acid Rain Formation) in *K¹² Language Arts Activity Book*.

1. Make sure students have their copy of *K¹² World: Weather or Not*. Tell them they will need to refer to the article "Let It Rain" to answer the questions on the Activity Book pages.

Objectives

- Describe the logical connection between particular sentences and paragraphs in a text (for example, comparison, cause-effect, first-second-third in a sequence).
- Sequence events in a text.
- Summarize text and maintain accurate sequence.
- Distinguish one's own opinion from the author's.
- Write a series of ordered steps or directions.

2. Direct students' attention to the Activity Book pages and have them read the directions.

3. Have students complete the Activity Book pages about the water cycle and acid rain.

TIP Keep the Activity Book pages in a safe place so students can refer to them later.

Making Connections

Explore "Let It Rain"

Sequence Events in the Text: The Water Cycle

Fill in the steps of the water cycle in sequence. Use the diagram on page 17 of the magazine to help you. Look in the text on page 16 for order words such as *first, next,* and *once.*

Steps in the Water Cycle

First
Precipitation falls to the ground from clouds.

Next
Some of the water goes into the ground or into lakes, rivers, and oceans.

Then
Water evaporates from storage or from the leaves of plants through transpiration.

Finally
Condensation happens, and water becomes liquid again and forms clouds.

LC 31

Write a summary of the water cycle in your own words. Keep the sequence of events in order. Use order words such as *first, second, next, then, finally,* and *at last.*

Students should explain the water cycle in sequence using the steps from the graphic organizer. They should also include transition words to signal each step in the process.

LC 32

Making Connections

Explore "Let It Rain"

Sequence Events in the Text: Acid Rain Formation

Fill in the steps that produce acid rain. Use the sidebar on page 19 of the magazine to help you. Use order words in your chart, such as *first, next, then,* and *finally.*

Steps in Acid Rain Formation

First
First, pollution puts chemicals into the air.

Next
Next, the chemicals react with water in clouds to form acids.

Then
Then, the acids fall to the earth as acid rain.

Finally
Finally, acid rain harms aquatic animals.

LC 33

Write a summary of how acid rain forms in your own words. Keep the sequence of events in order. Use order words such as *first, second, next, then, finally,* and *at last.*

Students should explain the steps in the formation of acid rain using the graphic organizer. They should also include transition words to signal each step in the process.

LC 34

Introduce "Winter Storms"

Lesson Overview

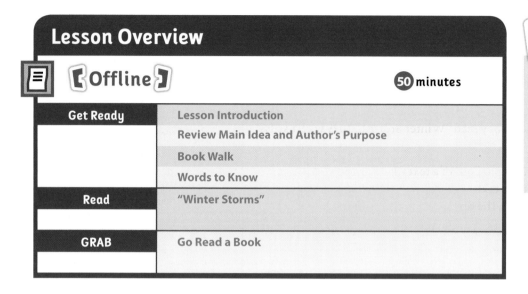

Offline   **50** minutes

Get Ready	Lesson Introduction
	Review Main Idea and Author's Purpose
	Book Walk
	Words to Know
Read	"Winter Storms"
GRAB	Go Read a Book

Big Ideas

▶ Active, strong readers employ reading strategies such as using existing knowledge to make sense of texts.

▶ Nonfiction texts differ from fiction texts in that they describe real or true things in life, rather than things made up by the author.

▶ Readers need to be able to sequence, summarize, and articulate the main idea.

▶ Readers must understand the relationship between main idea and supporting details.

▶ Readers identify the underlying implications of a text and use this information to form an opinion or make a decision.

[Materials]

Supplied

• "Winter Storms,"
  K¹² World: Weather or Not,
  pp. 26–37
• Reading Strategies
  bookmark

Article Synopsis

This article describes what causes snow and winter storms, including blizzards and ice storms.

Keywords

author's purpose – the reason the author wrote a text: to entertain, to inform, to express an opinion, or to persuade

graphic – a picture, photograph, map, diagram, or other image

main idea – the most important point the author makes; it may be stated or unstated

supporting details – the sentences that give information about the main idea or topic sentence

 **Offline** **50** minutes

Work **together** with students to complete offline Get Ready, Read, and GRAB activities.

Get Ready ....

Lesson Introduction
Prepare students to read "Winter Storms."

1. Explain to students that before they read "Winter Storms," they will discuss with you

   ▸ The main idea and author's purpose of a text
   ▸ Their predictions about the text
   ▸ Important words to know in the text

2. Tell students that while they read, you will check in to make sure they understand what they are reading.

3. Tell students that after they read, they will answer questions about the article.

Objectives
- Identify main idea and supporting details in a text.
- Identify author's purpose.
- Identify the main ideas and supporting details of a text read aloud or information presented in a variety of media and formats.
- Compare and contrast the most important points presented by two texts on the same topic.
- Use before-reading strategies.
- Increase concept and content vocabulary.

Review Main Idea and Author's Purpose
Read aloud a new text about rain, and have students identify the main idea and author's purpose, as well as compare and contrast this new text to the article "Let It Rain."

1. Review with students that they read an article about rain called "Let It Rain."

2. Tell students that you are going to read a short text that is also on the topic of rain. Have them listen closely for the main idea and the author's purpose in writing this new text.

3. **Read aloud** the following passage.

Rain brings some of the worst disasters know to humankind. Every year people who live in Asia must deal with terrible rainstorms. These are called typhoons. Typhoons come with very strong winds and heavy downpours. The water causes flooding and mudslides that can bury an entire village. Hundreds of people die in these monstrous storms every year.

Dangerous rainstorms also strike the United States. The eastern part of the country gets hurricanes. Hurricanes are another name for typhoons. They bring heavy rains and fierce winds. One of the worst hurricanes ever to hit the United States struck in 2005. It was called Katrina. Katrina killed about 1,500 people. The worst-hit areas included New Orleans, Louisiana, and the coast of Mississippi. There was devastating damage from the flooding and wind.

Rain has value. It brings much-needed water to people, plants, and animals. But rain is also a dangerous element of nature. It can bring destruction and hardship.

4. Ask students questions to help them compare and contrast this passage with the article "Let It Rain."

  ▶ **What is the main idea of the passage you just heard?** Possible answer: Rain causes destruction when it comes in terrible storms.

  ▶ **What are two details that the author describes to support this main idea?** Possible answers: Typhoons in Asia cause flooding and mudslides that bury towns. Hurricanes such as Katrina in the United States kill people.

  ▶ **What do you think is the author's purpose in writing this passage? Think of two.** One purpose is to inform readers of the damage that terrible rain storms can do. Another purpose is to persuade readers that rain can do harm as well as good.

  ▶ **Compare and contrast this passage with the article "Let It Rain." Describe how the main idea, details, and author's purpose are similar and different.** Possible answers: The texts are similar because they both talk about what happens when it rains, and both mention bad storms and floods. One purpose of the articles is to inform the reader about rain. The texts are different because the magazine article describes the good things about rain and what it can do. The magazine article also describes how rain happens. This passage talks about the damage that rain can do and focuses on storms rather than on how rain forms.

Book Walk

Have students lead you through a Book Walk of "Winter Storms." Remind them to use the **title** and **graphics** to make predictions about what the article is about.

Words to Know

Before reading "Winter Storms," remind students that the Words to Know are the words in boldfaced type within the article. They can find the definitions of these words in the glossary at the back of the magazine.

Read

"Winter Storms"

Have students read "Winter Storms." Remind them to use the strategies on their Reading Strategies bookmark. For example, they may want to go back and reread anything that they found confusing.

⮑ **Learning Coach Check-In** This reading assignment should take about 15 minutes. After students finish reading, ask the following questions to assess their comprehension of the selection:

▶ How is snow different from rain? Possible answer: Water vapor in clouds freezes, and precipitation comes down frozen as ice or snow instead of as water.

▶ What is the weather like in a blizzard? Possible answer: There is a lot of snow that falls hard, and there are very strong winds.

If students have trouble answering these questions, ask them what reading strategies they used and suggest they reread the selection.

Objectives

- Read literature independently and proficiently.
- Apply information read to answer questions.
- Evaluate reading strategies.

GRAB

Go Read a Book

Have students read a book or magazine of their own choosing for at least 20 minutes. Remind students to use the strategies on their Reading Strategies bookmark before and during reading to help them understand the text.

Objectives

- Read literature independently and proficiently.
- Read a variety of texts for information and pleasure.

Explore "Winter Storms"

Lesson Overview

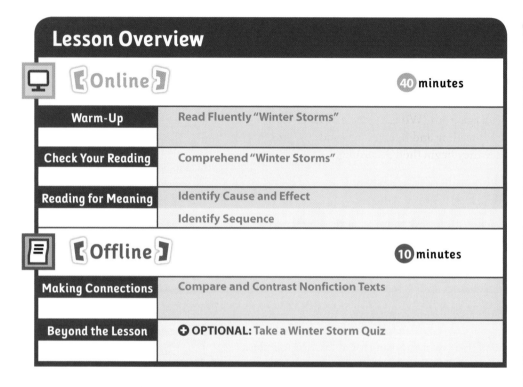

Online		40 minutes
Warm-Up	Read Fluently "Winter Storms"	
Check Your Reading	Comprehend "Winter Storms"	
Reading for Meaning	Identify Cause and Effect	
	Identify Sequence	

Offline		10 minutes
Making Connections	Compare and Contrast Nonfiction Texts	
Beyond the Lesson	⊕ OPTIONAL: Take a Winter Storm Quiz	

Materials

Supplied

- "Winter Storms,"
  K¹² World: Weather or Not,
  pp. 26–37
- *K¹² Language Arts Activity Book,* pp. LC 35–37

Keywords

cause – the reason something happens

compare – to explain how two or more things are alike

contrast – to explain how two or more things are different

effect – the result of a cause

sequence – the order in which things happen

Advance Preparation

Students will need access to a computer to go to a website for Making Connections and Beyond the Lesson.

Big Ideas

▸ Comprehension entails an understanding of the organizational patterns of text.
▸ Signal words—such as *before, consequently, compare/contrast, therefore*— are a guide to understanding the relationship between and among ideas.

 **40 minutes**

Students will work **independently** to complete online Warm-Up, Check Your Reading, and Reading for Meaning activities.

Warm-Up

Read Fluently "Winter Storms"
Students will read aloud and record a passage from "Winter Storms." The purpose of this activity is to improve students' oral reading and fluency. Remind students to listen to the model on each screen before they begin their recording.

Objectives
- Read poetry and prose aloud.
- Read aloud grade-level text with appropriate automaticity, prosody, accuracy and rate.

Check Your Reading

Comprehend "Winter Storms"
Students will answer questions about "Winter Storms" to demonstrate their literal and inferential comprehension of the article.

Objectives
- Sequence events in a text.
- Use graphics to answer a question.
- Use graphics and visuals to comprehend meaning and answer questions (diagrams, charts, captions).
- Identify main idea.
- Identify opinion.

Reading for Meaning

Identify Cause and Effect
Students will learn that authors of nonfiction texts may organize their writing using cause-and-effect relationships to explain why things happen. They will learn how to recognize cause-and-effect organization and identify examples of these relationships in the article "Winter Storms." Understanding the way authors structure text will help students with their comprehension and their own writing skills.

Identify Sequence
Students will practice identifying the sequence of events in a process. They will also recognize that nonfiction authors use sequence to help them achieve their purpose of informing the reader about how events occur.

Objectives
- Define *cause and effect*.
- Identify how one event may cause another event.
- Identify cause and effect.
- Describe the logical connection between particular sentences and paragraphs in a text (for example, comparison, cause-effect, first-second-third in a sequence).
- Describe the relationship between a series of steps.
- Sequence events in a text.
- Identify author's purpose.

 **10 minutes**

Work **together** with students to complete the offline Making Connections and Beyond the Lesson activities.

Making Connections

Compare and Contrast Nonfiction Texts

Students will compare and contrast two nonfiction texts about winter storms. Turn to pages LC 35–37 in *K¹² Language Arts Activity Book*.

1. Make sure students have their copy of the magazine *K¹² World: Weather or Not*. Tell them they will need to refer to the article "Winter Storms" to answer the questions on the Activity Book pages.

2. Follow the link provided in the online lesson to access the website booklet "Winter Storms." Have students read the website booklet.

3. Direct students' attention to the Activity Book pages and have them read the directions.

4. Have students complete the Activity Book pages.

Objectives

- Compare and contrast using evidence from the text.
- Compare and contrast the most important points and key details presented in two texts on the same topic.
- Identify author's purpose.
- Use text features and search tools (for example, keywords, sidebars, hyperlinks) to efficiently locate information relevant to a given topic.
- Write an opinion.
- Support an opinion with reasons.

Making Connections

Explore "Winter Storms"

Compare and Contrast Nonfiction Texts

Compare and contrast the website booklet "Winter Storms" with the magazine article "Winter Storms."

Similar	Different
They are both about winter storms. They both give facts about storms. They both tell how to be safe in winter weather.	The website booklet gives more information on how to be safe in winter weather. The magazine article tells more about how winter storms form and different kinds of storms.

LANGUAGE ARTS PURPLE LC 35

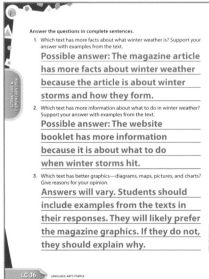

LC 36 LANGUAGE ARTS PURPLE

Answer the questions in complete sentences.

1. Which text has more facts about what winter weather is? Support your answer with examples from the text.
Possible answer: The magazine article has more facts about winter weather because the article is about winter storms and how they form.

2. Which text has more information about what to do in winter weather? Support your answer with examples from the text.
Possible answer: The website booklet has more information because it is about what to do when winter storms hit.

3. Which text has better graphics—diagrams, maps, pictures, and charts? Give reasons for your opinion.
Answers will vary. Students should include examples from the texts in their responses. They will likely prefer the magazine graphics. If they do not, they should explain why.

4. What do you think the magazine article "Winter Storms" could have done better?
Answers will vary, but students should give examples of how the article could be improved.

5. What do you think the website booklet "Winter Storms" could have done better?
Answers will vary, but students should give examples of how the website booklet could be improved.

6. What do you think is the author's purpose in the magazine article "Winter Storms"?
Possible answer: The author's purpose is to explain how winter storms form and what happens in winter storms.

7. What do you think is the author's purpose in the website booklet "Winter Storms"?
Possible answer: The author's purpose is to explain what to do to stay safe in winter storms.

 LANGUAGE ARTS PURPLE LC 37

Beyond the Lesson

OPTIONAL: Take a Winter Storm Quiz

This activity is OPTIONAL. It is intended for students who have extra time and would benefit from completing a quiz on winter storms. Feel free to skip this activity.

1. Have students refer to the website booklet "Winter Storms" (http://www.nws.noaa.gov/os/brochures/owlie/Owlie-winter.pdf).

2. Have them take the quiz on the last page of the booklet.

3. When students have completed the quiz, review the answers with them.

Fill in the Blanks

1. watch
2. warning
3. kitty litter
4. antenna
5. carbon monoxide
6. layers
7. mittens
8. winter
9. wind chill
10. snowdrift

True or False

1. T
2. F
3. T
4. F
5. F
6. T
7. T
8. T
9. F
10. F

Objectives

- Apply information read to answer questions about text(s).
- Use text features and search tools (for example, keywords, sidebars, hyperlinks) to efficiently locate information relevant to a given topic.

Introduce "Wind"

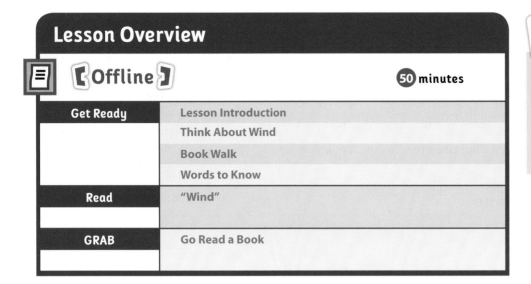

Lesson Overview

[Offline]   **50 minutes**

Get Ready	Lesson Introduction
	Think About Wind
	Book Walk
	Words to Know
Read	"Wind"
GRAB	Go Read a Book

Big Ideas

- Active, strong readers employ reading strategies such using existing knowledge to make sense of texts.
- Nonfiction texts differ from fiction texts in that they describe real or true things in life, rather than things made up by the author.
- Active strong readers monitor their comprehension as they read.

[Materials]

Supplied

- "Wind," *K¹² World: Weather or Not,* pp. 38–47
- Reading Strategies bookmark

Article Synopsis

This article describes various types of wind and how meteorologists measure wind. The article also presents the ways that wind can do damage and the ways it can be helpful.

Keywords

fact – something that can be proven true

nonfiction – writings about true things

topic – the subject of a text

Offline 50 minutes

Work **together** with students to complete offline Get Ready, Read, and GRAB activities.

Get Ready

Lesson Introduction
Prepare students to read "Wind."

1. Explain to students that before they read "Wind," they will discuss with you

    ► What they already know about wind and what they want to know about wind
    ► Their predictions about the text
    ► Important words to know in the text

2. Tell students that while they read, you will check in to make sure they understand what they are reading.

3. Tell students that after they read, they will answer questions about the article.

Objectives
- Make connections between text and self, text and world, and text to text.
- Connect text to prior knowledge.
- Use before-reading strategies.
- Increase concept and content vocabulary.

Think About Wind
Have students set up a KWL (Know-Wonder-Learn) chart to help them begin thinking about wind in preparation for reading the article "Wind."

1. Have students draw a three-column chart and label the columns "What I Know," "What I Wonder," and "What I Learn."

2. Have students tell what they know about wind and write it in the first column.

3. Ask students what they wonder, or would like to know, about wind and write it in the second column. If necessary, prompt students with questions.

    ► Would you like to know about different kinds of wind?
    ► Would you like to know how to measure wind?
    ► Would you like to know how wind can be useful?
    ► Would you like to know about dangerous winds?

4. Tell students they are going to read an article about the wind. When they finish reading, they should fill in the third column with things they learned about the wind.

Book Walk
Have students lead you through a Book Walk of "Wind." Remind them to use the **title** and **illustrations** to make predictions about what the article is about.

Words to Know

Before reading "Wind," remind students that the Words to Know are the words in boldfaced type within the article. They can find the definitions of these words in the glossary at the back of the magazine.

Read

"Wind"

Have students read "Wind." Remind them to use the strategies on their Reading Strategies bookmark. For example, they may want to adjust their speed and read more slowly to make sure they understand the text.

○ **Learning Coach Check-In** This reading assignment should take about 15 minutes. After students finish reading, ask the following questions to assess their comprehension of the selection:

▶ Look at your KWL chart. What did you learn about the wind? Answers will vary.

▶ Did you find answers to any of the questions you wondered about? Answers will vary.

▶ What is one useful thing and one harmful thing that you read that wind can do? Possible answers: useful things: power windmills that grind grains, power wind turbines that make electricity; harmful things: becomes dangerous when it blows very hard, destroys things

If students have trouble answering these questions, ask them what reading strategies they used and suggest they reread the selection.

Objectives
- Read literature independently and proficiently.
- Apply information read to answer questions.
- Evaluate reading strategies.

GRAB

Go Read a Book

Have students read a book or magazine of their own choosing for at least 20 minutes. Remind students to use the strategies on their Reading Strategies bookmark before and during reading to help them understand the text.

Objectives
- Read literature independently and proficiently.
- Read a variety of texts for information and pleasure.

Explore "Wind"

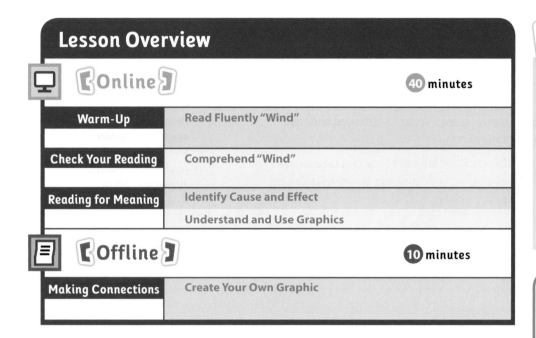

Lesson Overview

Online — 40 minutes

Warm-Up	Read Fluently "Wind"
Check Your Reading	Comprehend "Wind"
Reading for Meaning	Identify Cause and Effect
	Understand and Use Graphics

Offline — 10 minutes

Making Connections	Create Your Own Graphic

Materials

Supplied
- "Wind," *K¹² World: Weather or Not* pp. 38–47
- *K¹² Language Arts Activity Book*, pp. LC 39–41

Also Needed
- ruler
- crayons

Keywords

cause – the reason something happens

compare – to explain how two or more things are alike

contrast – to explain how two or more things are different

effect – the result of a cause

graphic – a picture, photograph, map, diagram, or other image

sequence – the order in which things happen

Advance Preparation

Students will need to access references, such as a library, an encyclopedia, or the Internet, for Making Connections.

Big Ideas

- ▸ Comprehension entails an understanding of the organizational patterns of text.
- ▸ Comprehension is facilitated by an understanding of physical presentation (headings, subheads, graphics, and other features).

 **40 minutes**

Students will work **independently** to complete online Warm-Up, Check Your Reading, and Reading for Meaning activities.

Warm-Up

Read Fluently "Wind"

Students will read aloud and record a passage from "Wind." The purpose of this activity is to improve students' oral reading and fluency. Remind students to listen to the model on each screen before they begin their recording.

Objectives
- Read poetry and prose aloud.
- Read aloud grade-level text with appropriate automaticity, prosody, accuracy and rate.

Check Your Reading

Comprehend "Wind"

Students will answer questions about "Wind" to demonstrate their literal and inferential comprehension of the article.

Objectives
- Identify cause and effect.
- Use information gained from illustrations (such as maps and photographs) and text to demonstrate understanding of the text (for example, where, when, why, and how key events occur).
- Identify author's purpose.
- Identify main idea.
- Identify opinion.

Reading for Meaning

Identify Cause and Effect
Students will look at how the author of "Wind" uses cause and effect to explain where wind comes from and what it can do.

_____

Understand and Use Graphics
Students will learn how to interpret graphics such as charts, diagrams, maps, and graphs to help them understand important information in a nonfiction text.

Objectives
- Define *cause and effect*.
- Identify how one event may cause another event.
- Identify a cause and its effect on events and/or relationships.
- Describe the logical connection between particular sentences and paragraphs in a text (for example, comparison, cause-effect, first-second-third in a sequence).
- Identify author's purpose.
- Use graphics to comprehend meaning and answer questions (diagrams, charts, captions).

 **10 minutes**

Work **together** with students to complete the offline Making Connections activity.

Making Connections

Create Your Own Graphic
Students will explore how graphics explain important information. Gather the ruler and crayons, and turn to pages LC 39–41 in *K¹² Language Arts Activity Book*.

1. Make sure students have their copy of the magazine *K¹² World: Weather or Not.* Tell them they will need to refer to the article "Wind" to complete the Activity Book pages.

2. Make sure students have access to references, such as the library, an encyclopedia, or the Internet, to gather additional data or other information for the graphic they will create.

3. Direct students' attention to the Activity Book pages and have them read the directions.

Objectives
- Compare and contrast using evidence from the text.
- Incorporate graphic features in writing.
- Identify author's purpose.
- Use text features and search tools (for example, keywords, sidebars, hyperlinks) to efficiently locate information relevant to a given topic.
- Use a visual display to enhance facts or details.

4. Discuss the information students are going to present and what type of graphic would give the best possible visual representation of this information. Review the uses of each type of graphic as necessary:

   ▸ **Maps** show location and are best suited to showing where winds or storms are located.

   ▸ **Charts** show information by category and are good for comparing and contrasting information or providing lists. A chart would be useful for listing the characteristics of wind measuring tools or comparing the wind speeds of various famous storms.

   ▸ **Graphs** illustrate numbers. Bar graphs are good for showing comparisons, such as the speeds of various winds. Line graphs show the changes in data over time, such as measurements of wind speed at the same location at different times.

   ▸ **Diagrams** show how something works and would be good tools for showing how hurricanes or tornadoes form, or how windmills or wind turbines work.

5. Have students complete the Activity Book pages.

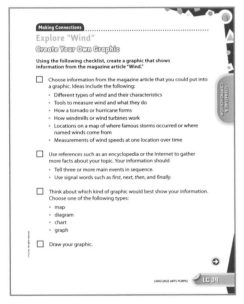

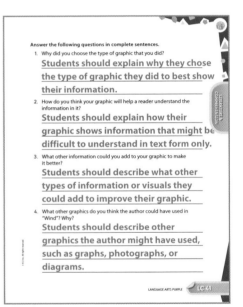

Introduce "Storm Chasers"

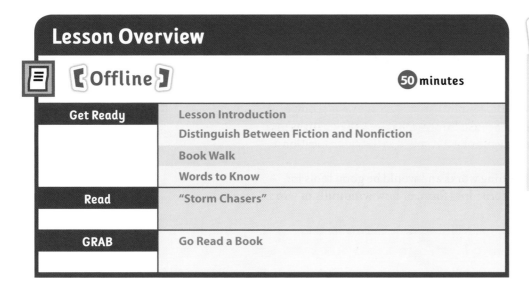

Lesson Overview

Offline — 50 minutes

Get Ready	Lesson Introduction
	Distinguish Between Fiction and Nonfiction
	Book Walk
	Words to Know
Read	"Storm Chasers"
GRAB	Go Read a Book

Big Ideas

▶ Active, strong readers employ reading strategies such as using existing knowledge to make sense of texts.
▶ Nonfiction texts differ from fiction texts in that they describe real or true things in life, rather than things made up by the author.
▶ Narrative and expository text differ significantly, for example, in structure, content, and purpose.

Materials

Supplied

- "Storm Chasers," *K¹² World: Weather or Not,* pp. 48–59
- Reading Strategies bookmark

Article Synopsis

This article describes the work of storm chasers, people who track and gather data about severe storms such as hurricanes and tornadoes. The article also includes a section about how tornadoes form, as well as a section about two fictional characters chasing a tornado, which is presented in a cartoon format.

Keywords

fact – something that can be proven true
fiction – make-believe stories
nonfiction – writings about true things

 **50 minutes**

Work **together** with students to complete offline Get Ready, Read, and GRAB activities.

Get Ready ....

Lesson Introduction

Prepare students to read "Storm Chasers."

1. Explain to students that before they read "Storm Chasers," they will discuss with you

   ▸ The difference between fiction and nonfiction
   ▸ Their predictions about the text
   ▸ Important words to know in the text

2. Tell students that while they read, you will check in to make sure they understand what they are reading.

3. Tell students that after they read, they will answer questions about the article.

> **Objectives**
> - Connect text to prior knowledge.
> - Use before-reading strategies.
> - Increase concept and content vocabulary.

Distinguish Between Fiction and Nonfiction

Discuss with students the differences between fiction and nonfiction and how to identify facts in texts that combine the two genres.

1. Remind students that **nonfiction** is writing that contains **facts**. Have students tell what a fact is and give an example. A fact is something that can be proven true, such as that the earth is round.

2. Review that **fiction** is writing about make-believe things. Sometimes an author combines fiction and nonfiction: The characters, setting, and plot might be imagined, but the story is mostly facts about real-life things. Ask students why an author might write a story that is made up but contains facts. Possible answer: The author might want to make the factual information more interesting and fun to read.

3. Tell students that one way to distinguish between fiction and fact in a story is to ask this question about anything that might be a fact: Could I find this information in a reference source, such an encyclopedia, a dictionary, or on a reference website?

4. Tell students that they are going to read a nonfiction article that includes a short story that mixes fact and fiction.

Book Walk

Have students lead you through a Book Walk of "Storm Chasers." Remind them to use the **title** and **illustrations** to make predictions about what the article is about.

Words to Know

Before reading "Storm Chasers," remind students that the Words to Know are the words in boldfaced type within the article. They can find the definitions of these words in the glossary at the back of the magazine.

Read

"Storm Chasers"

Have students read "Storm Chasers." Remind them to use the strategies on their Reading Strategies bookmark. For example, they may want to look for the answers to questions in the text. Tell students that they may want to do the crossword puzzle on page 57 as they read.

⊃ **Learning Coach Check-In** This reading assignment should take about 15 minutes. After students finish reading, ask the following questions to assess their comprehension of the selection:

► Who are storm chasers? People who follow storms to gather information about them or to make forecasts about them.

► What's the name of one tool that storm chasers use, and what does it do? Answers may include: Doppler radar to collect data about storms; a TOTO to measure tornadoes; a dropsonde to gather data about hurricanes.

If students have trouble answering these questions, ask them what reading strategies they used and suggest they reread the selection.

Objectives

- Read literature independently and proficiently.
- Apply information read to answer questions.
- Evaluate reading strategies.

GRAB

Go Read a Book

Have students read a book or magazine of their own choosing for at least 20 minutes. Remind students to use the strategies on their Reading Strategies bookmark before and during reading to help them understand the text.

Objectives

- Read literature independently and proficiently.
- Read a variety of texts for information and pleasure.

Explore "Storm Chasers"

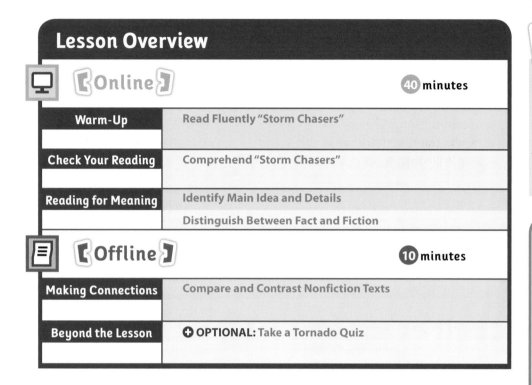

Lesson Overview

🖥 【Online】   ④⓪ minutes

Warm-Up	Read Fluently "Storm Chasers"
Check Your Reading	Comprehend "Storm Chasers"
Reading for Meaning	Identify Main Idea and Details
	Distinguish Between Fact and Fiction

📄 【Offline】   ①⓪ minutes

Making Connections	Compare and Contrast Nonfiction Texts
Beyond the Lesson	⊕ OPTIONAL: Take a Tornado Quiz

【Materials】

Supplied
- "Storm Chasers,"
  K¹² World: Weather or Not,
  pp. 48–59
- *K¹² Language Arts Activity
  Book,* pp. LC 43–45

Keywords

fact – something that can be proven true

fiction – make-believe stories

main idea – the most important point the author makes; it may be stated or unstated

supporting details – the details that give information about the main idea or topic sentence

topic – the subject of a text

Advance Preparation

Students will need access to a computer to go to a website for Making Connections and Beyond the Lesson.

Big Ideas

▸ Nonfiction texts differ from fiction texts in that they describe real or true things in life, rather than things made up by the author.

▸ Readers must understand the relationship between main idea and supporting details.

▸ Writing varies by genre. Different kinds of writing, whether creative, academic, or personal, vary in form and structure.

 **40 minutes**

Students will work **independently** to complete online Warm-Up, Check Your Reading, and Reading for Meaning activities.

Warm-Up

Read Fluently "Storm Chasers"
Students will read aloud and record a passage from "Storm Chasers." The purpose of this activity is to improve students' oral reading and fluency. Remind students to listen to the model on each screen before they begin their recording.

Objectives
- Read poetry and prose aloud.
- Read aloud grade-level text with appropriate automaticity, prosody, accuracy, and rate.

Check Your Reading

Comprehend "Storm Chasers"
Students will answer questions about "Storm Chasers" to demonstrate their literal and inferential comprehension of the article.

Objectives
- Identify concrete answers to questions.
- Apply information read to answer questions.
- Use graphics to answer a question about a reading.
- Sequence events in a text.
- Identify opinion.

Reading for Meaning

Identify Main Idea and Details
Students will identify the main idea and important supporting details of the article "Storm Chasers."

Distinguish Between Fact and Fiction
Students will learn that sometimes authors use a fictional format to present facts and information. They will practice distinguishing fact from fiction in a graphic story about chasing tornadoes.

Objectives
- Define *main idea* and *supporting details*.
- Identify main idea and supporting details in a text.
- Distinguish between main idea and details.
- Identify main idea.
- Define *fact*.
- Distinguish between fiction and nonfiction.
- Identify facts.

[Offline] 🔟 minutes

Work **together** with students to complete the offline Making Connections and Beyond the Lesson activities.

Making Connections

Compare and Contrast Nonfiction Texts

Students will compare and contrast two nonfiction texts about tornadoes and storm chasers. Turn to pages LC 43–45 in *K¹² Language Arts Activity Book*.

1. Make sure students have their copy of the magazine *K¹² World: Weather or Not*. Tell them they will need to refer to the article "Storm Chasers" to answer the questions on the Activity Book pages.

2. Follow the link provided online to access the website booklet "Tornadoes." Have students read the website booklet.

3. Direct students' attention to the Activity Book pages and have them read the directions.

4. Have students complete the Activity Book pages.

Objectives

- Compare and contrast using evidence from the text.
- Compare and contrast the most important points and key details presented in two texts on the same topic.
- Identify author's purpose.
- Use text features and search tools (for example, keywords, sidebars, hyperlinks) to efficiently locate information relevant to a given topic.
- Create and use graphic organizers, diagrams, charts, Venn diagrams, and time lines to demonstrate and support comprehension.
- State an opinion.
- Provide reasons that support an opinion.

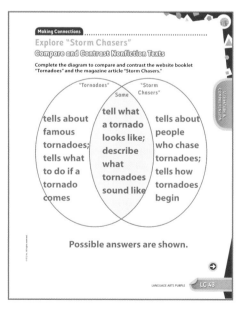

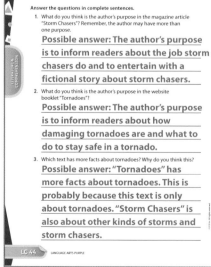

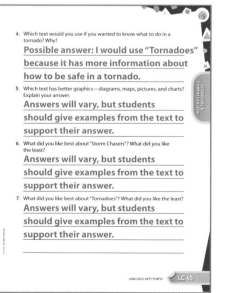

Beyond the Lesson

⊕ OPTIONAL: Take a Tornado Quiz

This activity is OPTIONAL. It is intended for students who have extra time and would benefit from completing a quiz on tornadoes. Feel free to skip this activity.

1. Have students refer to the website booklet "Tornadoes" (http://www.nws. noaa.gov/os/brochures/owlie/Owlie-tornadoes.pdf).

2. Have them take the quiz on the last page of the booklet.

3. When students have completed the quiz, review the answers with them.

Objectives

- Apply information read to answer questions about text(s).
- Use text features and search tools (for example, keywords, sidebars, hyperlinks) to efficiently locate information relevant to a given topic.

Fill in the Blanks

1. tornado
2. funnel and top
3. black clouds
4. watch
5. warning
6. train
7. ditch
8. basement
9. hail
10. bathroom
11. windows
12. mobile home
13. sky
14. radio

True or False

1. T
2. F
3. T
4. T
5. T
6. F
7. F
8. T
9. T
10. F

Reflections on *Weather or Not*

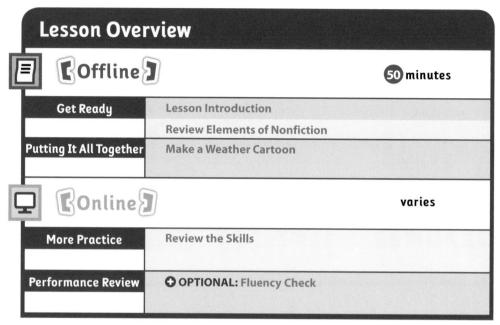

Lesson Overview

Offline
50 minutes

Get Ready	Lesson Introduction
	Review Elements of Nonfiction
Putting It All Together	Make a Weather Cartoon

Online
varies

More Practice	Review the Skills
Performance Review	⊕ OPTIONAL: Fluency Check

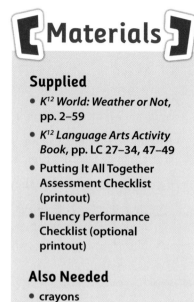

Materials

Supplied
- *K¹² World: Weather or Not*, pp. 2–59
- *K¹² Language Arts Activity Book*, pp. LC 27–34, 47–49
- Putting It All Together Assessment Checklist (printout)
- Fluency Performance Checklist (optional printout)

Also Needed
- crayons

Advance Preparation

Gather pages LC 27–30 (Main Idea, Details, and Author's Purpose), 31–32 (Sequence Events in the Text: The Water Cycle), and 33–34 (Sequence Events in the Text: Acid Rain Formation) in *K¹² Language Arts Activity Book*.

Big Ideas

▶ Nonfiction texts differ from fiction texts in that they describe real or true things in life, rather than things made up by the author.

▶ Readers must understand the relationship between main idea and supporting details.

▶ Writing varies by genre. Different kinds of writing, whether creative, academic, or personal, vary in form and structure.

Keywords

author's purpose – the reason the author wrote a text: to entertain, to inform, to express an opinion, or to persuade

cause – the reason something happens

effect – the result of a cause

fact – something that can be proven true

fiction – make-believe stories

main idea – the most important point the author makes; it may be stated or unstated

nonfiction – writings about true things

sequence – the order in which things happen

supporting details – the sentences that give information about the main idea or topic sentence

topic – the subject of a text

 **Offline** **50 minutes**

Work **together** with students to complete the offline Get Ready and Putting It All Together activities.

Get Ready

Lesson Introduction

Prepare students for creating their own cartoon about a weather topic.

1. Explain to students that they are going to create their own cartoon or graphic story about a weather topic.

2. Tell students that before they do the project, they will discuss with you

   ‣ The elements of nonfiction
   ‣ An author's purpose in writing nonfiction
   ‣ How nonfiction texts are organized

Review Elements of Nonfiction

Review the main features of nonfiction texts to prepare students to write their own nonfiction.

1. Have students tell what **nonfiction** is. writing about true things.

2. Remind students that authors of nonfiction may have more than one **purpose**, or reason, for writing. Have students tell what purposes an author of nonfiction might have. to inform, to entertain, to persuade, or to express an opinion or emotion

3. Remind students that nonfiction writing is about a **topic**, or subject, and that the author always has a **main idea** about the topic. Have students tell what a main idea and supporting details are. A main idea is the most important point the author makes. It may be stated or unstated. A supporting detail is a detail that gives more information about a main idea.

4. Point out that authors organize the information and facts in their texts in many different ways. Review two of the structures of nonfiction by having students define each of the following:

   ‣ sequence the order in which things happen
   ‣ cause and effect the reason something happens; the result of a cause

5. Tell students to keep in mind these qualities of nonfiction when they do the Putting It All Together activity.

Objectives

- Use text organizational features to locate and comprehend information (table of contents).
- Summarize the plot of a story.
- Define *character*.
- Define *narrator*.
- Define *point of view*.
- Identify third person narrator.
- Identify point of view in a selection.
- Describe the effect point of view has on a story.

Putting It All Together

Make a Weather Cartoon

Students will demonstrate their understanding of how authors weave together fiction and nonfiction to inform and entertain readers about factual topics. Have them gather their completed pages LC 27–34 and turn to pages LC 47–49 in *K¹² Language Arts Activity Book*.

1. Direct students' attention to the Activity Book pages. Tell them that they are going to create their own graphic story, or cartoon, about a weather topic, like the tornado chase cartoon in "Storm Chasers."

2. Have students complete the Activity Book pages.

   ⮕ **Learning Coach Check-In** Check in with students after about 40 minutes to see if they have completed the assignment.

3. When they have completed their cartoon, have them present it to an audience.

4. Use the materials and instructions in the online lesson to evaluate students' work.

5. Enter the answers (Yes or No) for each line of the assessment checklist online.

Objectives

- Distinguish between fiction and nonfiction.
- State the topic directly.
- Identify main idea.
- Identify supporting details.
- Identify facts.
- Sequence events in a story.
- Write dialogue.
- Write a fictional story.
- Create a cartoon.
- Choose a topic.

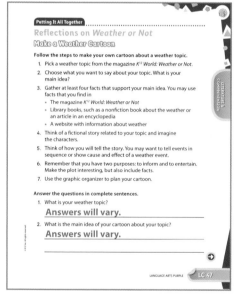

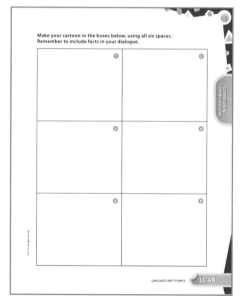

 **varies**

Students will work **independently** to complete the online More Practice activity.

More Practice

Review the Skills
If students scored less than 80 percent or had difficulty meeting the objectives of the Putting It All Together activity, have them go online for more practice.

 Reward: If students score 80 percent or more on the Putting It All Together activity, add a sticker for this unit on the My Accomplishments chart. If students did not score 80 percent or more, work with them to revise their writing until they do score 80 percent and then add a sticker to the My Accomplishments chart.

Objectives
- Define *main idea* and *supporting details*.
- Identify main idea and supporting details in a text.
- Identify the main idea.
- Distinguish between main idea and details.
- Describe the relationship between a series of steps.
- Sequence events in a text.
- Identify how one event may cause another event.
- Describe the logical connection between particular sentences and paragraphs in a text (for example, comparison, cause-effect, first-second-third in a sequence).
- Distinguish between fiction and nonfiction.
- Identify facts.

Performance Review

⊕ OPTIONAL: Fluency Check
Listen to students' recordings and use the Fluency Performance Checklist to review fluency and track performance. Keep the completed checklist so you can review students' progress over time.

Objectives
- Read aloud grade-level text with appropriate automaticity, prosody, accuracy, and rate.
- Read poetry and prose aloud.

Animal Friends Poetry

Unit Focus

In this unit, students will learn about the poetic techniques, such as rhyme and sensory language, that poets use to make their writing more vivid and interesting. Students will explore these poems:

- ▶ "The Hairy Dog"
- ▶ "I've Got a Dog"
- ▶ "A Kitten"
- ▶ "Cat"
- ▶ "The Elephant"
- ▶ "The Silent Snake"

Unit Plan		[Online]	[Offline]
Lesson 1	Introduce Poems About Cats and Dogs		50 minutes
Lesson 2	Explore Poems About Cats and Dogs	40 minutes	10 minutes
Lesson 3	Introduce "The Elephant" and "The Silent Snake"		50 minutes
Lesson 4	Explore "The Elephant" and "The Silent Snake"	40 minutes	10 minutes
Lesson 5	Reflections on Animal Friends Poetry	varies	50 minutes
Lesson 6	Your Choice		50 minutes

Introduce Poems About Cats and Dogs

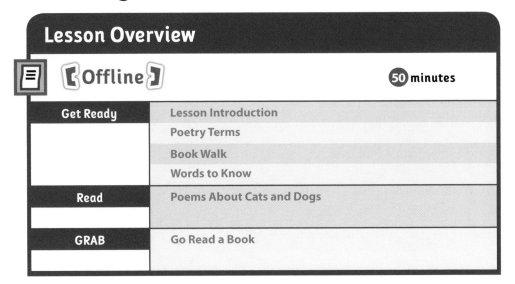

Lesson Overview

Offline 50 minutes

Get Ready	Lesson Introduction
	Poetry Terms
	Book Walk
	Words to Know
Read	Poems About Cats and Dogs
GRAB	Go Read a Book

Big Ideas

▸ Active, strong readers employ reading strategies such as making connections between text and self, between and among texts, and between text and the real world.

▸ Poems are different from prose in structure and content. They are generally organized in lines and often contain rhymes.

Materials

Supplied

- "The Hairy Dog," "I've Got a Dog," "A Kitten," "Cat," *K¹² Classics for Young Readers, Volume C*, pp. 66–73
- Poetry Reading Strategies bookmark
- Reading Strategies bookmark

Poetry Synopsis

In the four short poems in this lesson, the speakers describe their pet dogs and cats. The speakers in "The Hairy Dog" and "I've Got a Dog" tell what their pets look like. The speakers in "A Kitten" and "Cat" describe how their pets move and behave.

Keywords

poem – a piece of poetry

poet – one who writes poetry

poetry – writing that uses language, sound, and rhythm to make readers feel, experience, or imagine something

rhyme – the use of words that end with the same sounds; for example, *cat* and *hat* rhyme

speaker – the narrator of a poem

stanza – a group of lines in a poem

 **50** minutes

Work **together** with students to complete offline Get Ready, Read, and GRAB activities.

Get Ready

Lesson Introduction
Prepare students to read "The Hairy Dog," "I've Got a Dog," "A Kitten," and "Cat."

1. Explain to students that before they read the poems they will discuss with you

   ▸ How poems are different from other kinds of writing
   ▸ Their predictions about the poems they will read

2. Tell students that while they read, you will check in to make sure they understand what they are reading.

3. Tell students that after they read, they will answer questions about the poems.

Poetry Terms
Discuss what poetry is and how it is different from other kinds of writing.

1. Have students use the **table of contents** in *K¹² Classics for Young Readers, Volume C*, to find the "The Hairy Dog." Ask students what a **poem** is. Possible answers: writing in lines; writing that rhymes; writing that is not in complete paragraphs like fiction and nonfiction; writing that creates pictures in the reader's mind

2. Review the definition of **poetry**. writing that is made up of lines that often rhyme and follow a specific rhythm

3. Ask students if they remember what we call authors who write poems. poets

4. Tell students that a poem also has a **speaker**. The speaker is not the same as the poet. The speaker is the character who is speaking in the poem or telling the poem. Ask students if they can remember what we call the speaker in fiction writing. narrator

5. Have students look at the structure of "The Hairy Dog."

   ▸ Review that the rows of text in the poem are called lines.
   ▸ Point out that there are two groups of lines and ask students if they know what these groups are called. stanzas
   ▸ Explain that many poems use **stanzas**. Stanzas in a poem are like paragraphs in writing. Stanzas break ideas apart.

6. Tell students that many poems also use **rhyme**. Have students define *rhyme* or review it with them, and have them give examples of rhyming words. *Rhyme* is the use of words that end with the same sounds; some examples of rhyming word pairs are *cat* and *bat*, *dog* and *log*, and *pet* and *wet*.

Objectives
- Recognize various genres of literature.
- Define *poetry* as a genre.
- Define *speaker*.
- Distinguish between speaker and author.
- Define *stanza*.
- Identify stanzas.
- Refer to parts of stories, dramas, and poems when writing or speaking about a text, using terms such as *chapter*, *scene*, and *stanza*.
- Define *rhyme*.
- Use text organizational features to locate and comprehend information (table of contents).
- Use text features to make a prediction (illustrations, title).
- Increase concept and content vocabulary.

Book Walk

Have students lead you through a Book Walk of "The Hairy Dog," "I've Got a Dog," "A Kitten," and "Cat." Remind them to use the **titles** and **illustrations** to make predictions about what each poem will be about.

Words to Know

Remind students that they will find the Words to Know at the bottom of the pages in the selections. There are Words to Know in "The Hairy Dog" and "A Kitten."

 Read •

Poems About Cats and Dogs

Have students read "The Hairy Dog," "I've Got a Dog," "A Kitten," and "Cat." Remind them to use the strategies on their Poetry Reading Strategies bookmark. For example, they may want to read each poem once silently to themselves and then a second time aloud so that they can hear the sounds in the poem.

Objectives
- Read literature independently and proficiently.
- Apply information read to answer questions.
- Evaluate reading strategies.

  ↪ **Learning Coach Check-In** This reading assignment should take about 10 minutes. After students finish reading, ask the following questions to assess their comprehension of the selections:

   ▸ The first two poems are about dogs. What are the dogs in the poems like? Possible answers: In "The Hairy Dog," the dog is so hairy people can't see his eyes and don't know what kind of dog he is. In "I've Got a Dog," the dog is thin and has a lot of fleas.

   ▸ How do the cats in the last two poems behave? Possible answers: In "A Kitten," the kitten jumps and paws at the air and chases invisible things. In "Cat," the cat creeps around and crawls into dark places.

If students have trouble answering these questions, ask them what reading strategies they used and suggest they reread the selections.

GRAB •

Go Read a Book

Have students read a book or magazine of their own choosing for at least 20 minutes. Remind students to use the strategies on their Reading Strategies bookmark before and during reading to help them understand the text.

 Remember: The more students read, the better readers they become.

Objectives
- Read literature independently and proficiently.
- Read a variety of texts for information and pleasure.

Explore Poems About Cats and Dogs

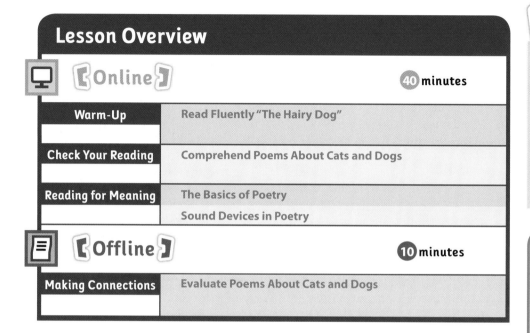

Lesson Overview

🖥 【Online】   40 minutes

Warm-Up	Read Fluently "The Hairy Dog"
Check Your Reading	Comprehend Poems About Cats and Dogs
Reading for Meaning	The Basics of Poetry
	Sound Devices in Poetry

☰ 【Offline】   10 minutes

Making Connections	Evaluate Poems About Cats and Dogs

Big Ideas

▸ Active, strong readers employ reading strategies such as making connections between text and self, between and among texts, and between text and the real world.

▸ Readers need to synthesize, draw conclusions about, and interpret what they have read.

▸ Poems are different from prose in structure and content. They are generally organized in lines and often contain rhymes.

【 Materials 】

Supplied

- "The Hairy Dog," "I've Got a Dog," "A Kitten," "Cat," *K¹² Classics for Young Readers, Volume C,* pp. 66–73
- *K¹² Language Arts Activity Book,* p. LC 51–52

Keywords

alliteration – the use of words with the same or close to the same beginning sounds

couplet – two successive lines of poetry that work together and often rhyme

onomatopoeia (AH-nuh-MAH-tuh-PEE-uh) – the use of words that show sounds; for example, *moo, woof, quack, squash*

rhyme – the use of words that end with the same sounds; for example, *cat* and *hat* rhyme

rhyme scheme – the pattern of rhymes made by the last sounds in the lines of a poem, shown by a different letter of the alphabet to represent each rhyme

 **minutes**

Students will work **independently** to complete online Warm-Up, Check Your Reading, and Reading for Meaning activities.

Warm-Up

Read Fluently "The Hairy Dog"

Students will read aloud and record the poem "The Hairy Dog." The purpose of this activity is to improve students' oral reading and fluency. Remind students to listen to the model on each screen before they begin their recording.

Objectives

- Read poetry and prose aloud.
- Read aloud grade-level text with appropriate automaticity, prosody, accuracy, and rate.
- Create engaging audio recordings of stories or poems that demonstrate fluid reading at an understandable pace.

Check Your Reading

Comprehend Poems About Cats and Dogs

Students will answer questions about "The Hairy Dog," "I've Got a Dog," "A Kitten," and "Cat" to demonstrate their literal and inferential comprehension of the poems.

Objectives

- Identify concrete answers to questions.
- Infer answers to questions.
- Apply information read to answer questions.
- Explain how specific aspects of a text's illustrations contribute to the meaning of the text.

Reading for Meaning

The Basics of Poetry
Students will learn how to identify the rhyme scheme and rhyming couplets in a poem.

Sound Devices in Poetry
Students will learn about two sound devices—alliteration and onomatopoeia—poets use to make their poetry more interesting and to draw attention to ideas and images they want to emphasize.

Objectives
- Refer to parts of stories, dramas, and poems when writing or speaking about a text, using terms such as *chapter*, *scene*, and *stanza*.
- Define *rhyme scheme*.
- Identify rhyme in a literary selection.
- Identify rhyme scheme.
- Define *rhyming couplet*.
- Recognize rhyming couplets.
- Define *sound devices*.
- Listen to and identify sound elements in poetry.
- Define *alliteration*.
- Identify alliteration.
- Define *onomatopoeia*.
- Identify author's use of onomatopoeia.

[Offline] **10** minutes

Work **together** with students to complete the offline Making Connections activity.

Making Connections

Evaluate Poems About Cats and Dogs
Students will analyze and evaluate the poets' techniques in poems about cats and dogs. Turn to pages LC 51 and 52 in *K¹² Language Arts Activity Book*.

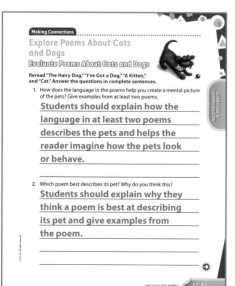

Making Connections

Explore Poems About Cats and Dogs

Evaluate Poems About Cats and Dogs

Reread "The Hairy Dog," "I've Got a Dog," "A Kitten," and "Cat." Answer the questions in complete sentences.

1. How does the language in the poems help you create a mental picture of the pets? Give examples from at least two poems.
   Students should explain how the language in at least two poems describes the pets and helps the reader imagine how the pets look or behave.

2. Which poem best describes its pet? Why do you think this?
   Students should explain why they think a poem is best at describing its pet and give examples from the poem.

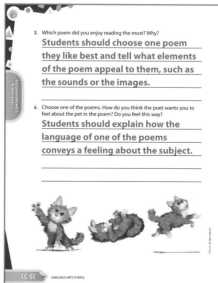

3. Which poem did you enjoy reading the most? Why?
   Students should choose one poem they like best and tell what elements of the poem appeal to them, such as the sounds or the images.

4. Choose one of the poems. How do you think the poet wants you to feel about the pet in the poem? Do you feel this way?
   Students should explain how the language of one of the poems conveys a feeling about the subject.

Objectives
- Answer evaluative questions based on reading.
- Compare and contrast literary elements in poetry.
- Describe methods the authors use to influence readers' feelings.
- Distinguish one's own opinion from the author's.
- Make connections between text and self, text and world, and text to text.
- State an opinion.
- Give reasons for opinion.

Introduce "The Elephant" and "The Silent Snake"

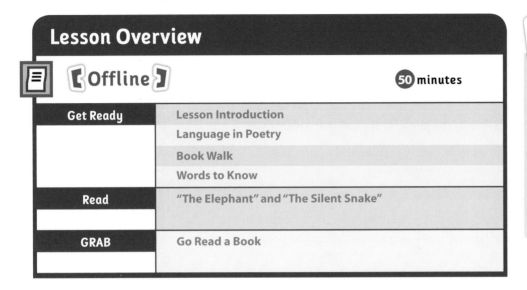

Lesson Overview

Offline — 50 minutes

Get Ready	Lesson Introduction
	Language in Poetry
	Book Walk
	Words to Know
Read	"The Elephant" and "The Silent Snake"
GRAB	Go Read a Book

Big Ideas

▶ Active, strong readers employ reading strategies such as making connections between text and self, between and among texts, and between text and the real world.

▶ Poems are different from prose in structure and content. They are generally organized in lines and often contain rhymes.

▶ The use of imagery and sensory language creates detailed pictures in the reader's mind, so the reader can understand and appreciate the ideas and feelings the writer conveys.

Materials

Supplied

- "The Elephant," "The Silent Snake," *K¹² Classics for Young Readers, Volume C*, pp. 74–77
- Poetry Reading Strategies bookmark
- Reading Strategies bookmark

Poetry Synopsis

In "The Elephant," the poet uses similes to describe the size and behavior of an elephant. In "The Silent Snake," the poet uses vivid verbs and sound devices such as rhymes and alliteration to create a mental image of a silently slithering snake.

Keywords

alliteration – the use of words with the same or close to the same beginning sounds

onomatopoeia (AH-nuh-MAH-tuh-PEE-uh) – the use of words that show sounds; for example, *moo, woof, quack, squash*

poem – a piece of poetry

rhyme – the use of words that end with the same sounds; for example, *cat* and *hat* rhyme

 **50** minutes

Work **together** with students to complete offline Get Ready, Read, and GRAB activities.

Get Ready

 Objectives
- Define *rhyme*.
- Use text organizational features to locate and comprehend information (table of contents).
- Use text features to make a prediction (illustrations, title).
- Increase concept and content vocabulary.

Lesson Introduction
Prepare students to read "The Elephant" and "The Silent Snake."

1. Explain to students that before they read the poems, they will discuss with you

   ▶ What they remember about poetry, including rhymes and sound devices
   ▶ Their predictions about the poems they will read

2. Tell students that while they read, you will check in to make sure they understand what they are reading.

3. Tell students that after they read, they will answer questions about the poems.

Language in Poetry
Review one of the sound elements of poetry—rhyme. Also, have students begin thinking about how poets use language to create images in the reader's mind.

1. Have students tell what they remember about one of the sound devices that poets use to make their poems more interesting.

   ▶ What is a **rhyme**? Give some examples. *Rhyme* is the use of words that end with the same sounds; some examples include *hat* and *bat* and *frog* and *log*.

2. Tell students that poets also use language to describe things and create an image, or picture, in the reader's mind.

3. Ask students to describe an orange. Have them use words that would help someone understand how the orange looks, feels, smells, and tastes. Possible answers: It's round and orange, has a rough skin, smells sweet like a flower, and tastes sour and sweet at the same time.

4. Tell students that in the poems they are going to read, the poets use language and sound devices to describe two animals.

Book Walk
Have students lead you through a Book Walk of "The Elephant" and "The Silent Snake." Remind them to use the **titles** and **illustrations** to make predictions about what each poem will be about.

Words to Know

Remind students that they will find the Words to Know at the bottom of the pages in the selections.

Read

"The Elephant" and "The Silent Snake"

Have students read "The Elephant" and "The Silent Snake." Remind them to use the strategies on their Poetry Reading Strategies bookmark. For example, they may want to listen for rhyming words and other sound devices.

➲ **Learning Coach Check-In** This reading assignment should take about 10 minutes. After students finish reading, ask the following questions to assess their comprehension of the selections:

- ► In the poem "The Elephant," what are some of the words the speaker uses to describe the elephant? Possible answers: gentle; mild; good; large
- ► In "The Silent Snake," what are some of the animals the poet compares the snake to? Possible answers: birds; rabbits; squirrels; mayflies

If students have trouble answering these questions, ask them what reading strategies they used and suggest they reread the selections.

Objectives
- Read literature independently and proficiently.
- Apply information read to answer questions.
- Evaluate reading strategies.

GRAB

Go Read a Book

Have students read a book or magazine of their own choosing for at least 20 minutes. Remind students to use the strategies on their Reading Strategies bookmark before and during reading to help them understand the text.

Objectives
- Read literature independently and proficiently.
- Read a variety of texts for information and pleasure.

Explore "The Elephant" and "The Silent Snake"

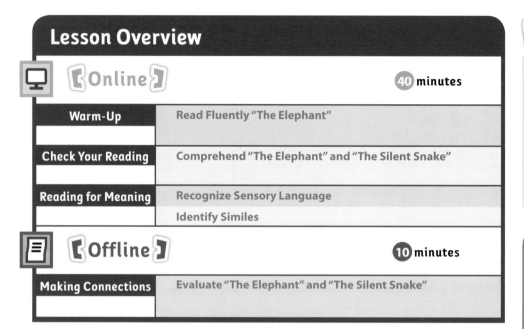

Lesson Overview

Online — 40 minutes

Warm-Up	Read Fluently "The Elephant"
Check Your Reading	Comprehend "The Elephant" and "The Silent Snake"
Reading for Meaning	Recognize Sensory Language
	Identify Similes

Offline — 10 minutes

Making Connections	Evaluate "The Elephant" and "The Silent Snake"

Materials

Supplied

- "The Elephant," "The Silent Snake," K[12] *Classics for Young Readers, Volume C,* pp. 74–77
- K[12] *Language Arts Activity Book*, pp. LC 53–54

Keywords

alliteration – the use of words with the same or close to the same beginning sounds

compare – to explain how two or more things are alike

figurative language – words that describe something by comparing it to something completely different
Example: Rain fell in buckets and the streets looked like rivers.

onomatopoeia (AH-nuh-MAH-tuh-PEE-uh) – the use of words that show sounds; for example, *moo, woof, quack, squash*

simile – a comparison between two things using the word *like* or *as*
Example: I didn't hear him come in because he was as quiet as a mouse.

Big Ideas

- Active, strong readers employ reading strategies such as making connections between text and self, between and among texts, and between text and the real world.
- Readers need to synthesize, draw conclusions about, and interpret what they have read.
- Poems are different from prose in structure and content. They are generally organized in lines and often contain rhymes.
- The use of imagery and sensory language creates detailed pictures in the reader's mind, so the reader can understand and appreciate the ideas and feelings the writer conveys.
- Good writing paints pictures with words to create a visual image of the text in the reader's mind's eye.

 **40 minutes**

Students will work **independently** to complete online Warm-Up, Check Your Reading, and Reading for Meaning activities.

Warm-Up

Read Fluently "The Elephant"
Students will read aloud and record the poem "The Elephant." The purpose of this activity is to improve students' oral reading and fluency. Remind students to listen to the model on each screen before they begin their recording.

 Objectives
- Read poetry and prose aloud.
- Create engaging audio recordings of stories or poems that demonstrate fluid reading at an understandable pace.
- Read aloud grade-level text with appropriate automaticity, prosody, accuracy, and rate.

Check Your Reading

Comprehend "The Elephant" and "The Silent Snake"
Students will answer questions about "The Elephant" and "The Silent Snake" to demonstrate their literal and inferential comprehension of the poems.

 Objectives
- Infer answers to questions.
- Identify rhyme scheme.
- Identify stanzas.
- Recognize rhyming couplets.
- Identify alliteration.

Reading for Meaning

Recognize Sensory Language
Students will learn how poets use sensory language, especially vivid verbs, to help readers form a mental picture of the action, events, objects, feelings, or people being described.

Identify Similes
Students will learn the difference between literal and figurative language and identify similes as one type of figurative language. They will identify similes in the poems they read.

 Objectives
- Define *sensory language.*
- Identify sensory language.
- Identify sensory language: vivid verbs.
- Define *literal language.*
- Define *figurative language.*
- Distinguish between literal and nonliteral or figurative language.
- Define *similes.*
- Identify similes.

 **10 minutes**

Work **together** with students to complete the offline Making Connections activity.

Making Connections ••

Evaluate "The Elephant" and "The Silent Snake"
Students will analyze and evaluate the poets' techniques in "The Elephant" and "The Silent Snake." Turn to pages LC 53 and 54 in *K¹² Language Arts Activity Book*.

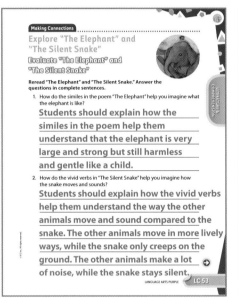

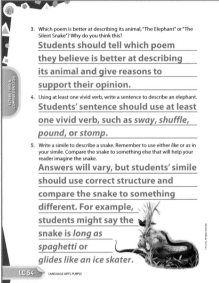

Objectives

- Answer evaluative questions based on reading.
- Compare and contrast literary elements in poetry.
- Describe methods authors use to influence readers' feelings.
- Make connections between text and self, text and world, and text to text.
- Write a simile.
- Write an opinion.
- Give reasons for opinion.

Reflections on Animal Friends Poetry

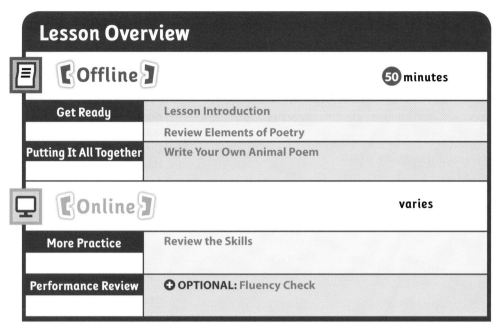

Lesson Overview

Offline — 50 minutes

Get Ready	Lesson Introduction
	Review Elements of Poetry
Putting It All Together	Write Your Own Animal Poem

Online — varies

More Practice	Review the Skills
Performance Review	⊕ OPTIONAL: Fluency Check

Big Ideas

▶ Poems are different from prose in structure and content. They are generally organized in lines and often contain rhymes.

▶ The use of imagery and sensory language creates detailed pictures in the reader's mind, so the reader can understand and appreciate the ideas and feelings the writer conveys.

▶ Good writing paints pictures with words to create a visual image of the text in the reader's mind's eye.

Materials

Supplied

- "The Hairy Dog," "I've Got a Dog," "A Kitten," "Cat," "The Elephant," "The Silent Snake," *K¹² Classics for Young Readers, Volume C*, pp. 66–77
- *K¹² Language Arts Activity Book*, pp. LC 55–57
- Putting It All Together Assessment Checklist (printout)
- Fluency Performance Checklist (optional printout)

Also Needed

- pencils, coloring, or crayons

Keywords

alliteration – the use of words with the same or close to the same beginning sounds

figurative language – words that describe something by comparing it to something completely different
Example: Rain fell in buckets and the streets looked like rivers.

rhyme scheme – the pattern of rhymes made by the last sounds in the lines of a poem, shown by a different letter of the alphabet to represent each rhyme

sensory language – language that appeals to the five senses

simile – a comparison between two things using the word *like* or *as*
Example: I didn't hear him come in because he was as quiet as a mouse.

stanza – a group of lines in a poem

 **Offline** 🔟 **minutes**

Work **together** with students to complete the offline Get Ready and Putting It All Together activities.

Get Ready ···

Lesson Introduction

Prepare students to write their own poem. Tell students they are going to write their own poem. Before they write, they will discuss with you

▶ The elements of poetry they have learned about in this unit
▶ Their favorite poem from the unit and why it is their favorite

 Objectives
• Recognize the characteristics of poetry.

Review Elements of Poetry

Review the elements of poetry that students have learned about in this unit.

▶ lines and stanzas
▶ rhymes and rhyme scheme
▶ alliteration and onomatopoeia
▶ sensory language and vivid verbs
▶ figurative language such as simile

Putting It All Together ·····································

✏️ **Write Your Own Animal Poem**

Students will write and illustrate their own poem using the elements of poetry learned in the unit. Gather the coloring pencils or crayons and turn to pages LC 55–57 in *K¹² Language Arts Activity Book*.

1. Have students choose their favorite poem from the unit and tell why they liked it.

2. Tell students to find their favorite poem in *K¹² Language Arts Classics for Young Readers, Volume C.*

3. Direct students' attention to the Activity Book pages and have them read the directions.

4. Tell them that the checklist will guide them to use the poetic elements and language that they learned about in the unit to write their own poem about an animal and then illustrate it.

5. Have students complete the Activity Book pages. Remind them to use their best cursive handwriting and leave spaces between words so that others can read what they wrote.

 Objectives
• Write poetry that includes sensory language.
• Write poetry that includes rhythm and rhyme scheme.
• Write poetry that includes figurative language.
• Deliver a dramatic interpretation.
• Create a visual.
• Follow directions to complete a task.

6. Have students create an illustration that reflects the language of their poem.

⊃ **Learning Coach Check-In** Check in with students after about 40 minutes to see if they have completed the assignment.

7. When students have completed their poem, have them read the poem aloud using a clear, expressive voice.

8. Use the materials and instructions in the online lesson to evaluate students' work.

9. Enter the answers (Yes or No) for each line of the assessment checklist online.

TIP If students have access to a multimedia program, they may use the software to create the visual for their poem. They could also record their poem and listen to their own recording.

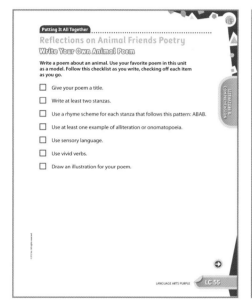

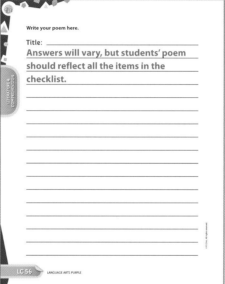

 **Varies**

Students will work **independently** to complete the online More Practice activity.

More Practice

Review the Skills

If students scored less than 80 percent or had difficulty meeting the objectives of the Putting It All Together activity, have them go online for more practice.

 Reward: If students score 80 percent or more on the Putting it All Together activity, add a sticker for this unit on the My Accomplishments chart. If students did not score 80 percent or more, work with them to revise their writing until they do score 80 percent and then add a sticker to the My Accomplishments chart.

Objectives
- Identify stanzas.
- Identify rhyme in a literary selection.
- Recognize rhyming couplets.
- Identify sensory language.
- Identify alliteration.
- Identify author's use of onomatopoeia.
- Identify similes.

Performance Review

○ OPTIONAL: Fluency Check

Listen to students' recordings and use the Fluency Performance Checklist to review fluency and track performance. Keep the completed checklist so you can review students' progress over time.

Objectives
- Read aloud grade-level text with appropriate automaticity, prosody, accuracy, and rate.

Critical Skills Practice 2

Unit Focus

In this unit, students will read nonfiction passages, poetry, and fiction passages, and practice answering multiple choice questions about those readings. Students will practice questions and formats similar to those found on standardized tests.

Unit Plan		**Offline**	**Online**
Lesson 1	Nonfiction Passages (A)		50 minutes
Lesson 2	Poetry (A)		50 minutes
Lesson 3	Fiction Passages (C)		50 minutes
Lesson 4	Nonfiction Passages (B)		50 minutes
Lesson 5	Unit Checkpoint	50 minutes	varies

Nonfiction Passages (A)

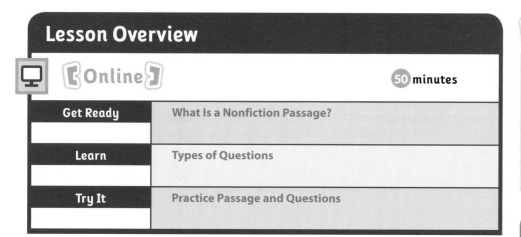

Lesson Overview

Online   50 minutes

Get Ready	What Is a Nonfiction Passage?
Learn	Types of Questions
Try It	Practice Passage and Questions

Big Ideas

▶ Comprehension entails asking and answering questions about the text.
▶ Comprehension strategies can be taught through explicit instruction.
▶ Reading strategies are conscious plans that readers apply and adapt to make sense of text.
▶ Comprehension requires an understanding of story structure.

Materials

Supplied

- Types of Questions (optional printout)
- Practice Passage and Questions (optional printout)

Keywords

autobiography – the story of a person's life written by that person

biography – the story of someone's life written by another person

caption – writing under a picture that describes the picture

glossary – a list of important terms and their meanings that is usually found in the back of a book

 **Online** 🕐 **minutes**

Students will work online to complete Get Ready, Learn, and Try It activities.

Get Ready

What Is a Nonfiction Passage?

Students will review what a nonfiction passage is. They will also review types of nonfiction, including **autobiography** and **biography**, and refresh their memory about important features of nonfiction texts, such as titles, **captions**, and **glossaries**. Before they begin, ask students what nonfiction is and then have them do the activity to see if they were correct.

Objectives
- Identify examples of fiction and nonfiction.
- Identify features of a nonfiction text.

Learn

Types of Questions

Students will learn about different types of multiple choice questions. The questions will be about genre, features of nonfiction texts, the difference between biography and autobiography, sequence, and understanding the most important ideas of a passage.

- ▸ A **biography** is a work of nonfiction about a real person's life that is written by someone else.
- ▸ An **autobiography** is a work of nonfiction that is a real person's written account of his or her own life.
- ▸ The **sequence** of events in a text is the order in which they happen.
- ▸ A **caption** is writing under a picture that describes the picture.

Students will learn about these question types in the context of a passage about Benjamin Franklin.

TIP If students are not comfortable reading the passage for this activity online, print Types of Questions and have students read the printout.

Objectives
- Identify examples of fiction and nonfiction.
- Identify features of a nonfiction text.
- Distinguish between biography and autobiography.
- Sequence events in a text.
- Demonstrate comprehension of text.

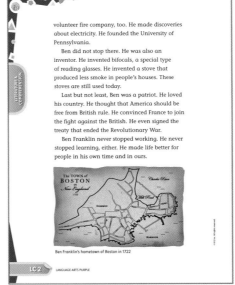

Try It

Practice Passage and Questions

Students will practice answering multiple choice questions using a nonfiction passage about Eleanor Roosevelt.

TIP If students are not comfortable reading the passage for this activity online, print Practice Passage and Questions and have students read the printout.

Try It

Nonfiction Passages (A)
Practice Passage and Questions

Read the passage. Then go online to answer the questions.

Eleanor Roosevelt: A Friend to Everyone

Eleanor Roosevelt was married to Franklin D. Roosevelt, president of the United States. Yet Eleanor Roosevelt was much more than First Lady. Her kindness and belief in equality made the world a better place.

Eleanor was born in New York in 1884. Life was not easy for her. Her mother and father died when she was a child. One of her brothers died, too. As a teenager, she did not fit in.

These hard times shaped Eleanor. She learned to care about people who were not treated well. She wanted fairness for all. She wanted to fix problems in America.

Eleanor became a social worker. She visited poor areas of New York City. She made sure people who lived there could visit doctors. She helped their children stay safe.

Eleanor also worked for equality. At one time, women in the United States could not vote. Eleanor thought this was unfair. She joined a group called the suffragists. They worked to get women the

LANGUAGE ARTS PURPLE   LC 1

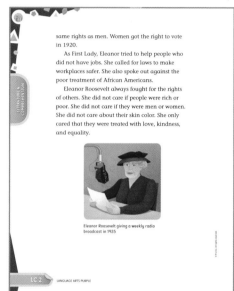

LC 2   LANGUAGE ARTS PURPLE

same rights as men. Women got the right to vote in 1920.

As First Lady, Eleanor tried to help people who did not have jobs. She called for laws to make workplaces safer. She also spoke out against the poor treatment of African Americans.

Eleanor Roosevelt always fought for the rights of others. She did not care if people were rich or poor. She did not care if they were men or women. She did not care about their skin color. She only cared that they were treated with love, kindness, and equality.

Eleanor Roosevelt giving a weekly radio broadcast in 1935

Objectives

- Identify examples of fiction and nonfiction.
- Identify features of a nonfiction text.
- Distinguish between biography and autobiography.
- Sequence events in a text.
- Demonstrate comprehension of text.

Poetry (A)

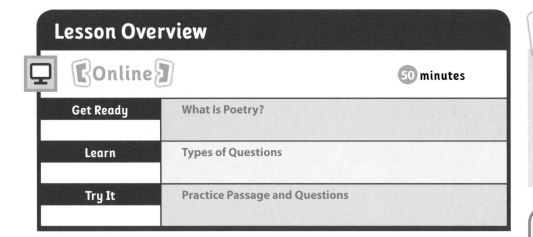

Lesson Overview

Online — 50 minutes

Get Ready	What Is Poetry?
Learn	Types of Questions
Try It	Practice Passage and Questions

Big Ideas

► Poems are different from prose in structure and content. They are generally organized in lines and often contain rhymes.
► The use of imagery and sensory language creates detailed pictures in the reader's mind, so the reader can understand and appreciate the ideas and feelings the writer conveys.
► Good writing paints pictures with words to create a visual image of the text in the reader's mind's eye.

Materials

Supplied

- Types of Questions (optional printout)
- Practice Passage and Questions (optional printout)

Keywords

alliteration – the use of words with the same or close to the same beginning sounds

onomatopoeia (AH-nuh-MAH-tuh-PEE-uh) – the use of words that show sounds; for example, *moo, woof, quack, squash*

rhyme – the use of words that end with the same sounds; for example, *cat* and *hat* rhyme

rhyme scheme – the pattern of rhymes made by the last sounds in the lines of a poem, shown by a different letter of the alphabet to represent each rhyme

stanza – a group of lines in a poem

 **50 minutes**

Students will work online to complete Get Ready, Learn, and Try It activities.

Get Ready ●

What Is Poetry?

Students will review important elements of poetry and poetic techniques. These elements include **stanza**, **rhyme**, and **rhyme scheme**, as well as the sound devices **alliteration** and **onomatopoeia**. Students will also review the importance of action words in poetry.

Objectives

- Identify defining characteristics of common genres (for example, poetry, drama, fiction, nonfiction).

Learn ●

Types of Questions

Students will learn about different types of multiple choice questions associated with poetry passages. The questions will be about identifying stanzas in a poem; recognizing rhyme scheme; and identifying examples of alliteration, onomatopoeia, and action words.

TIP If students are not comfortable reading the passage for this activity online, print Types of Questions and have students read the printout.

Objectives

- Identify defining characteristics of common genres (for example, poetry, drama, fiction, nonfiction).
- Identify rhyme scheme.
- Identify alliteration.
- Indentify sound patterns (for example, onomatopoeia, alliteration) in a third-grade passage.
- Identify action verbs in a poem.

Try It

Practice Passage and Questions

Students will practice answering multiple choice questions about poetry passages.

 TIP If students are not comfortable reading the passage for this activity online, print Practice Passage and Questions and have students read the printout.

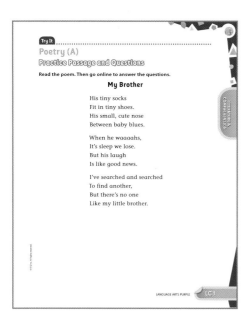

Fiction Passages (C)

Lesson Overview

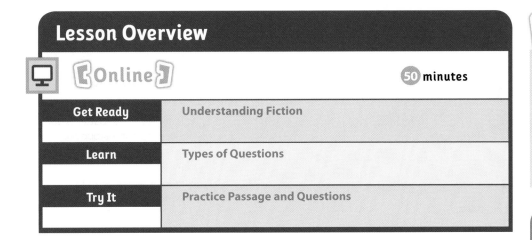

Online	**50 minutes**
Get Ready	Understanding Fiction
Learn	Types of Questions
Try It	Practice Passage and Questions

Big Ideas

▶ Comprehension entails asking and answering questions about the text.
▶ Comprehension strategies can be taught through explicit instruction.
▶ Reading strategies are conscious plans that readers apply and adapt to make sense of text.
▶ Comprehension requires an understanding of story structure.

Materials

Supplied

- Types of Questions (optional printout)
- Practice Passage and Questions (optional printout)

Keywords

conclusion – a decision made about something not stated, using information provided and what is already known

problem – an issue a character must solve in a story

solution – how a character solves a problem in a story

theme – the author's message or big idea

 **50 minutes**

Students will work online to complete Get Ready, Learn, and Try It activities.

Get Ready

Understanding Fiction

Students will review some concepts key to understanding fiction passages.

▶ Fiction passages are about characters who face **problems** and attempt to find **solutions**.

▶ Readers learn about characters based on what characters say, what they do, and what others say about them, as well as how to draw **conclusions** based on evidence in the text.

▶ **Theme** is the author's message or big idea.

 Objectives
• Identify defining characteristics of common genres (for example, poetry, drama, fiction, nonfiction).

Learn

Types of Questions

Students will learn about different types of multiple choice questions associated with fiction passages. The questions will be about identifying problems and solutions, describing characters and drawing conclusions, and identifying theme.

TIP If students are not comfortable reading the passage for this activity online, print Types of Questions and have students read the printout.

Objectives
• Identify the problem a character faces in a text.
• Identify the solution to a problem a character faces in a text.
• Describe characters by what they say, what they do, how others feel about them.
• Draw conclusions using evidence from text.
• Identify theme.

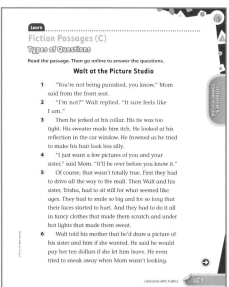

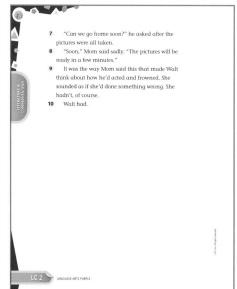

Try It

Practice Passage and Questions

Students will practice answering multiple choice questions about fiction passages.

 TIP If students are not comfortable reading the passage for this activity online, print Practice Passage and Questions and have students read the printout.

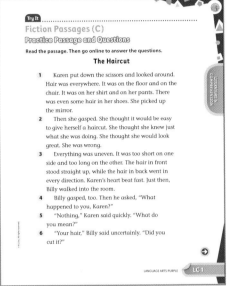

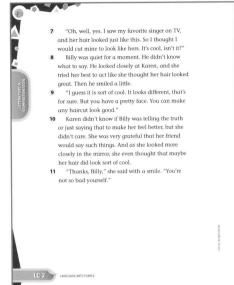

Objectives

- Identify the problem a character faces in a text.
- Identify the solution to a problem a character faces in a text.
- Describe characters by what they say, what they do, how others feel about them.
- Draw conclusions using evidence from text.
- Identify theme.

Nonfiction Passages (B)

Lesson Overview

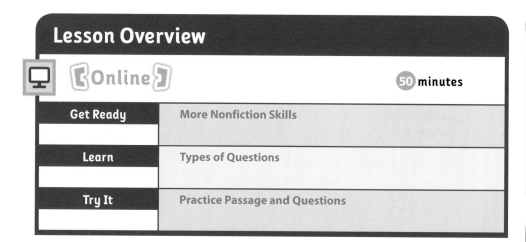

Online	50 minutes
Get Ready	More Nonfiction Skills
Learn	Types of Questions
Try It	Practice Passage and Questions

Big Ideas

▶ Comprehension entails asking and answering questions about the text.
▶ Comprehension strategies can be taught through explicit instruction.
▶ Reading strategies are conscious plans that readers apply and adapt to make sense of text.
▶ Comprehension requires an understanding of story structure.

Materials

Supplied

• Types of Questions (optional printout)
• Practice Passage and Questions (optional printout)

Keywords

fact – something that can be proven true

main idea – the most important point the author makes; it may be stated or unstated

nonfiction – writings about true things

opinion – something that a person thinks or believes, but which cannot be proven to be true

supporting details – the sentences that give information about the main idea or topic sentence

 **minutes**

Students will work online to complete Get Ready, Learn, and Try It activities.

Get Ready

More Nonfiction Skills

Students will review important skills related to reading nonfiction passages, including differentiating between **facts** and **opinions** and between the **main idea** of a paragraph and its **supporting details**. Students will also review how to determine the author's purpose for writing a work of nonfiction.

 Objectives
- Identify defining characteristics of common genres (for example, poetry, drama, fiction, nonfiction).

Learn

Types of Questions

Students will learn about different types of multiple choice questions associated with nonfiction passages. The questions will be about identifying facts and opinions, recognizing the main idea and supporting details, and understanding the author's purpose.

TIP If students are not comfortable reading the passage for this activity online, print Types of Questions and have students read the printout.

 Objectives
- Identify fact.
- Distinguish between a fact and an opinion.
- Identify author's purpose.
- Identify the main idea and supporting details in a text.
- Differentiate the main idea and supporting details in a third-grade passage.

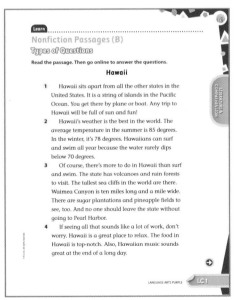

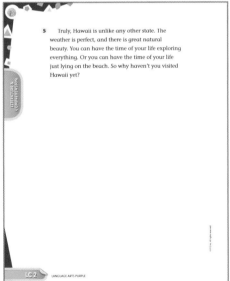

Try It

Practice Passage and Questions

Students will practice answering multiple choice questions about nonfiction passages.

TIP If students are not comfortable reading the passage for this activity online, print Practice Passage and Questions and have students read the printout.

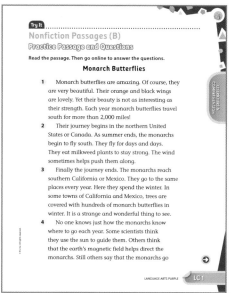

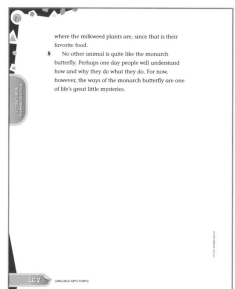

Unit Checkpoint

Lesson Overview

Offline   **50** minutes

Unit Checkpoint	Part 1: Nonfiction Passage
	Part 2: Poem
	Part 3: Fiction Passage

Online   varies

More Practice	Review the Skills

Materials

Supplied

- *K¹² Language Arts Assessments*, pp. LC 13–23

Objectives

- Identify examples of fiction and nonfiction.
- Identify features of a nonfiction text.
- Distinguish between biography and autobiography.
- Sequence events in a text.
- Demonstrate comprehension of text.
- Identify fact.
- Distinguish between a fact and an opinion.
- Identify author's purpose.
- Identify the main idea and supporting details in a text.
- Differentiate the main idea and supporting details in a third-grade passage.
- Identify defining characteristics of common genres (for example, poetry, drama, fiction, nonfiction).
- Identify rhyme scheme.
- Identify alliteration.
- Indentify sound patterns (for example, onomatopoeia, alliteration) in a third-grade passage.
- Identify action verbs in a poem.
- Identify the problem a character faces in a text.
- Identify the solution to a problem a character faces in a text.
- Describe characters by what they say, what they do, how others feel about them.
- Draw conclusions using evidence from text.
- Identify theme.

 **50 minutes**

Unit Checkpoint

Explain that students are going to show what they have learned about reading and answering questions about nonfiction passages, poems, and fiction passages.

1. Give students the Unit Checkpoint pages.

2. Read the directions together.

3. Use the Answer Key to score the Checkpoint and then enter the results online.

4. Review each exercise with students. Work with students to correct any exercise that they missed.

Part 1: Nonfiction Passage
Have students read "Jackie Robinson" and answer the questions.

Part 2: Poem
Have students read "April Showers" and answer the questions.

Part 3: Fiction Passage
Have students read "The Discovery" and answer the questions.

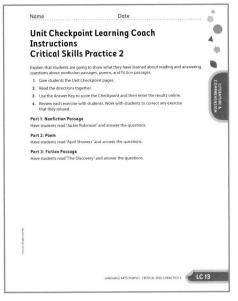

Name _____ Date _____

Unit Checkpoint Learning Coach Instructions
Critical Skills Practice 2

Explain that students are going to show what they have learned about reading and answering questions about nonfiction passages, poems, and fiction passages.

1. Give students the Unit Checkpoint pages.
2. Read the directions together.
3. Use the Answer Key to score the Checkpoint and then enter the results online.
4. Review each exercise with students. Work with students to correct any exercise that they missed.

Part 1: Nonfiction Passage
Have students read "Jackie Robinson" and answer the questions.

Part 2: Poem
Have students read "April Showers" and answer the questions.

Part 3: Fiction Passage
Have students read "The Discovery" and answer the questions.

LANGUAGE ARTS PURPLE | CRITICAL SKILLS PRACTICE 2   LC 13

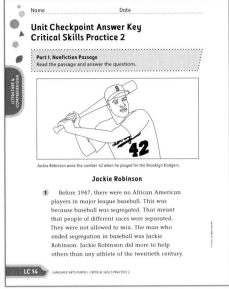

Name _____ Date _____

Unit Checkpoint Answer Key
Critical Skills Practice 2

Part 1. Nonfiction Passage
Read the passage and answer the questions.

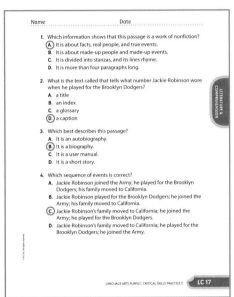

Jackie Robinson wore the number 42 when he played for the Brooklyn Dodgers.

Jackie Robinson

1   Before 1947, there were no African American players in major league baseball. This was because baseball was segregated. That meant that people of different races were separated. They were not allowed to mix. The man who ended segregation in baseball was Jackie Robinson. Jackie Robinson did more to help others than any athlete of the twentieth century.

LANGUAGE ARTS PURPLE | CRITICAL SKILLS PRACTICE 2   LC 14

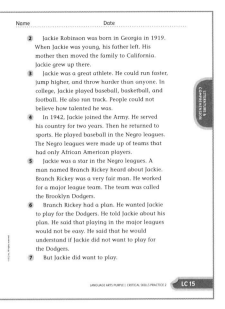

2   Jackie Robinson was born in Georgia in 1919. When Jackie was young, his father left. His mother then moved the family to California. Jackie grew up there.

3   Jackie was a great athlete. He could run faster, jump higher, and throw harder than anyone. In college, Jackie played baseball, basketball, and football. He also ran track. People could not believe how talented he was.

4   In 1942, Jackie joined the Army. He served his country for two years. Then he returned to sports. He played baseball in the Negro leagues. The Negro leagues were made up of teams that had only African American players.

5   Jackie was a star in the Negro leagues. A man named Branch Rickey heard about Jackie. Branch Rickey was a very fair man. He worked for a major league team. The team was called the Brooklyn Dodgers.

6   Branch Rickey had a plan. He wanted Jackie to play for the Dodgers. He told Jackie about his plan. He said that playing in the major leagues would not be easy. He said that he would understand if Jackie did not want to play for the Dodgers.

7   But Jackie did want to play.

LANGUAGE ARTS PURPLE | CRITICAL SKILLS PRACTICE 2   LC 15

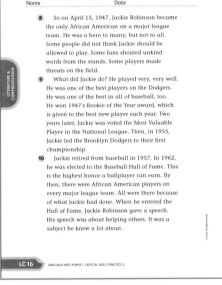

8   So on April 15, 1947, Jackie Robinson became the only African American on a major league team. He was a hero to many, but not to all. Some people did not think Jackie should be allowed to play. Some fans shouted unkind words from the stands. Some players made threats on the field.

9   What did Jackie do? He played very, very well. He was one of the best players on the Dodgers. He was one of the best in all of baseball, too. He won 1947's Rookie of the Year award, which is given to the best new player each year. Two years later, Jackie was voted the Most Valuable Player in the National League. Then, in 1955, Jackie led the Brooklyn Dodgers to their first championship.

10   Jackie retired from baseball in 1957. In 1962, he was elected to the Baseball Hall of Fame. This is the highest honor a ballplayer can earn. By then, there were African American players on every major league team. All were there because of what Jackie had done. When he entered the Hall of Fame, Jackie Robinson gave a speech. His speech was about helping others. It was a subject he knew a lot about.

LANGUAGE ARTS PURPLE | CRITICAL SKILLS PRACTICE 2   LC 16

Name _____ Date _____

1. Which information shows that this passage is a work of nonfiction?
   A. It is about facts, real people, and true events.
   B. It is about made-up people and made-up events.
   C. It is divided into stanzas, and its lines rhyme.
   D. It is more than four paragraphs long.

2. What is the text called that tells what number Jackie Robinson wore when he played for the Brooklyn Dodgers?
   A. a title
   B. an index
   C. a glossary
   D. a caption

3. Which best describes this passage?
   A. It is an autobiography.
   B. It is a biography.
   C. It is a user manual.
   D. It is a short story.

4. Which sequence of events is correct?
   A. Jackie Robinson joined the Army; he played for the Brooklyn Dodgers; his family moved to California.
   B. Jackie Robinson played for the Brooklyn Dodgers; he joined the Army; his family moved to California.
   C. Jackie Robinson's family moved to California; he joined the Army; he played for the Brooklyn Dodgers.
   D. Jackie Robinson's family moved to California; he played for the Brooklyn Dodgers; he joined the Army.

LANGUAGE ARTS PURPLE | CRITICAL SKILLS PRACTICE 2   LC 17

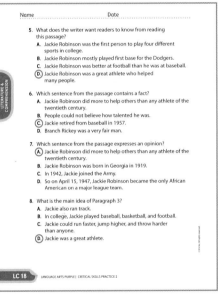

Name _____ Date _____

5. What does the writer want readers to know from reading this passage?
   A. Jackie Robinson was the first person to play four different sports in college.
   B. Jackie Robinson mostly played first base for the Dodgers.
   C. Jackie Robinson was better at football than he was at baseball.
   D. Jackie Robinson was a great athlete who helped many people.

6. Which sentence from the passage contains a fact?
   A. Jackie Robinson did more to help others than any athlete of the twentieth century.
   B. People could not believe how talented he was.
   C. Jackie retired from baseball in 1957.
   D. Branch Rickey was a very fair man.

7. Which sentence from the passage expresses an opinion?
   A. Jackie Robinson did more to help others than any athlete of the twentieth century.
   B. Jackie Robinson was born in Georgia in 1919.
   C. In 1942, Jackie joined the Army.
   D. So on April 15, 1947, Jackie Robinson became the only African American on a major league team.

8. What is the main idea of Paragraph 3?
   A. Jackie also ran track.
   B. In college, Jackie played baseball, basketball, and football.
   C. Jackie could run faster, jump higher, and throw harder than anyone.
   D. Jackie was a great athlete.

LANGUAGE ARTS PURPLE | CRITICAL SKILLS PRACTICE 2   LC 18

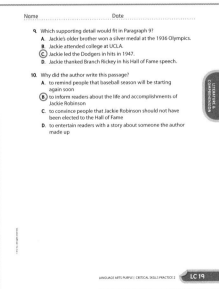

Name _____ Date _____

9. Which supporting detail would fit in Paragraph 9?
   A. Jackie's older brother won a silver medal at the 1936 Olympics.
   B. Jackie attended college at UCLA.
   C. Jackie led the Dodgers in hits in 1947.
   D. Jackie thanked Branch Rickey in his Hall of Fame speech.

10. Why did the author write this passage?
    A. to remind people that baseball season will be starting again soon
    B. to inform readers about the life and accomplishments of Jackie Robinson
    C. to convince people that Jackie Robinson should not have been elected to the Hall of Fame
    D. to entertain readers with a story about someone the author made up

LANGUAGE ARTS PURPLE | CRITICAL SKILLS PRACTICE 2   LC 19

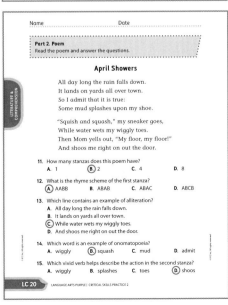

Name _____ Date _____

Part 2. Poem
Read the poem and answer the questions.

April Showers

All day long the rain falls down.
It lands on yards all over town.
So I admit that it is true:
Some mud splashes upon my shoe.

"Squish and squash," my sneaker goes,
While water wets my wiggly toes.
Then Mom yells out, "My floor, my floor!"
And shoos me right on out the door.

11. How many stanzas does this poem have?
    A. 1   B. 2   C. 4   D. 8

12. What is the rhyme scheme of the first stanza?
    A. AABB   B. ABAB   C. ABAC   D. ABCB

13. Which line contains an example of alliteration?
    A. All day long the rain falls down.
    B. It lands on yards all over town.
    C. While water wets my wiggly toes.
    D. And shoos me right on out the door.

14. Which word is an example of onomatopoeia?
    A. wiggly   B. squash   C. mud   D. admit

15. Which vivid verb helps describe the action in the second stanza?
    A. wiggly   B. splashes   C. toes   D. shoos

LANGUAGE ARTS PURPLE | CRITICAL SKILLS PRACTICE 2   LC 20

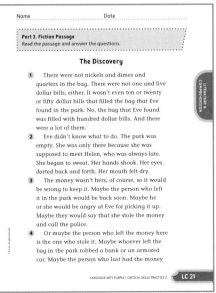

Name _____ Date _____

Part 3. Fiction Passage
Read the passage and answer the questions.

The Discovery

1   There were not nickels and dimes and quarters in the bag. There were not one and five dollar bills, either. It wasn't even ten or twenty or fifty dollar bills that filled the bag that Eve found in the park. No, the bag that Eve found was filled with hundred dollar bills. And there were a lot of them.

2   Eve didn't know what to do. The park was empty. She was only there because she was supposed to meet Helen, who was always late. She began to sweat. Her hands shook. Her eyes darted back and forth. Her mouth felt dry.

3   The money wasn't hers, of course, so it would be wrong to keep it. Maybe the person who left it in the park would be back soon. Maybe he or she would be angry at Eve for picking it up. Maybe they would say that she stole the money and call the police.

4   Or maybe the person who left the money here is the one who stole it. Maybe whoever left the bag in the park robbed a bank or an armored car. Maybe the person who last had the money

LANGUAGE ARTS PURPLE | CRITICAL SKILLS PRACTICE 2   LC 21

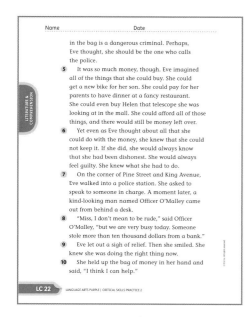

Name _____ Date _____

in the bag is a dangerous criminal. Perhaps, Eve thought, she should be the one who calls the police.

5   It was so much money, though. Eve imagined all of the things that she could buy. She could get a new bike for her son. She could pay for her parents to have dinner at a fancy restaurant. She could even buy Helen that telescope she was looking at in the mall. She could afford all of those things, and there would still be money left over.

6   Yet even as Eve thought about all that she could do with the money, she knew that she could not keep it. If she did, she would always know that she had been dishonest. She would always feel guilty. She knew what she had to do.

7   On the corner of Pine Street and King Avenue, Eve walked into a police station. She asked to speak to someone in charge. A moment later, a kind-looking man named Officer O'Malley came out from behind a desk.

8   "Miss, I don't mean to be rude," said Officer O'Malley, "but we are very busy today. Someone stole more than ten thousand dollars from a bank."

9   Eve let out a sigh of relief. Then she smiled. She knew she was doing the right thing now.

10   She held up the bag of money in her hand and said, "I think I can help."

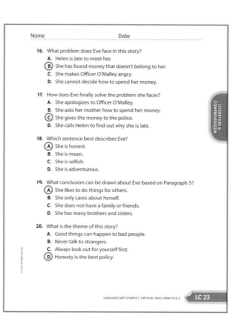

Name _____ Date _____

16. What problem does Eve face in this story?
   A. Helen is late to meet her.
   B. She has found money that doesn't belong to her.
   C. She makes Officer O'Malley angry.
   D. She cannot decide how to spend her money.

17. How does Eve finally solve the problem she faces?
   A. She apologizes to Officer O'Malley.
   B. She asks her mother how to spend her money.
   C. She gives the money to the police.
   D. She calls Helen to find out why she is late.

18. Which sentence best describes Eve?
   A. She is honest.
   B. She is mean.
   C. She is selfish.
   D. She is adventurous.

19. What conclusion can be drawn about Eve based on Paragraph 5?
   A. She likes to do things for others.
   B. She only cares about herself.
   C. She does not have a family or friends.
   D. She has many brothers and sisters.

20. What is the theme of this story?
   A. Good things can happen to bad people.
   B. Never talk to strangers.
   C. Always look out for yourself first.
   D. Honesty is the best policy.

varies

Students will work **independently** to complete the online More Practice activity.

More Practice

Review the Skills

If students scored less than 80 percent or had difficulty meeting the objectives of the Unit Checkpoint, have them go online for more practice.

> **Objectives**
> • Evaluate Unit Checkpoint results and choose activities for more practice.

Reward: If students score 80 percent or more on the Unit Checkpoint, add a sticker for this unit on the My Accomplishments chart. If students did not score 80 percent or more, work with them to revise their work until they do score 80 percent, and then add a sticker to the My Accomplishments chart.

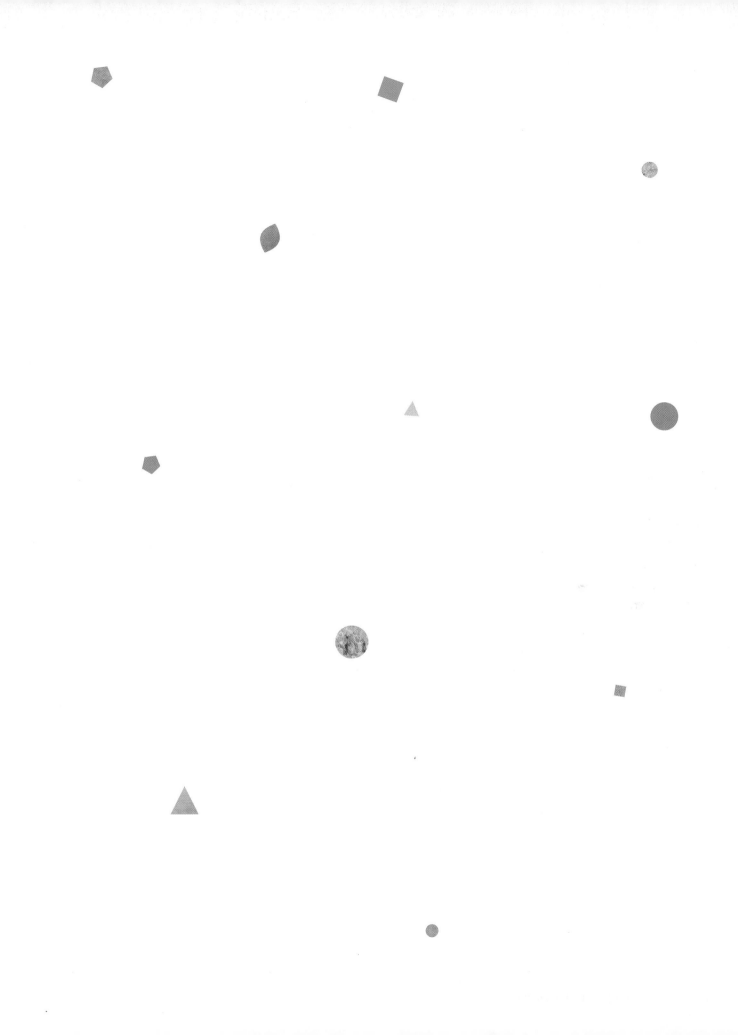

George Washington: Soldier, Hero, President

Unit Focus

Students will read *George Washington: Soldier, Hero, President* by Justine and Ron Fontes. In the accompanying lessons, they will learn about

▶ What a biography is
▶ The features of some biographies, such as captions and headings
▶ Main ideas and details
▶ Causes and effects
▶ Sequences of important events

Unit Plan		[Online]	[Offline]
Lesson 1	Introduce *George Washington: Soldier, Hero, President* (A)		50 minutes
Lesson 2	Explore *George Washington: Soldier, Hero, President* (A)	40 minutes	10 minutes
Lesson 3	Introduce *George Washington: Soldier, Hero, President* (B)		50 minutes
Lesson 4	Explore *George Washington: Soldier, Hero, President* (B)	40 minutes	10 minutes
Lesson 5	Introduce *George Washington: Soldier, Hero, President* (C)		50 minutes
Lesson 6	Explore *George Washington: Soldier, Hero, President* (C)	40 minutes	10 minutes
Lesson 7	Reflections on *George Washington: Soldier, Hero, President*	varies	50 minutes
Lesson 8	Your Choice		50 minutes

Introduce *George Washington: Soldier, Hero, President* (A)

Lesson Overview

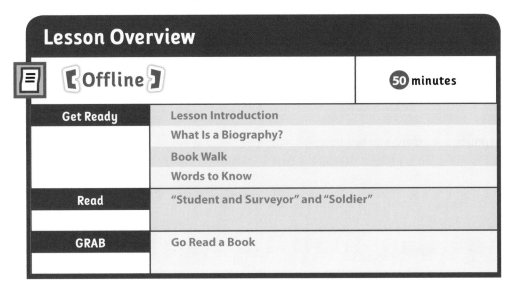

Offline		**50 minutes**
Get Ready	Lesson Introduction	
	What Is a Biography?	
	Book Walk	
	Words to Know	
Read	"Student and Surveyor" and "Soldier"	
GRAB	Go Read a Book	

Advance Preparation

Read the first two chapters of *George Washington: Soldier, Hero, President* to locate Words to Know in the text before beginning the Get Ready.

Big Ideas

- ▶ Nonfiction texts differ from fiction texts in that they describe real or true things in life, rather than things made up by the author.
- ▶ Biographies are a type of nonfiction meant to inform the reader about a person's life.
- ▶ To understand important information in a text, readers must be familiar with text features and their purposes.

Materials

Supplied

- *George Washington: Soldier, Hero, President* by Justine and Ron Fontes
- Reading Strategies bookmark

Chapter Synopses

"Student and Surveyor" tells of George Washington's early years growing up in colonial Virginia. At a young age, Washington teaches himself how to survey land and then takes over the family plantation, Mount Vernon. In "Soldier," Washington becomes a soldier in the British army and fights in the French and Indian War.

Keywords

autobiography – the story of a person's life written by that person

biography – the story of someone's life written by another person

caption – writing printed with a picture that describes or explains the picture

fact – something that can be proven true

fiction – make-believe stories

nonfiction – writings about true things

table of contents – a list at the start of a book that gives the titles of the book's stories, poems, articles, chapters, or nonfiction pieces and the pages where they can be found

 **50 minutes**

Work **together** with students to complete offline Get Ready, Read, and GRAB activities.

Get Ready

Lesson Introduction

Prepare students to read the first two chapters of *George Washington: Soldier, Hero, President*.

1. Tell students that they are going to read a short chapter book called *George Washington: Soldier, Hero, President*. Today they will read the first two chapters of the book.

2. Explain that before students read the book, they will get ready by discussing with you

   ▸ What a biography is
   ▸ What they will find in a biography
   ▸ Their predictions about the text
   ▸ Important words to know in the text

3. Tell students that after they read, you will check to make sure they understood what they read.

4. Tell students that after they read, they will answer questions about what they read.

What Is a Biography?

Discuss the genre of biography and the features of biographies to prepare students for reading the first two chapters in *George Washington: Soldier, Hero, President*.

1. Ask students what they know about George Washington. Students should know that George Washington was a real person. They should also know he was the first president of the United States.

2. Have students tell whether they think a biography is a type of **fiction** or **nonfiction** and explain why. Students should know that a biography is nonfiction because nonfiction is writing about real or true things, and a biography is the story of a real person's life.

3. Explain that books written about the lives of real people, such as George Washington, fall into two categories: **biography** and **autobiography**. Have students tell the difference between the two. A biography is the story of someone's life written by another person, while an autobiography is the story of a person's life written by that person.

Objectives

- Define *biography*.
- Define *autobiography*.
- Identify biography.
- Distinguish between biography and autobiography.
- Identify author's purpose.
- Identify features of a nonfiction text.
- Use text organizational features to locate and comprehend information (table of contents).
- Use text features to make a prediction (illustration).
- Use chapter titles to make predictions and comprehend text.
- Increase concept and content vocabulary.
- Understand grade-appropriate words and phrases from various subject-matter areas that appear in a text.

4. Show students the book *George Washington: Soldier, Hero, President* and have them read the title and author. Ask whether they think the book is a biography or an autobiography and how they know. The book is a biography because it was written by Justine and Ron Fontes, not by George Washington.

5. Remind students that authors have a purpose for writing: to entertain, to inform, to express an opinion, or to persuade. Sometimes authors may have more than one purpose. Ask students what they think is the purpose of a biography. Students may say that the purpose of a biography is to inform readers about the person who is the subject of the biography. They may also say that the purpose could also be to entertain readers, if the person had an interesting life. It might even be to persuade readers about the author's opinion of the person who is the subject of the biography.

6. Have students tell what they know about nonfiction writing. Possible answer: Nonfiction writing contains facts and information.

7. Remind students that nonfiction writing often has pictures or other visual features to give readers information. Have students use the **table of contents** to find the first chapter in the book, "Student and Surveyor." Point out the words next to the picture on page 7 and review that these words make a **caption**, one feature that nonfiction texts may include. Ask students to name other features and point to examples in the first two chapters of the book. Possible answers: chapter titles in the table of contents and on pages 4 and 14; map on page 5; sidebars on page 5, 6, and 15; headings in the sidebars; other captions on pages 5, 9, 12, and 13

8. Tell students to look for the features of nonfiction and recall their purposes as they read.

Book Walk

Have students lead you through a Book Walk of the first two chapters of *George Washington: Soldier, Hero, President*, "Student and Surveyor" and "Soldier." Make sure students point to the **glossary** and the **index**. Remind students to use the **chapter titles** and **illustrations** to make predictions about the text.

Words to Know

Before reading the first two chapters of *George Washington: Soldier, Hero, President*, go over Words to Know with students.

- ▶ **claimed** – took as one's own
- ▶ **hostile** – having to do with an enemy; unfriendly
- ▶ **smallpox** – a disease that spread easily among people and caused fevers and blisters

Read

"Student and Surveyor" and "Soldier"

Have students read "Student and Surveyor" and "Soldier" in *George Washington: Soldier, Hero, President*. Remind students to use the strategies on their Reading Strategies bookmark. For example, they may want to stop at the end of each page and make a mental summary of what they just read.

➲ **Learning Coach Check-In** This reading assignment should take about 15 minutes. After students finish reading, ask the following questions to assess their comprehension of the selection:

▸ Where and when was George Washington born? in Virginia when it was a colony of England, in the 1700s

▸ What did Washington do in these two chapters that made him special? Possible answers: He became a surveyor when he was only a teenager; he delivered a message for the British army to the French army; he fought in the French and Indian War and helped lead some troops to safety.

If students have trouble answering these questions, ask them what reading strategies they used and suggest they reread the selection.

Objectives

- Read literature independently and proficiently.
- Apply information read to answer questions.
- Evaluate reading strategies.

GRAB

Go Read a Book

Have students read a book or magazine of their own choosing for at least 20 minutes. Remind students to use the strategies on their Reading Strategies bookmark before and during reading to help them understand the text.

TIP Remember: The more students read, the better readers they become.

Objectives

- Read literature independently and proficiently.
- Read a variety of texts for information and pleasure.

Explore *George Washington: Soldier, Hero, President* (A)

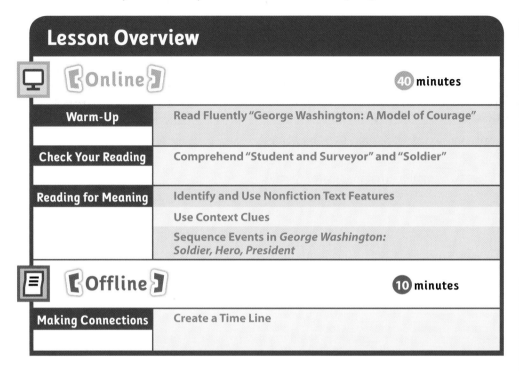

Lesson Overview

Online — 40 minutes

Warm-Up	Read Fluently "George Washington: A Model of Courage"
Check Your Reading	Comprehend "Student and Surveyor" and "Soldier"
Reading for Meaning	Identify and Use Nonfiction Text Features
	Use Context Clues
	Sequence Events in *George Washington: Soldier, Hero, President*

Offline — 10 minutes

Making Connections	Create a Time Line

Big Ideas

▸ Readers need to be able to sequence, summarize, and articulate the main idea.

▸ Active, strong readers employ reading strategies such as drawing inferences during and after reading.

▸ Readers must understand the relationship between main idea and supporting details.

▸ Readers should be able to retell the story (or information) in their own words, not repeat what was written.

▸ Knowing how to use context clues to extract meaning from unfamiliar words is critical to determining what is important in text.

Materials

Supplied

● *George Washington: Soldier, Hero, President* by Justine and Ron Fontes
● *K¹² Language Arts Activity Book*, pp. LC 59–61

Also Needed

● tape, clear

Keywords

caption – writing printed with a picture that describes or explains the picture

context clue – a word or phrase in a text that helps you figure out the meaning of an unknown word

glossary – a list of important terms and their meanings that is usually found in the back of a book

heading – a title within the body of a text that tells the reader something about a section of the text

index – an alphabetical list at the end of a book or magazine that tells the pages where a subject or name can be found

main idea – the most important point the author makes; it may be stated or unstated

sequence – the order in which things happen

sidebar – a short text within a larger text that tells something related but not necessary to the main story

time line – a line showing dates and events in the order that they happened

 **minutes**

Students will work **independently** to complete online Warm-Up, Check Your Reading, and Reading for Meaning activities.

Warm-Up

Read Fluently "George Washington: A Model of Courage"
Students will read aloud and record the passage "George Washington: A Model of Courage." The purpose of this activity is to improve students' oral reading and fluency. Remind students to listen to the model on each screen before they begin their recording.

Objectives
- Read poetry and prose aloud.
- Read aloud grade-level text with appropriate automaticity, prosody, accuracy, and rate.

Check Your Reading

Comprehend "Student and Surveyor" and "Soldier"
Students will answer questions about the first two chapters of *George Washington: Soldier, Hero, President*, "Student and Surveyor" and "Soldier," to demonstrate their literal and inferential comprehension of the story.

Objectives
- Identify concrete answers to questions.
- Infer answers to questions.
- Apply information read to answer questions.

Reading for Meaning

Identify and Use Nonfiction Text Features
Students will use nonfiction text features, such as **sidebars**, **captions**, a **glossary**, and an **index**, to locate and understand information in *George Washington: Soldier, Hero, President*. Knowing how to locate and use the information in these nonfiction features is an important aspect of reading comprehension.

Use Context Clues
Students will use **context clues** to define unfamiliar words in the first two chapters of *George Washington: Soldier, Hero, President*. Being able to decipher the meaning of new words from the context clues provided in the text is an important aspect of reading comprehension.

Sequence Events in *George Washington: Soldier, Hero, President*
Students will learn that a time line is a way to organize important events in chronological or time order. They will begin to identify important events in *George Washington: Soldier, Hero, President* that can be used to create a time line of Washington's life.

Objectives

- Identify features of a nonfiction text.
- Use resources or other tools to determine the meaning of a word (use glossary).
- Use text features to comprehend text meaning (bold, italic, headers, etc.).
- Use text organizational features to locate and comprehend information (table of contents, glossary, chapter, index, title, author, illustrator, caption).
- Use context clues to determine word meanings.
- Define *sequence*.
- Define *main idea* and *supporting details*.
- Distinguish between main idea and details.
- Use temporal words and phrases to signal event order.
- Determine the meaning of general academic and domain-specific words and phrases in a text.

[Offline] ⏱ 10 minutes

Work **together** with students to complete the offline Making Connections activity.

Making Connections •••

Create a Time Line

Students will sequence important events from the first two chapters of *George Washington: Soldier, Hero, President*. They will work on this time line throughout the unit and use it to create a summary. Gather the tape and turn to pages LC 59–61 in *K¹² Language Arts Activity Book*.

1. Tell students they are going to record important events from Washington's life as they read the book. Have them tear out the Activity Book pages and tape together the time line.

2. Have them begin their time line by selecting events from the first two chapters. They should add at least one event from the first two chapters. Possible answers: 1752: Washington becomes master of Mount Vernon. 1753: Washington goes on a mission to Fort LeBoeuf that starts the French and Indian War. 1755: Major General Braddock comes to America and Washington tries to warn him about how to fight.

3. Remind students to look for the important events, or **main ideas** and their dates, from the chapters they read.

4. Tell students they may write events above or below the line, depending on what fits best on the time line.

TIP Have students keep the Activity Book pages in a safe place so they can add to the time line as they read the book.

Objectives
- Identify main idea.
- Sequence events in a text.
- Use a graphic organizer to organize information.

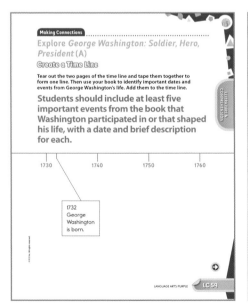

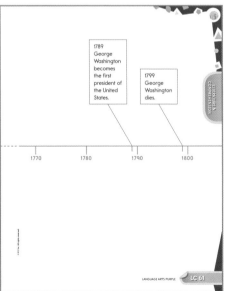

Introduce *George Washington: Soldier, Hero, President* (B)

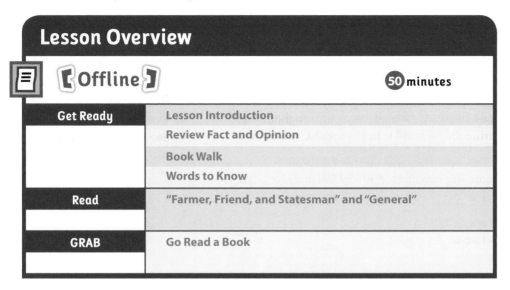

Lesson Overview

Offline
50 minutes

Get Ready	Lesson Introduction
	Review Fact and Opinion
	Book Walk
	Words to Know
Read	"Farmer, Friend, and Statesman" and "General"
GRAB	Go Read a Book

Advance Preparation

Read the next two chapters of *George Washington: Soldier, Hero, President* to locate Words to Know in the text before beginning the Get Ready.

Big Ideas

- ▶ Nonfiction texts differ from fiction texts in that they describe real or true things in life, rather than things made up by the author.
- ▶ Biographies are a type of nonfiction meant to inform the reader about a person's life.
- ▶ Active, strong readers employ reading strategies such as monitoring their comprehension (for example, self-check) as they read.

Materials

Supplied
- *George Washington: Soldier, Hero, President* by Justine and Ron Fontes
- Reading Strategies bookmark

Chapter Synopses

"Farmer, Friend, and Statesman" describes the beginnings of the war between the colonies and England. The colonists protest the high British taxes, and Washington becomes commander-in-chief of the Continental Army. In "General," the Continental Army is poorly supplied and trained, so it suffers many defeats in battling the British. America declares independence from England, and Washington and his troops achieve some surprise victories against the British and their hired troops.

Keywords

biography – the story of someone's life written by another person

fact – something that can be proven true

nonfiction – writings about true things

opinion – something that a person thinks or believes, but which cannot be proven to be true

table of contents – a list at the start of a book that gives the titles of the book's stories, poems, articles, chapters, or nonfiction pieces and the pages where they can be found

 **minutes**

Work **together** with students to complete offline Get Ready, Read, and GRAB activities.

Get Ready

Lesson Introduction
Prepare students to read the next two chapters of *George Washington: Soldier, Hero, President*.

1. Explain to students that before they read the next two chapters of *George Washington: Soldier, Hero, President*, they will discuss with you

   ▶ What they read in the first two chapters
   ▶ The difference between fact and opinion
   ▶ Their predictions about the text
   ▶ Important words to know in the text

2. Tell students that while they read, you will check in to make sure they understand what they are reading.

3. Tell students that after they read, they will answer questions about what they read.

> **Objectives**
> • Define *fact*.
> • Define *opinion*.
> • Distinguish between fact and opinion.
> • Identify facts.
> • Use text organizational features to locate and comprehend information (table of contents).
> • Use before-reading strategies.
> • Increase concept and content vocabulary.

Review Fact and Opinion
Review the difference between fact and opinion.

1. Have students tell what a **fact** is and give an example.

2. Have students tell how a fact is different from an **opinion** and give an example of an opinion.

3. Remind students that **nonfiction** books may contain both facts and opinions, but they should focus on the facts. Authors offer opinions to help persuade readers, but facts are meant for information.

4. Have students look through the first chapter in the book and identify a fact. Students should identify one fact from the "Student and Surveyor" chapter, such as George Washington was born in Virginia in 1732, or George's father died suddenly when George was 11.

5. Have students use the **table of contents** to find the chapter "Soldier." Then have them skim the last few paragraphs at the end of the chapter before the point where they stopped reading and give a summary of the events from the first two chapters.

Book Walk

Have students lead you through a Book Walk of the next two chapters of *George Washington: Soldier, Hero, President*, "Farmer, Friend, and Statesman" and "General." Remind students to use the **illustrations** and **chapter titles** to make their predictions about what will happen in the story.

Words to Know

Before reading the next two chapters of *George Washington: Soldier, Hero, President*, go over Words to Know with students.

- ▶ **backwoodsmen** – people who live deep in the woods
- ▶ **cobblers** – people who make shoes
- ▶ **dockworkers** – people who load and unload boats in a port
- ▶ **frontier** – the edge or border of a settlement
- ▶ **industries** – businesses that make things

Read

"Farmer, Friend, and Statesman" and "General"

Have students read "Farmer, Friend, and Statesman" and "General" of *George Washington: Soldier, Hero, President*. Remind students to use the strategies on their Reading Strategies bookmark. For example, they may want to stop at the end of each page of the story and ask themselves questions about what they just read.

 Learning Coach Check-In This reading assignment should take about 15 minutes. After students finish reading, ask the following questions to assess their comprehension of the selection:

- ▶ What did the American colonists do when England made them pay high taxes? They refused to buy goods from England and threw English tea into the sea.
- ▶ What was the American army like? Describe it. The army wasn't well trained. It didn't have many supplies. The army wanted to defeat the British. The soldiers were smart and surprised the Hessians and the English army.

If students have trouble answering these questions, ask them what reading strategies they used and suggest they reread the selection.

Objectives
- Read literature independently and proficiently.
- Apply information read to answer questions.
- Evaluate reading strategies.

GRAB

Go Read a Book

Have students read a book or magazine of their own choosing for at least 20 minutes. Remind students to use the strategies on their Reading Strategies bookmark before and during reading to help them understand the text.

Objectives
- Read literature independently and proficiently.
- Read a variety of texts for information and pleasure.

Explore *George Washington: Soldier, Hero, President* (B)

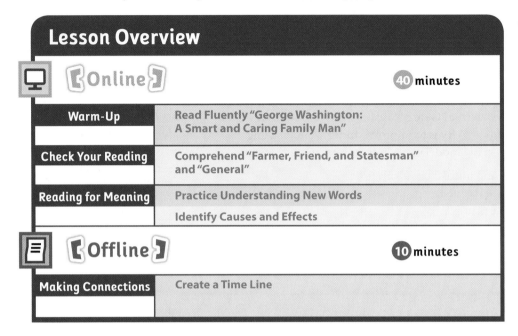

Lesson Overview

Online — 40 minutes

Warm-Up	Read Fluently "George Washington: A Smart and Caring Family Man"
Check Your Reading	Comprehend "Farmer, Friend, and Statesman" and "General"
Reading for Meaning	Practice Understanding New Words
	Identify Causes and Effects

Offline — 10 minutes

Making Connections	Create a Time Line

Materials

Supplied

- *George Washington: Soldier, Hero, President* by Justine and Ron Fontes
- *K¹² Language Arts Activity Book*, pp. LC 59–61

Keywords

cause – the reason something happens

context clue – a word or phrase in a text that helps you figure out the meaning of an unknown word

effect – the result of a cause

glossary – a list of important terms and their meanings that is usually found in the back of a book

main idea – the most important point the author makes; it may be stated or unstated

sequence – the order in which things happen

Advance Preparation

Have students gather their partially completed time line on pages LC 59–61 (Create a Time Line) in *K¹² Language Arts Activity Book*.

Big Ideas

▶ Active, strong readers employ reading strategies such as drawing inferences during and after reading.

▶ Comprehension entails an understanding of the organizational patterns of text.

▶ Knowing how to use context clues to extract meaning from unfamiliar words is critical to determining what is important in text.

▶ Signal words—such as *before, consequently, compare/contrast, therefore*—are a guide to understanding the relationship between and among ideas.

 **40** minutes

Students will work **independently** to complete online Warm-Up, Check Your Reading, and Reading for Meaning activities.

Warm-Up

Read Fluently "George Washington: A Smart and Caring Family Man"
Students will read aloud and record the passage "George Washington: A Smart and Caring Family Man." The purpose of this activity is to improve students' oral reading and fluency. Remind students to listen to the model on each screen before they begin their recording.

 Objectives
- Read poetry and prose aloud.
- Read aloud grade-level text with appropriate automaticity, prosody, accuracy, and rate.

Check Your Reading

Comprehend "Farmer, Friend, and Statesman" and "General"
Students will answer questions about the next two chapters of *George Washington: Soldier, Hero, President*, "Farmer, Friend, and Statesman" and "General," to demonstrate their literal and inferential comprehension of the story.

 Objectives
- Identify concrete answers to questions.
- Apply information read to answer questions.
- Identify features of nonfiction text.

Reading for Meaning

Practice Understanding New Words
Students will use the glossary and context clues to help them define unfamiliar words in *George Washington: Soldier, Hero, President*.

Identify Causes and Effects
Students will identify **cause-and-effect** relationships in the "Farmer, Friend, and Statesman" and "General" chapters of *George Washington: Soldier, Hero, President*. These relationships will help students better understand Washington and the historical period.

 Objectives
- Use resources or other tools to determine the meaning of a word (use glossary).
- Use context clues to determine word meaning.
- Define *cause* and *effect*.
- Identify a cause and its effect on events and/or relationships.
- Make relevant cause-and-effect connections between earlier events and later events in a text.
- Identify how one event may cause another event.

 **10** minutes

Work **together** with students to complete the offline Making Connections activity.

Making Connections ....

Create a Time Line

Students will add to their time line with important events from the next two chapters of *George Washington: Soldier, Hero, President*. Gather the partially completed time line.

1. Tell students they are going to add new important events from George Washington's life to their time line. They should add at least one event from each of the chapters they just read: "Farmer, Friend, and Statesman" and "General." Possible answers: 1775: Washington takes command of the Continental Army. 1776: The colonies sign the Declaration of Independence. 1776: America gets its first flag. 1776: The Continental Army wins a victory against the Hessians in New Jersey.

2. Remind students to look for the important events, or **main ideas** and their dates, from the chapters they read.

3. Tell students they may write events above or below the line, depending on what fits best on the time line.

TIP Have students keep the Activity Book pages in a safe place so they can add to the time line as they read the book.

> **Objectives**
> - Identify main idea.
> - Sequence events in a text.
> - Use a graphic organizer to organize information.
> - Acquire grade-appropriate words and phrases from various subject-matter areas and use them accurately, including terms having to do with space and time relationships.

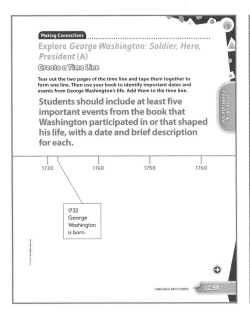

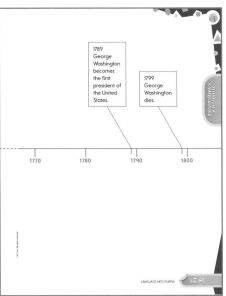

Introduce *George Washington: Soldier, Hero, President* (C)

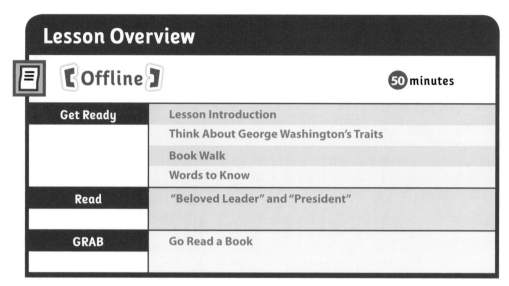

Lesson Overview

Offline   **50** minutes

Get Ready	Lesson Introduction
	Think About George Washington's Traits
	Book Walk
	Words to Know
Read	"Beloved Leader" and "President"
GRAB	Go Read a Book

Advance Preparation

Read the last two chapters of *George Washington: Soldier, Hero, President* to locate Words to Know in the text before beginning the Get Ready.

Big Ideas

- ▸ Nonfiction texts differ from fiction texts in that they describe real or true things in life, rather than things made up by the author.
- ▸ Biographies are a type of nonfiction meant to inform the reader about a person's life.
- ▸ Active, strong readers employ reading strategies such as monitoring their comprehension (for example, self-check) as they read.

[Materials]

Supplied

- *George Washington: Soldier, Hero, President* by Justine and Ron Fontes
- Reading Strategies bookmark

Chapter Synopses

In "Beloved Leader," France sends help and America wins the war and its independence. Washington is called upon to lead the creation of the new Constitution. "President" describes Washington's efforts to be a fair first president of the United States. This last chapter also tells of Washington's death and the construction of a monument to him in Washington, D.C.

Keywords

trait – a quality of a person or character

 **50 minutes**

Work **together** with students to complete offline Get Ready, Read, and GRAB activities.

Get Ready

Lesson Introduction
Prepare students to read the last two chapters of *George Washington: Soldier, Hero, President.*

1. Explain to students that before they read the last two chapters of *George Washington: Soldier, Hero, President*, they will discuss with you

   ▶ What they read in the last two chapters
   ▶ George Washington's traits
   ▶ Their predictions about the text
   ▶ Important words to know in the text

2. Tell students that while they read, you will check in to make sure they understand what they are reading.

3. Tell students that after they read, they will answer questions about what they read.

 Objectives
- Identify character traits.
- Use text organizational features to locate and comprehend information (table of contents).
- Use before-reading strategies.
- Increase concept and content vocabulary.

Think About George Washington's Traits
Review what a trait is and have students begin thinking about George Washington's traits to prepare for a later activity on the main idea and purpose of the book.

1. Have students tell what a **trait** is and give an example of one of their own traits. Remind students of the difference between a trait and a temporary feeling or condition. An emotion like sadness or a condition like hunger may change, while a trait like bravery usually doesn't. A trait is a quality of a person or character; some traits that students might mention include friendly, kind, smart, shy, hardworking, artistic, caring, and nervous.

2. Have students describe George Washington by telling one or two of his traits and one fact from the book that shows each trait. Students may say that Washington is hardworking, because he runs Mount Vernon and stays up all night one time to write a report. They might say he's smart, because he teaches himself how to be a surveyor, and he figures out how to win battles against stronger British forces. They may say he's brave, because he leads his troops into battles against the British, even though he knows his soldiers are not as well prepared as their enemies. They may say he's loyal to his country, because he takes the job of commanding the American army without pay.

3. Ask students why they think the authors wanted to write about Washington's traits. Possible answers: They want readers to know why Washington was so famous and why he became the first U.S. president. They want readers to admire Washington and be more like him.

4. Tell students to continue to look for evidence of Washington's traits as they read the last two chapters of the book.

Book Walk

Have students lead you through a Book Walk of the last two chapters of *George Washington: Soldier, Hero, President*, "Beloved Leader" and "President." Remind students to use the **illustrations** and **chapter titles** to make their predictions about what will happen in the story.

Words to Know

Before reading the last two chapters of *George Washington: Soldier, Hero, President*, go over Words to Know with students.

- **foreign policy** – ways that one country deals with other countries
- **ideals** – beliefs about what is best or right
- **modestly** – without wanting to take credit for abilities or achievements
- **monument** – a statue or other structure built to remember or honor a person or event
- **representatives** – people who are elected to make laws or vote for others
- **unanimously** – agreed to by everyone

Read

"Beloved Leader" and "President"

Have students read "Beloved Leader" and "President" of *George Washington: Soldier, Hero, President*. Remind students to use the strategies on their Reading Strategies bookmark. For example, they may want to stop at the end of each page of the story and ask themselves questions about what they just read.

⟳ **Learning Coach Check-In** This reading assignment should take about 15 minutes. After students finish reading, ask the following questions to assess their comprehension of the selection:

▸ What group did Washington lead after America won the war against England? the group that wrote the Constitution

▸ How many times was Washington elected president of the United States? twice

If students have trouble answering these questions, ask them what reading strategies they used and suggest they reread the selection.

Objectives
- Read literature independently and proficiently.
- Apply information read to answer questions.
- Evaluate reading strategies.

GRAB

Go Read a Book

Have students read a book or magazine of their own choosing for at least 20 minutes. Remind students to use the strategies on their Reading Strategies bookmark before and during reading to help them understand the text.

Objectives
- Read literature independently and proficiently.
- Read a variety of texts for information and pleasure.

Explore *George Washington: Soldier, Hero, President* (C)

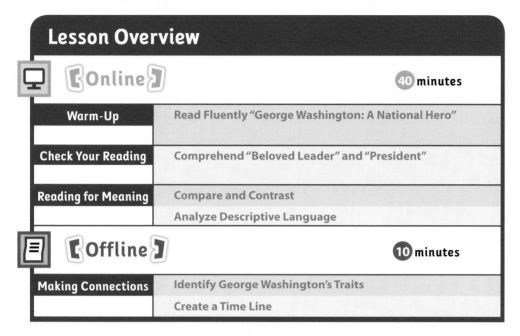

Lesson Overview

🖥 [Online] **40** minutes

Warm-Up	Read Fluently "George Washington: A National Hero"
Check Your Reading	Comprehend "Beloved Leader" and "President"
Reading for Meaning	Compare and Contrast
	Analyze Descriptive Language

[Offline] **10** minutes

Making Connections	Identify George Washington's Traits
	Create a Time Line

Advance Preparation

Have students gather their partially completed time line on pages LC 59–61 (Create a Time Line) in *K¹² Language Arts Activity Book*.

Big Ideas

- ▶ Active, strong readers employ reading strategies such as drawing inferences during and after reading.
- ▶ Readers should be able to retell the story (or information) in their own words, not repeat what was written.
- ▶ Signal words—such as *before, consequently, compare/contrast,* and *therefore*— are a guide to understanding the relationship between and among ideas.
- ▶ Readers must focus on the specific language of a text to aid in interpretation.

[Materials]

Supplied

- *George Washington: Soldier, Hero, President* by Justine and Ron Fontes
- *K¹² Language Arts Activity Book*, pp. LC 59–61, 63–64

Keywords

author's purpose – the reason the author wrote a text: to entertain, to inform, to express an opinion, or to persuade

compare – to explain how two or more things are alike

contrast – to explain how two or more things are different

main idea – the most important point the author makes; it may be stated or unstated

sensory language – language that appeals to the five senses

trait – a quality of a person or character

 **minutes**

Students will work **independently** to complete online Warm-Up, Check Your Reading, and Reading for Meaning activities.

Warm-Up

Read Fluently "George Washington: A National Hero"
Students will read aloud and record the passage "George Washington: A National Hero." The purpose of this activity is to improve students' oral reading and fluency. Remind students to listen to the model on each screen before they begin their recording.

Objectives
- Read poetry and prose aloud.
- Read aloud grade-level text with appropriate automaticity, prosody, accuracy, and rate.

Check Your Reading

Comprehend "Beloved Leader" and "President"
Students will answer questions about the last two chapters of *George Washington: Soldier, Hero, President*, "Beloved Leader" and "President," to demonstrate their literal and inferential comprehension of the story.

Objectives
- Identify concrete answers to questions.
- Infer answers to questions.
- Apply information read to answer questions.
- Explain how specific aspects of a text's illustrations contribute to the meaning of the text.

Reading for Meaning

Compare and Contrast
Students will compare and contrast the Continental and British armies as they are described in *George Washington: Soldier, Hero, President*. The purpose of this activity is to help students draw conclusions about why the Americans won the Revolutionary War despite the challenges they faced.

Analyze Descriptive Language
Students will explore descriptive language and its effect in *George Washington: Soldier, Hero, President*.

Objectives
- Define *compare* and *contrast*.
- Compare and contrast using evidence from the text.
- Draw conclusions using evidence from text.
- Identify sensory language.
- Identify sensory language: vivid verbs.
- Use text to create mental image.
- Describe methods authors use to influence readers' feelings.
- Identify language that shows, not tells.

 **10 minutes**

Work **together** with students to complete the offline Making Connections activities.

Making Connections

Identify George Washington's Traits
Students will identify George Washington's traits and support them with evidence from *George Washington: Soldier, Hero, President*. Turn to pages LC 63 and 64 in *K¹² Language Arts Activity Book*.

1. Have students tell what a **trait** is. a quality of a person or character

2. Remind students that they discussed George Washington's traits before they read the last two chapters of the book *George Washington: Soldier, Hero, President*. Have students tell what trait they identified.

Objectives
- Define *trait*.
- Identify character traits.
- Identify main idea.
- Identify author's purpose.
- Sequence events in a text.
- Use a graphic organizer to organize information.

3. Tell students to read the directions carefully before they complete the Activity Book pages.

4. Have students complete the Activity Book pages.

TIP Have students keep the Activity Book pages in a safe place so they can use them for the final activity of the unit.

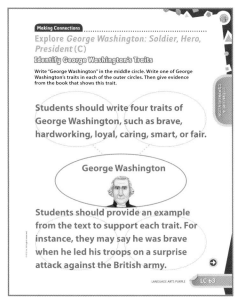
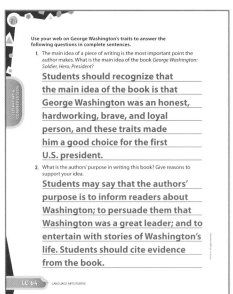

Create a Time Line

Students will add important events from the last two chapters of *George Washington: Soldier, Hero, President*. Gather the partially completed time line.

1. Tell students they are going to add new important events from George Washington's life to their time line. They should add at least one event from each of the chapters they just read: "Beloved Leader" and "President." Possible answers: 1777: The British march into Philadelphia. 1778: France sends troops and money to help America. 1783: The war ends, and America becomes free. 1787: Washington leads a group to write a new constitution. 1788: The Constitution is approved. 1789: Washington becomes the first president of the United States. 1792: Washington is elected president a second time.

2. Remind students to look for the important events, or **main ideas** and their dates, from the chapters they read.

3. Tell students they may write events above or below the line, depending on what fits best on the time line.

(TIP) Have students keep the Activity Book pages in a safe place so they can use them for the final activity of the unit.

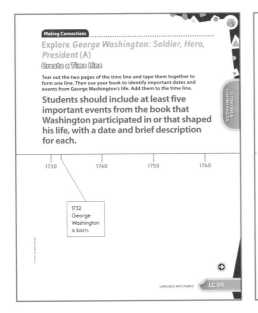

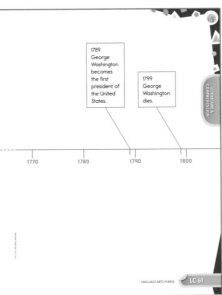

Reflections on *George Washington: Soldier, Hero, President*

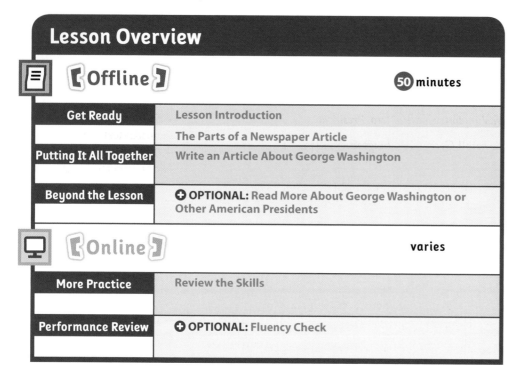

Lesson Overview

📄 [Offline]   **50** minutes

Get Ready	Lesson Introduction
	The Parts of a Newspaper Article
Putting It All Together	Write an Article About George Washington
Beyond the Lesson	➕ OPTIONAL: Read More About George Washington or Other American Presidents

🖥️ [Online]   varies

More Practice	Review the Skills
Performance Review	➕ OPTIONAL: Fluency Check

[Materials]

Supplied

- *George Washington: Soldier, Hero, President* by Justine and Ron Fontes
- *K¹² Language Arts Activity Book*, pp. LC 59–61, 63–64, 65–67
- Putting It All Together Assessment Checklist (printout)
- Fluency Performance Checklist (optional printout)

Also Needed

- pencils, coloring, or crayons
- newspaper (optional)

Advance Preparation

Have students gather their completed time line on pages LC 59–61 (Create a Time Line) and traits web on pages LC 63 and 64 (Identify George Washington's Traits) in *K¹² Language Arts Activity Book*. Locate the front page of a newspaper or an article from an online news website.

Big Ideas

▸ Readers need to be able to sequence, summarize, and articulate the main idea.
▸ Readers should be able to retell the story (or information) in their own words, not repeat what was written.
▸ Readers must understand the relationship between main idea and supporting details.
▸ Readers need to synthesize, draw conclusions about, and interpret what they have read.
▸ Writers must be able to articulate a main idea and support it with appropriate details.
▸ Writing requires organization and structure.

Keywords

main idea – the most important point the author makes; it may be stated or unstated

sequence – the order in which things happen

summarize – to tell in order the most important ideas or events of a text

summary – a short retelling that includes only the most important ideas or events of a text

topic – the subject of a text

 **50 minutes**

Work **together** with students to complete the offline Get Ready, Putting It All Together, and Beyond the Lesson activities.

Get Ready ....

Lesson Introduction

Prepare students for retelling *George Washington: Soldier, Hero, President*.

1. Tell students that they are going to retell *George Washington: Soldier, Hero, President*.

2. Have them retell what happens in the book. If they have trouble remembering, suggest that students take a Book Walk through the story to refresh their memory.

Objectives
- Summarize text and maintain accurate sequence.
- Identify important questions that need to be answered (5Ws and H).

The Parts of a Newspaper Article

Teach students about the 5Ws and H—the questions that news articles answer—in preparation for writing their own article about George Washington.

1. If you have one, show students an article from the front page of a newspaper or online news website.

2. Explain that news articles tell the **topic** and **main idea** of the article in the very first or second paragraph, so readers know quickly what the article is about. To get the important information in the first paragraph, news writers follow the 5Ws and H guideline for writing. Tell students what these letters stand for.

   - **W**ho is the article about?
   - **W**hat happened to this person or group?
   - **W**here did this event happen?
   - **W**hen did this event happen?
   - **W**hy did the event occur?
   - **H**ow did the event take place?

3. Look at your sample article. Read the first paragraph. Help students indentify the 5Ws and H of the article. If the information isn't in the first paragraph, read the second paragraph and look for the information there.

4. Explain that after the introduction to the article, news writers use the body of the article to give details about the 5Ws and H. They may tell more about what happened, why or how something happened, or additional information or quotations from the people involved.

5. Tell students that they need to know the 5Ws and H for Putting It All Together.

Putting It All Together

Write an Article About George Washington

Students will write an article about George Washington in which they summarize the book *George Washington: Soldier, Hero, President* and demonstrate their understanding of the main ideas, Washington's character, and purpose of the book. Gather the time line, traits web, and coloring pencils or crayons, and turn to pages LC 65–67 in *K¹² Language Arts Activity Book*.

1. Tell students that they are going to write a summary of the book using a newspaper article format.

2. Have students read all instructions carefully before beginning the assignment. Have them complete the Activity Book pages.

3. After they complete the Activity Book pages, have students look back at what they wrote. Did they use language that helps readers picture the people and events in the article? Allow students to revise their work and add more descriptive language to help readers understand the article. Have students proofread their draft for mistakes in grammar, spelling, and punctuation, noting any errors or other changes they need to make.

4. Have them rewrite their article as a final copy on their own paper and illustrate it with a picture. Students should include a caption—in a complete sentence—that describes the picture. (Remind students to use their best cursive handwriting and leave spaces between words so that others can read what they wrote.)

5. When students have completed their article, use the materials and instructions in the online lesson to evaluate students' work.

Objectives

- Identify the main idea and supporting details in a text.
- Organize information around a main idea.
- Summarize text and maintain accurate sequence.
- Write a summary.
- State the topic directly.
- Identify important questions that need to be answered (5Ws and H).
- Include details in draft.
- Write a caption relating to an illustration.
- Write a headline.
- Write an introduction.
- Use vivid images that relate to the main idea.
- Write a concluding statement.
- Apply the conventions of grammar, usage, mechanics, and spelling.
- Create a visual.

6. Enter the answers (Yes or No) for each line of the assessment checklist online.

↪ **Learning Coach Check-In** Check in with students after about 40 minutes to see if they have completed the assignment.

 If students are interested, they could write their final draft on a computer using publishing tools to make it look like a newspaper article, or they could even write their article online as a blog post.

Reward: If students score 80 percent or more on the Putting It All Together activity, add a sticker for this unit on the My Accomplishments chart. If students did not score 80 percent or more, work with them to revise their writing until they do score 80 percent and then add a sticker to the My Accomplishments chart.

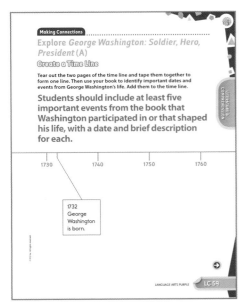

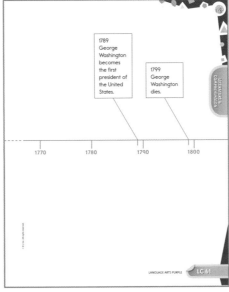

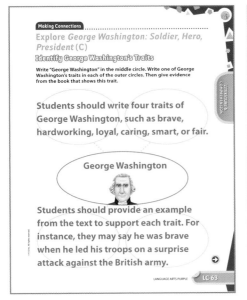

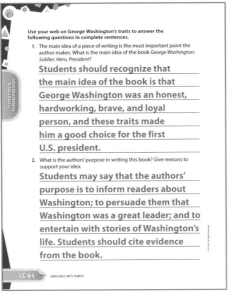

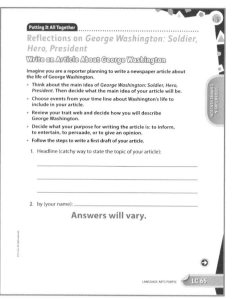

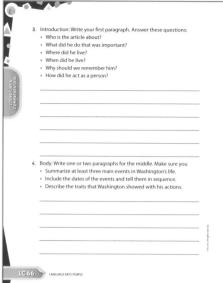

Putting It All Together

Reflections on *George Washington: Soldier, Hero, President*

Write an Article About George Washington

Imagine you are a reporter planning to write a newspaper article about the life of George Washington.

- Think about the main idea of *George Washington: Soldier, Hero, President*. Then decide what the main idea of your article will be.
- Choose events from your time line about Washington's life to include in your article.
- Review your trait web and decide how you will describe George Washington.
- Decide what your purpose for writing the article is: to inform, to entertain, to persuade, or to give an opinion.
- Follow the steps to write a first draft of your article.

1. Headline (catchy way to state the topic of your article):

2. by (your name): _____

Answers will vary.

3. Introduction: Write your first paragraph. Answer these questions:
   - Who is the article about?
   - What did he do that was important?
   - Where did he live?
   - When did he live?
   - Why should we remember him?
   - How did he act as a person?

4. Body: Write one or two paragraphs for the middle. Make sure you
   - Summarize at least three main events in Washington's life.
   - Include the dates of the events and tell them in sequence.
   - Describe the traits that Washington showed with his actions.

5. Conclusion: Write the last paragraph of your article. Make sure you
   - Summarize the main idea of your article.
   - Tell why Washington should be remembered.

Beyond the Lesson

⊕ OPTIONAL: Read More About George Washington or Other American Presidents

This activity is OPTIONAL. It is intended for students who have extra time and would benefit from reading more about George Washington or reading about other American presidents. Feel free to skip this activity.

1. Ask students if they would like to read more about George Washington or another American president and, if so, why.

2. Have students get another book on George Washington or a book on a different U.S. president. Some possible choices include

   - Thomas Jefferson
   - John Adams
   - James Monroe
   - Theodore Roosevelt
   - Franklin Delano Roosevelt
   - Harry S. Truman
   - Ronald Reagan
   - William Clinton
   - George H.W. Bush
   - George W. Bush
   - Barack Obama

3. If students read another book about George Washington, have them compare and contrast that book and *George Washington: Soldier, Hero, President*. Discuss with them how the books are similar and how they are different.

Objectives

- Compare and contrast the most important points and details on two texts on the same topic.
- Compare and contrast using evidence from the text.
- Use a graphic organizer to organize information.
- Read a variety of texts for information and pleasure.
- Make connections between text and self, text and world, and text to text.

4. If students read a book about another president, have them create and discuss a trait web on the new president, like the one they did for George Washington.

   ▶ Tell them to put the president's name at the center of the web and write four traits of the person in the outer circles of the web.

   ▶ For each trait, have them summarize an event from the book about the president's life that shows this trait.

   ▶ Discuss with students how this president is similar to and different from George Washington.

 **varies**

Students will work **independently** to complete the online More Practice activity.

More Practice

Review the Skills

If students scored less than 80 percent or had difficulty meeting the objectives of the Putting It All Together activity, have them go online for more practice.

Objectives

- Identify the main idea and supporting details in a text.
- Organize information around a main idea.
- Summarize text and maintain accurate sequence.
- Write a summary.
- State the topic directly.
- Identify important questions that need to be answered (5Ws and H).
- Include details in draft.
- Write a caption relating to an illustration.

Performance Review

⊕ **OPTIONAL: Fluency Check**

Listen to students' recordings and use the Fluency Performance Checklist to review fluency and track performance. Keep the completed checklist so you can review students' progress over time.

Objectives

- Read aloud grade-level text with appropriate automaticity, prosody, accuracy, and rate.

Critical Skills Practice 3

Unit Focus

In this unit, students will focus on reading nonfiction passages, fiction passages, paired passages, and poetry and on answering multiple choice questions about those readings in a test format.

Unit Plan		Offline	Online
Lesson 1	Nonfiction Passages (C)		50 minutes
Lesson 2	Fiction Passages (D)		50 minutes
Lesson 3	Paired Passages (A)		50 minutes
Lesson 4	Poetry (B)		50 minutes
Lesson 5	Unit Checkpoint	50 minutes	varies

Nonfiction Passages (C)

Lesson Overview

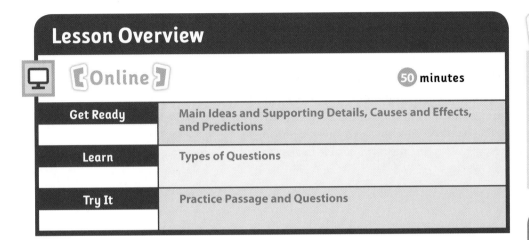

Online	50 minutes

Get Ready	Main Ideas and Supporting Details, Causes and Effects, and Predictions
Learn	Types of Questions
Try It	Practice Passage and Questions

Big Ideas

▸ Comprehension entails asking and answering questions about the text.

▸ Comprehension strategies can be taught through explicit instruction.

▸ Reading strategies are conscious plans that readers apply and adapt to make sense of text.

▸ Comprehension requires an understanding of story structure.

Materials

Supplied

- Types of Questions (optional printout)
- Practice Passage and Questions (optional printout)

Keywords

cause – the reason something happens

effect – the result of a cause

main idea – the most important point the author makes; it may be stated or unstated

prediction – a guess about what might happen that is based on information in a story and what you already know

supporting details – the sentences that give information about the main idea or topic sentence

 **Online** 🕐 **minutes**

Students will work online to complete Get Ready, Learn, and Try It activities.

Get Ready

Main Ideas and Supporting Details, Causes and Effects, and Predictions
Students will focus on several important elements of nonfiction passages. They will review main ideas and supporting details, causes and effects, facts and evidence in support of predictions, and the relationship between questions and specific portions of text. Be sure students understand these terms so that they will be able to answer the questions in the activities.

Objectives
- Define *main idea*.
- Define *supporting details*.
- Define *cause* and *effect*.
- Define *prediction*.

Learn

Types of Questions
Students will learn about different types of multiple choice questions. The questions will be about understanding how passages are organized with main ideas and supporting details, identifying causes and effects, recognizing how specific parts of a passage answer a question, and making predictions based on facts and textual evidence.

Objectives
- Identify organization by main idea and supporting details.
- Identify causes.
- Identify effects.
- Generate questions about what has been read.
- Use text to make a prediction.

- ▶ A **main idea** is the most important idea in a paragraph or text. **Supporting details** are sentences that give information about the main idea. Many nonfiction passages contain paragraphs that are organized to present a main idea and several supporting details.
- ▶ A **cause** is the reason something happens, while an **effect** is the result of a cause.
- ▶ A **prediction** is a guess about what might happen that is based on facts, textual evidence, and what is already known.

TIP If students are not comfortable reading the passage for this activity online, print Types of Questions and have students read the printout.

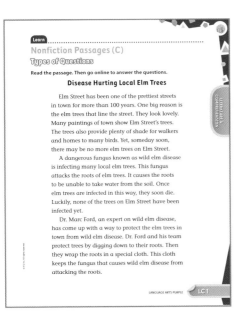

Learn

Nonfiction Passages (C)

Types of Questions

Read the passage. Then go online to answer the questions.

Disease Hurting Local Elm Trees

Elm Street has been one of the prettiest streets in town for more than 100 years. One big reason is the elm trees that line the street. They look lovely. Many paintings of town show Elm Street's trees. The trees also provide plenty of shade for walkers and homes to many birds. Yet, someday soon, there may be no more elm trees on Elm Street.

A dangerous fungus known as wild elm disease is infecting many local elm trees. This fungus attacks the roots of elm trees. It causes the roots to be unable to take water from the soil. Once elm trees are infected in this way, they soon die. Luckily, none of the trees on Elm Street have been infected yet.

Dr. Marc Ford, an expert on wild elm disease, has come up with a way to protect the elm trees in town from wild elm disease. Dr. Ford and his team protect trees by digging down to their roots. Then they wrap the roots in a special cloth. This cloth keeps the fungus that causes wild elm disease from attacking the roots.

LANGUAGE ARTS PURPLE LC 1

Try It

Practice Passage and Questions

Students will practice answering multiple choice questions about a nonfiction passage.

 If students are not comfortable reading the passage for this activity online, print Practice Passage and Questions and have students read the printout.

Try It

Nonfiction Passages (C)

Practice Passage and Questions

Read the passage. Then go online to answer the questions.

Beach Street Sharks Win Big

The Beach Street Sharks are a special 10-and-under soccer team. They proved that yesterday when they beat the Cedar Park Comets 5–3. What made the game so amazing? The Sharks scored five goals in less than 10 minutes!

With eight minutes left in the game, the Sharks were down 3–0. Things looked bad. Then Susan Murray, the team captain, called everyone together during a break in the game. Murray told the team that they could still turn the game around. She said that she was going to try her hardest to score a goal or two. She said that she believed in them.

Suddenly, the Sharks began to play better. Betty Lakofski, the Sharks goalie, made a great save. She then passed the ball to Anna Lewis, who dribbled and passed to Susan Murray. Murray then made the team's first goal.

LANGUAGE ARTS PURPLE LC 1

LC 2 LANGUAGE ARTS PURPLE

Before long, the rest of the Sharks got in on the act. Cara Buckley, Ella Reese, and Erin Brown each scored a goal. The Comets were shocked by the sudden scoring surge. With a minute to play, the Sharks were winning 4–3! Susan Murray scored the final goal, a perfect ending because she was the one who inspired her team.

Objectives

- Identify organization by main idea and supporting details.
- Identify causes.
- Identify effects.
- Generate questions about what has been read.
- Use text to make a prediction.

Fiction Passages (D)

Lesson Overview

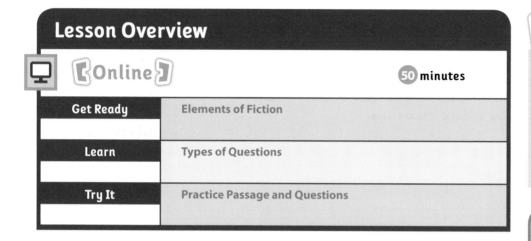

Online — 50 minutes

Get Ready	Elements of Fiction
Learn	Types of Questions
Try It	Practice Passage and Questions

Materials

Supplied
- Types of Questions (optional printout)
- Practice Passage and Questions (optional printout)

Keywords

author – a writer

context clue – a word or phrase in a text that helps you figure out the meaning of an unknown word

first-person point of view – the telling of a story by a character in that story, using pronouns such as *I*, *me*, and *we*

narrator – the teller of a story

trait – a quality of a person or character

Big Ideas

▶ Readers analyze a text to determine more about how the text's parts work as a whole, and how its parts contribute to meaning.

▶ Interpreting text requires close attention to content and literary elements.

▶ To understand and interpret a story, readers need to understand and describe characters and what they do.

▶ Readers should pay close attention to the visual elements (for example, illustrations) that accompany a story to help create and describe the meaning of a text.

▶ The point of view that a story is told from determines how much information readers have about plot events and characters' feelings.

▶ Knowing how to use context clues to extract meaning from unfamiliar words is critical to determining what is important in text.

 **50 minutes**

Students will work online to complete Get Ready, Learn, and Try It activities.

Get Ready

Elements of Fiction

Students will review important elements of fiction passages. These elements include **author**, **narrator**, and character **traits**, as well as **context clues**.

Objectives
- Define *author*.
- Define *narrator*.
- Define *character traits*.
- Define *context clues*.

Learn

Types of Questions

Students will learn about different types of multiple choice questions having to do with fiction passages. The questions will be about distinguishing between author and narrator; identifying first-person narrators; describing characters and their traits; using illustrations to help understand characters, plot, and setting; and using context clues to determine what unfamiliar words mean.

TIP If students are not comfortable reading the passage for this activity online, print Types of Questions and have students read the printout.

Objectives
- Distinguish between author and narrator.
- Identify first-person narrator(s).
- Describe characters and their traits.
- Use information from visuals to develop an understanding of the characters, setting, and plot.
- Use context to determine the meaning of unfamiliar words.

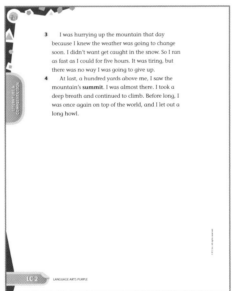

Try It

Practice Passage and Questions

Students will practice answering multiple choice questions about a fiction passage.

TIP If students are not comfortable reading the passage for this activity online, print Practice Passage and Questions and have students read the printout.

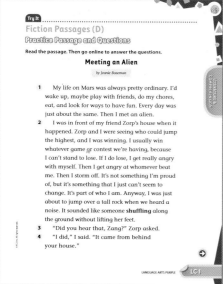

Paired Passages (A)

Lesson Overview

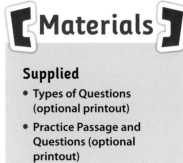

[Online]   (50) minutes

Get Ready	Paired Passages
Learn	Types of Questions
Try It	Practice Passage and Questions

[Materials]

Supplied

- Types of Questions (optional printout)
- Practice Passage and Questions (optional printout)

Keywords

trait – a quality of a person or character

Big Ideas

▸ Readers must focus on the specific language of a text to aid in interpretation.

▸ To understand and interpret a story, readers need to understand and describe characters and what they do.

▸ Signal words—such as *before, consequently, compare/contrast, therefore*—are a guide to understanding the relationship between and among ideas.

 **Online** 🕐 50 **minutes**

Students will work online to complete Get Ready, Learn, and Try It activities.

Get Ready ....

Paired Passages

Students will review what paired passages are, the ways in which they are often related, and some common elements they may be asked to compare when answering questions about paired passages.

 Objectives
- Define *paired passages*.

Learn ....

Types of Questions

Students will learn about different types of multiple choice questions associated with paired fiction passages. The questions will be about comparing the two passages, demonstrating understanding of the texts, and identifying the similarities and differences of the characters in the texts.

TIP If students are not comfortable reading the passages for this activity online, print Types of Questions and have students read the printout.

 Objectives
- Compare and contrast descriptions that support comprehension.
- Demonstrate comprehension of text.
- Compare and contrast characters from different stories.

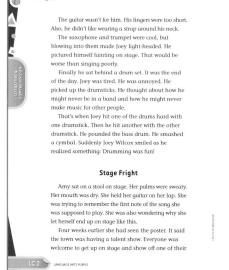

Try It

Practice Passages and Questions

Students will practice answering multiple choice questions about paired nonfiction passages.

TIP If students are not comfortable reading the passages for this activity online, print Practice Passage and Questions and have students read the printout.

Objectives
- Infer answers to questions about text(s).
- Demonstrate comprehension of text.
- Compare and contrast literary elements in two or more literary selections.
- Compare and contrast descriptions that support comprehension.

Try It

Paired Passages (A)

Practice Passages and Questions

Read the passages. Then go online to answer the questions.

The City Needs a New Park

There is an empty lot on Elm Street. If you live here, you know it well. The lot is where the library stood until last year's fire. Now there is just a patch of dirt and bit of grass there.

Yet why should the empty lot stay empty? We should turn it into a park. A park could have swings and slides. It could have a sandbox and a jungle gym, too. A park would look so nice. Kids could go there to play, and adults could go there to relax.

Turning the empty lot into a park wouldn't cost much money. Most of the work could be done by volunteers. We would not have to build anything. There would be no bricks or steel beams to buy. There would be no cranes to rent or bulldozer drivers to pay.

The day we lost the old library was a terrible one. Yet now we can change our city for the better. Every person should agree. We can make our city better. Let's turn that empty lot into a park!

LANGUAGE ARTS PURPLE LC 1

Let's Build a New Library

Last year, a fire burned down the Elm Street Library. It was one of the darkest days in our city's history. Today there is an empty lot where the library stood.

Yet we can change things. We can build a new library, and we can build it right on Elm Street. The new library could be even better than the old one. It could have books, as well as a computer lab. Everyone could use the new library.

Building a new library wouldn't cost much. Volunteers would donate their time and money. Cole Construction has said that they will help work on building a new library. Jones Lumberyard has promised the city plenty of wood.

The empty lot on Elm Street has been there for too long. The people of our city must unite. We can turn that empty lot into a new library that we can all be proud of.

LC 2 LANGUAGE ARTS PURPLE

Poetry (B)

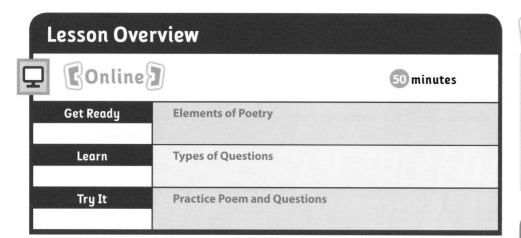

Lesson Overview

[Online]   50 minutes

Get Ready	Elements of Poetry
Learn	Types of Questions
Try It	Practice Poem and Questions

Big Ideas

▶ Poems are different from prose in structure and content. They are generally organized in lines and often contain rhymes.

▶ The use of imagery and sensory language creates detailed pictures in the reader's mind, so the reader can understand and appreciate the ideas and feelings the writer conveys.

▶ Good writing paints pictures with words to create a visual image of the text in the reader's mind's eye.

[Materials]

Supplied

- Types of Questions (optional printout)
- Practice Poem and Questions (optional printout)

Keywords

figurative language – words that describe something by comparing it to something completely different
Example: Rain fell in buckets and the streets looked like rivers.

literal meaning – following the usual, or exact, meaning of words

metaphor – a figure of speech that compares two unlike things, without using the words *like* or *as*
Example: The cat's eyes were emeralds shining in the night.

sensory language – language that appeals to the five senses

simile – a comparison between two things using the words *like* or *as*
Example: I didn't hear him come in because he was as quiet as a mouse.

 **50 minutes**

Students will work online to complete Get Ready, Learn, and Try It activities.

Get Ready

Elements of Poetry
Students will review important elements of poetry. These elements include **figurative language**, **metaphors**, and **similes**, as well as **sensory language** in the form of vivid verbs.

Objectives
- Define *figurative language*.
- Define *literal meaning*.
- Define *metaphor*.
- Define *simile*.
- Define *sensory language*.

Learn

Types of Questions
Students will learn about different types of multiple choice questions that are frequently asked about poems on standardized assessments. The questions will be about recognizing figurative language and distinguishing between literal and figurative meaning, as well as identifying similes, metaphors, and sensory language in the form of vivid verbs.

TIP If students are not comfortable reading the poem for this activity online, print Types of Questions and have students read the printout.

Objectives
- Recognize figurative language.
- Distinguish between literal and nonliteral or figurative language in poetry.
- Identify metaphor.
- Identify similes.
- Identify sensory language: vivid verbs.

Learn
Poetry (B)
Types of Questions

Read the poem. Then go online to answer the questions.

Home Sweet Home

1 My house is built
   Of stone and brick.
   Its roof is black.
   Its walls are thick.

2 Its windows are
   Like open eyes.
   They see hellos.
   They see good-byes.

3 The kitchen is
   The house's heart:
   The perfect place
   For each day's start.

4 The porch is like
   The house's lap:
   An ideal spot
   For a catnap.

5 The floorboards groan.
   The stairway creaks.
   They are the voice
   When the house speaks.

6 No matter where
   I choose to roam,
   My house is still
   My only home.

Try It

Practice Poem and Questions

Students will practice answering multiple choice questions associated with poetry.

TIP If students are not comfortable reading the poem for this activity online, print Practice Passage and Questions and have students read the printout.

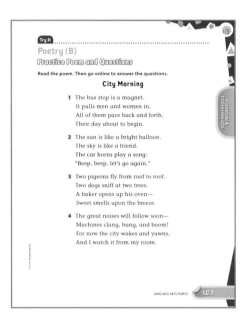

Objectives

- Recognize figurative language.
- Distinguish between literal and nonliteral or figurative language in poetry.
- Identify metaphor.
- Identify similes.
- Identify sensory language: vivid verbs.

Unit Checkpoint

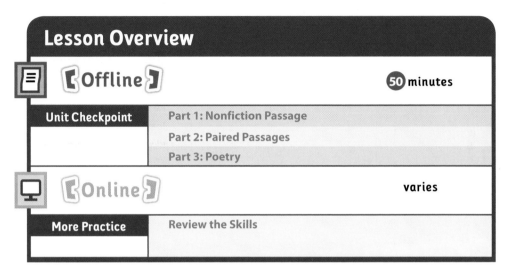

Lesson Overview

Offline   50 minutes

Unit Checkpoint	Part 1: Nonfiction Passage
	Part 2: Paired Passages
	Part 3: Poetry

Online   varies

More Practice	Review the Skills

Materials

Supplied

- *K¹² Language Arts Assessments*, pp. LC 25–37

Objectives

- Identify organization by main idea and supporting details.
- Identify causes.
- Identify effects.
- Generate questions about what has been read.
- Use text to make a prediction.
- Distinguish between author and narrator.
- Identify first-person narrator(s).
- Describe characters and their traits.
- Use information from visuals to develop an understanding of the characters, setting, and plot.
- Use context to determine the meaning of unfamiliar words.
- Infer answers to questions about text(s).
- Demonstrate comprehension of text.
- Compare and contrast characters from different stories.
- Compare and contrast literary elements in two or more literary selections.
- Compare and contrast descriptions that support comprehension.
- Recognize figurative language.
- Distinguish between literal and nonliteral or figurative language in poetry.
- Identify metaphor.
- Identify similes.
- Identify sensory language: vivid verbs.

 **50 minutes**

Unit Checkpoint

Lesson Introduction

Explain that students are going to show what they have learned about answering questions about nonfiction passages, paired fiction passages, and poems.

1. Give students the Unit Checkpoint pages.

2. Read the directions together.

3. Use the Answer Key to score the Checkpoint and then enter the results online.

4. Review each exercise with students. Work with students to correct any exercises they missed.

Part 1: Nonfiction Passage

Have students read "A Successful Concert" and answer the questions.

Part 2: Paired Passages

Have students read "A Topsy-Turvy World" and "The Morning of the Green Snow" and answer the questions.

Part 3: Poetry

Have students read "Up, Up, and Away" and answer the questions.

Panel 1 (LC 25)

Name _____ Date _____

Unit Checkpoint Learning Coach Instructions
Critical Skills Practice 3

Explain that students are going to show what they have learned about answering questions about nonfiction passages, paired fiction passages, and poems.

1. Give students the Unit Checkpoint pages.
2. Read the instructions together.
3. Use the Answer Key to score the Checkpoint and then enter the results online.
4. Review each exercise with students. Work with students to correct any exercises they missed.

Part 1: Nonfiction Passage
Have students read "A Successful Concert" and answer the questions.

Part 2: Paired Passages
Have students read "A Topsy-Turvy World" and "The Morning of the Green Snow" and answer the questions.

Part 3: Poetry
Have students read "Up, Up, and Away" and answer the questions.

Panel 2 (LC 26)

Name _____ Date _____

Unit Checkpoint Answer Key
Critical Skills Practice 3

Part 1. Nonfiction Passage
Read the passage and answer the questions.

A Successful Concert

1   Last night's concert at the new Roberts Theater was wonderful. First of all, the music was amazing. Second, the crowd was full of energy. Last but not least, the theater is the most beautiful one in the entire state.

2   The evening began with Neil Foreman on stage. He wore a black suit, and he played five classic pieces by Mozart. Each note was perfect. As soon as his fingers touched the keys, every eye in the theater was on him. When he finished and stood, the whole audience stood, too. The building then erupted in cheers and delighted shouts. Mr. Foreman was clearly glad that the crowd was happy. He smiled and blew kisses to everyone.

3   Ursula Carr stepped up to the piano next. Unlike Mr. Foreman, she played only new music. Still, her songs were quite powerful. It was as if Miss Carr used the piano to touch the hearts of her listeners. Some audience members were

Panel 3 (LC 27)

Name _____ Date _____

so moved that they began to cry. A young man handed Miss Carr a dozen roses as she walked off stage.

4   The last performer was a young boy. His name was Adam Moore, and he played just one song. It was a song he wrote himself, and it had no words. Yet that was perfect. The melody stood alone. It reached the high ceilings of the Roberts Theater. It filled the room. The music seemed to be coming from everywhere, and people listened as if they were in a trance. Mr. Moore's song was the perfect ending to a perfect evening.

1. How is the passage's first paragraph organized?
   A. It tells readers about the writer.
   B. It places events in time order.
   C. It states the least important ideas first.
   (D) It states a main idea and then provides supporting details.

2. What causes the whole audience to stand in Paragraph 2?
   A. the beauty of the Roberts Theater
   (B) Neil Foreman's performance
   C. Ursula Carr's performance
   D. Neil Foreman's blowing kisses to the audience

3. Which is one effect of Ursula Carr's music in Paragraph 3?
   (A) Some audience members begin to cry.
   B. Neil Foreman stands and waves to the crowd.
   C. She chooses to play only modern music.
   D. Adam Moore decides to play just one song.

Panel 4 (LC 28)

Name _____ Date _____

4. Read these sentences from the passage:

> Ursula Carr stepped up to the piano next. Unlike Mr. Foreman, she played only new music. Still, her songs were quite powerful.

Which question do these sentences answer?
   A. What did Ursula Carr wear while she played the piano?
   B. Did Ursula Carr's songs have words?
   (C) How was Ursula Carr's performance different from Neil Foreman's?
   D. Why did Ursula Carr play her music before Adam Moore?

5. Which prediction might readers make after reading this passage?
   (A) The writer will go to hear these people play the piano again.
   B. Tickets for future concerts at the Roberts Theater will not cost a lot of money.
   C. Neil Foreman will never perform with Ursula Carr or Adam Moore again.
   D. Adam Moore will decide to write words for the song he played at the concert.

Part 2. Paired Passages
Read the passages and answer the questions.

A Topsy-Turvy World
by Michelle Frye

1   At first, I didn't even notice that anything was strange. It seemed like a regular morning in June. I woke up, got out of bed, and walked

Panel 5 (LC 29)

Name _____ Date _____

to the kitchen. I yawned and rubbed my eyes. My stomach rumbled, so I decided to have some cereal. That's when I reached for the door of the refrigerator and noticed that I was standing on the ceiling.

2   That sounds crazy, but it's true. The floor was high above my head. The tallest shelf in the cabinets only came up to my knees. The drawer with the forks and spoons, which was under the kitchen counter, was too high for me to reach. I was so confused that I stepped on the smoke detector.

3   Once the alarm stopped blaring and I could hear again, I began looking for a solution to my problem. That's how I am. I can figure out anything, even something as strange as finding myself walking on the ceiling, if I just work hard enough. I thought for a moment.

4   "Shannon Sue Lopez," I said to myself, "this must be a dream. You ate three slices of pizza last night. You are having a nightmare."

5   So I pinched myself to see if I would wake up. I didn't, of course. I just hurt my arm where I pinched it. Still, I couldn't give up.

6   Next I tried to climb down to the floor. I thought that maybe, once I reached the ground, everything would be normal again. Yet I couldn't

Panel 6 (LC 30)

Name _____ Date _____

get to the floor. Every time I tried, I fell back up to the ceiling. So I came up with a different plan.

7   I hoped that it was only the kitchen that was upside down. Maybe if I went into the living room or my bedroom, I'd find my feet back on the carpet. But that wasn't true, either. I scratched my head and paced.

8   Because I was so deep in thought, I didn't see the ceiling fan in the dining room. So I tripped on it. I bumped my head on a hook that held one of my mom's hanging plants. That hurt, too, but it gave me an idea.

9   It made me think of my mom's garden, which is outside. There's no ceiling outside. I thought that if I went outside, I'd have to end up back on the ground. I stood and went to the front door.

10   It wasn't easy to reach the door knob. I had to jump a few times before I grabbed it. Then I had to pull as hard as I could to turn the knob. When the knob finally turned, the door opened just a crack. I used all of my strength to pull myself up. Then I strained to see what was outside. Of course, what I saw really surprised me.

11   Right there on my doorstep was the wing of an airplane. Under it was an engine, and it roared loudly. I looked up and saw that all

Panel 7 (LC 31)

Name _____ Date _____

of the passengers on the plane were staring at me. I looked down and saw the ground. It was thousands of feet below.

12   From the cockpit, the pilot smiled and waved to me. I waved back just to be polite.

13   Then I shouted, "I hope you know that I'm not giving up! I'm going to figure out what is going on here! I'm going to solve this problem and get things back to normal around here!"

14   The pilot just winked.

The Morning of the Green Snow
by Max Wilson

1   January in the tiny town of Hale, Wisconsin, is always a cold time. Icicles hang from rooftops, and people dress in warm coats, hats, and gloves. It snows a lot. Those who live in Hale are used to winter weather. Yet no one expected what happened here last Monday. That was the day that Josh Martin opened his bedroom window and woke up everyone in town with his shouts.

2   "The snow is green! The snow is green!" he hollered.

3   Josh was right, of course. The snow was green. It was the color of healthy grass and tree leaves

Panel 8 (LC 32)

Name _____ Date _____

in summer. Yet the green snow wasn't falling on the whole town. No, the green snow was only falling on Josh's house and property. As it piled up on his roof and his yard, it made Josh's house look like it was slowly rising up from a big field—or slowly sinking in one.

4   "It's still coming down," said Josh, and everyone agreed.

5   By nine o'clock, the green snow was already quite deep. By ten, there were 18 inches of it on Josh's house and yard. Flakes continued to fall at eleven. By noon, the whole first floor was buried.

6   "This could be dangerous!" Josh yelled from his bed. "What if my house is totally buried? Won't someone do something?"

7   Of course, Josh did not say what the people of Hale should do. He did not do anything himself, either. If he did, that would have been almost as surprising as the green snow. For Josh was great at spotting problems, but he was terrible at solving them.

8   Two months ago, he let his friend Shauna have his clock radio because he did not feel like replacing its dead battery. Just a day before the green snow hit, Josh noticed that he was getting sick, but he did not bother to take any medicine.

Panel 9 (LC 33)

Name _____ Date _____

9   It wasn't that Josh was foolish. It was that he was lazy. In fact, Josh was the laziest person in all of Hale, Wisconsin. To Josh, it was always easier to do nothing than do something. Whenever something did have to be done, Josh just sat there and hoped that someone else would solve whatever problem he faced.

10   This wasn't fair to Josh's friends and neighbors, of course. They were tired of always having to solve his problems for him. So this time, no one came to Josh's aid. If the problems caused by the green snow were going to be solved, Josh would have to solve them himself.

11   So the green snow fell and fell, and Josh looked at his neighbors from his bedroom window. They looked back at Josh. Neither moved. And the green snow fell and fell.

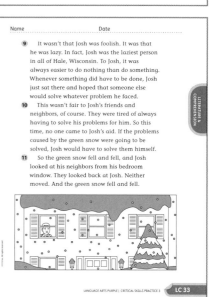

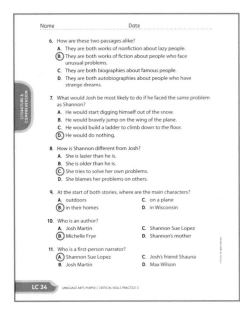

Name _____ Date _____

6. How are these two passages alike?
   A. They are both works of nonfiction about lazy people.
   B. They are both works of fiction about people who face unusual problems.
   C. They are both biographies about famous people.
   D. They are both autobiographies about people who have strange dreams.

7. What would Josh be most likely to do if he faced the same problem as Shannon?
   A. He would start digging himself out of the snow.
   B. He would bravely jump on the wing of the plane.
   C. He would build a ladder to climb down to the floor.
   D. He would do nothing.

8. How is Shannon different from Josh?
   A. She is lazier than he is.
   B. She is older than he is.
   C. She tries to solve her own problems.
   D. She blames her problems on others.

9. At the start of both stories, where are the main characters?
   A. outdoors   C. on a plane
   B. in their homes   D. in Wisconsin

10. Who is an author?
    A. Josh Martin   C. Shannon Sue Lopez
    B. Michelle Frye   D. Shannon's mother

11. Who is a first-person narrator?
    A. Shannon Sue Lopez   C. Josh's friend Shauna
    B. Josh Martin   D. Max Wilson

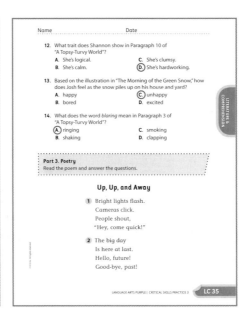

Name _____ Date _____

12. What trait does Shannon show in Paragraph 10 of "A Topsy-Turvy World"?
    A. She's logical.   C. She's clumsy.
    B. She's calm.   D. She's hardworking.

13. Based on the illustration in "The Morning of the Green Snow," how does Josh feel as the snow piles up on his house and yard?
    A. happy   C. unhappy
    B. bored   D. excited

14. What does the word blaring mean in Paragraph 3 of "A Topsy-Turvy World"?
    A. ringing   C. smoking
    B. shaking   D. clapping

Part 3. Poetry
Read the poem and answer the questions.

Up, Up, and Away

1 Bright lights flash.
   Cameras click.
   People shout,
   "Hey, come quick!"

2 The big day
   Is here at last.
   Hello, future!
   Good-bye, past!

Name _____ Date _____

3 I run as fast
   As a rocket ship.
   My legs are engines.
   I dare not trip.

4 My mouth is a desert.
   My heart's a drum.
   I see a man
   Raise his thumb.

5 I watch a girl
   Begin to float,
   But not on water
   Like a boat.

6 She's floating on
   Nothing but air.
   She wears a smile.
   She hasn't a care.

7 And there's no need
   To wonder why:
   For finally
   People can fly!

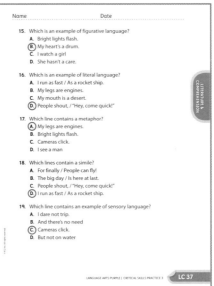

Name _____ Date _____

15. Which is an example of figurative language?
    A. Bright lights flash.
    B. My heart's a drum.
    C. I watch a girl
    D. She hasn't a care.

16. Which is an example of literal language?
    A. I run as fast / As a rocket ship.
    B. My legs are engines.
    C. My mouth is a desert.
    D. People shout, "Hey, come quick!"

17. Which line contains a metaphor?
    A. My legs are engines.
    B. Bright lights flash.
    C. Cameras click.
    D. I see a man

18. Which lines contain a simile?
    A. For finally / People can fly!
    B. The big day / Is here at last.
    C. People shout, / "Hey, come quick!"
    D. I run as fast / As a rocket ship.

19. Which line contains an example of sensory language?
    A. I dare not trip.
    B. And there's no need
    C. Cameras click.
    D. But not on water

 **varies**

Students will work **independently** to complete the online More Practice activity.

More Practice

Review the Skills

If students scored less than 80 percent or had difficulty meeting the objectives of the Unit Checkpoint, have them go online for more practice.

 Objectives
- Evaluate Unit Checkpoint results and choose activities for more practice.

 Reward: If students score 80 percent or more on the Unit Checkpoint, add a sticker for this unit on the My Accomplishments chart. If students did not score 80 percent or more, work with them to revise their work until they do score 80 percent, and then add a sticker to the My Accomplishments chart.

Semester Review and Checkpoint

Unit Focus

In this unit, students will review what they have learned about reading and understanding poetry, fiction texts, nonfiction texts, directions, and forms. Then they will complete the Semester Checkpoint to demonstrate their skills in literature comprehension.

Unit Plan		[Online]	[Offline]
Lesson 1	Semester Review	35 minutes	15 minutes
Lesson 2	Semester Checkpoint	35 minutes	15 minutes

Semester Review

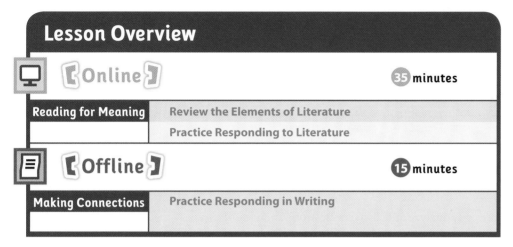

Lesson Overview

Online — 35 minutes

Reading for Meaning	Review the Elements of Literature
	Practice Responding to Literature

Offline — 15 minutes

Making Connections	Practice Responding in Writing

Materials

Supplied

- *K¹² Language Arts Activity Book*, pp. LC 69–73

Content Background

The Semester Review and Checkpoint marks the halfway point in the course. If students are not able to score above 70 percent on the Semester Review activities, Learning Coaches should seek assistance from a professional.

 **35 minutes**

Work **together** with students to complete the Get Ready and Reading for Meaning activities.

 **Reading for Meaning** •

Review the Elements of Literature

Students will play a game to help them review the elements of fiction, nonfiction, poetry, directions, and forms.

Practice Responding to Literature

Students will help the K[12] characters properly analyze and answer questions about a poem, a nonfiction passage, and a form.

Objectives

- Complete a semester review on the elements of literature and responding to literature, nonfiction, and practical writing.

[Offline] **15 minutes**

Work **together** with students to complete the offline Making Connections activity.

Making Connections •

Practice Responding in Writing

Students will review how to write responses to paired passages. Turn to pages LC 69–73 in K[12] *Language Arts Activity Book.*

1. Direct students' attention to the Activity Book pages and have them read the directions.

2. Have students read the stories and answer all questions.

3. Go over students' answers with them to make sure they understand how to respond to paired passages.

Objectives

- Differentiate among various literary genres.
- Summarize a work of literature and maintain accurate sequence.
- Write a summary.
- Identify problems and solutions in a story.
- Identify the moral or lesson in a fable.
- Compare and contrast literary elements in two or more literary selections.

Semester Review

Semester Review
Practice Responding in Writing

Read the two stories, and then answer the questions.

The Jay and the Peacocks
adapted from Aesop's fables

Once there was a jay who wanted to be a peacock. "Peacocks are such fine, beautiful birds," he thought. "They have such bright, colorful feathers that shine blue and green in the sun. And look at me just a plain, brown bird. Oh, I wish I could be a peacock!"

One morning, the jay flew down into the yard where the peacocks liked to walk. Peacock feathers were lying around the yard, glowing like blue-green jewels in the sun. The jay collected all the cast-off peacock feathers, tied them to his tail, and walked down to the peacocks. "How fine I look!" he thought.

But when the jay got close to the peacocks, they saw that he was only pretending. So they pecked at him and tore away all his fake feathers.

The jay was embarrassed. He flew back to sit with the other jays.

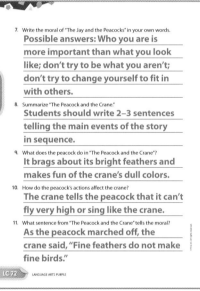

LANGUAGE ARTS PURPLE LC 69

But the other jays had watched him from the trees. They were angry with him, too. As they flew away, they cried, "Fine feathers do not make fine birds."

The Peacock and the Crane
adapted from Aesop's fables

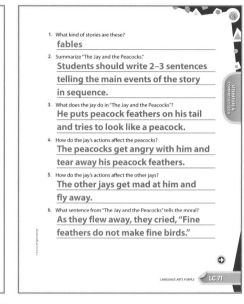

A peacock passed by a crane. The peacock spread its beautiful tail. It made fun of the crane's dull gray feathers.

"Look at me! I am dressed like a king, in all the bright colors of the rainbow," the peacock boasted. "You, however, have no color on your wings."

"This is true," answered the crane. "But I can fly as high as the heavens. My voice rises to the stars when I sing. You, on the other hand, can hardly fly at all. You are left to walk on the ground and drag your tail in the dirt."

As the peacock marched off, the crane said, "Fine feathers do not make fine birds."

LC 70 LANGUAGE ARTS PURPLE

---

1. What kind of stories are these?
   fables

2. Summarize "The Jay and the Peacocks."
   Students should write 2–3 sentences telling the main events of the story in sequence.

3. What does the jay do in "The Jay and the Peacocks"?
   He puts peacock feathers on his tail and tries to look like a peacock.

4. How do the jay's actions affect the peacocks?
   The peacocks get angry with him and tear away his peacock feathers.

5. How do the jay's actions affect the other jays?
   The other jays get mad at him and fly away.

6. What sentence from "The Jay and the Peacocks" tells the moral?
   As they flew away, they cried, "Fine feathers do not make fine birds."

LANGUAGE ARTS PURPLE LC 71

---

7. Write the moral of "The Jay and the Peacocks" in your own words.
   Possible answers: Who you are is more important than what you look like; don't try to be what you aren't; don't try to change yourself to fit in with others.

8. Summarize "The Peacock and the Crane."
   Students should write 2–3 sentences telling the main events of the story in sequence.

9. What does the peacock do in "The Peacock and the Crane"?
   It brags about its bright feathers and makes fun of the crane's dull colors.

10. How do the peacock's actions affect the crane?
    The crane tells the peacock that it can't fly very high or sing like the crane.

11. What sentence from "The Peacock and the Crane" tells the moral?
    As the peacock marched off, the crane said, "Fine feathers do not make fine birds."

LC 72 LANGUAGE ARTS PURPLE

---

12. Write the moral of "The Peacock and the Crane" in your own words.
    Possible answers: Don't brag, because everyone has something to be proud of; people who brag are not beautiful; beauty is what is on the inside not the outside.

13. Write a paragraph in which you compare and contrast the two fables.
    Students should write 4–5 sentences comparing and contrasting the two stories. For similarities, students may say the stories are fables, they are both about birds, there are peacocks in both stories, and the moral is the same. The differences include different birds (jays and cranes) and plots.

LANGUAGE ARTS PURPLE LC 73

Semester Checkpoint

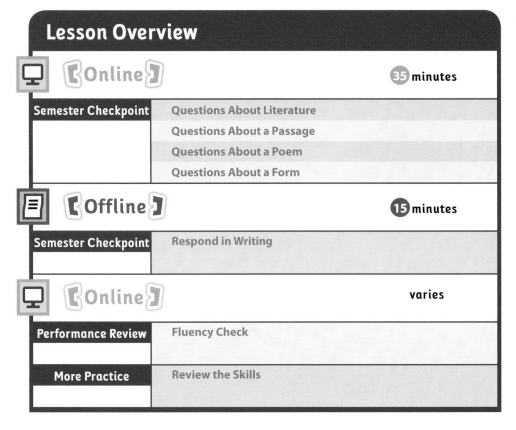

Lesson Overview

🖥 [Online]   35 minutes

Semester Checkpoint	Questions About Literature
	Questions About a Passage
	Questions About a Poem
	Questions About a Form

📄 [Offline]   15 minutes

Semester Checkpoint	Respond in Writing

🖥 [Online]   varies

Performance Review	Fluency Check
More Practice	Review the Skills

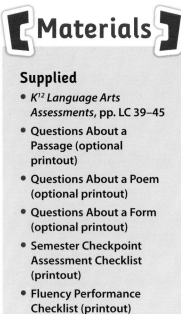

[Materials]

Supplied

- *K¹² Language Arts Assessments*, pp. LC 39–45
- Questions About a Passage (optional printout)
- Questions About a Poem (optional printout)
- Questions About a Form (optional printout)
- Semester Checkpoint Assessment Checklist (printout)
- Fluency Performance Checklist (printout)

Content Background

The Semester Review and Checkpoint marks the halfway point in the course. If students are not able to score above 70 percent on the Semester Checkpoint, Learning Coaches should seek assistance from a professional.

 **35 minutes**

Students will work **independently** to complete online Semester Checkpoint.

Semester Checkpoint ....

Questions About Literature

Students will answer multiple choice questions about the elements of fiction, nonfiction, and poetry. Questions will assess their knowledge of key terms and the names of significant characters in literature.

Questions About a Passage

Students will read a nonfiction passage and answer multiple choice questions about the text.

TIP If students are not comfortable reading the passage for this activity online, print Questions About a Passage and have students read the printout.

Objectives

- Complete a Semester Checkpoint on the elements of literature and responding to literature, nonfiction, and practical writing.
- Demonstrate knowledge of authors, characters, and events in significant works of literature.

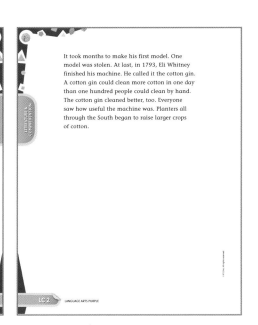

Questions About a Poem

Students will read a poem and answer multiple choice questions about the text.

TIP If students are not comfortable reading the passage for this activity online, print Questions About a Poem and have students read the printout.

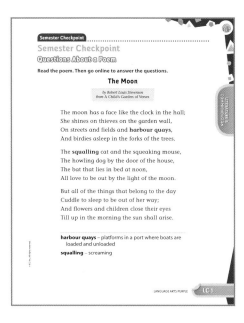

Questions About a Form

Students will answer questions about how to complete a form.

TIP If students are not comfortable reading the passage for this activity online, print Questions About a Form and have students read the printout.

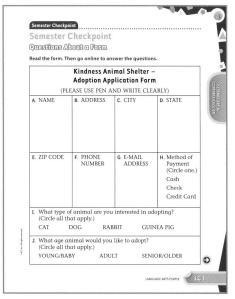

[Offline] 15 minutes

Work **together** with students to complete the offline Semester Checkpoint.

Semester Checkpoint

Respond in Writing
Explain that students are going to show what they have learned about comparing and contrasting two fables.

1. Give students the Semester Checkpoint pages.

2. Read the directions together.

3. Use the Answer Key to score the Checkpoint and the Semester Checkpoint Assessment Checklist to evaluate students' response to Question 12. Then enter the results online.

4. Review each exercise with students. Work with students to correct any exercise that they missed.

Part 1: Read Two Fables
Have students read "Lion's Surprise" and "The Dove and the Ant."

Part 2: Respond in Writing
Have students answer the questions.

Objectives
- Differentiate among various literary genres. (Identify fable.)
- Summarize a work of literature and maintain accurate sequence.
- Write a summary.
- Identify problems and solutions in a story.
- Identify the moral or lesson in a fable.
- Compare and contrast literary elements in two or more literary selections.

Name _____ Date _____

Semester Checkpoint Learning Coach Instructions
Respond in Writing

Explain that students are going to show what they have learned about comparing and contrasting two fables.

1. Give students the Semester Checkpoint pages.
2. Read the directions together.
3. Use the Answer Key to score the Checkpoint and the Semester Checkpoint Assessment Checklist to evaluate students' response to Question 12. Then enter the results online.
4. Review each exercise with students. Work with students to correct any exercise they missed.

Part 1: Read Two Fables
Have students read "Lion's Surprise" and "The Dove and the Ant."

Part 2: Respond in Writing
Have students answer the questions.

Name _____ Date _____

Semester Checkpoint Answer Key
Respond in Writing

Part 1. Read Two Fables
Read the two stories.

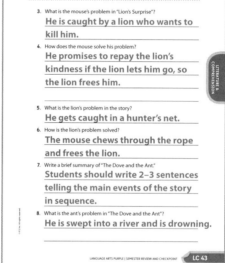

Lion's Surprise
by Anonymous

Lion was curled up in a sunny spot, taking his afternoon nap. A little mouse scurried over his face and woke him up from a pleasant dream.

Lion angrily clasped the mouse in his huge paw and was about to kill him when the mouse cried, "If you spare my life, I will repay your kindness someday."

Name _____ Date _____

"How could someone as small and weak as you help someone as great and powerful as me?" said Lion. Still, he laughed and let the little mouse go.

Later that day, Lion was caught by a hunter in a net made of rope. The mouse heard him roar, came and chewed through the rope, and set him free.

"I laughed when you said you could help me," said Lion, "but now I know that even a mouse can save a lion."

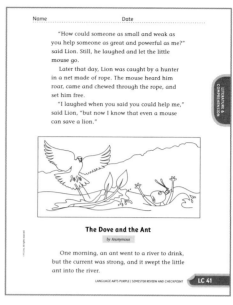

The Dove and the Ant
by Anonymous

One morning, an ant went to a river to drink, but the current was strong, and it swept the little ant into the river.

Name _____ Date _____

A dove saw the ant drowning, so she threw a stick into the river. The ant climbed up onto it and floated safely to shore. The dove had saved the ant's life.

"Thank you!" said the ant. "I hope that someday I can help you as you have helped me."

The dove laughed kindly. "My little friend," she said, "I thank you for your kind wishes, but I do not look for help from someone so small."

Later, the ant saw a man aim a gun at the dove. The ant stung the man's foot sharply. This made the man miss his shot and saved the dove's life.

So little friends can be great friends after all!

Part 2. Respond in Writing
Answer the questions.

1. What type of writing are these two stories?
   fables

2. Write a brief summary of "Lion's Surprise."
   Students should write 2–3 sentences telling the main events of the story in sequence.

Name _____ Date _____

3. What is the mouse's problem in "Lion's Surprise"?
   He is caught by a lion who wants to kill him.

4. How does the mouse solve his problem?
   He promises to repay the lion's kindness if the lion lets him go, so the lion frees him.

5. What is the lion's problem in the story?
   He gets caught in a hunter's net.

6. How is the lion's problem solved?
   The mouse chews through the rope and frees the lion.

7. Write a brief summary of "The Dove and the Ant."
   Students should write 2–3 sentences telling the main events of the story in sequence.

8. What is the ant's problem in "The Dove and the Ant"?
   He is swept into a river and is drowning.

Name _____ Date _____

9. How is the ant's problem solved?
   A dove saves him by throwing a stick into the river for the ant to climb onto.

10. What is the dove's problem in the story?
    A hunter is about to shoot her.

11. How is the dove's problem solved?
    The ant stings the hunter on the foot so that he misses his shot and the dove is saved.

12–17. Compare and contrast the two fables in a paragraph of at least five sentences.
- First, tell the titles of both stories.
- Then, tell how the stories are similar.
- Next, tell how they are different.
- Finally, tell about the morals of the stories and what a reader can learn from them

Use the rubric to score the paragraph. Enter the results online.

_____
_____
_____
_____

 **varies**

Review students' performance on the Warm-Up activities from the semester. Students will work **independently** to complete the online More Practice activity.

Performance Review

Fluency Check

Listen to students' recordings and use the Fluency Performance Checklist to review fluency and track performance. Keep the completed checklist so you can review students' progress over time.

 Objectives
- Read poetry and prose aloud.
- Create engaging audio recordings of stories or poems that demonstrate fluid reading at an understandable pace.

More Practice

Review the Skills

If students scored less than 80 percent on or had difficulty meeting the objectives of the Semester Checkpoint, have them go online for more practice.

If students are not able to score above 70 percent on the Semester Checkpoint, Learning Coaches should seek assistance from a professional.

 Objectives
- Evaluate Checkpoint results and choose activities to review.

 Reward: If students score 80 percent or more on the Semester Checkpoint, add a sticker for this unit on the My Accomplishments chart.

Writing Skills

Journals

Unit Focus

In this unit, students will learn about journals and journal writing. Before you begin working with students in this unit, watch Introduction to Writing Skills in Lesson 1 online. This introduction will give you important information about the Writing Skills program. Then read the K^{12} Language Arts Purple Course Overview at the beginning of this Lesson Guide. You do not have any other work to do for Lesson 1.

Beginning in Lesson 2, you will work with students on journal writing. Students will keep a journal and write in it frequently as they work through the units and lessons in this program. Their journal is a place for students to respond to prompts and to write independently. The writing that students do in their journal can be creative, thoughtful, and personal. It is writing that is not meant to be graded, and the intended audience for anything written in the journal is the student. While writing clearly and correctly is always encouraged, students should not worry if the writing they do in their journal contains mistakes in grammar, usage, or mechanics. By writing in a journal, students will practice and hone their ability to express themselves in writing. Such practice will lead to their becoming better writers.

A key way to excite students about writing in their journal is to stress the freedom that comes with journal writing. When students are about to write in their journal, encourage them to be creative, honest, and open-minded. Encourage them to follow where their imagination leads. Through journal writing, students can learn that writing can be fulfilling and fun.

Unit Plan		[Online]	[Offline]
Lesson 1	Introduction to Writing Skills	10 minutes	25 minutes
Lesson 2	Introduction to Journals	15 minutes	20 minutes
Lesson 3	Look Around	15 minutes	20 minutes
Lesson 4	Ideas and Dreams	15 minutes	20 minutes
Lesson 5	Write in Your Journal		35 minutes

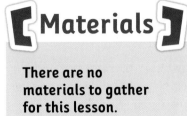

Introduction to Writing Skills

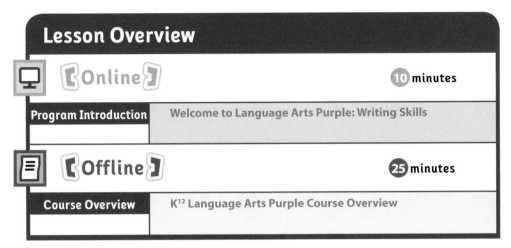

Lesson Overview

🖥 【Online】   ⏱ **10** minutes

Program Introduction	Welcome to Language Arts Purple: Writing Skills

📄 【Offline】   **25** minutes

Course Overview	K¹² Language Arts Purple Course Overview

【Materials】

There are no materials to gather for this lesson.

【Online】 **10** minutes

View the K¹² Language Arts Purple: Writing Skills Program Introduction with students.

Program Introduction ....

Welcome to Language Arts Purple: Writing Skills
Students will go online to view the introduction to learn how to navigate through the program and successfully complete their learning journey. View this introduction with students to learn more about your role in the program.

 Objectives
- Navigate the K¹² Language Arts Purple Writing Skills program online.

【Offline】 **25** minutes

Review the General Course Structure and Overview and the K¹² Language Arts Purple Writing Skills Program Overview.

Course Overview ....

K¹² Language Arts Purple Course Overview
Review the information on pages x–xxi and xxx–xxxv in *K¹² Language Arts Lesson Guide* if you have not already done so. Go to page viii to get started.

 Objectives
- Understand the general course overview and structure in K¹² Language Arts Purple.

Introduction to Journals

Lesson Overview

Online		**15** minutes
Composition	What Is a Journal?	
Offline		**20** minutes
Composition	Journal: Write About Yourself	

Big Ideas

- Journal writing is a form of freewriting. It is an opportunity to get ideas on paper without regard for correctness of the language or for the format of a piece of writing.
- To improve, writers require frequent practice.

Materials

Supplied
- *K¹² My Journal*, pp. 2–3

Keywords

freewriting – a way for a writer to pick a topic and write as much as possible about it within a set time limit

journal – a notebook where a writer regularly records experiences and ideas

journal entry – a response to a specific prompt or an instance of recording one's thoughts and experiences

writing prompt – a sentence or sentences that ask for a particular kind of writing

Online — 15 minutes

Students will work online to learn about journals and journal writing. Help students locate the online activity.

Composition

What Is a Journal?

By exploring what journals are and what purpose they serve, as well as seeing an example of the writing that Johnny does in his journal, students will learn what will be expected of them when they are told to write in their journal.

Objectives
- Recognize a journal prompt.
- Respond to a journal prompt.
- Freewrite about a topic.

[Offline] ⏱ 20 minutes

Have students complete the offline Composition activity.

Composition ●

✎ Journal: Write About Yourself

Students will respond to a journal prompt by writing about themselves. Gather *K¹² My Journal* and have students turn to pages 2 and 3.

> **Objectives**
> - Recognize a journal prompt.
> - Respond to a journal prompt.
> - Freewrite about a topic.

1. Tell students they are going to write in their journal about themselves and some of the things that are important to them. To help students respond to the prompt, ask them to think about their answers to the following questions.

   ▶ What are some of your favorite things? What are some of your least favorite things? Why?

   ▶ How would someone else describe you? What might that person say about what you are like or the way you behave?

   ▶ What are some of the things that matter most to you? Is it your family? Your friends? Your beliefs or ideas? Is it an activity or a hobby?

2. Have students respond to the prompt in their journal. Remind them to include details about themselves and the things they like, dislike, or consider important. Encourage students to write in complete sentences, although it is not a requirement when they are freewriting in their journal. Also, remind students that their writing will not be graded, so they need not be overly concerned with errors in spelling or mistakes in grammar, usage, or mechanics.

TIP Students should write for about 20 minutes. Freewriting allows students to use their imagination to write what they want without worrying about being graded, so encourage them to keep writing for the entire time. If students have trouble writing for 20 minutes, use the prompts in Step 1 or have them list ideas or words. If they want to keep writing beyond 20 minutes, praise them for their enthusiasm and offer to let them complete their entry later in the day as a reward.

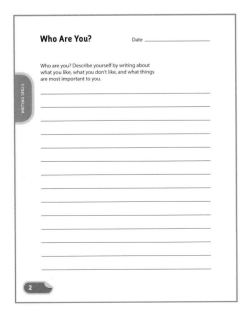

Look Around

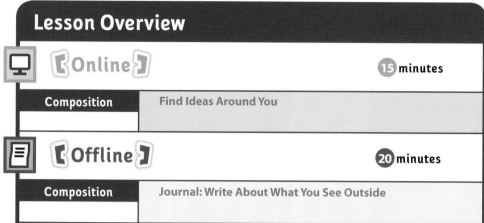

Lesson Overview

Online — 15 minutes

Composition	Find Ideas Around You

Offline — 20 minutes

Composition	Journal: Write About What You See Outside

Big Ideas

▸ Journal writing is a form of freewriting. It is an opportunity to get ideas on paper without regard for correctness of the language or for the format of a piece of writing.

▸ To improve, writers require frequent practice.

Materials

Supplied
- *K¹² My Journal*, pp. 4–5

Keywords

freewriting – a way for a writer to pick a topic and write as much as possible about it within a set time limit

journal – a notebook where a writer regularly records experiences and ideas

journal entry – a response to a specific prompt or an instance of recording one's thoughts and experiences

writing prompt – a sentence or sentences that ask for a particular kind of writing

Online 15 minutes

Students will work online to learn about using their powers of observation to provide ideas for a journal entry. Help students locate the online activity.

Composition ....

Find Ideas Around You
By seeing an example of how to use their senses to observe the world in order to describe it, students will learn how to respond to a writing prompt in their journal.

Objectives
- Recognize a journal prompt.
- Respond to a journal prompt.
- Freewrite about a topic.

 **20 minutes**

Have students complete the offline Composition activity.

Composition

 Journal: Write About What You See Outside

Students will respond to a journal prompt by writing about the world around them. Gather *K¹² My Journal* and have students turn to pages 4 and 5.

> **Objectives**
> - Recognize a journal prompt.
> - Respond to a journal prompt.
> - Freewrite about a topic.

1. Tell students they are going to write in their journal about what they observe when they look outside. To help students think of how to respond to the prompt, ask them to think about their answers to the following questions.

   ▸ What objects do you see? What shapes are the objects? Are they big or small? What colors are they? Do they remind you of anything? If so, what?

   ▸ What do you hear? Are the sounds loud or quiet? Do they come from nearby or far away? How would you write out the sounds if they were words?

   ▸ Do you smell anything? Are the smells good or bad? What do they remind you of?

   ▸ How do things that you see feel? Are they hard or soft? Rough or smooth? Warm or cold?

2. Have students respond to the prompt in their journal. Remind them to include details about what they see, hear, smell, taste, and touch. Encourage students to write in complete sentences, although it is not a requirement when they are freewriting in their journal. Also, remind students that their writing will not be graded, so they need not be overly concerned with errors in spelling or mistakes in grammar, usage, or mechanics.

TIP Students should write for about 20 minutes. Freewriting allows students to use their imagination to write what they want without worrying about being graded, so encourage them to keep writing for the entire time. If students have trouble writing for 20 minutes, use the prompts in Step 1 or have them list ideas or words. If they want to keep writing beyond 20 minutes, praise them for their enthusiasm and offer to let them complete their entry later in the day as a reward.

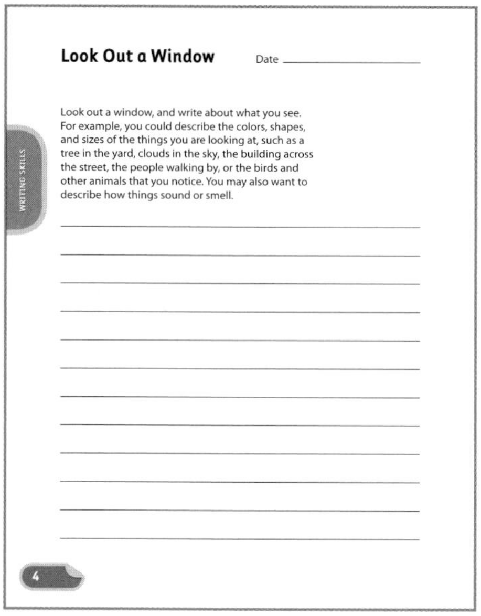

Look Out a Window   Date _____

Look out a window, and write about what you see.
For example, you could describe the colors, shapes,
and sizes of the things you are looking at, such as a
tree in the yard, clouds in the sky, the building across
the street, the people walking by, or the birds and
other animals that you notice. You may also want to
describe how things sound or smell.

_____

_____

_____

_____

_____

_____

_____

_____

_____

_____

_____

_____

4

Ideas and Dreams

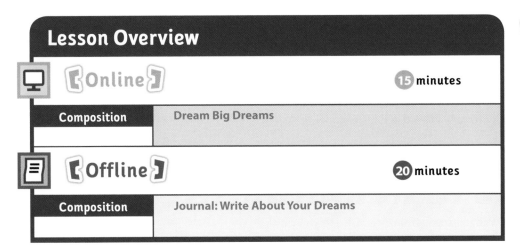

Lesson Overview

Online   **15** minutes

Composition	Dream Big Dreams

Offline   **20** minutes

Composition	Journal: Write About Your Dreams

Big Ideas

- ▶ Journal writing is a form of freewriting. It is an opportunity to get ideas on paper without regard for correctness of the language or for the format of a piece of writing.
- ▶ To improve, writers require frequent practice.

Materials

Supplied
- *K¹² My Journal*, pp. 6–7

Keywords

freewriting – a way for a writer to pick a topic and write as much as possible about it within a set time limit

journal – a notebook where a writer regularly records experiences and ideas

journal entry – a response to a specific prompt or an instance of recording one's thoughts and experiences

writing prompt – a sentence or sentences that ask for a particular kind of writing

 **15** minutes

Students will work online to learn about using a journal as a place to imagine and write about the future. Help students locate the online activity.

Composition

Dream Big Dreams

By seeing an example of how Johnny uses his journal as a place to write about some of his hopes and dreams for the future, students will learn about how to respond to a similar writing prompt in their journal.

Objectives
- Recognize a journal prompt.
- Respond to a journal prompt.
- Freewrite about a topic.

 **20 minutes**

Have students complete the offline Composition activity.

 Composition •

Journal: Write About Your Dreams

Students will respond to a journal prompt by writing about some of their own dreams and ideas for their future. Gather *K¹² My Journal* and have students turn to pages 6 and 7.

Objectives
- Recognize a journal prompt.
- Respond to a journal prompt.
- Freewrite about a topic.

1. Tell students they are going to write in their journal about what they hope to be or do when they are older. To help students think about how to respond to the prompt, ask them to think about their answers to the following questions.

   ▸ What do you like to do now? What are you interested in? Do you think there's a job that might let you keep doing the things you like to do when you're older?
   ▸ If you had your dream job, what would a day at work be like? For example, would you meet special people or go to special places?
   ▸ What would you have to learn or know to be able to do your dream job?
   ▸ Where would you go or what would you do to learn these things?

2. Have students respond to the prompt in their journal. Remind them to include details about the job they're thinking about having one day and explain why. Encourage students to write in complete sentences, although it is not a requirement when they are freewriting in their journal. Also, remind students that their writing will not be graded, so they need not be overly concerned with errors in spelling or mistakes in grammar, usage, or mechanics.

TIP Students should write for about 20 minutes. Freewriting allows students to use their imagination to write what they want without worrying about being graded, so encourage them to keep writing for the entire time. If students have trouble writing for 20 minutes, use the prompts in Step 1 or have them list ideas or words. If they want to keep writing beyond 20 minutes, praise them for their enthusiasm and offer to let them complete their entry later in the day as a reward.

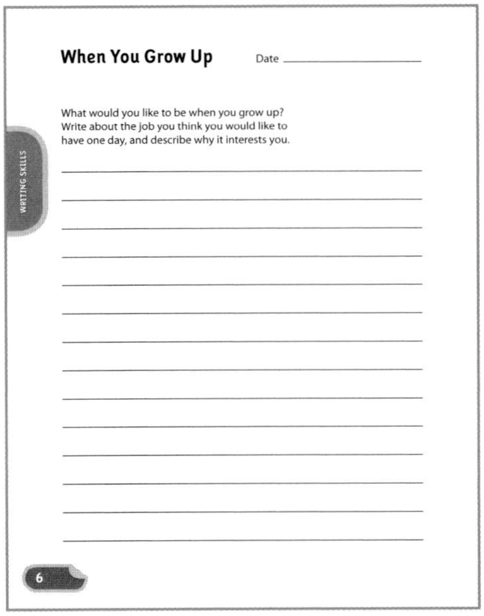

When You Grow Up   Date _____

What would you like to be when you grow up? Write about the job you think you would like to have one day, and describe why it interests you.

_____
_____
_____
_____
_____
_____
_____
_____
_____
_____
_____
_____
_____

6

Write in Your Journal

Lesson Overview

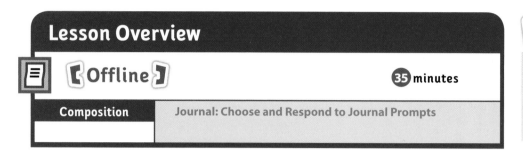Offline		35 minutes
Composition	Journal: Choose and Respond to Journal Prompts	

Materials

Supplied
• *K¹² My Journal*, pp. 8–15, 50–93

Keywords

freewriting – a way for a writer to pick a topic and write as much as possible about it within a set time limit

journal – a notebook where a writer regularly records experiences and ideas

journal entry – a response to a specific prompt or an instance of recording one's thoughts and experiences

writing prompt – a sentence or sentences that ask for a particular kind of writing

Big Ideas

▶ Journal writing is a form of free writing. It is an opportunity to get ideas on paper without regard for correctness of the language or for the format of a piece of writing.
▶ To improve, writers require frequent practice.

 35 minutes

Have students complete the offline Composition activity.

Composition ....

 Journal: Choose and Respond to Journal Prompts

Students will choose and respond to two journal prompts. Gather *K¹² My Journal* and have students turn to pages 8–15, as well as pages 50–93.

1. Tell students they are going to choose two prompts in their journal and respond to them. Give them time to page through pages 8–15 and pages 50–93 of their journal to read over the prompts and make their choice. If students have trouble choosing two prompts to respond to, ask them the following questions.

   ▶ Which prompts seem most interesting to you? Which ones deal with subjects that you like?
   ▶ Which prompts did you read and quickly begin to imagine what you would say? If you were going to discuss two prompts with your best friend, which ones would you talk about?

Objectives
• Respond to a journal prompt.
• Freewrite about a topic.

2. If students have trouble responding to one or both of the prompts they've selected, ask them to think about their answers to the following questions.

  ▸ What do you think of first when you think about this prompt? If you could talk about your response to this prompt rather than write it down, what would you say?

  ▸ Where else does your mind go when you think about this subject? Is there a way to connect what you are thinking about to what this prompt is asking or telling you to write?

  ▸ Would a family member or friend respond to this prompt differently than you would? If so, how would their response be different, and why?

3. Have students respond to the two prompts of their choosing in their journal. Remind them to include as many details as they can in their responses. Encourage students to write in complete sentences, although it is not a requirement when they are freewriting in their journal. Also, remind students that their writing will not be graded, so they need not be overly concerned with errors in spelling or mistakes in grammar, usage, or mechanics.

TIP Students should write for about 35 minutes. Freewriting allows students to use their imagination to write what they want without worrying about being graded, so encourage them to keep writing for the entire time. If students have trouble choosing prompts or writing for 35 minutes, use the prompts in Steps 1 and 2 or have them list ideas or words. If students want to keep writing beyond 35 minutes, praise them for their enthusiasm and offer to let them complete their entry later in the day as a reward.

Reward: When students complete both journal entries, add a sticker for this unit on the My Accomplishments chart.

Sentences

Unit Focus

In this unit, students will learn about sentences. They will

▶ Learn what a complete sentence is and how to identify one.

▶ Learn how to write a complete sentence correctly, avoiding errors in capitalization and punctuation at the start and end of the sentence.

▶ Identify the four kinds of sentences—declarative, interrogative, exclamatory, and imperative—and write each kind.

▶ Identify simple sentences, including those with compound parts, and practice writing them.

▶ Learn the difference between simple and compound sentences, as well as how to write compound sentences correctly.

▶ Examine the role of coordinating conjunctions in compound sentences.

▶ Identify complex sentences and their parts.

▶ Learn how to write complex sentences and examine the role of subordinating conjunctions in complex sentences.

Unit Plan

		[Online]	[Offline]
Lesson 1	Complete Sentences and Journal Entry	15 minutes	20 minutes
Lesson 2	Kinds of Sentences	20 minutes	15 minutes
Lesson 3	Simple Sentences (A)	20 minutes	15 minutes
Lesson 4	Simple Sentences (B)	20 minutes	15 minutes
Lesson 5	Compound Sentences (A)	20 minutes	15 minutes
Lesson 6	Compound Sentences (B)	20 minutes	15 minutes
Lesson 7	Complex Sentences (A)	20 minutes	15 minutes
Lesson 8	Complex Sentences (B)	20 minutes	15 minutes
Lesson 9	Unit Review	35 minutes	
Lesson 10	Unit Checkpoint	20 minutes	15 minutes

Complete Sentences and Journal Entry

Lesson Overview

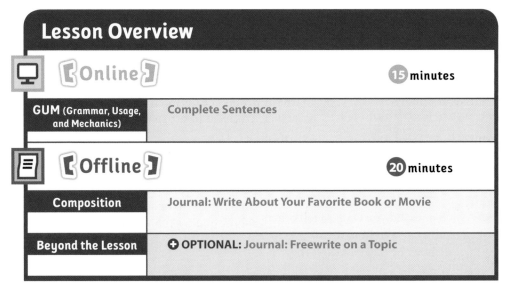

Online		**15** minutes
GUM (Grammar, Usage, and Mechanics)	Complete Sentences	
Offline		**20** minutes
Composition	Journal: Write About Your Favorite Book or Movie	
Beyond the Lesson	⊕ OPTIONAL: Journal: Freewrite on a Topic	

Materials

Supplied
- *K¹² My Journal*, pp. 16–17
- *Grammar Reference Guide* Online Book (optional)

Keywords

sentence – a group of words that tells a complete thought

Advance Preparation

To prepare for this lesson, review Complete Sentences in the *Grammar Reference Guide* (linked in the online lesson) to familiarize yourself with the topic.

Big Ideas

To be effective communicators, writers and speakers should recognize and use complete sentences.

Online   **15** minutes

Students will work online to complete activities on complete sentences. Help students locate the online activities.

GUM (Grammar, Usage, and Mechanics)

Complete Sentences

Students will learn what a complete sentence is and practice identifying complete sentences. They will also learn about proper capitalization and punctuation at the start and end of a complete sentence.

Objectives
- Identify a complete sentence.
- Recognize that a complete sentence begins with a capital letter and has an end mark.

 **20 minutes**

Have students complete the offline Composition and Beyond the Lesson activities.

Composition

 Journal: Write About Your Favorite Book or Movie

Students will respond to a journal prompt by describing their favorite book or movie. Gather *K¹² My Journal* and have students turn to pages 16 and 17.

Objectives
- Respond to a journal prompt.
- Freewrite about a topic.

1. Tell students they are going to write in their journal about their favorite book or movie. To help students think of a book that they enjoyed or a movie that they loved, ask them to think about their answers to the following questions.

   ▶ What books have you read? What movies have you seen? Which ones made you laugh or think a lot? Which ones did you want to tell others about as soon as you had finished reading or watching them?

   ▶ What was so good about your favorite book or movie? Was it the characters? Was it what happened? Was it the way reading or seeing it made you feel?

   ▶ Do you know anyone else who loves this book or movie? Why do they like it? Have you ever spoken to this person about the book or movie? If so, what did you say? If not, what would you say?

   ▶ Why should other people read this book or see this movie?

2. Have students respond to the prompt in their journal. Suggest that they include details about the characters, plot, and setting or settings of the book or movie, as well as to explain why the book or movie affected them as it did. Encourage students to write in complete sentences, although it is not a requirement when they are freewriting in their journal.

TIP Students should write for about 20 minutes. Freewriting allows students to use their imaginations to write what they want without worrying about being graded, so encourage them to keep writing for the entire time. If students have trouble writing for 20 minutes, use the prompting questions in Step 1 or have them list ideas or words. If they want to keep writing beyond 20 minutes, praise them for their enthusiasm and offer to let them complete their entry later in the day as a reward.

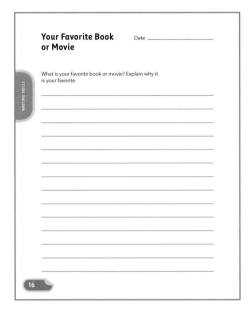

Beyond the Lesson

✏ ⊕ OPTIONAL: Journal: Freewrite on a Topic

This activity is OPTIONAL. It is intended for students who have extra time and would benefit from extra practice. Feel free to skip this activity. Gather *K¹² My Journal*.

1. Have students either respond to a prompt in Thoughts and Experiences (pages 50–93) or write about their own topic on the next available page in Ideas (pages 96–139).

2. Encourage students to explore their thoughts and write as much as they want. There are no rules. If students wish, ideas can be fleshed out into a more developed composition at a later time.

3. If students feel comfortable sharing what they wrote, encourage them to share with you or their peers.

TIP Studies show that students who write more frequently become better writers.

Objectives
- Respond to a journal prompt.
- Freewrite about a topic.

Kinds of Sentences

Lesson Overview

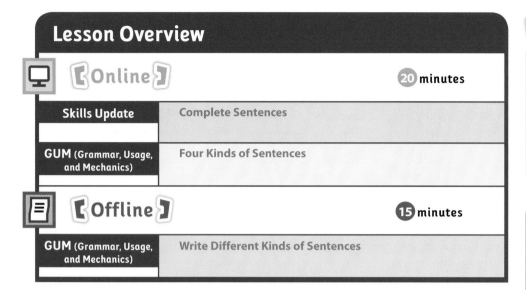

Online   20 minutes

Skills Update	Complete Sentences
GUM (Grammar, Usage, and Mechanics)	Four Kinds of Sentences

Offline   15 minutes

GUM (Grammar, Usage, and Mechanics)	Write Different Kinds of Sentences

Advance Preparation

To prepare for this lesson, review Kinds of Sentences in the *Grammar Reference Guide* (linked in the online lesson) to familiarize yourself with the topic.

Big Ideas

▶ By using the four kinds of sentences, writers and speakers can communicate a full range of ideas.
▶ Using different kinds of sentences helps writers and speakers express their ideas accurately.

Materials

Supplied

• *K¹² Language Arts Activity Book*, p. WS 1
• *Grammar Reference Guide* Online Book (optional)

Keywords

declarative sentence – a group of words that makes a statement

exclamatory sentence – a group of words that shows strong feeling

imperative sentence – a group of words that gives a command or makes a request

interrogative sentence – a group of words that asks a question

 **20 minutes**

Students will work online to review complete sentences and to complete activities on the four kinds of sentences. Help students locate the online activities.

Skills Update

Complete Sentences

Students will review how to identify complete sentences by answering Skills Update questions. Sit with students as they do this activity and note if they answer correctly.

⤷ **Learning Coach Check-In** How did students do on the Skills Update?

▸ **All answers correct:** Great! Skip the review screen and go on to the next activity.

▸ **Any answers incorrect:** Take a few minutes to review complete sentences now. Use the links on the screen after the Skills Update to take another look at the online activities or review Complete Sentences in the *Grammar Reference Guide* together.

 This activity will require extra time if students need to review complete sentences. Take the extra 5–10 minutes to review now because new skills build on what students have already learned.

Objectives
- Identify a complete sentence.
- Recognize that a complete sentence begins with a capital letter and has an end mark.

GUM (Grammar, Usage, and Mechanics)

Four Kinds of Sentences

Students will learn about the four kinds of sentences: declarative, exclamatory, imperative, and interrogative. They will then practice identifying the kinds of sentences and punctuating them correctly.

Objectives
- Identify declarative sentences.
- Identify exclamatory sentences.
- Identify imperative sentences.
- Identify interrogative sentences.
- Recognize that a complete sentence begins with a capital letter and has an end mark.

 **15 minutes**

Have students complete the offline GUM activity.

GUM (Grammar, Usage, and Mechanics) ....

Write Different Kinds of Sentences

Students will write one of each kind of sentence. Turn to page WS 1 in *K¹² Language Arts Activity Book.*

Objectives
- Use declarative sentences.
- Use exclamatory sentences.
- Use imperative sentences.
- Use interrogative sentences.

1. Direct students' attention to the Activity Book page and have them read the directions.

2. Have students complete the Activity Book page. Provide support as necessary, reminding students that the rules of capitalization and punctuation apply, no matter what kind of sentence they are writing.

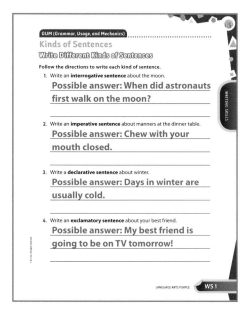

Simple Sentences (A)

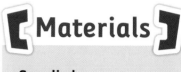

Lesson Overview

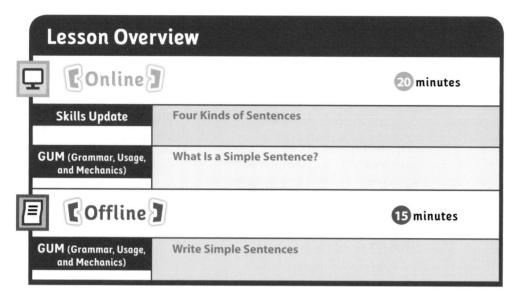

🖥 **[Online]**		**20** minutes
Skills Update	Four Kinds of Sentences	
GUM (Grammar, Usage, and Mechanics)	What Is a Simple Sentence?	
📄 **[Offline]**		**15** minutes
GUM (Grammar, Usage, and Mechanics)	Write Simple Sentences	

Advance Preparation

To prepare for this lesson, review Structure of Sentences (Simple Sentence) in the *Grammar Reference Guide* (linked in the online lesson) to familiarize yourself with the topic.

Big Ideas

Varying the structure of sentences—simple, compound, complex, compound-complex—makes writing more interesting to readers.

[Materials]

Supplied

• *K¹² Language Arts Activity Book*, p. WS 2
• *Grammar Reference Guide* Online Book (optional)

Keywords

simple sentence – a sentence that is one independent part, a group of words with one subject and one verb that express a complete thought

 **minutes**

Students will work online to review the four kinds of sentences and to complete activities on simple sentences. Help students locate the online activities.

Skills Update

Four Kinds of Sentences

Students will review how to identify declarative, exclamatory, imperative, and interrogative sentences by answering Skills Update questions. Sit with students as they do this activity and note if they answer correctly.

⮑ **Learning Coach Check-In** How did students do on the Skills Update?

- ▸ **All answers correct:** Great! Skip the review screen and go on to the next activity.
- ▸ **Any answers incorrect:** Take a few minutes to review the four kinds of sentences now. Use the links on the screen after the Skills Update to take another look at the online activities or review Kinds of Sentences in the *Grammar Reference Guide* together.

TIP This activity will require extra time if students need to review the four kinds of sentences. Take the extra 5–10 minutes to review now because new skills build on what students have already learned.

> **Objectives**
> - Identify declarative sentences.
> - Identify exclamatory sentences.
> - Identify imperative sentences.
> - Identify interrogative sentences.

GUM (Grammar, Usage, and Mechanics)

What Is a Simple Sentence?

Students will learn what a simple sentence is and practice identifying simple sentences.

> **Objectives**
> - Identify simple sentences.

 **Offline** **15 minutes**

Have students complete the offline GUM activity.

GUM (Grammar, Usage, and Mechanics)

Write Simple Sentences

Students will write some simple sentences. Turn to page WS 2 in *K¹² Language Arts Activity Book*.

1. Direct students' attention to the Activity Book page and have them read the directions.

2. Have students complete the Activity Book page. Provide support as necessary, reminding students that the rules of capitalization and punctuation apply to all sentences.

Objectives
• Write simple sentences.

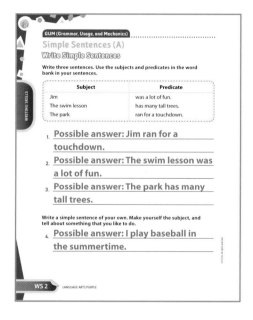

Simple Sentences (B)

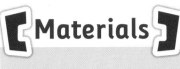

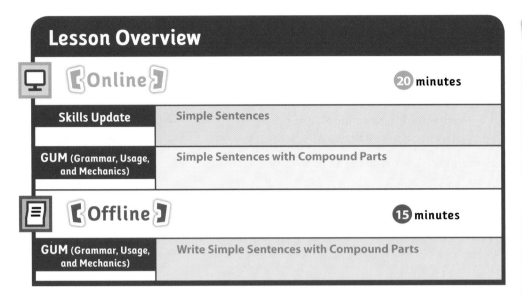

Lesson Overview

🖥 【Online】   20 minutes

Skills Update	Simple Sentences
GUM (Grammar, Usage, and Mechanics)	Simple Sentences with Compound Parts

☰ 【Offline】   15 minutes

GUM (Grammar, Usage, and Mechanics)	Write Simple Sentences with Compound Parts

【Materials】

Supplied
- *K¹² Language Arts Activity Book*, p. WS 3
- *Grammar Reference Guide* Online Book (optional)

Keywords

simple sentence – a sentence that is one independent part, a group of words with one subject and one verb that express a complete thought

Advance Preparation

To prepare for this lesson, review Structure of Sentences (Simple Sentence) in the *Grammar Reference Guide* (linked in the online lesson) to familiarize yourself with the topic.

Big Ideas

Varying the structure of sentences—simple, compound, complex, compound-complex—makes writing more interesting to readers.

 ⟨20⟩ **minutes**

Students will work online to review simple sentences and to complete activities on simple sentences with compound parts. Help students locate the online activities.

Skills Update ●

Simple Sentences
Students will review how to identify simple sentences by answering Skills Update questions. Sit with students as they do this activity and note if they answer correctly.

 Objectives
• Identify simple sentences.

⤵ **Learning Coach Check-In** How did students do on the Skills Update?
▸ **All answers correct:** Great! Skip the review screen and go on to the next activity.
▸ **Any answers incorrect:** Take a few minutes to review simple sentences now. Use the links on the screen after the Skills Update to take another look at the online activities or review Structure of Sentences (Simple Sentence) in the *Grammar Reference Guide* together.

TIP This activity will require extra time if students need to review simple sentences. Take the extra 5–10 minutes to review now because new skills build on what students have already learned.

GUM (Grammar, Usage, and Mechanics) ●

Simple Sentences with Compound Parts
Students will learn what a simple sentence with a compound part is and practice identifying simple sentences with compound parts.

 Objectives
• Identify simple sentences.

 **15 minutes**

Have students complete the offline GUM activity.

GUM (Grammar, Usage, and Mechanics)

Write Simple Sentences with Compound Parts

Students will write some simple sentences with compound parts. Turn to page WS 3 in *K¹² Language Arts Activity Book*.

1. Direct students' attention to the activity page and have them read the directions.

2. Have students complete the Activity Book page. Provide support as necessary, reminding students that the rules of capitalization and punctuation apply to all sentences.

Objectives
- Write simple sentences.

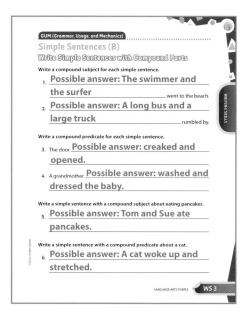

Compound Sentences (A)

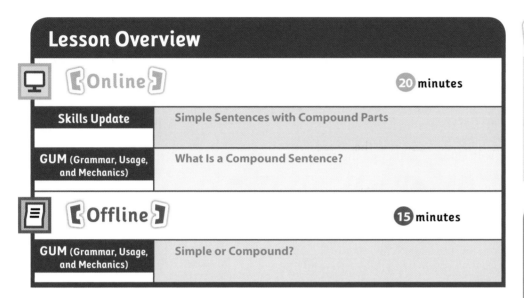

Lesson Overview

🖥 〔Online〕 — 20 minutes

Skills Update	Simple Sentences with Compound Parts
GUM (Grammar, Usage, and Mechanics)	What Is a Compound Sentence?

≣ 〔Offline〕 — 15 minutes

GUM (Grammar, Usage, and Mechanics)	Simple or Compound?

〔Materials〕

Supplied
- *K¹² Language Arts Activity Book*, p. WS 4
- *Grammar Reference Guide* Online Book (optional)

Keywords

compound sentence – a sentence that has at least two independent parts

conjunction – a word used to join parts of a sentence, such as *and*, *but*, and *or*

Advance Preparation

To prepare for this lesson, review Structure of Sentences (Compound Sentence) in the *Grammar Reference Guide* (linked in the online lesson) to familiarize yourself with the topic.

Big Ideas

Varying the structure of sentences—simple, compound, complex, compound-complex —makes writing more interesting to readers.

 **20 minutes**

Students will work online to review simple sentences with compound parts and to complete activities on compound sentences. Help students locate the online activities.

Skills Update

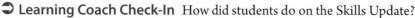

Simple Sentences with Compound Parts

Students will review how to identify simple sentences with compound parts by answering Skills Update questions. Sit with students as they do this activity and note if they answer correctly.

> ➲ **Learning Coach Check-In** How did students do on the Skills Update?
>
> ▸ **All answers correct:** Great! Skip the review screen and go on to the next activity.
>
> ▸ **Any answers incorrect:** Take a few minutes to review simple sentences with compound parts now. Use the links on the screen after the Skills Update to take another look at the online activities or review Structure of Sentences (Simple Sentence) in the *Grammar Reference Guide* together.

TIP This activity will require extra time if students need to review simple sentences with compound parts. Take the extra 5–10 minutes to review now because new skills build on what students have already learned.

Objectives
- Identify simple sentences.

GUM (Grammar, Usage, and Mechanics)

What Is a Compound Sentence?

Students will learn what a compound sentence is, what a conjunction is, and will practice identifying compound sentences and conjunctions.

TIP The conjunctions used in compound sentences are called *coordinating conjunctions*. However, we are not using that term with students and are just referring to them as *conjunctions*.

Objectives
- Identify compound sentences.
- Identify coordinating conjunctions.
- Use coordinating conjunctions.

 **Offline** **15** minutes

Have students complete the offline GUM activity.

GUM (Grammar, Usage, and Mechanics) ....

Simple or Compound?

Students will identify whether sentences are simple or compound. Then they will identify the conjunctions in compound sentences. Turn to page WS 4 in *K¹² Language Arts Activity Book.*

1. Direct students' attention to the Activity Book page and have them read the directions.

2. Have students complete the Activity Book page. Provide support as necessary, reminding students that compound sentences are made up of at least two independent parts that are joined with a conjunction.

Objectives
- Identify compound sentences.
- Identify coordinating conjunctions.
- Use coordinating conjunctions.

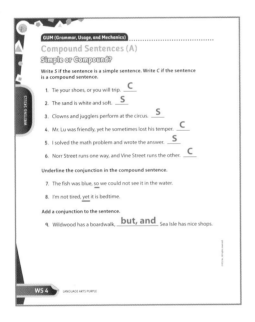

Compound Sentences (B)

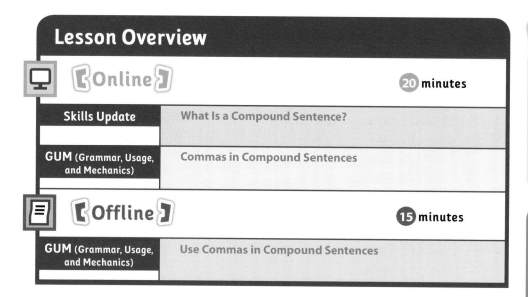

Lesson Overview

🖥 【Online】   20 minutes

Skills Update	What Is a Compound Sentence?
GUM (Grammar, Usage, and Mechanics)	Commas in Compound Sentences

📄 【Offline】   15 minutes

GUM (Grammar, Usage, and Mechanics)	Use Commas in Compound Sentences

【Materials】

Supplied

- *K¹² Language Arts Activity Book*, p. WS 5
- *Grammar Reference Guide*, Online Book (optional)

Keywords

compound sentence – a sentence that has at least two independent parts

conjunction – a word used to join parts of a sentence, such as *and*, *but*, and *or*

Advance Preparation

To prepare for this lesson, review Structure of Sentences (Compound Sentence) in the *Grammar Reference Guide* (linked in the online lesson) to familiarize yourself with the topic.

Big Ideas

Varying the structure of sentences—simple, compound, complex, compound-complex—makes writing more interesting to readers.

 **minutes**

Students will work online to review compound sentences and complete activities on using commas in compound sentences. Help students locate the online activities.

Skills Update

What Is a Compound Sentence?
Students will review how to identify compound sentences by answering Skills Update questions. Sit with students as they do this activity and note if they answer correctly.

> **⟳ Learning Coach Check-In**   How did students do on the Skills Update?
> - ▶ **All answers correct:** Great! Skip the review screen and go on to the next activity.
> - ▶ **Any answers incorrect:** Take a few minutes to review compound sentences now. Use the links on the screen after the Skills Update to take another look at the online activities or review Structure of Sentences (Compound Sentence) in the *Grammar Reference Guide* together.

TIP This activity will require extra time if students need to review compound sentences. Take the extra 5–10 minutes to review now because new skills build on what students have already learned.

Objectives
- Identify compound sentences.

GUM (Grammar, Usage, and Mechanics)

Commas in Compound Sentences
Students will learn how to form and punctuate compound sentences correctly. Then they will practice identifying correctly written compound sentences.

Objectives
- Form compound sentences.
- Use coordinating conjunctions.
- Use a comma before the conjunction in a compound sentence.

 **Offline** ⏱ **15** minutes

Have students complete the offline GUM activity.

GUM (Grammar, Usage, and Mechanics) ··

Use Commas in Compound Sentences

Students will place commas in compound sentences and form compound sentences from simple sentences. Turn to page WS 5 in *K¹² Language Arts Activity Book.*

1. Direct students' attention to the Activity Book page and have them read the directions.

2. Have students complete the Activity Book page. Provide support as necessary, reminding students that commas come before conjunctions in compound sentences.

Objectives
- Use a comma before the conjunction in a compound sentence.
- Write compound sentences.
- Use coordinating conjunctions.

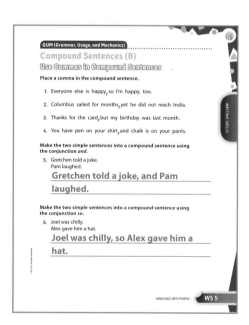

Complex Sentences (A)

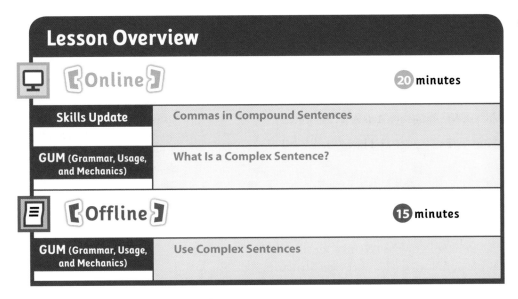

Lesson Overview

Online — 20 minutes

Skills Update	Commas in Compound Sentences
GUM (Grammar, Usage, and Mechanics)	What Is a Complex Sentence?

Offline — 15 minutes

GUM (Grammar, Usage, and Mechanics)	Use Complex Sentences

Materials

Supplied
- *K¹² Language Arts Activity Book*, p. WS 6
- *Grammar Reference Guide* Online Book (optional)

Keywords

complex sentence – a sentence that has one independent part and at least one dependent part

Advance Preparation

To prepare for this lesson, review Structure of Sentences (Complex Sentence) in the *Grammar Reference Guide* (linked in the online lesson) to familiarize yourself with the topic.

Big Ideas

Varying the structure of sentences—simple, compound, complex, compound-complex—makes writing more interesting to readers.

 **Online** 20 **minutes**

Students will work online to review commas in compound sentences and complete activities on identifying complex sentences. Help students locate the online activities.

Skills Update

Commas in Compound Sentences

Students will review how to use commas in compound sentences by answering Skills Update questions. Sit with students as they do this activity and note if they answer correctly.

⮌ **Learning Coach Check-In** How did students do on the Skills Update?

▸ **All answers correct:** Great! Skip the review screen and go on to the next activity.

▸ **Any answers incorrect:** Take a few minutes to review how to use commas in compound sentences now. Use the links on the screen after the Skills Update to take another look at the online activities or review Structure of Sentences (Compound Sentence) in the *Grammar Reference Guide* together.

 TIP This activity will require extra time if students need to review how to use commas in compound sentences. Take the extra 5–10 minutes to review now because new skills build on what students have already learned.

Objectives
- Identify compound sentences.
- Use a comma before the conjunction in a compound sentence.

GUM (Grammar, Usage, and Mechanics)

What Is a Complex Sentence?

Students will learn what a complex sentence is. Then they will practice identifying complex sentences.

Objectives
- Identify complex sentences.

 **15 minutes**

Have students complete the offline GUM activity.

GUM (Grammar, Usage, and Mechanics) ••

Use Complex Sentences

Students will practice forming complex sentences. Turn to page WS 6 in
K¹² Language Arts Activity Book.

Objectives
• Use complex sentences.

1. Direct students' attention to the Activity Book page and have them read
   the directions.

2. Have students complete the Activity Book page. Provide support as necessary,
   reminding students that all rules regarding capitalization and punctuation
   apply. Also remind them that if the dependent part begins a complex sentence,
   a comma must follow the dependent part.

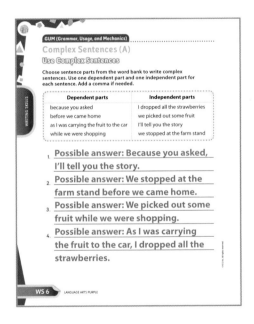

Complex Sentences (B)

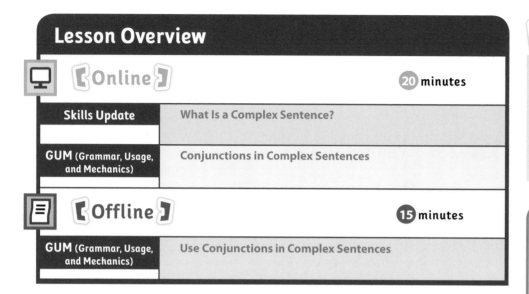

Lesson Overview

🖥 〖Online〗   20 minutes

Skills Update	What Is a Complex Sentence?
GUM (Grammar, Usage, and Mechanics)	Conjunctions in Complex Sentences

📄 〖Offline〗   15 minutes

GUM (Grammar, Usage, and Mechanics)	Use Conjunctions in Complex Sentences

〖Materials〗

Supplied

- *K¹² Language Arts Activity Book*, p. WS 7
- *Grammar Reference Guide* Online Book (optional)

Keywords

complex sentence – a sentence that has one independent part and at least one dependent part

conjunction – a word used to join parts of a sentence, such as *and*, *but*, and *or*

Advance Preparation

To prepare for this lesson, review Structure of Sentences (Complex Sentence) in the *Grammar Reference Guide* (linked in the online lesson) to familiarize yourself with the topic.

Big Ideas

Varying the structure of sentences—simple, compound, complex, compound-complex—makes writing more interesting to readers.

 **20 minutes**

Students will work online to review how to identify complex sentences and to complete activities on using conjunctions in complex sentences. Help students locate the online activities.

Skills Update

What Is a Complex Sentence?

Students will review how to identify complex sentences by answering Skills Update questions. Sit with students as they do this activity and note if they answer correctly.

 Objectives
- Identify complex sentences.

⟳ **Learning Coach Check-In** How did students do on the Skills Update?
  ▸ **All answers correct:** Great! Skip the review screen and go on to the next activity.
  ▸ **Any answers incorrect:** Take a few minutes to review how to identify complex sentences now. Use the links on the screen after the Skills Update to take another look at the online activities or review Structure of Sentences (Complex Sentence) in the *Grammar Reference Guide* together.

TIP This activity will require extra time if students need to review how to identify complex sentences. Take the extra 5–10 minutes to review now because new skills build on what students have already learned.

GUM (Grammar, Usage, and Mechanics)

Conjunctions in Complex Sentences

Students will learn about the parts of complex sentences and how to use conjunctions in complex sentences. Then they will practice identifying the parts of complex sentences and using appropriate conjunctions in complex sentences.

 Objectives
- Identify complex sentences.
- Use subordinating conjunctions in a complex sentence.

TIP Subordinating conjunctions are the kind of conjunctions that are used in complex sentences. Although students will use subordinating conjunctions to create complex sentences, we will not be using the word *subordinating* with them.

Offline 15 minutes

Have students complete the offline GUM activity.

GUM (Grammar, Usage, and Mechanics) ·

Use Conjunctions in Complex Sentences

Students will practice using appropriate conjunctions in complex sentences and writing complex sentences of their own. Turn to page WS 7 in *K¹² Language Arts Activity Book*.

1. Direct students' attention to the Activity Book page and have them read the directions.

2. Have students complete the Activity Book page. Provide support as necessary, reminding students that the meaning of a complex sentence often relies on its conjunction.

Objectives

* Use subordinating conjunctions in a complex sentence.
* Write complex sentences.

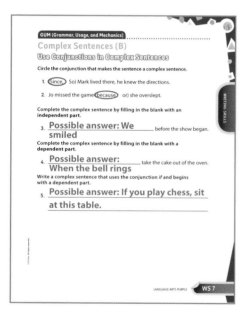

Unit Review

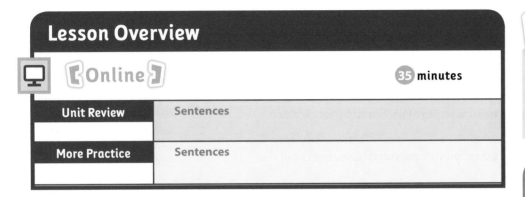

Lesson Overview

Online   **35** minutes

Unit Review	Sentences
More Practice	Sentences

Keywords

complex sentence – a sentence that has one independent part and at least one dependent part

compound sentence – a sentence that has at least two independent parts

conjunction – a word used to join parts of a sentence, such as *and*, *but*, and *or*

declarative sentence – a group of words that makes a statement

exclamatory sentence – a group of words that shows strong feeling

imperative sentence – a group of words that gives a command or makes a request

interrogative sentence – a group of words that asks a question

sentence – a group of words that tells a complete thought

simple sentence – a sentence that is one independent part, a group of words with one subject and one verb that express a complete thought

 **minutes**

Students will work online to review the grammar, usage, and mechanics skills learned in the unit. Help students locate the online activities.

Unit Review

Sentences

Students will review what they have learned about sentences to prepare for the Unit Checkpoint.

 TIP A full list of objectives covered in the Unit Review can be found in the online lesson.

Objectives
- Complete a review of grammar, usage, and mechanics skills.

More Practice

Sentences

Go over students' results on the Unit Review and, if necessary, have them complete the appropriate review activities listed in the table online. Help students locate the activities and provide support as needed.

 TIP The time students need to complete this activity will vary. Set aside enough time for students to complete all review activities if they need to do so.

Objectives
- Evaluate Unit Review results and choose activities for more practice.

Unit Checkpoint

Lesson Overview

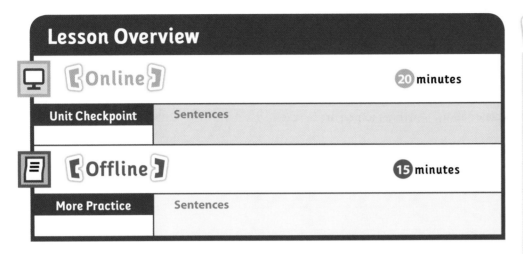

Online — 20 minutes

Unit Checkpoint	Sentences

Offline — 15 minutes

More Practice	Sentences

Materials

Supplied

- *Grammar Reference Guide* Online Book (optional)
- Complete Sentences (optional printout)
- Kinds of Sentences (optional printout)
- Simple Sentences (optional printout)
- Compound Sentences (optional printout)
- Complex Sentences (optional printout)

Keywords

complex sentence – a sentence that has one independent part and at least one dependent part

compound sentence – a sentence that has at least two independent parts

conjunction – a word used to join parts of a sentence, such as *and*, *but*, and *or*

declarative sentence – a group of words that makes a statement

exclamatory sentence – a group of words that shows strong feeling

imperative sentence – a group of words that gives a command or makes a request

interrogative sentence – a group of words that asks a question

sentence – a group of words that tells a complete thought

simple sentence – a sentence that is one independent part, a group of words with one subject and one verb that express a complete thought

 **Online** **minutes**

Students will work online **independently** to complete the Unit Checkpoint. Help students locate the Unit Checkpoint and provide support as necessary.

Unit Checkpoint

Sentences

Students will complete an online Unit Checkpoint about sentences. If necessary, read the directions to students.

TIP A full list of objectives covered in the Unit Checkpoint can be found in the online lesson.

> **Objectives**
> • Complete a Unit Checkpoint on grammar, usage, and mechanics skills.

Offline **minutes**

Work **together** with students to complete the offline More Practice activity.

More Practice

Sentences

Go over students' results on the Unit Checkpoint and, if necessary, print out and have them complete the appropriate practice pages listed in the table online. Students can complete all necessary pages now, or if more time is needed, they can spread them out over the next few days. If students scored less than 80 percent on the Unit Checkpoint, you may want them to retake the checkpoint after completing the additional activity pages.

TIP The time students need to complete this activity will vary. Set aside enough time for students to complete some or all activity pages and to retake the Unit Checkpoint, if they need to do so. Students may retake the Unit Checkpoint immediately, but having them complete the practice pages and then retake it might be more effective.

> **Objectives**
> • Evaluate Unit Checkpoint results and choose activities for more practice.

 Reward: When students score 80 percent or above on the Unit Checkpoint, add a sticker for this unit on the My Accomplishments chart.

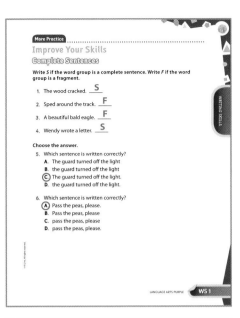

More Practice

Improve Your Skills

Complete Sentences

Write *S* if the word group is a complete sentence. Write *F* if the word group is a fragment.

1. The wood cracked. **S**
2. Sped around the track. **F**
3. A beautiful bald eagle. **F**
4. Wendy wrote a letter. **S**

Choose the answer.

5. Which sentence is written correctly?
   A. The guard turned off the light
   B. the guard turned off the light
   C. The guard turned off the light.
   D. the guard turned off the light.

6. Which sentence is written correctly?
   A. Pass the peas, please.
   B. Pass the peas, please
   C. pass the peas, please.
   D. pass the peas, please.

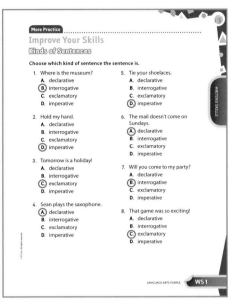

More Practice

Improve Your Skills

Kinds of Sentences

Choose which kind of sentence the sentence is.

1. Where is the museum?
   A. declarative
   B. interrogative
   C. exclamatory
   D. imperative

2. Hold my hand.
   A. declarative
   B. interrogative
   C. exclamatory
   D. imperative

3. Tomorrow is a holiday!
   A. declarative
   B. interrogative
   C. exclamatory
   D. imperative

4. Sean plays the saxophone.
   A. declarative
   B. interrogative
   C. exclamatory
   D. imperative

5. Tie your shoelaces.
   A. declarative
   B. interrogative
   C. exclamatory
   D. imperative

6. The mail doesn't come on Sundays.
   A. declarative
   B. interrogative
   C. exclamatory
   D. imperative

7. Will you come to my party?
   A. declarative
   B. interrogative
   C. exclamatory
   D. imperative

8. That game was so exciting!
   A. declarative
   B. interrogative
   C. exclamatory
   D. imperative

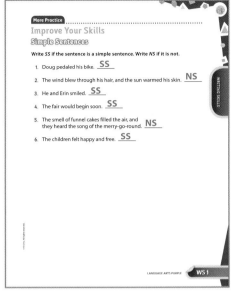

More Practice

Improve Your Skills

Simple Sentences

Write *SS* if the sentence is a simple sentence. Write *NS* if it is not.

1. Doug pedaled his bike. **SS**
2. The wind blew through his hair, and the sun warmed his skin. **NS**
3. He and Erin smiled. **SS**
4. The fair would begin soon. **SS**
5. The smell of funnel cakes filled the air, and they heard the song of the merry-go-round. **NS**
6. The children felt happy and free. **SS**

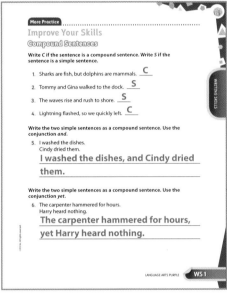

More Practice

Improve Your Skills

Compound Sentences

Write *C* if the sentence is a compound sentence. Write *S* if the sentence is a simple sentence.

1. Sharks are fish, but dolphins are mammals. **C**
2. Tommy and Gina walked to the dock. **S**
3. The waves rise and rush to shore. **S**
4. Lightning flashed, so we quickly left. **C**

Write the two simple sentences as a compound sentence. Use the conjunction *and*.

5. I washed the dishes.
   Cindy dried them.

   I washed the dishes, and Cindy dried them.

Write the two simple sentences as a compound sentence. Use the conjunction *yet*.

6. The carpenter hammered for hours.
   Harry heard nothing.

   The carpenter hammered for hours, yet Harry heard nothing.

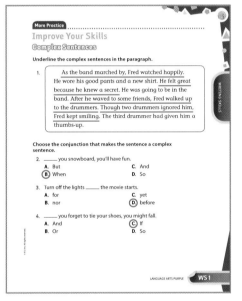

More Practice

Improve Your Skills

Complex Sentences

Underline the complex sentences in the paragraph.

1.
   > As the band marched by, Fred watched happily. He wore his good pants and a new shirt. He felt great because he knew a secret. He was going to be in the band. After he waved to some friends, Fred walked up to the drummers. Though two drummers ignored him, Fred kept smiling. The third drummer had given him a thumbs-up.

Choose the conjunction that makes the sentence a complex sentence.

2. _____ you snowboard, you'll have fun.
   A. But   C. And
   B. When   D. So

3. Turn off the lights _____ the movie starts.
   A. for   C. yet
   B. nor   **D.** before

4. _____ you forget to tie your shoes, you might fall.
   A. And   **C.** If
   B. Or   D. So

Paragraphs

Unit Focus

In the grammar, usage, and mechanics (GUM) part of the unit, students will review sentences and learn about the dictionary and thesaurus. They will

- ▶ Recall what a complete sentence is.
- ▶ Practice identifying complete sentences.
- ▶ Review capitalizing the first word in a sentence.
- ▶ Review punctuation marks to end a sentence.
- ▶ Learn how to use a dictionary.
- ▶ Learn how to use a thesaurus.

In the composition part of the unit, students will write an opinion paragraph. They will

- ▶ Use their journal to freewrite.
- ▶ Brainstorm a topic and plan their opinion paragraph.
- ▶ Write a draft of their opinion paragraph that contains a topic sentence that expresses an opinion, at least three supporting reasons, and a concluding sentence.
- ▶ Use a dictionary and a thesaurus to improve their writing.
- ▶ Revise and proofread their opinion paragraph.
- ▶ Write a final copy of their opinion paragraph to share.

Unit Plan		〖Online〗	〖Offline〗
Lesson 1	Review Sentences and Journal Entry	15 minutes	20 minutes
Lesson 2	Model Opinion Paragraph	20 minutes	15 minutes
Lesson 3	Brainstorm Topics	15 minutes	20 minutes
Lesson 4	Plan Your Paragraph	15 minutes	20 minutes
Lesson 5	Draft Your Opinion Paragraph (A)	10 minutes	25 minutes
Lesson 6	Draft Your Opinion Paragraph (B)	10 minutes	25 minutes
Lesson 7	Use a Dictionary and Thesaurus	15 minutes	20 minutes
Lesson 8	Revise Your Paragraph	10 minutes	25 minutes
Lesson 9	Proofread Your Paragraph	10 minutes	25 minutes
Lesson 10	Publish Your Paragraph	10 minutes	25 minutes

Review Sentences and Journal Entry

Lesson Overview

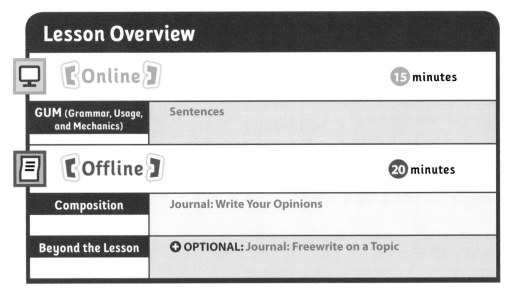

💻 **【Online】**		**15** minutes
GUM (Grammar, Usage, and Mechanics)	Sentences	
📄 **【Offline】**		**20** minutes
Composition	Journal: Write Your Opinions	
Beyond the Lesson	⊕ OPTIONAL: Journal: Freewrite on a Topic	

【Materials】

Supplied
- *K¹² My Journal*, pp. 18–19
- *Grammar Reference Guide* Online Book (optional)

Keywords

sentence – a group of words that tells a complete thought

Advance Preparation

To prepare for the GUM portion of this lesson, review Complete Sentences in the *Grammar Reference Guide* (linked in the online lesson) to familiarize yourself with the topic. While students complete their journal writing, review the online How to Evaluate Writing activity at the end of the lesson.

 **【Online】** **15** minutes

Students will work online **independently** to complete activities on sentences. Help students locate the online activities.

GUM (Grammar, Usage, and Mechanics)

Sentences

Students will review what a complete sentence is and practice identifying complete sentences. They will also review what they have learned about capitalization and punctuation in sentences.

Objectives
- Recall what a sentence is.
- Identify a complete sentence.
- Recognize that a complete sentence begins with a capital letter and has an end mark.

 **Offline** **20** minutes

Work **together** with students to complete the offline Composition activity.

Composition

 Journal: Write Your Opinions

Students will respond to a journal prompt by expressing some of their opinions. Gather *K[12] My Journal* and have students turn to pages 18 and 19.

Objectives

- Respond to a journal prompt.
- Freewrite about a topic.

1. Tell students they are going to write in their journal about some of their opinions. To help students think of some opinions they have, ask them to think about their answers to the following questions.

   ▸ Which is better, summer or winter? Spring or fall? Why?
   ▸ Should a person be fined for littering? Why or why not?
   ▸ What is your favorite kind of music? What is your least favorite kind of music? Why do you like one but dislike the other?

2. Have students respond to the prompt in their journal. Remind them to include details about what they think or feel and why they hold the opinions that they do. Encourage students to write in complete sentences, although it is not a requirement when they are freewriting in their journal.

TIP Students should write for about 20 minutes. Freewriting allows students to use their imagination to write what they want without worrying about being graded, so encourage them to keep writing for the entire time. If students have trouble writing for 20 minutes, use the prompts in Step 1 or have them list ideas or words. If they want to keep writing beyond the suggested time, praise them for their enthusiasm and offer to let them complete their entry later in the day as a reward.

Three Opinions Date _____

Some people think pizza is the best food. Other people think basketball is the best game. What are three opinions you have?

1. _____
2. _____
3. _____

18

19

Beyond the Lesson

 ○ OPTIONAL: Journal: Freewrite on a Topic

This activity is OPTIONAL. It is intended for students who have extra time and would benefit from extra practice. Feel free to skip this activity. Gather *K¹² My Journal.*

1. Have students either respond to a prompt in Thoughts and Experiences (pages 50–93) or write about their own topic on the next available page in Ideas (pages 96–139).

2. Encourage students to explore their thoughts and write as much as they want. There are no rules. If students wish, ideas can be fleshed out into a more developed composition at a later time.

3. If students feel comfortable sharing what they wrote, encourage them to share with you or their peers.

TIP Studies show that students who write more frequently become better writers.

Objectives
- Respond to a journal prompt.
- Freewrite about a topic.

Model Opinion Paragraph

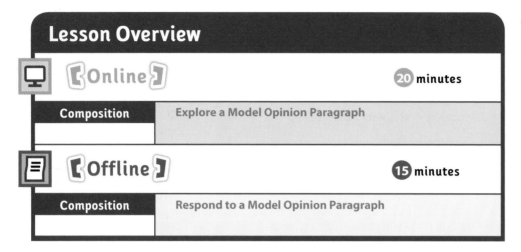

Lesson Overview

🖥️ 〖Online〗		20 minutes
Composition	Explore a Model Opinion Paragraph	

📄 〖Offline〗		15 minutes
Composition	Respond to a Model Opinion Paragraph	

〖Materials〗

Supplied

- *K¹² Language Arts Activity Book*, pp. WS 9–12

Keywords

paragraph – a group of sentences about one topic

topic sentence – the sentence that expresses the main idea of the paragraph

Advance Preparation

In this lesson, students begin to accumulate documents they will need as they work on their opinion paragraph. You might want to provide students with a folder or large envelope in which to keep these documents.

Big Ideas

The study of writing models provides students with opportunities to read, analyze, and emulate good models.

 **20 minutes**

Students will work online to read and explore a model opinion paragraph. Help students locate the online activity.

Composition •••

Explore a Model Opinion Paragraph

By reading and exploring a model opinion paragraph, students will learn what an opinion paragraph is and how it is organized.

 TIP If students are not comfortable reading the model opinion paragraph for this activity online, they may read the model on page WS 9 in *K¹² Language Arts Activity Book*.

Objectives

- Describe the elements of a paragraph.
- Identify the topic sentence that expresses the main idea of the paragraph.
- Identify reasons that support an opinion.
- Identify transitions that connect ideas.
- Identify the concluding sentence.

 **15 minutes**

Have students complete the offline Composition activity.

Composition •••

Respond to a Model Opinion Paragraph

Students will review what they learned about the model opinion paragraph. Turn to pages WS 11 and 12 in *K¹² Language Arts Activity Book*.

1. Have students reread Alexander's opinion paragraph on page WS 9.

2. Have students complete the Activity Book pages about Alexander's opinion paragraph. Encourage students to write in complete sentences. Provide support as necessary. Students should refer to Alexander's opinion paragraph as needed.

Objectives

- Describe the elements of a paragraph.
- Identify the topic sentence that expresses the main idea of the paragraph.
- Identify reasons that support an opinion.
- Identify transitions that connect ideas.
- Identify the concluding sentence.

(TIP) Keep Alexander's opinion paragraph in a safe place so students can refer to it later.

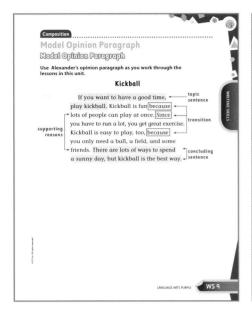

Composition

Model Opinion Paragraph
Model Opinion Paragraph

Use Alexander's opinion paragraph as you work through the lessons in this unit.

Kickball

If you want to have a good time, play kickball. Kickball is fun because lots of people can play at once. Since you have to run a lot, you get great exercise. Kickball is easy to play, too, because you only need a ball, a field, and some friends. There are lots of ways to spend a sunny day, but kickball is the best way.

topic sentence

transition

supporting reasons

concluding sentence

WS 9

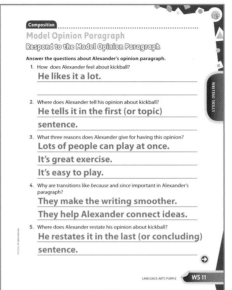

Composition

Model Opinion Paragraph
Respond to the Model Opinion Paragraph

Answer the questions about Alexander's opinion paragraph.

1. How does Alexander feel about kickball?
   He likes it a lot.

2. Where does Alexander tell his opinion about kickball?
   He tells it in the first (or topic) sentence.

3. What three reasons does Alexander give for having this opinion?
   Lots of people can play at once.
   It's great exercise.
   It's easy to play.

4. Why are transitions like *because* and *since* important in Alexander's paragraph?
   They make the writing smoother.
   They help Alexander connect ideas.

5. Where does Alexander restate his opinion about kickball?
   He restates it in the last (or concluding) sentence.

WS 11

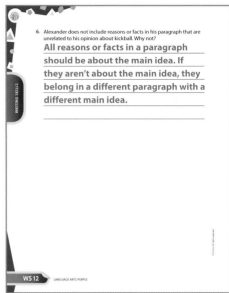

6. Alexander does not include reasons or facts in his paragraph that are unrelated to his opinion about kickball. Why not?
   All reasons or facts in a paragraph should be about the main idea. If they aren't about the main idea, they belong in a different paragraph with a different main idea.

WS 12

Brainstorm Topics

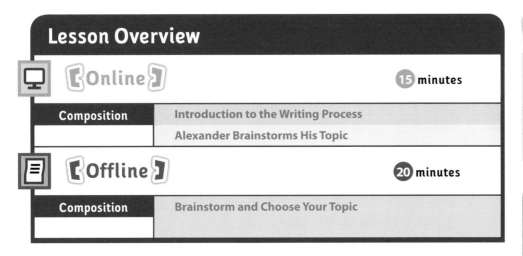

Lesson Overview

Online — 15 minutes

Composition	Introduction to the Writing Process
	Alexander Brainstorms His Topic

Offline — 20 minutes

Composition	Brainstorm and Choose Your Topic

Materials

Supplied
- *K¹² Language Arts Activity Book*, p. WS 13
- *K¹² My Journal* (optional)

Keywords

brainstorming – before writing, a way for the writer to come up with ideas

 **15 minutes**

Students will work online to learn how to brainstorm topics for their opinion paragraph. Help students locate the online activities.

Composition

Introduction to the Writing Process
Students will explore the stages in the writing process.

Alexander Brainstorms His Topic
By watching Alexander brainstorm his topic, students will learn how to brainstorm topics for their own opinion paragraph.

Objectives
- Explore the writing process.
- Brainstorm ideas for an opinion paragraph.
- Choose a topic.

 **20 minutes**

Have students complete the offline Composition activity.

Composition ·

Brainstorm and Choose Your Topic

Students will brainstorm and choose a topic for their own opinion paragraph.
Turn to page WS 13 in *K¹² Language Arts Activity Book*.

1. Allow students to use the Three Opinions topic in their journal (pages 18 and 19) for their opinion paragraph, if they wish. If students choose to do so, then no further brainstorming is necessary, and students do not need to complete the Activity Book page. For students needing a topic, continue with Step 2.

2. Have students complete the Activity Book page. Provide support as necessary. Remind students that during brainstorming, no idea is a bad idea. The point is to list as many ideas as possible before choosing a topic.

Objectives
- Brainstorm ideas for an opinion paragraph.
- Choose a topic.

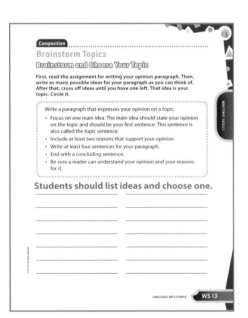

Plan Your Paragraph

Lesson Overview

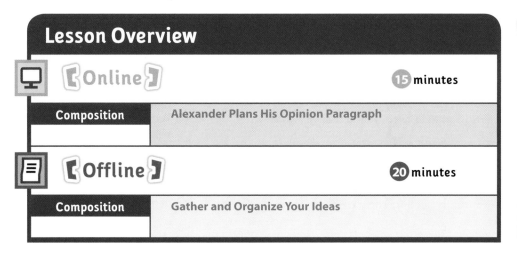

💻 **Online**		15 minutes
Composition	Alexander Plans His Opinion Paragraph	
📄 **Offline**		20 minutes
Composition	Gather and Organize Your Ideas	

Materials

Supplied
- *K¹² Language Arts Activity Book*, pp. WS 15

Keywords

topic sentence – the sentence that expresses the main idea of the paragraph

Big Ideas

Writers must be able to articulate a main idea and support it with appropriate details.

 **Online** 15 minutes

Students will work online to learn how to use a graphic organizer to organize ideas for their opinion paragraph. Help students locate the online activity.

Composition ••

Alexander Plans His Opinion Paragraph
By watching how Alexander uses a graphic organizer, students will learn how to organize ideas for their opinion paragraph.

 Objectives
- Use a graphic organizer to plan.
- Distinguish between details that do and do not support the topic sentence.

[Offline] 20 minutes

Have students complete the offline Composition activity.

Composition

Gather and Organize Your Ideas

Students will use a graphic organizer to gather and organize ideas about the topic of their opinion paragraph. Turn to page WS 15 in *K¹² Language Arts Activity Book*.

1. Direct students' attention to the Activity Book page. Remind students that they do not need to use complete sentences on the graphic organizer.

2. Have students fill in the main idea box with their opinion on the topic they have chosen. The main idea will eventually become the paragraph's topic sentence.

3. For the rest of the graphic organizer, have students write reasons that support their opinion. Finally students should restate their main idea in the last box. The restated main idea will eventually become the paragraph's concluding sentence. Provide support as necessary.

 Keep the completed graphic organizer in a safe place so students can refer to it later.

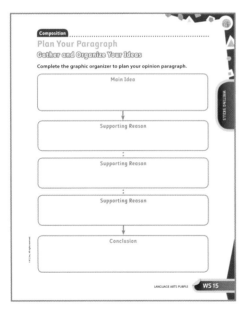

Objectives
- Use a graphic organizer to plan.
- Distinguish between details that do and do not support the topic sentence.

Draft Your Opinion Paragraph (A)

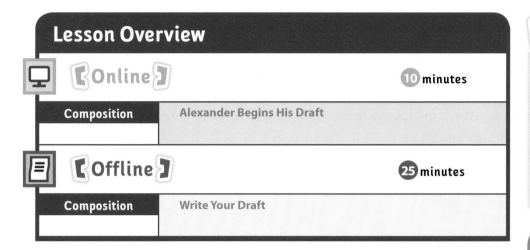

Lesson Overview

🖥️ **Online**		**10** minutes
Composition	Alexander Begins His Draft	

📄 **Offline**		**25** minutes
Composition	Write Your Draft	

Materials

Supplied
- *Grammar Reference Guide* Online Book (optional)
- *K¹² Language Arts Activity Book*, pp. WS 9, 15, 17–18
- drafting page (optional printout)

Keywords

drafting – of writing, the stage or step of the process in which the writer first writes the piece

Advance Preparation

Gather pages WS 9 (Model Opinion Paragraph) and WS 15 (Gather and Organize Your Ideas, students' completed graphic organizer) in *K¹² Language Arts Activity Book*.

Big Ideas

Writers must be able to articulate a main idea and support it with appropriate details.

 **10 minutes**

Students will work online to learn how to begin drafting an opinion paragraph. Help students locate the online activity.

Composition

Alexander Begins His Draft
By watching how Alexander begins to draft his opinion paragraph, students will learn how to begin drafting their own opinion paragraph.

Objectives
- Use a graphic organizer to write a paragraph.
- Write an opinion paragraph.
- State an opinion.
- Provide reasons that support the opinion.
- Use linking words and phrases to connect opinions and reasons.
- Provide a concluding statement or section.

 **25 minutes**

Have students complete the offline Composition activity.

Composition

 Write Your Draft
Students will begin drafting their opinion paragraph. Have them gather the model opinion paragraph and their completed graphic organizer on the Gather and Organize Your Ideas page. Turn to pages WS 17 and 18 in *K¹² Language Arts Activity Book*.

1. Help students start drafting by reminding them to refer to Alexander's opinion paragraph and the information on their completed Gather and Organize Your Ideas page as necessary. The model will help students remember what elements their paragraph should include, and the information on the Gather and Organize Your Ideas page will help them remember which reasons to include and where to place them.

2. Remind students that a draft does not have to be perfect. It's just a first try at putting ideas on paper. Tell students that they will start writing their draft in this lesson and finish in the next lesson.

Objectives
- Use a graphic organizer to write a paragraph.
- Write an opinion paragraph.
- State an opinion.
- Provide reasons that support the opinion.
- Use linking words and phrases to connect opinions and reasons.
- Provide a concluding statement or section.

3. Have students use the lined Activity Book pages to begin drafting their opinion paragraph. Students should write only in the white rows, because the purple rows will be used for making revisions to the draft later.

Start here ▶

If needed, additional drafting pages can be printed from the online lesson.

4. If students want to use a reference material such as the *Grammar Reference Guide* or a dictionary while drafting, suggest that they wait until they are revising or proofreading. Looking up information while drafting can interfere with students' flow of ideas.

TIP Keep students' drafting pages in a safe place so students can continue working on them later.

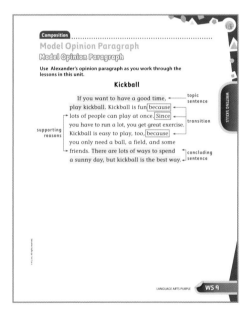

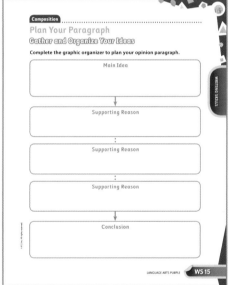

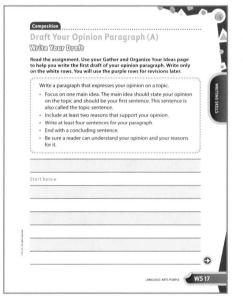

Draft Your Opinion Paragraph (B)

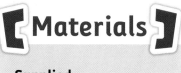

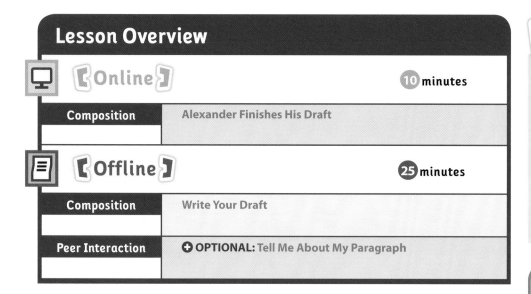

Lesson Overview

🖥 [Online]   **10** minutes

Composition	Alexander Finishes His Draft

📝 [Offline]   **25** minutes

Composition	Write Your Draft
Peer Interaction	➕ **OPTIONAL:** Tell Me About My Paragraph

[Materials]

Supplied
- *K¹² Language Arts Activity Book*, pp. WS 9, 15, 17–20
- *Grammar Reference Guide* Online Book (optional)
- drafting page (optional printout)
- Opinion Paragraph: Feedback Sheet (printout)

Keywords

drafting – of writing, the stage or step of the process in which the writer first writes the piece

Advance Preparation

Gather pages WS 9 (Model Opinion Paragraph), 15 (Gather and Organize Your Ideas, students' completed graphic organizer), and 17 and 18 (Write Your Draft, students' partially completed opinion paragraph draft) in *K¹² Language Arts Activity Book*. Print Opinion Paragraph: Feedback Sheet from the online lesson.

Big Ideas

Writing is the communication of ideas in a structured, orderly form.

 **minutes**

Students will work online independently to learn how to finish drafting an opinion paragraph. Help students locate the online activity.

Composition

Alexander Finishes His Draft

By watching how Alexander finishes drafting his opinion paragraph, students will learn how to finish drafting their own opinion paragraph.

 Objectives

- Use a graphic organizer to write a paragraph.
- Write an opinion paragraph.
- State an opinion.
- Provide reasons that support the opinion.
- Use linking words and phrases to connect opinions and reasons.
- Provide a concluding statement or section.

 **minutes**

Work **together** with students to complete the offline Composition and Peer Interaction activities.

Composition

 Write Your Draft

Students will finish drafting their opinion paragraph, and you will review it. Have them gather the model opinion paragraph, their completed graphic organizer on the Gather and Organize Your Ideas page, and their opinion paragraph draft. You will also need the Opinion Paragraph: Feedback Sheet, printable from the online lesson.

1. Have students finish drafting their opinion paragraph, continuing to write only in the white rows. If needed, additional drafting pages can be printed from the online lesson.

2. As students write, remind them to refer to Alexander's opinion paragraph and their Gather and Organize Your Ideas page as necessary. Continue to emphasize that drafts are not meant to be perfect. They are a work in progress.

 Objectives

- Use a graphic organizer to write a paragraph.
- Write an opinion paragraph.
- State an opinion.
- Provide reasons that support the opinion.
- Use linking words and phrases to connect opinions and reasons.
- Provide a concluding statement or section.

3. If students want to use a reference material such as the *Grammar Reference Guide* or a dictionary while drafting, suggest that they wait until they are revising or proofreading. Looking up information while drafting can interfere with students' flow of ideas.

⮌ **Learning Coach Check-In** When students have finished their draft, read and review it using the Opinion Paragraph: Feedback Sheet, but do not go over the feedback sheet with students now. The notes you take on this sheet will guide your feedback to students as they revise their draft in a later lesson. Keep the feedback sheet in a safe place until students are ready to revise their draft.

TIP Keep students' opinion paragraph draft and the Opinion Paragraph: Feedback Sheet in a safe place so they can be used later.

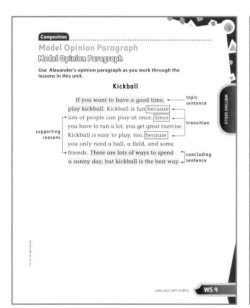

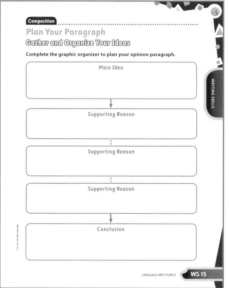

Peer Interaction

OPTIONAL: Tell Me About My Paragraph

This activity is OPTIONAL. It is intended for students who have extra time and would benefit from extra practice. Feel free to skip this activity.

Students can benefit from exchanging opinion paragraphs with another student. Each writer should receive feedback. To complete this optional activity, turn to pages WS 19 and 20 in *K¹² Language Arts Activity Book*. (Additional copies of the Peer Interaction form can be printed from the online lesson.)

Objectives
- Use guidance from adults and peers to revise writing.
- Collaborate with peers on writing projects.

1. Have students exchange drafts with other students.

2. Have students use the Activity Book pages to provide others with feedback about their writing.

3. In the upcoming revising lesson, students may use the feedback provided from other students to improve their opinion paragraph.

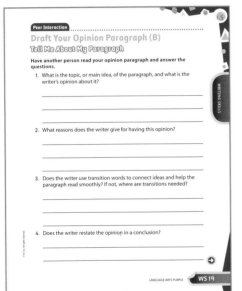

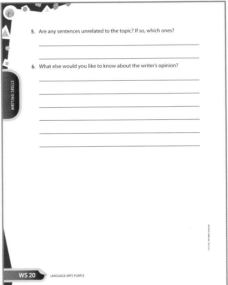

Use a Dictionary and Thesaurus

Lesson Overview

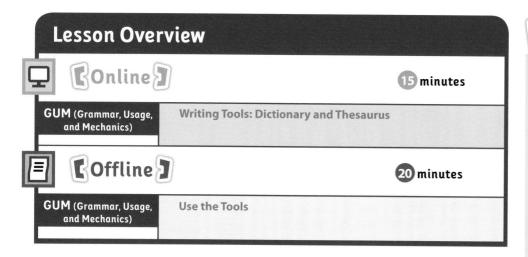

Online	15 minutes
GUM (Grammar, Usage, and Mechanics)	Writing Tools: Dictionary and Thesaurus

Offline	20 minutes
GUM (Grammar, Usage, and Mechanics)	Use the Tools

[Materials]

Supplied
- *K¹² Language Arts Activity Book*, pp. WS 21
- *Grammar Reference Guide* Online Book (optional)
- Opinion Paragraph: Feedback Sheet (printout)

Also Needed
- dictionary
- thesaurus

Keywords

dictionary – a reference work made up of words with their definitions, in alphabetical order

thesaurus – a reference work that gives synonyms and antonyms for words

Advance Preparation

To prepare for this lesson, review the dictionary and thesaurus entries in the Resources of the *Grammar Reference Guide* (linked in the online lesson) to familiarize yourself with the topics. If you have not already completed the Opinion Paragraph: Feedback Sheet, do so during this lesson while students work independently. You will need to share this form with students in the next lesson.

 **15 minutes**

Students will work online to complete activities on using a dictionary and a thesaurus. Help students locate the online activity.

GUM (Grammar, Usage, and Mechanics)

Writing Tools: Dictionary and Thesaurus
Students will learn about the types of information found in a dictionary and a thesaurus and why both resources are valuable to writers.

Objectives
- Recognize the kind of information found in a dictionary.
- Recognize the kind of information found in a thesaurus.

 **minutes**

Have students complete the offline GUM activity.

GUM (Grammar, Usage, and Mechanics)

Use the Tools
Students will practice using a dictionary and a thesaurus. Turn to pages WS 21 in *K¹² Language Arts Activity Book* and have students complete the page.

Turn to pages WS 21

Objectives
- Use a dictionary.
- Use a thesaurus.

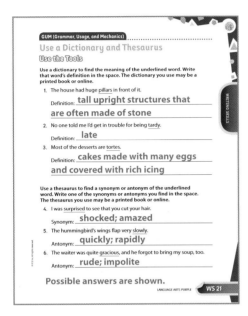

GUM (Grammar, Usage, and Mechanics)

Use a Dictionary and Thesaurus

Use the Tools

Use a dictionary to find the meaning of the underlined word. Write that word's definition in the space. The dictionary you use may be a printed book or online.

1. The house had huge <u>pillars</u> in front of it.

   Definition: tall upright structures that are often made of stone

2. No one told me I'd get in trouble for being <u>tardy</u>.

   Definition: late

3. Most of the desserts are <u>tortes</u>.

   Definition: cakes made with many eggs and covered with rich icing

Use a thesaurus to find a synonym or antonym of the underlined word. Write one of the synonyms or antonyms you find in the space. The thesaurus you use may be a printed book or online.

4. I was <u>surprised</u> to see that you cut your hair.

   Synonym: shocked; amazed

5. The hummingbird's wings flap very <u>slowly</u>.

   Antonym: quickly; rapidly

6. The waiter was quite <u>gracious</u>, and he forgot to bring my soup, too.

   Antonym: rude; impolite

Possible answers are shown.

LANGUAGE ARTS PURPLE WS 21

Revise Your Paragraph

Lesson Overview

 **Online**   **10** minutes

Composition	Alexander Revises His Draft

Offline   **25** minutes

Composition	Revise with a Checklist

Materials

Supplied
- *K¹² Language Arts Activity Book*, pp. WS 17–20, 23
- drafting page (optional printout)
- Opinion Paragraph: Feedback Sheet (printout)

Keyword

revising – the stage or step of the writing process in which the writer rereads and edits the draft, correcting errors and making changes in content or organization that improve the piece

Advance Preparation

Gather pages WS 17 and 18 (Write Your Draft, students' draft of their opinion paragraph) and 19 and 20 (Tell Me About My Paragraph, if completed) in *K¹² Language Arts Activity Book* and the completed Opinion Paragraph: Feedback Sheet. You will review the feedback with students.

Big Ideas

- Teaching the writing process encourages students to organize their ideas before they write and revise their work after they write.
- One of the most powerful ways to improve writing is to directly teach strategies for planning and revising until students can use these strategies on their own.

 **minutes**

Students will work online to learn how to revise an opinion paragraph. Help students locate the online activity.

Composition •

Alexander Revises His Draft
By watching how Alexander revises his opinion paragraph draft, students will learn how to revise their draft.

 Objectives
- Revise the draft of a paragraph.
- Delete any ideas that spoil the unity.
- Strengthen the topic sentence.
- Use a thesaurus to check word choice.

 **minutes**

Work **together** with students to complete the offline Composition activity.

Composition •

Revise with a Checklist
Students will revise their opinion paragraph. Have them gather their opinion paragraph draft and any completed Peer Interaction forms. Turn to page WS 23 in *K¹² Language Arts Activity Book* and gather the Opinion Paragraph: Feedback Sheet that you filled out.

1. Use the Opinion Paragraph: Feedback Sheet to guide your discussion with students.

   ▶ Tell students the strengths of their paragraph. Provide positive comments about the main idea, language, reasons, or other elements of the paragraph you enjoyed.

 Objectives
- Revise the draft of a paragraph.
- Delete any ideas that spoil the unity.
- Strengthen the topic sentence.
- Use a thesaurus to check word choice.

▶ Walk through the Purpose and Content and Structure and Organization sections of the feedback sheet with students. Do not address your comments in the Grammar and Mechanics section at this time. You can work with students on grammar and mechanics when they proofread. Providing these corrections at this time may distract students from the real work of revising for content and structure.

▶ As you go through the feedback sheet with students, encourage them to actively revise their draft based on your feedback. Reassure students that it's okay to remove ideas or sentences from their paragraph. Doing so may help their paragraph stay focused on their topic, even if something they cut was included in the graphic organizer on their Gather and Organize Your Ideas page.

▶ As students revise their draft, have them use the purple rows to mark their revisions.

Start here ▶

2. Once you've reviewed your comments on the first two sections of the feedback sheet with students, have them review their draft once more, using the revising checklist on the Activity Book page. Students should check off each box on the checklist as they complete each item.

3. If students received feedback from peers, discuss with them how they might use it to improve their paragraph. Help students decide what peer feedback would be useful to include in their revisions.

4. If students' revised opinion paragraph has many changes that make the paragraph difficult to understand, encourage students to make a clean copy before they proofread in a later lesson. Additional drafting pages can be printed from the online lesson.

TIP Keep students' revised opinion paragraph in a safe place so students can refer to it later.

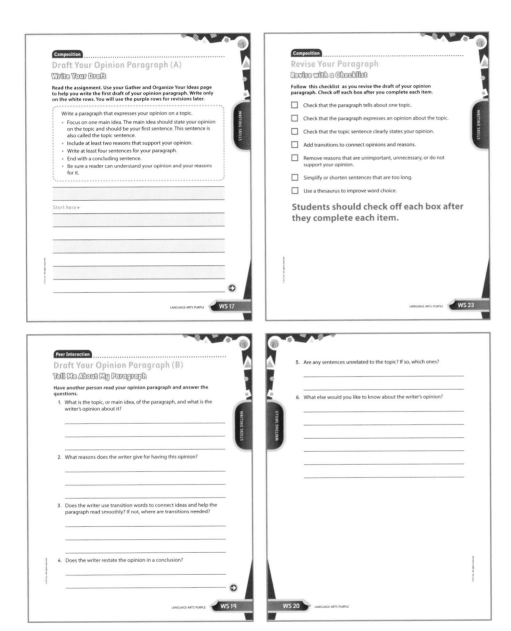

Composition

Draft Your Opinion Paragraph (A)

Write Your Draft

Read the assignment. Use your Gather and Organize Your Ideas page to help you write the first draft of your opinion paragraph. Write only on the white rows. You will use the purple rows for revisions later.

Write a paragraph that expresses your opinion on a topic.
- Focus on one main idea. The main idea should state your opinion on the topic and should be your first sentence. This sentence is also called the topic sentence.
- Include at least two reasons that support your opinion.
- Write at least four sentences for your paragraph.
- End with a concluding sentence.
- Be sure a reader can understand your opinion and your reasons for it.

Start here ▶

LANGUAGE ARTS PURPLE   WS 17

Composition

Revise Your Paragraph

Revise with a Checklist

Follow this checklist as you revise the draft of your opinion paragraph. Check off each box after you complete each item.

☐ Check that the paragraph tells about one topic.

☐ Check that the paragraph expresses an opinion about the topic.

☐ Check that the topic sentence clearly states your opinion.

☐ Add transitions to connect opinions and reasons.

☐ Remove reasons that are unimportant, unnecessary, or do not support your opinion.

☐ Simplify or shorten sentences that are too long.

☐ Use a thesaurus to improve word choice.

Students should check off each box after they complete each item.

LANGUAGE ARTS PURPLE   WS 23

Peer Interaction

Draft Your Opinion Paragraph (B)

Tell Me About My Paragraph

Have another person read your opinion paragraph and answer the questions.

1. What is the topic, or main idea, of the paragraph, and what is the writer's opinion about it?

2. What reasons does the writer give for having this opinion?

3. Does the writer use transition words to connect ideas and help the paragraph read smoothly? If not, where are transitions needed?

4. Does the writer restate the opinion in a conclusion?

LANGUAGE ARTS PURPLE   WS 19

5. Are any sentences unrelated to the topic? If so, which ones?

6. What else would you like to know about the writer's opinion?

WS 20   LANGUAGE ARTS PURPLE

Proofread Your Paragraph

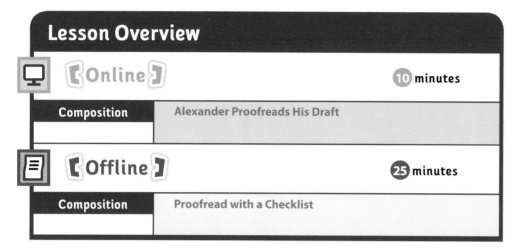

Lesson Overview

Online — 10 minutes

| Composition | Alexander Proofreads His Draft |

Offline — 25 minutes

| Composition | Proofread with a Checklist |

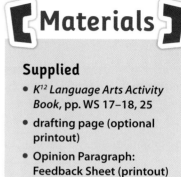

Materials

Supplied
- *K¹² Language Arts Activity Book*, pp. WS 17–18, 25
- drafting page (optional printout)
- Opinion Paragraph: Feedback Sheet (printout)

Keywords

dictionary – a reference work made up of words with their definitions, in alphabetical order

proofreading – the stage or step of the writing process in which the writer checks for errors in grammar, punctuation, capitalization, and spelling

Advance Preparation

Gather pages WS 17 and 18 (Write Your Draft, students' draft of their opinion paragraph) in *K¹² Language Arts Activity Book* and the completed Opinion Paragraph: Feedback Sheet. If students' revised paragraph has many changes that make it difficult to read and understand, you may want to encourage them to make a clean copy before they proofread in this lesson. Additional drafting pages can be printed from the online lesson.

Big Ideas

Good writers carefully check their work for errors.

 **Online** 10 minutes

Students will work online to learn how to proofread an opinion paragraph.
Help students locate the online activity.

Composition

Alexander Proofreads His Draft

By watching how Alexander proofreads his opinion paragraph draft, students will learn how to proofread their draft.

 Objectives
- Proofread a paragraph.
- Use a dictionary to check spelling.
- Capitalize the first word of a sentence.

Offline · ⟨25⟩ minutes

Work **together** with students to complete the offline Composition activity.

Composition ·

Proofread with a Checklist

Students will proofread their opinion paragraph. Have them gather their opinion paragraph draft. Gather the Opinion Paragraph: Feedback Sheet that you filled out, and turn to page WS 25 in *K¹² Language Arts Activity Book*.

1. Review with students your comments in the Grammar and Mechanics section of the feedback sheet. As you go through the feedback sheet with them, encourage students to use the purple rows on their drafting pages to actively mark changes based on your feedback.

2. Once you've reviewed your comments in the Grammar and Mechanics section of the feedback sheet with students, have them review their draft once more using the Proofread with a Checklist activity page. Students should check off each box on the checklist as they complete each item.

3. If students' revised opinion paragraph has many changes that make the paragraph difficult to read and understand, encourage them to make a clean copy before they proofread. Additional drafting pages can be printed from the online lesson.

TIP Keep students' proofread opinion paragraph in a safe place so students can refer to it later.

Objectives
- Proofread a paragraph.
- Use a dictionary to check spelling.
- Capitalize the first word of a sentence.

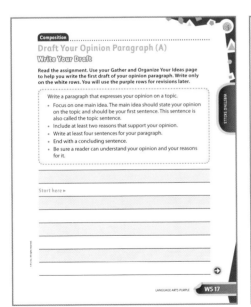

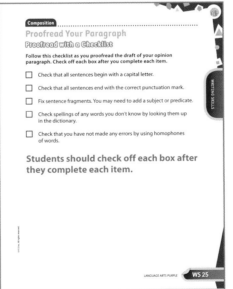

Publish Your Paragraph

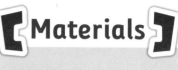
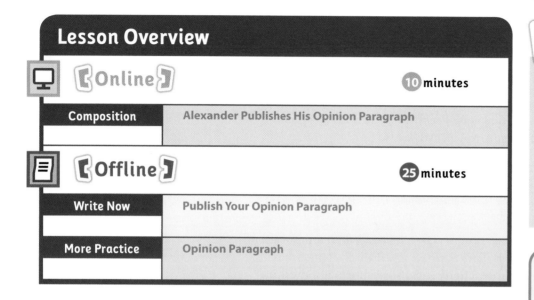

Lesson Overview

Online — 10 minutes

| Composition | Alexander Publishes His Opinion Paragraph |

Offline — 25 minutes

| Write Now | Publish Your Opinion Paragraph |
| More Practice | Opinion Paragraph |

Materials

Supplied

- *K¹² Language Arts Activity Book*, pp. WS 17–18, 27
- Opinion Paragraph: Rubric and Sample Responses (printout)
- lined writing page (optional printout)

Keywords

publishing – the stage or step of the writing process in which the writer makes a clean copy of the piece and shares it

Advance Preparation

Gather pages WS 17 and 18 (Write Your Draft, students' draft of their opinion paragraph) in *K¹² Language Arts Activity Book*, which students should have revised and proofread.

Big Ideas

Working collaboratively with other students during various stages of the writing process can improve student writing.

 **Online** 10 minutes

Students will work online to learn how to publish an opinion paragraph. Help students locate the online activity.

Composition

Alexander Publishes His Opinion Paragraph

By watching how Alexander publishes his opinion paragraph, students will learn how to publish theirs.

Objectives

- Create a clean copy of the opinion paragraph.
- Include illustrations when useful.

 **[Offline]** **25** minutes

Work **together** with students to complete the offline Write Now and More Practice activities.

 Write Now ....

 Publish Your Opinion Paragraph

Students will publish their opinion paragraph. Have them gather their proofread draft. Turn to page WS 27 in *K¹² Language Arts Activity Book*.

> **Objectives**
> - Create a clean copy of the opinion paragraph.
> - Include illustrations when useful.

1. Explain to students that they will finish their opinion paragraph by completing the last step in the writing process—publishing their work.
   Say: Publishing your writing means making a clean and final copy that is ready for sharing with others.

   ▸ To be ready to publish your opinion paragraph, you should have finished revising and proofreading your draft.

   ▸ The final copy should be your best effort and should not have any errors.

2. Explain that the final copy should be written clearly and neatly on clean sheets of paper. Tell students that they should use good handwriting and leave spaces between words so that others can read what they wrote.

3. Have students use the lined Activity Book pages to write their final copy. If needed, additional lined writing pages can be printed from the online lesson.

4. Use the materials and instructions in the online lesson to evaluate students' finished writing. You will be looking at students' writing to evaluate the following:

   ▸ **Purpose and Content:** The paragraph states the writer's opinion on a topic and contains at least two reasons that explain why the writer holds this opinion. There is no more than one superfluous detail in the paragraph. The writing achieves some measure of sentence fluency.

   ▸ **Structure and Organization:** The paragraph has been revised. The paragraph contains at least three of the following elements in the following order: a topic sentence that states the main idea, several sentences that contain supporting reasons, and a concluding sentence that restates the main idea. Some attempt at using transition words to connect opinions and reasons has been made.

   ▸ **Grammar and Mechanics:** The paragraph has been proofread using a checklist, and few if any errors remain.

5. Enter students' scores online for each rubric category.

6. If students' writing scored a 1 in any category, work with them to revise and proofread their work.

7. Suggest that students illustrate any part of the paragraph that a reader may need help understanding or that will make the paragraph more convincing. Encourage students to share their opinion paragraph with anyone who might agree or disagree with their opinion. In addition, people who are special to students, such as grandparents, would likely enjoy hearing the paragraph read to them or having a copy of the paragraph to keep.

TIP Tell students that producing a piece of writing that is ready to publish and share with others is a great accomplishment. Let students know that the effort they make to publish an opinion paragraph is something to be proud of.

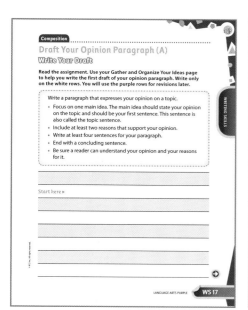

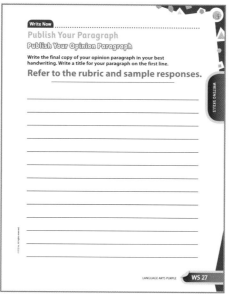

More Practice

Opinion Paragraph

If students' writing did not meet objectives, have them complete the appropriate review activities listed in the table online. Follow the online instructions to help students revise and edit their work. Impress upon students that revising makes their work better. Writing is a process, and each time they revise their opinion paragraph they are improving their writing. Always begin with something positive to say. If there is one reason, for example, mention it and say how this reason helps you better understand and appreciate the writer's opinion on the topic.

Help students locate the activities and provide support as needed.

Objectives
• Revise the draft of a paragraph.

Reward: When students' writing is Level 2 or higher on the Opinion Paragraph grading rubric, add a sticker for this unit on the My Accomplishments chart.

UNIT OVERVIEW Combining Sentences and Personal Story

Unit Focus

In the grammar part of the unit, students will learn about sentence parts, combining sentences, and adding details to sentences. They will

- ▶ Learn the definition of *complete subject* and how to identify it in a sentence.
- ▶ Learn the definition of *complete predicate* and how to identify it in a sentence.
- ▶ Combine two sentences that have the same subject into one sentence with a compound predicate.
- ▶ Combine two sentences that have the same predicate into one sentence with a compound subject.
- ▶ Combine two simple sentences to form a compound sentence.
- ▶ Expand a sentence by adding details.

In the composition part of the unit, students will write a personal story. They will

- ▶ Use their journal to freewrite.
- ▶ Brainstorm a topic and plan their story.
- ▶ Write a draft that has a beginning, middle, and end.
- ▶ Add details to make their writing stronger.
- ▶ Revise and proofread their personal story.
- ▶ Write a final copy of their personal story to share.

Unit Plan · [Online] [Offline]

Lesson	Topic	Online	Offline
Lesson 1	Complete Subjects and Journal Entry	15 minutes	20 minutes
Lesson 2	Complete Predicates and Model Personal Story	20 minutes	15 minutes
Lesson 3	Combine Sentences and Brainstorm Your Topic	20 minutes	15 minutes
Lesson 4	Combine Sentences and Plan Your Personal Story	20 minutes	15 minutes
Lesson 5	Draft Your Personal Story	10 minutes	25 minutes
Lesson 6	Combine Sentences and Draft Your Personal Story	15 minutes	20 minutes
Lesson 7	Improve Sentences with Details	15 minutes	20 minutes
Lesson 8	Revise Your Personal Story	10 minutes	25 minutes
Lesson 9	Unit Review and Proofread Your Personal Story	20 minutes	15 minutes
Lesson 10	Unit Checkpoint and Publish Your Personal Story	15 minutes	20 minutes

Complete Subjects and Journal Entry

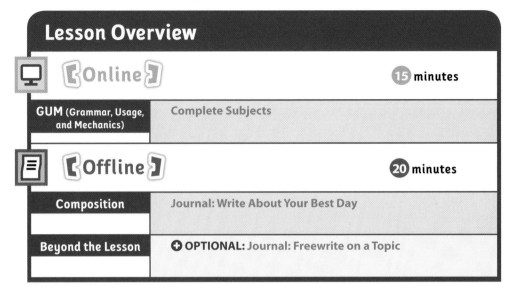

Lesson Overview

🖥️ **【Online】**		**15** minutes
GUM (Grammar, Usage, and Mechanics)	Complete Subjects	

📄 **【Offline】**		**20** minutes
Composition	Journal: Write About Your Best Day	
Beyond the Lesson	➕ OPTIONAL: Journal: Freewrite on a Topic	

【Materials】

Supplied
- *K¹² My Journal*, pp. 20–21
- *Grammar Reference Guide* Online Book (optional)

Keywords

complete subject – the part of the sentence that tells whom or what the sentence is about

Advance Preparation

To prepare for the GUM portion of this lesson, review Parts of a Sentence (Complete Subject) in the *Grammar Reference Guide* (linked in the online lesson) to familiarize yourself with the topic.

 **15** minutes

Students will work online **independently** to complete activities on complete subjects. Help students locate the online activities.

GUM (Grammar, Usage, and Mechanics) ....

Complete Subjects
Students will learn what a complete subject is and practice identifying complete subjects in sentences.

 Objectives
- Identify the subject of a sentence.
- Identify the subject of an imperative sentence.

 **20 minutes**

Work **together** with students to complete the offline Composition and Beyond the Lesson activities.

Composition

🖊 **Journal: Write About Your Best Day**

Students will respond to a journal prompt by describing their greatest day. Gather *K¹² My Journal* and have students turn to pages 20 and 21.

1. Tell students they are going to write in their journal about their best day ever. To help students think of a great day they have had, ask them to think about their answers to the following questions.

   ▶ What do you like to do? Do you remember a day when you did this?
   ▶ Where do you like to go? When did you go there?
   ▶ Whom do you like to spend time with? Do you usually do something you enjoy with that person?

2. Have students respond to the prompt in their journal. Remind them to include details about where they were, who was with them, and how they felt. Encourage students to write in complete sentences although it is not a requirement when they are freewriting in their journal.

3. If students feel comfortable sharing what they wrote, have them share with you or their peers.

TIP Students should write for about 20 minutes. Freewriting allows students to use their imagination to write what they want without worrying about being graded, so encourage them to keep writing for the entire time. If students have trouble writing for 20 minutes, use the prompts in Step 1 or have them list ideas or words. If they want to keep writing, praise them for their enthusiasm and offer to let them complete their entry later in the day as a reward.

Objectives
- Respond to a journal prompt.
- Freewrite about a topic.

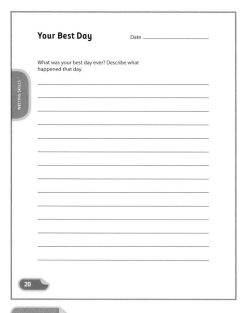

Your Best Day   Date _____

What was your best day ever? Describe what happened that day.

WRITING SKILLS

20

Beyond the Lesson •••

OPTIONAL: Journal: Freewrite on a Topic

This activity is OPTIONAL. It is intended for students who have extra
time and would benefit from extra practice. Feel free to skip this activity. Gather
K¹² My Journal.

1. Have students either respond to a prompt in Thoughts and Experiences
   (pages 50–93) or write about their own topic on the next available page in
   Ideas (pages 96–139).

2. Encourage students to explore their thoughts and write as much as they want.
   There are no rules. If students wish, ideas can be fleshed out into a more
   developed composition at a later time.

3. If students feel comfortable sharing what they wrote, encourage them to share
   with you or their peers.

TIP Studies show that students who write more frequently become better writers.

Objectives

- Respond to a journal
  prompt.
- Freewrite about a topic.

Complete Predicates and Model Personal Story

Lesson Overview

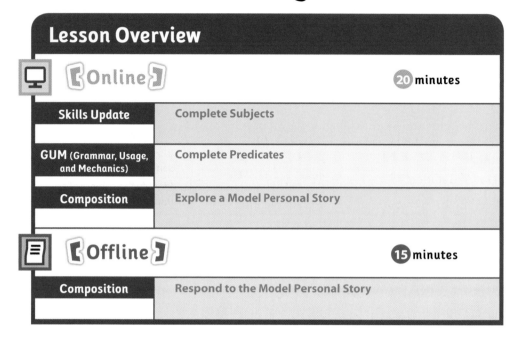

Online	**20** minutes
Skills Update	Complete Subjects
GUM (Grammar, Usage, and Mechanics)	Complete Predicates
Composition	Explore a Model Personal Story

Offline	**15** minutes
Composition	Respond to the Model Personal Story

Materials

Supplied
- *K¹² Language Arts Activity Book,* pp. WS 29–32
- *Grammar Reference Guide* Online Book (optional)

Keywords

chronological order – a way to organize that puts details in time order

complete predicate – the verb in a sentence and all the words that belong with and describe the verb

Advance Preparation

To prepare for the GUM portion of this lesson, review Parts of a Sentence (Complete Predicate) in the *Grammar Reference Guide* (linked in the online lesson) to familiarize yourself with the topic. In this lesson, students begin to accumulate documents they will need as they work on their personal story. You might want to provide students with a folder or large envelope in which to keep these documents.

Big Ideas

▸ Sequencing ideas is the beginning of writing a personal narrative or experience story.
▸ Experience stories relate a meaningful event that made a lasting impression on the writer and can be communicated to a reader.

 **minutes**

Students will work online to review complete subjects, to complete activities on complete predicates, and to read and explore a model personal story. Help students locate the online activities.

Skills Update

Complete Subjects

Students will review how to identify complete subjects by answering Skills Update questions. Sit with students as they do this activity and note if they answer correctly.

↶ **Learning Coach Check-In** How did students do on the Skills Update?

> ▸ **All questions correct:** Great! Skip the review screen and go on to the next activity.
>
> ▸ **Any questions incorrect:** Take a few minutes to review complete subjects now. Use the links on the screen after the Skills Update questions to take another look at the online activities or review Parts of a Sentence (Complete Subject) in the *Grammar Reference Guide* together.

TIP This activity will require extra time if students need to review complete subjects. Take the extra 5–10 minutes to review now because new skills build on what students have already learned.

> **Objectives**
> - Identify the subject of a sentence.
> - Identify the subject of an imperative sentence.

GUM (Grammar, Usage, and Mechanics)

Complete Predicates

Students will learn what a complete predicate is and practice identifying complete predicates in sentences.

> **Objectives**
> - Identify the predicate of a sentence.

Composition

Explore a Model Personal Story

By reading and exploring a model personal story, students will learn what a personal story is and how it is organized.

TIP If students are not comfortable reading the model personal story for this activity online, they may read the model on pages WS 29 and 30 in *K¹² Language Arts Activity Book*.

> **Objectives**
> - Describe the elements of a personal story.

 **15 minutes**

Have students complete the offline Composition activity.

Composition

Respond to the Model Personal Story

Students will review what they learned about the model personal story. Gather pages WS 31 and 32 in *K¹² Language Arts Activity Book*.

1. Have students reread Winnie's personal story on pages WS 29 and 30.

2. Have students complete the Activity Book pages about Winnie's personal story. Provide support as necessary. Students should refer to Winnie's personal story as needed.

TIP Keep Winnie's personal story in a safe place so students can refer to it later.

Objectives

- Describe the elements of a personal story.
- Identify the beginning, middle, and end of a story.
- Explain the significance of a story.
- Recognize that a story is told in chronological order.

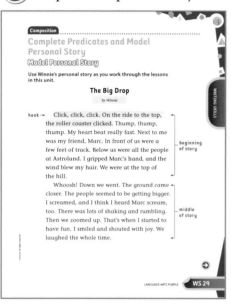

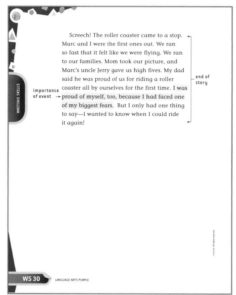

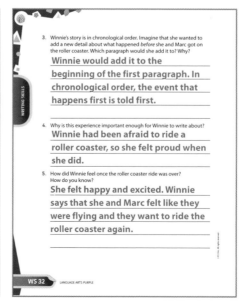

Combine Sentences and Brainstorm Your Topic

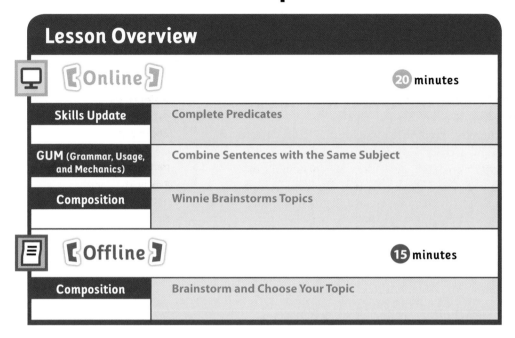

Lesson Overview

Online — 20 minutes

Skills Update	Complete Predicates
GUM (Grammar, Usage, and Mechanics)	Combine Sentences with the Same Subject
Composition	Winnie Brainstorms Topics

Offline — 15 minutes

Composition	Brainstorm and Choose Your Topic

Materials

Supplied

- *K¹² Language Arts Activity Book,* p. WS 33
- *K¹² My Journal* (optional)
- *Grammar Reference Guide* Online Book (optional)

Keywords

brainstorming – before writing, a way for the writer to come up with ideas

compound predicate – two or more predicates that have the same subject

conjunction – a word used to join parts of a sentence, such as *and*, *but*, and *or*

personal narrative – an essay about a personal experience of the writer

sentence combining – joining two sentences that have similar parts into one sentence

Advance Preparation

To prepare for the GUM portion of this lesson, review Combining Sentences in the *Grammar Reference Guide* (linked in the online lesson) to familiarize yourself with the topic.

Big Ideas

- ► Sentence combining—teaching students to construct complex, sophisticated sentences—is an effective instructional strategy and an important element in learning how to write well.
- ► Experience stories should relate a meaningful event that made a lasting impression on the writer and can be communicated to a reader.
- ► Knowing how to combine sentences that have similar subjects or similar predicates helps writers avoid monotony.

 **20 minutes**

Students will work online to review complete predicates, to complete activities on combining sentences, and to learn how to brainstorm topics for their personal story. Help students locate the online activities.

Skills Update

Complete Predicates
Students will review how to identify complete predicates by answering Skills Update questions. Sit with students as they do this activity and note if they answer correctly.

 Learning Coach Check-In How did students do on the Skills Update?

> ▸ **All questions correct:** Great! Skip the review screen and go on to the next activity.
> ▸ **Any questions incorrect:** Take a few minutes to review complete predicates now. Use the links on the screen after the Skills Update questions to take another look at the online activities or review Parts of a Sentence (Complete Predicate) in the *Grammar Reference Guide* together.

TIP This activity will require extra time if students need to review complete predicates. Take the extra 5–10 minutes to review now because new skills build on what students have already learned.

Objectives
* Identify the predicate of a sentence.

GUM (Grammar, Usage, and Mechanics)

Complete Sentences with the Same Subject
Students will learn what a compound predicate is and practice combining sentences and forming sentences with compound predicates.

Objectives
* Combine sentences to form one sentence with a compound predicate.
* Use conjunctions to form compound predicates.

Composition

Winnie Brainstorms Topics
By watching Winnie brainstorm her topic, students will learn how to brainstorm topics for their personal story.

Objectives
* Brainstorm topics for a personal story.

 **Offline** ⏱ **15 minutes**

Have students complete the offline Composition activity.

Composition ●

Brainstorm and Choose Your Topic

Students will brainstorm and choose a topic for their personal story. Turn to page WS 33 in *K¹² Language Arts Activity Book*.

Objectives
- Brainstorm topics for a personal story.
- Choose a topic.

1. Allow students to use the Your Best Day topic in their journal (pages 20 and 21) for their personal story, if they wish. If students choose to do so, then no further brainstorming is necessary, and students do not need to complete the Activity Book page. For students needing a topic, continue with Step 2.

2. Have students complete the Activity Book page to brainstorm and choose a story topic. Provide support as necessary. Remind students that during brainstorming, no idea is a bad idea. The point is to list as many ideas as possible before choosing a topic.

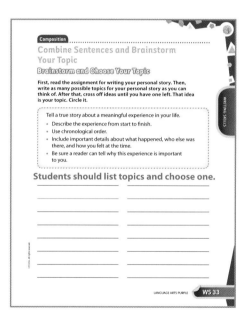

Combine Sentences and Plan Your Personal Story

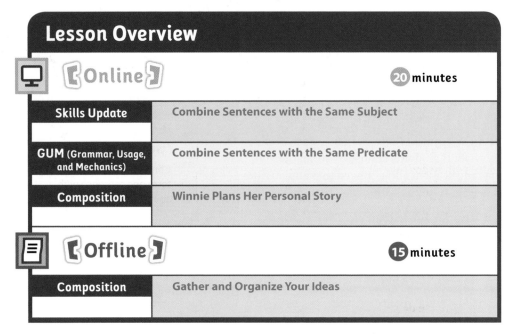

Lesson Overview

Online — 20 minutes

Skills Update	Combine Sentences with the Same Subject
GUM (Grammar, Usage, and Mechanics)	Combine Sentences with the Same Predicate
Composition	Winnie Plans Her Personal Story

Offline — 15 minutes

Composition	Gather and Organize Your Ideas

Materials

Supplied

- K¹² Language Arts Activity Book, pp. WS 35–36
- Grammar Reference Guide Online Book (optional)

Keywords

compound subject – two or more subjects that have the same predicate

conjunction – a word used to join parts of a sentence, such as *and*, *but*, and *or*

personal narrative – an essay about a personal experience of the writer

sentence combining – joining two sentences that have similar parts into one sentence

Advance Preparation

To prepare for the GUM portion of this lesson, review Combining Sentences in the *Grammar Reference Guide* (linked in the online lesson) to familiarize yourself with the topic.

Big Ideas

- ▶ Sentence combining—teaching students to construct complex, sophisticated sentences—is an effective instructional strategy and an important element in learning how to write well.
- ▶ Knowing how to combine sentences that have similar subjects or similar predicates helps writers avoid monotony.
- ▶ Sequencing ideas is the beginning of writing a personal narrative or experience story.
- ▶ Experience stories relate a meaningful event that made a lasting impression on the writer and can be communicated to a reader.

 **Online** **20** minutes

Students will work online to review combining sentences with the same subject, to complete activities on combining sentences with the same predicate, and to learn how to use a graphic organizer to organize ideas for their personal story. Help students locate the online activities.

Skills Update

Combine Sentences with the Same Subject
Students will review how to combine sentences with the same subject by answering Skills Update questions. Sit with students as they do this activity and note if they answer correctly.

⮌ **Learning Coach Check-In** How did students do on the Skills Update?

▸ **All questions correct:** Great! Skip the review screen and go on to the next activity.

▸ **Any questions incorrect:** Take a few minutes to review combining sentences with the same subject now. Use the links on the screen after the Skills Update questions to take another look at the online activities or review Parts of a Sentence (Compound Verb) in the *Grammar Reference Guide* together.

TIP This activity will require extra time if students need to review combining sentences with the same subject. Take the extra 5–10 minutes to review now because new skills build on what students have already learned.

> **Objectives**
> • Combine sentences to form one sentence with a compound predicate.
> • Use conjunctions to form compound predicates.

GUM (Grammar, Usage, and Mechanics)

Combine Sentences with the Same Predicate
Students will learn what a compound subject is and practice combining sentences and forming sentences with a compound subject.

> **Objectives**
> • Combine sentences to form one sentence with a compound subject.
> • Use conjunctions to form compound subjects.

Composition

Winnie Plans Her Personal Story
By watching how Winnie uses a graphic organizer, students will learn how to organize ideas for their personal story.

> **Objectives**
> • Use a graphic organizer to put ideas in order of beginning, middle, and end.

[Offline] 15 minutes

Have students complete the offline Composition activity.

Composition

Gather and Organize Your Ideas

Students will gather details about their personal story and then use a graphic organizer to organize these ideas. Turn to pages WS 35 and 36 in *K¹² Language Arts Activity Book*.

1. Have students complete the form on page WS 35 by listing their story topic and then briefly describing who is part of their personal story, what happened during the event, and when and where the event took place. Remind students that they do not need to use complete sentences on the form.

2. Have students complete the graphic organizer on page WS 36 by filling it with ideas and details they want to include in their personal story. Provide support as necessary. Remind students that they do not need to use complete sentences on the graphic organizer.

TIP Keep students' completed graphic organizer in a safe place so they can refer to it later.

Objectives
- Develop details for a story by answering questions.
- Use a graphic organizer to put ideas in order of beginning, middle, and end.

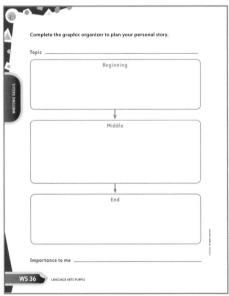

Draft Your Personal Story

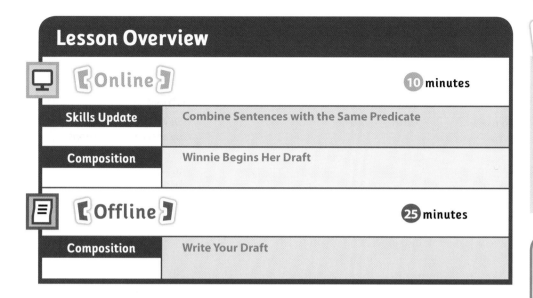

Lesson Overview

🖥 〔Online〕   **10** minutes

Skills Update	Combine Sentences with the Same Predicate
Composition	Winnie Begins Her Draft

📄 〔Offline〕   **25** minutes

Composition	Write Your Draft

〔Materials〕

Supplied

- *K¹² Language Arts Activity Book*, pp. WS 29–30, 35–38
- *Grammar Reference Guide* Online Book (optional)
- drafting page (optional printout)

Keywords

chronological order – a way to organize that puts details in time order

personal narrative – an essay about a personal experience of the writer

Advance Preparation

Gather pages WS 29 and 30 (Model Personal Story) and WS 35 and 36 (Gather and Organize Your Ideas, students' completed graphic organizer) in *K¹² Language Arts Activity Book*.

Big Ideas

- ▸ Sequencing ideas is the beginning of writing a personal narrative or experience story.
- ▸ Experience stories relate a meaningful event that made a lasting impression on the writer and can be communicated to a reader.

 **minutes**

Students will work online to review combining sentences with the same predicate and to learn how to begin drafting a personal story. Help students locate the online activities. So that students can concentrate on beginning their draft, this lesson does not contain any GUM activities.

Skills Update

Combine Sentences with the Same Predicate

Students will review how to combine sentences with the same predicate by answering Skills Update questions. Sit with students as they do this activity and note if they answer correctly.

➲ **Learning Coach Check-In** How did students do on the Skills Update?

> ▸ **All questions correct:** Great! Skip the review screen and go on to the next activity.
>
> ▸ **Any questions incorrect:** Take a few minutes to review combining sentences with the same predicate now. Use the links on the screen after the Skills Update questions to take another look at the online activities or review Parts of a Sentence (Compound Subject) in the *Grammar Reference Guide* together.

 This activity will require extra time if students need to review combining sentences with the same predicate. Take the extra 5–10 minutes to review now because new skills build on what students have already learned.

Objectives
- Combine sentences to form one sentence with a compound subject.
- Use conjunctions to form compound subjects.

Composition

Winnie Begins Her Draft

By watching how Winnie begins to draft her personal story, students will learn how to begin drafting their own personal story.

Objectives
- Draft a personal story.

 **minutes**

Have students complete the offline Composition activity.

Composition

Write Your Draft

Students will begin drafting their personal story. Have them gather the model personal story and their completed Gather and Organize Your Ideas pages. Turn to pages WS 37 and 38 in *K¹² Language Arts Activity Book*.

Objectives
- Draft a personal story.
- Put ideas in chronological order.

1. Help students start drafting by reminding them to refer to Winnie's personal story and the information on their completed Gather and Organize Your Ideas pages as necessary. The model will help students remember what elements their story should include, and the information on the Gather and Organize Your Ideas pages will help them remember which details to include and where to place them.

2. Remind students that a draft does not have to be perfect. It's just a first try at putting ideas on paper. Tell students that they will start writing their draft in this lesson and finish in the next lesson.

3. Have students use the lined Activity Book pages to begin drafting their personal story. Students should write only in the white rows, because the purple rows will be used for making revisions to the draft later.

Start here ▶ Students should write only in the white rows
while drafting.

If needed, additional drafting pages can be printed from the online lesson.

4. If students want to use a reference material such as the *Grammar Reference Guide* or a dictionary while drafting, suggest that they wait until they are revising or proofreading. Looking up information while drafting can interfere with students' flow of ideas.

TIP Keep students' drafting pages in a safe place so students can continue working on them later.

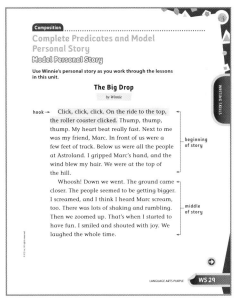

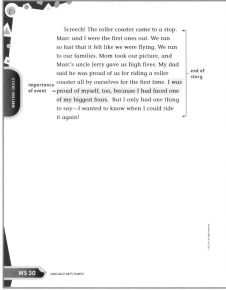

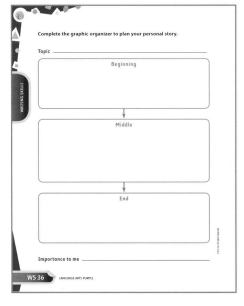

Combine Sentences and Draft Your Personal Story

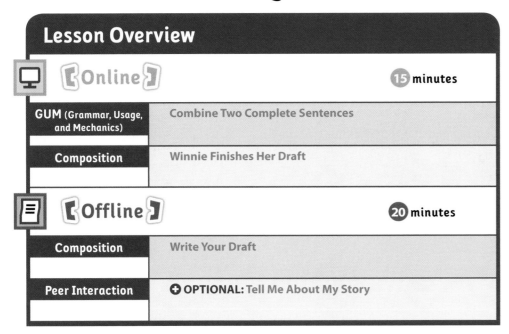

Lesson Overview

🖥️ 【Online】   15 minutes

GUM (Grammar, Usage, and Mechanics)	Combine Two Complete Sentences
Composition	Winnie Finishes Her Draft

📄 【Offline】   20 minutes

Composition	Write Your Draft
Peer Interaction	➕ OPTIONAL: Tell Me About My Story

【Materials】

Supplied
- *K¹² Language Arts Activity Book*, pp. WS 29–30, 35–40
- *Grammar Reference Guide* Online Book (optional)
- drafting page (optional printout)
- Personal Story: Feedback Sheet (printout)

Keywords

compound sentence – a sentence that has at least two independent clauses

conjunction – a word used to join parts of a sentence, such as *and*, *but*, and *or*

personal narrative – an essay about a personal experience of the writer

sentence combining – joining two sentences that have similar parts into one sentence

simple sentence – a sentence that is one independent clause

Advance Preparation

To prepare for the GUM portion of this lesson, review Combining Sentences in the *Grammar Reference Guide* (linked in the online lesson) to familiarize yourself with the topic. Gather pages WS 29 and 30 (Model Personal Story), 35 and 36 (Gather and Organize Your Idea, students' completed graphic organizer), and 37 and 38 (Write Your Draft, students' personal story draft) in *K¹² Language Arts Activity Book*. Print the Personal Story: Feedback Sheet from the online lesson.

Big Ideas

- ▶ Sentence combining—teaching students to construct complex, sophisticated sentences—is an effective instructional strategy and an important element in learning to write well.
- ▶ Experience stories relate a meaningful event that made a lasting impression on the writer and can be communicated to a reader.

[Online] minutes

Students will work online independently to complete activities on combining sentences with conjunctions and to learn how to finish drafting a personal story. Help students locate the online activities.

GUM (Grammar, Usage, and Mechanics)

Combine Two Complete Sentences

Students will learn and practice how to use conjunctions to combine two simple sentences into one longer compound sentence.

 Objectives
- Combine two simple sentences to form a compound sentence.
- Use conjunctions to form compound sentences.

Composition

Winnie Finishes Her Draft

By watching how Winnie finishes drafting her personal story, students will learn how to finish drafting their own personal story.

Objectives
- Draft a personal story.

[Offline] **20 minutes**

Work **together** with students to complete the offline Composition and Peer Interaction activities.

Composition ·

✏️ **Write Your Draft**

Students will finish drafting their personal story, and you will review it. Have them gather the model personal story, their completed Gather and Organize Your Ideas pages, and their personal story draft. You will also need the Personal Story: Feedback Sheet, printable from the online lesson.

1. Have students finish drafting their personal story, continuing to write only in the white rows. If needed, additional drafting pages can be printed from the online lesson.

2. As students write, remind them to refer to Winnie's personal story and their Gather and Organize Your Ideas pages as necessary. Continue to emphasize that drafts are not meant to be perfect. They are a work in progress.

3. If students want to use a reference material such as the *Grammar Reference Guide* or a dictionary while drafting, suggest that they wait until they are revising or proofreading. Looking up information while drafting can interfere with students' flow of ideas.

   ⊃ **Learning Coach Check-In** When students have finished their draft, read and review it using the Personal Story: Feedback Sheet, but do not go over the feedback sheet with students now. The notes you take on this sheet will guide your feedback to students as they revise their draft in a later lesson. Keep the feedback sheet in a safe place until students are ready to revise their draft.

TIP Keep students' story draft and the Personal Story: Feedback Sheet in a safe place so they can be used later.

> **Objectives**
> - Draft a personal story.
> - Put ideas in chronological order.
> - State the significance of a story.

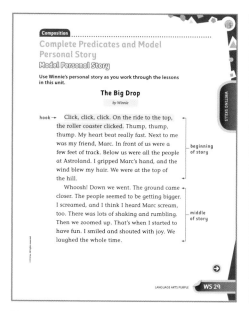

Composition

Complete Predicates and Model Personal Story

Model Personal Story

Use Winnie's personal story as you work through the lessons in this unit.

The Big Drop
by Winnie

hook → Click, click, click. On the ride to the top, the roller coaster clicked. Thump, thump, thump. My heart beat really fast. Next to me was my friend, Marc. In front of us were a few feet of track. Below us were all the people at Astroland. I gripped Marc's hand, and the wind blew my hair. We were at the top of the hill.

⟩ beginning of story

Whoosh! Down we went. The ground came closer. The people seemed to be getting bigger. I screamed, and I think I heard Marc scream, too. There was lots of shaking and rumbling. Then we zoomed up. That's when I started to have fun. I smiled and shouted with joy. We laughed the whole time.

⟩ middle of story

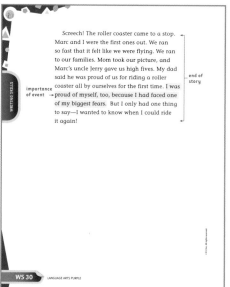

Screech! The roller coaster came to a stop. Marc and I were the first ones out. We ran so fast that it felt like we were flying. We ran to our families. Mom took our picture, and Marc's uncle Jerry gave us high fives. My dad said he was proud of us for riding a roller coaster all by ourselves for the first time. I was

⟩ end of story

importance of event → proud of myself, too, because I had faced one of my biggest fears. But I only had one thing to say—I wanted to know when I could ride it again!

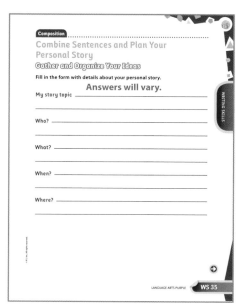

Composition

Combine Sentences and Plan Your Personal Story

Gather and Organize Your Ideas

Fill in the form with details about your personal story.

Answers will vary.

My story topic _____

Who? _____

What? _____

When? _____

Where? _____

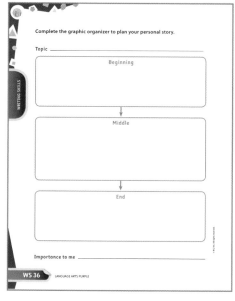

Complete the graphic organizer to plan your personal story.

Topic _____

Beginning

↓

Middle

↓

End

Importance to me _____

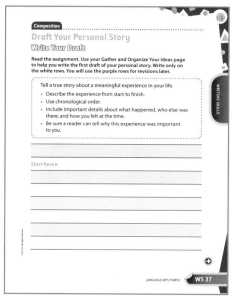

Composition

Draft Your Personal Story

Write Your Draft

Read the assignment. Use your Gather and Organize Your Ideas page to help you write the first draft of your personal story. Write only on the white rows. You will use the purple rows for revisions later.

Tell a true story about a meaningful experience in your life.
- Describe the experience from start to finish.
- Use chronological order.
- Include important details about what happened, who else was there, and how you felt at the time.
- Be sure a reader can tell why this experience was important to you.

Start here ▶

Peer Interaction

Objectives
- Use guidance from adults and peers to revise writing.
- Collaborate with peers on writing projects.

✚ OPTIONAL: Tell Me About My Story

This activity is OPTIONAL. It is intended for students who have extra time and would benefit from extra practice. Feel free to skip this activity.

Students can benefit from exchanging stories with another student. Each writer should receive feedback. To complete this optional activity, turn to pages WS 39 and 40 in *K¹² Language Arts Activity Book*. (Additional copies of the Peer Interaction Form can be printed from the online lesson.)

1. Have students exchange drafts with other students.

2. Have students use the Activity Book pages to provide others with feedback about their writing.

3. In the upcoming revising lesson, students may use the feedback provided from others to improve their story.

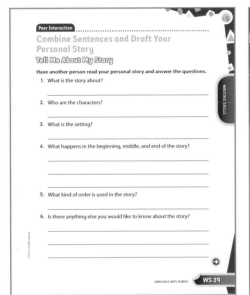

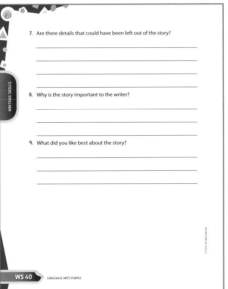

Improve Sentences with Details

Lesson Overview

[Online]   15 minutes

Skills Update	Combine Two Complete Sentences
GUM (Grammar, Usage, and Mechanics)	Details, Details

[Offline]   20 minutes

GUM (Grammar, Usage, and Mechanics)	Add Details to Sentences

[Materials]

Supplied
- *K¹² Language Arts Activity Book*, pp. WS 41–42
- *Grammar Reference Guide* Online Book (optional)
- Personal Story: Feedback Sheet (printout)

Keywords
sentence expanding – adding details, such as descriptive words and phrases, to sentences

Advance Preparation

To prepare for the GUM portion of this lesson, review Expanding and Reducing Sentences in the *Grammar Reference Guide* (linked in the online lesson) to familiarize yourself with the topic. If you have not already completed the Personal Story: Feedback Sheet, do so during this lesson while students work independently. You will need to share this form with students in the next lesson.

 **minutes**

Students will work online to review combining sentences and to complete an activity on adding details to sentences. Help students locate the online activities.

Skills Update

Combine Two Complete Sentences

Students will review how to combine two complete sentences by answering Skills Update questions. Sit with students as they do this activity and note if they answer correctly.

⮌ Learning Coach Check-In How did students do on the Skills Update?

> ▸ **All questions correct:** Great! Skip the review screen and go on to the next activity.

> ▸ **Any questions incorrect:** Take a few minutes to review combining two complete sentences now. Use the links on the screen after the Skills Update questions to take another look at the online activities or review Combining Sentences in the *Grammar Reference Guide* together.

 This activity will require extra time if students need to review combining two complete sentences. Take the extra 5–10 minutes to review now because new skills build on what students have already learned.

 Objectives
- Combine two simple sentences to form a compound sentence.
- Use conjunctions to form compound sentences.

GUM (Grammar, Usage, and Mechanics)

Details, Details

Students will learn how to expand sentences by adding details.

Objectives
- Expand sentences by adding details.

 **20 minutes**

Have students complete the offline GUM activity.

GUM (Grammar, Usage, and Mechanics) ....

Add Details to Sentences

Students will practice expanding sentences by adding details. Turn to pages WS 41 and 42 in *K¹² Language Arts Activity Book* and have students complete the pages.

Objectives
- Expand sentences by adding details.

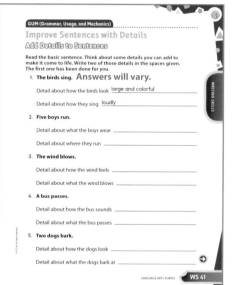

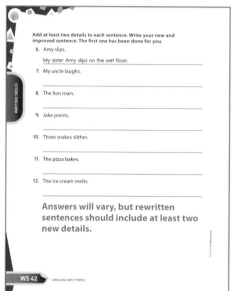

Revise Your Personal Story

Lesson Overview

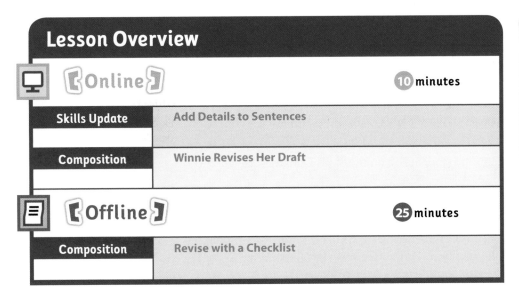

Online — 10 minutes

Skills Update	Add Details to Sentences
Composition	Winnie Revises Her Draft

Offline — 25 minutes

Composition	Revise with a Checklist

Advance Preparation

Gather pages WS 37 and 38 (Write Your Draft, students' draft of their personal story) and 39 and 40 (Tell Me About My Story, if completed) in *K¹² Language Arts Activity Book* and the completed Personal Story: Feedback Sheet. You will review the feedback sheet with students.

Big Ideas

▸ Teaching the writing process encourages students to organize their ideas before they write and revise their work after they write.

▸ One of the most powerful ways to improve writing is to directly teach strategies for planning and revising until students can use these strategies on their own.

▸ Experience stories relate a meaningful event that made a lasting impression on the writer and can be communicated to a reader.

▸ Knowing how to combine sentences that have similar subjects or similar predicates helps writers avoid monotony.

Materials

Supplied

- *K¹² Language Arts Activity Book*, pp. WS 37–40, 43
- *Grammar Reference Guide* Online Book (optional)
- drafting page (optional printout)
- Personal Story: Feedback Sheet (printout)

Keywords

chronological order – a way to organize that puts details in time order

revising – the stage or step of the writing process in which the writer rereads and edits the draft, correcting errors and making changes in content or organization that improve the piece

sentence expanding – adding details, such as descriptive words and phrases, to sentences

 **10 minutes**

Students will work online to review adding details to sentences and to learn how to revise a personal story. Help students locate the online activities.

Skills Update

Add Details to Sentences

Students will review how to add details to sentences by answering Skills Update questions. Sit with students as they do this activity and note if they answer correctly.

 Learning Coach Check-In How did students do on the Skills Update?

- ▸ **All questions correct:** Great! Skip the review screen and go on to the next activity.
- ▸ **Any questions incorrect:** Take a few minutes to review adding details to sentences now. Use the links on the screen after the Skills Update questions to take another look at the online activities or review Expanding and Reducing Sentences in the *Grammar Reference Guide* together.

TIP This activity will require extra time if students need to review adding details to sentences. Take the extra 5–10 minutes to review now because new skills build on what students have already learned.

> **Objectives**
> - Expand sentences by adding details.

Composition

Winnie Revises Her Draft

By watching how Winnie uses a checklist to revise her personal story draft, students will learn how to revise their draft.

> **Objectives**
> - Revise a personal story.

Offline **25** minutes

Work **together** with students to complete the offline Composition activity.

Composition

Revise with a Checklist

Students will revise their personal story. Have them gather their personal story draft and any completed Peer Interaction forms. Turn to page WS 43 in *K¹² Language Arts Activity Book* and gather the Personal Story: Feedback Sheet that you filled out.

Objectives

- Revise a personal story.
- Combine successive sentences that have the same subject or the same predicate.
- Expand sentences by adding details.
- Check for beginning, middle, and end and chronological order.

1. Use the Personal Story: Feedback Sheet to guide your discussion with students.

   ▶ Tell students the strengths of their story. Provide positive comments about the ideas, language, details, or other elements of the story you enjoyed.

   ▶ Walk through the Purpose and Content and Structure and Organization sections of the feedback sheet with students. Do not address your comments in the Grammar and Mechanics section at this time. You can work with students on grammar and mechanics when they proofread. Providing these corrections at this time may distract students from the real work of revising for content and structure.

   ▶ As you go through the feedback sheet with students, encourage them to actively revise their draft based on your feedback. Reassure students that it's okay to remove ideas or sentences from their story so that it stays focused and on track even if something was included in the graphic organizer on their Gather and Organize Your Ideas pages.

   ▶ As students revise their draft, have them use the purple rows to mark their revisions.

purple
Start here ▶ Students should write ~~only~~ in the ~~white~~ rows
revising
while ~~drafting.~~

2. Once you've reviewed your comments on the first two sections of the feedback sheet with students, have them review their draft once more, using the revising checklist on the Activity Book page. Students should check off each box on the checklist as they complete each item.

3. If students received feedback from peers, discuss with them how they might use it to improve their story. Help students decide which peer feedback would be useful to include in their revisions.

4. If students' revised personal story has many changes that make the story difficult to read and understand, encourage them to make a clean copy before they proofread in a later lesson. Additional drafting pages can be printed from the online lesson.

TIP Keep students' revised personal story in a safe place so students can refer to it later.

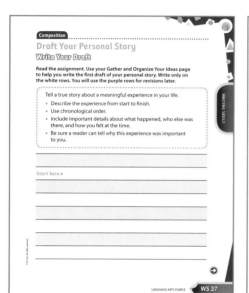

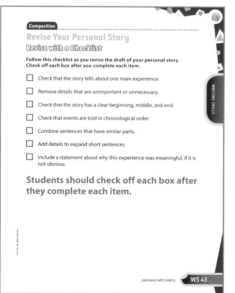

Unit Review and Proofread Your Personal Story

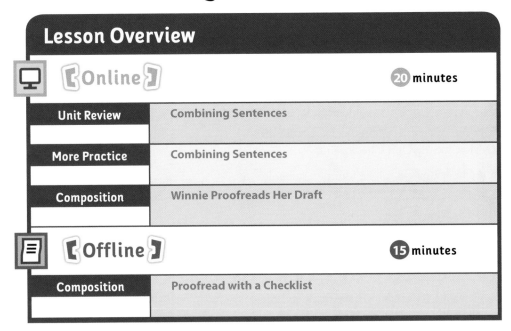

Lesson Overview

🖥️	**[Online]**	⏱️ **20 minutes**
Unit Review	Combining Sentences	
More Practice	Combining Sentences	
Composition	Winnie Proofreads Her Draft	
📄	**[Offline]**	⏱️ **15 minutes**
Composition	Proofread with a Checklist	

Advance Preparation

Gather pages WS 37 and 38 (Write Your Draft, students' draft of their personal story) in *K¹² Language Arts Activity Book* and the completed Personal Story: Feedback Sheet. If students' revised personal story has many changes that make the story difficult to read and understand, encourage them to make a clean copy before they proofread in this lesson. Additional drafting pages can be printed from the online lesson.

Big Ideas

▸ Good writers carefully check their work for errors.
▸ Experience stories relate a meaningful event that made a lasting impression on the writer and can be communicated to a reader.
▸ Knowing how to combine sentences that have similar subjects or similar predicates helps writers avoid monotony.
▸ Sentence combining—teaching students to construct complex, sophisticated sentences—is an effective instructional strategy and an important element in learning how to write well.

Materials

Supplied

- *K¹² Language Arts Activity Book*, pp. WS 37–38, 45
- *Grammar Reference Guide* Online Book (optional)
- drafting page (optional printout)
- Personal Story: Feedback Sheet (printout)

Keywords

compound predicate – two or more predicates that have the same subject

compound sentence – a sentence that has at least two independent clauses

compound subject – two or more subjects that have the same predicate

conjunction – a word used to join parts of a sentence, such as *and*, *but*, and *or*

predicate – the verb or verb phrase in a sentence

proofreading – the stage or step of the writing process in which the writer checks for errors in grammar, punctuation, capitalization, and spelling

sentence combining – joining two sentences that have similar parts into one sentence

sentence expanding – adding details, such as descriptive words and phrases, to sentences

simple sentence – a sentence that is one independent clause

subject – a word or words that tell whom or what the sentence is about

 **20 minutes**

Students will work online to review the grammar, usage, and mechanics skills learned in the unit and also to learn how to proofread a personal story. Help students locate the online activities.

Unit Review

Combining Sentences

Students will review what they have learned about subjects, predicates, combining sentences, and expanding sentences to review for the Unit Checkpoint.

TIP A full list of objectives covered in the Unit Review can be found in the online lesson.

Objectives
- Complete a review of grammar, usage, and mechanics skills.

More Practice

Combining Sentences

Go over students' results on the Unit Review and, if necessary, have them complete the appropriate review activities listed in the table online. Help students locate the activities and provide support as needed.

TIP The time students need to complete this activity will vary. Set aside enough time for students to complete all review activities, if they need to do so.

Objectives
- Evaluate Unit Review results and choose activities for more practice.

Composition

Winnie Proofreads Her Draft

By watching how Winnie proofreads her personal story draft, students will learn how to proofread their draft.

Objectives
- Proofread a personal story.
- Check capitalization and punctuation of sentences.

 **Offline** (15) minutes

Work **together** with students to complete the offline Composition activity.

Composition ....

Proofread with a Checklist

Students will proofread their personal story. Have them gather their personal story draft. Turn to page WS 45 in *K¹² Language Arts Activity Book* and gather the Personal Story: Feedback Sheet that you filled out.

 Objectives
- Proofread a personal story.
- Check capitalization and punctuation of sentences.

1. Review with students your comments in the Grammar and Mechanics section of the feedback sheet. As you go through the feedback sheet with students, encourage them to use the purple rows on their drafting pages to actively mark changes based on your feedback.

2. Once you've reviewed your comments in the Grammar and Mechanics section of the feedback sheet with students, have them review their draft once more using the proofreading checklist. Students should check off each box on the checklist as they complete each item.

3. If students' revised personal story has many changes that make the story difficult to read and understand, encourage them to make a clean copy before they proofread. Additional drafting pages can be printed from the online lesson.

TIP Keep students' proofread story in a safe place so they can refer to it later.

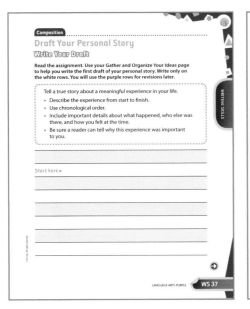

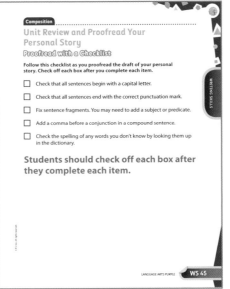

Unit Checkpoint and Publish Your Personal Story

Lesson Overview

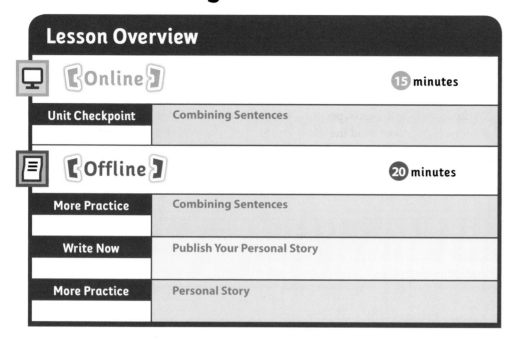

Online		15 minutes
Unit Checkpoint	Combining Sentences	

Offline		20 minutes
More Practice	Combining Sentences	
Write Now	Publish Your Personal Story	
More Practice	Personal Story	

Advance Preparation

Gather pages WS 37 and 38 (Write Your Draft, students' draft of their personal story) in *K¹² Language Arts Activity Book*, which students should have revised and proofread.

Big Ideas

▶ Working collaboratively with other students during various stages of the writing process can improve student writing.

▶ Experience stories relate a meaningful event that made a lasting impression on the writer and can be communicated to a reader.

▶ Knowing how to combine sentences that have similar subjects or similar predicates helps writers avoid monotony.

▶ Sentence combining—teaching students to construct complex, sophisticated sentences—is an effective instructional strategy and an important element in learning how to write well.

Materials

Supplied

● *K¹² Language Arts Activity Book*, pp. WS 37–38, 47–50

● *Grammar Reference Guide* Online Book (optional)

● Personal Story: Rubric and Sample Responses (printout)

● *Subjects and Predicates* (optional printout)

● Sentence Combining (optional printout)

● Add Details to Sentences (optional printout)

● lined writing page (optional printout)

Keywords

compound predicate – two or more predicates that have the same subject

compound sentence – a sentence that has at least two independent clauses

compound subject – two or more subjects that have the same predicate

conjunction – a word used to join parts of a sentence, such as *and*, *but*, and *or*

predicate – the verb or verb phrase in a sentence

publishing – the stage or step of the writing process in which the writer makes a clean copy of the piece and shares it

sentence combining – joining two sentences that have similar parts into one sentence

sentence expanding – adding details, such as descriptive words and phrases, to sentences

simple sentence – a sentence that is one independent clause

subject – a word or words that tell whom or what the sentence is about

 **15** minutes

Students will work online **independently** to complete the Unit Checkpoint. Help students locate the Unit Checkpoint and provide support as necessary.

 ....

Combining Sentences

Students will complete an online Unit Checkpoint about subjects, predicates, combining sentences, and expanding sentences. If necessary, read the directions to students.

 A full list of objectives covered in the Unit Checkpoint can be found in the online lesson.

Objectives
- Complete a Unit Checkpoint on grammar, usage, and mechanics skills.

[Offline] **20** minutes

Work **together** with students to complete the offline More Practice and Write Now activities.

More Practice ....

Combining Sentences

Go over students' results on the Unit Checkpoint and, if they missed **two or more** exercises in a section, print out and have them complete the activity page or pages listed in the table online. Students can complete all necessary pages now or spread them out over the next few days. They can also review the appropriate sections of the *Grammar Reference Guide* with you. If students scored less than 80 percent on the Unit Checkpoint, you may want them to retake the checkpoint after completing the additional activity pages.

 The time students need to complete this activity will vary. Set aside enough time for students to complete some or all activity pages and to retake the Unit Checkpoint, if they need to do so. Students may retake the Unit Checkpoint immediately, but having them complete the activity pages and then retake it might be more effective.

Objectives
- Evaluate Unit Checkpoint results and choose activities for more practice.

More Practice

Improve Your Skills
Subjects and Predicates

Choose the complete subject of the sentence.

1. Meg lives in Rhode Island.
   - (A) Meg
   - B. lives
   - C. lives in Rhode Island
   - D. Rhode Island

2. Many pretty flowers bloom in June.
   - A. pretty flowers
   - (B) Many pretty flowers
   - C. bloom
   - D. in June

3. The men at the bus stop wave to the driver.
   - (A) The men at the bus stop
   - B. bus stop
   - C. wave to the driver
   - D. driver

4. A loud silver helicopter landed on the roof.
   - A. loud
   - B. silver helicopter
   - (C) A loud silver helicopter
   - D. helicopter landed on the roof

5. Six people boarded the train.
   - A. people
   - B. people boarded the train
   - C. the train
   - (D) Six people

Underline the complete predicate in the sentence.

6. A small yellow bird chirps.
7. Kelly and Joe walked to the park after dinner.
8. Most of my friends play the drums.
9. You opened the envelope.
10. Come with me to the party.

More Practice

Improve Your Skills
Sentence Combining

Combine the pair of sentences to form one sentence. Your combined sentence should have a compound predicate joined by a conjunction.

1. Hannah sings.
   Hannah dances.

   Hannah sings and dances.

2. The bottle dropped into the sea.
   The bottle floated on the waves.

   The bottle dropped into the sea and floated on the waves.

3. My aunt stopped by.
   My aunt left quickly.

   My aunt stopped by but left quickly.

4. Sam picked up the game.
   He turned it on.

   Sam picked up the game and turned it on.

Read each pair of sentences. Then combine them to form one sentence with a compound subject joined by a conjunction.

5. Many Germans love to cook.
   Many Italians love to cook.

   Many Germans and Italians love to cook.

6. Mom came to my recital.
   Dad came to my recital.

   Mom and Dad came to my recital.

7. Geese fly south for the winter.
   Ducks fly south for the winter.

   Geese and ducks fly south for the winter.

8. Dogs make good pets.
   Gerbils make good pets.

   Dogs and gerbils make good pets.

Choose the compound sentence that correctly combines the pairs of sentences.

9. I washed the dishes.
   Jody dried them.
   - A. I washed the dishes Jody dried them.
   - B. I washed the dishes, Jody dried them.
   - C. I washed the dishes and Jody dried them.
   - (D) I washed the dishes, and Jody dried them.

---

10. Vanilla is good.
    Chocolate is better.
    - A. Vanilla is good but chocolate is better.
    - (B) Vanilla is good, but chocolate is better.
    - C. Vanilla is good, chocolate is better.
    - D. Vanilla is good chocolate is better.

Write a compound sentence that joins each pair of sentences.

11. The sidewalk was icy.
    I slipped.

    Answers may include:
    The sidewalk was icy, and I slipped.
    The sidewalk was icy, so I slipped.

12. Call me tonight.
    We will talk.

    Call me tonight, and we will talk.

More Practice

Improve Your Skills
Add Details to Sentences

Read the sentence. Think about its subject and its predicate. Then, add at least one detail to the subject and one detail to the predicate. The first one has been done for you.

1. The mouse ran.

   The small mouse ran quickly across the floor.

2. A leaf falls.

3. Two women laugh.

4. The car is red.

5. My shoes are in the closet.

6. The man was a quarterback.

   Students should add a detail to both the subject and predicate in each sentence they write.

Write Now

 Publish Your Personal Story

Students will publish their personal story. Have them gather their proofread draft. Turn to pages WS 47–50 in *K¹² Language Arts Activity Book*.

Objectives

- Make a clean copy of a personal story.

1. Explain to students that they will finish their personal story by completing the last step in the writing process—publishing their work.
   Say: Publishing your writing means making a clean and final copy that is ready for sharing with others.

   ▸ To be ready to publish your personal story, you should have finished revising and proofreading your draft.
   ▸ The final copy should be your best effort and should not have any errors.

2. Explain that the final copy should be written clearly and neatly on clean sheets of paper. Tell students that they should use good handwriting and leave spaces between words so that others can read what they wrote.

3. Have students use the lined Activity Book pages to write their final copy. If needed, additional lined writing pages can be printed from the online lesson.

4. Use the materials and instructions in the online lesson to evaluate students' finished writing. You will be looking at students' writing to evaluate the following:

   ▸ **Purpose and Content:** The story describes a meaningful experience, focuses mostly on the important moments of that experience, and includes few unnecessary details. The story tells how the author felt at the time and states why the experience is significant. The writing has some measure of sentence fluency and some descriptive details.
   ▸ **Structure and Organization:** The story has been revised. The piece has a beginning with a hook, middle, and end. Most events are described in chronological order.
   ▸ **Grammar and Mechanics:** The story has been proofread using a checklist, and few, if any, errors remain. Most sentences are complete, and any compound sentences have a conjunction.

5. Enter students' scores online for each rubric category.

6. If students' writing scored a 1 in any category, work with them to revise and proofread their work.

7. Suggest that, if possible, students share their personal story with anyone who played a part in the experience with them. In addition, people special to students, such as grandparents, would likely enjoy hearing the story read to them or having a copy of the story to keep.

TIP Tell students that producing a piece of writing that is ready to publish and share with others is a great accomplishment. Let students know that the effort they put in to publish a story is something to be proud of.

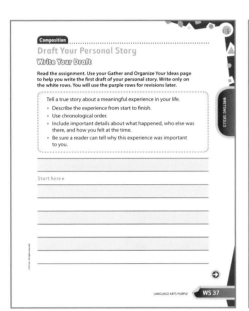

Composition

Draft Your Personal Story

Write Your Draft

Read the assignment. Use your Gather and Organize Your Ideas page to help you write the first draft of your personal story. Write only on the white rows. You will use the purple rows for revisions later.

> Tell a true story about a meaningful experience in your life.
> - Describe the experience from start to finish.
> - Use chronological order.
> - Include important details about what happened, who else was there, and how you felt at the time.
> - Be sure a reader can tell why this experience was important to you.

Start here ▶

LANGUAGE ARTS PURPLE **WS 37**

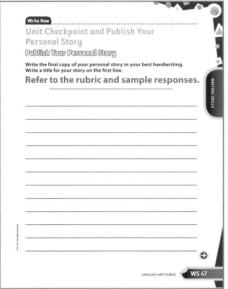

Write Now

Unit Checkpoint and Publish Your Personal Story

Publish Your Personal Story

Write the final copy of your personal story in your best handwriting. Write a title for your story on the first line.

Refer to the rubric and sample responses.

LANGUAGE ARTS PURPLE **WS 47**

More Practice

Personal Story

If students' writing did not meet objectives, have them complete the appropriate review activities listed in the table online. Follow the online instructions to help them revise and proofread their work. Impress upon students that revising makes their work better. Writing is a process, and each time they revise their story they are improving their writing. Always begin with something positive to say. If there is one detail, for example, mention it and say how this detail helps you picture what is being written about.

Help students locate the activities and provide support as needed.

Objectives
• Revise a personal story.

Reward: When students score 80 percent or above on the Unit Checkpoint and their writing is Level 2 or higher on the Personal Story grading rubric, add a sticker for this unit on the My Accomplishments chart.

Critical Skills Practice 1

Unit Focus

This is the first Critical Skills Practice unit of the Writing Skills program. Be sure to watch the Introduction to Critical Skills Practice in the online lesson.

In this unit, students will practice answering questions about skills associated with vocabulary, language, and spelling. They will

- ▶ Practice vocabulary skills by applying knowledge of prefixes and suffixes to determine the meaning of an unfamiliar word.
- ▶ Review what a complete sentence is and determine the difference between a complete sentence and a fragment.
- ▶ Practice recognizing correct agreement of a verb with its subject.
- ▶ Learn how to recognize and spell the correct homophone and to spell compound words.

Unit Plan		[Offline]	[Online]
Lesson 1	Vocabulary Skills (A)		35 minutes
Lesson 2	Language Skills (A)		35 minutes
Lesson 3	Spelling Skills (A)		35 minutes
Lesson 4	Vocabulary Skills (B)		35 minutes
Lesson 5	Unit Checkpoint	35 minutes	varies

Vocabulary Skills (A)

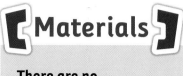

Lesson Overview

[Online]   **35** minutes

Get Ready	Prefixes
Learn	Questions About Prefixes
Try It	Answer Questions About Prefixes

Keywords

context clue – a word or phrase in a text that helps you figure out the meaning of an unknown word

prefix – a word part with its own meaning that can be added to the beginning of a base word or root to make a new word with a different meaning

Advance Preparation

Watch the Introduction to Critical Skills Practice with students before beginning the lesson.

Big Ideas

Practice answering the kinds of questions often found on standardized tests can make taking the tests less stressful for students.

[Online] **35** minutes

Students will work online **independently** to complete Get Ready, Learn, and Try It activities. Help students locate the online activities.

Get Ready ....

Prefixes
Students will review the definition of *prefix*, the meaning of some common prefixes, and the role that context clues play in unlocking the meanings of words with prefixes.

Objectives
- Define *prefix*.
- Recall the meanings of prefixes.
- Use sentence-level context as a clue to the meaning of a word or phrase.

Learn

Questions About Prefixes
Students will learn how to answer questions about words that begin with prefixes. They will read and work through several exercises about prefixes.

Objectives
- Identify and use prefixes to determine word meaning.
- Use sentence-level context as a clue to the meaning of a word or phrase.

Try It

Answer Questions About Prefixes
Students will show their comprehension of the skills they have learned by answering several questions about words with prefixes.

Objectives
- Identify and use prefixes to determine word meaning.
- Use sentence-level context as a clue to the meaning of a word or phrase.

Language Skills (A)

Lesson Overview

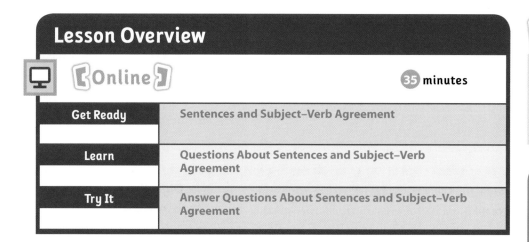

Get Ready	Sentences and Subject–Verb Agreement
Learn	Questions About Sentences and Subject–Verb Agreement
Try It	Answer Questions About Sentences and Subject–Verb Agreement

Online · 35 minutes

Advance Preparation

To prepare for this lesson, review Sentences (Complete Sentences) and Agreement (Subject and Verb Agreement) in the *Grammar Reference Guide* (linked in the online lesson) to familiarize yourself with the topics.

Big Ideas

Practice answering the kinds of questions often found on standardized tests can make taking the tests less stressful for students.

Materials

Supplied
- *Grammar Reference Guide* Online Book (optional)

Keywords

predicate – the verb or verb phrase in a sentence

sentence – a group of words that tells a complete thought

subject – a word or words that tell whom or what the sentence is about

subject–verb agreement – the way a subject and verb match when both are singular or both are plural

---

 **Online** · 35 minutes

Students will work online **independently** to complete Get Ready, Learn, and Try It activities. Help students locate the online activities.

Get Ready ....

Sentences and Subject–Verb Agreement
Students will review what a complete sentence is, how to add details to a sentence, and how to make a subject and verb agree in a sentence.

Objectives
- Define *complete sentence*.
- Identify subject and verb agreement.

Learn

Questions About Sentences and Subject–Verb Agreement

Students will learn how to answer questions that require them to identify complete sentences, expand sentences by adding details, and demonstrate their understanding of subject–verb agreement.

Objectives

- Identify a complete sentence.
- Expand sentences by adding details.
- Use a verb that agrees with its subject.

Try It

Answer Questions About Sentences and Subject–Verb Agreement

Students will show their comprehension of the skills they have learned by answering several questions about complete sentences, adding details to sentences, and subject–verb agreement.

Objectives

- Identify a complete sentence.
- Expand sentences by adding details.
- Use a verb that agrees with its subject.

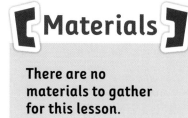

Spelling Skills (A)

Lesson Overview

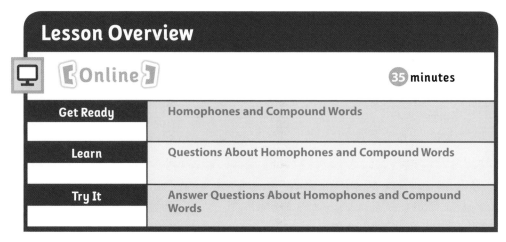

Online		35 minutes
Get Ready	Homophones and Compound Words	
Learn	Questions About Homophones and Compound Words	
Try It	Answer Questions About Homophones and Compound Words	

Materials

There are no materials to gather for this lesson.

Keywords

compound word – a word made from two smaller words

homophone – a word that sounds the same as another word but has a different spelling and meaning

Big Ideas

Practice answering the kinds of questions often found on standardized tests can make taking the tests less stressful for students.

 **35 minutes**

Students will work online **independently** to complete Get Ready, Learn, and Try It activities. Help students locate the online activities.

Get Ready

Homophones and Compound Words
Students will review what homophones are, how to use context clues to identify the meaning of a homophone, and how to recognize a compound word. Applying this knowledge will help students spell homophones and compound words.

Objectives

- Define *homophone*.
- Define *compound word*.
- Use sentence-level context as a clue to the meaning of a word or phrase.

Learn

Questions About Homophones and Compound Words
Students will learn how to answer questions that require them to spell homophones and compound words.

Objectives
- Spell homophones.
- Spell compound words.
- Use sentence-level context as a clue to the meaning of a word or phrase.

Try It

Answer Questions About Homophones and Compound Words
Students will show their comprehension of the skills they have learned by answering several questions about spelling homophones and compound words.

Objectives
- Spell homophones.
- Spell compound words.
- Use sentence-level context as a clue to the meaning of a word or phrase.

Vocabulary Skills (B)

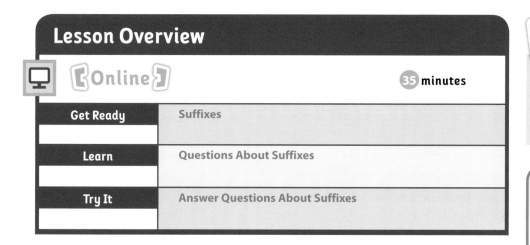

Lesson Overview

Online
35 minutes

Get Ready	Suffixes
Learn	Questions About Suffixes
Try It	Answer Questions About Suffixes

Big Ideas

Practice answering the kinds of questions often found on standardized tests can make taking the tests less stressful for students.

Materials

There are no materials to gather for this lesson.

Keywords

context clue – a word or phrase in a text that helps you figure out the meaning of an unknown word

suffix – a word part added to the end of a base word or root that changes the meaning or part of speech of a word

Online 35 minutes

Students will work online **independently** to complete Get Ready, Learn, and Try It activities. Help students locate the online activities.

Get Ready

Suffixes

Students will review the definition of *suffix*, the meaning of some common suffixes, and the role that context clues play in unlocking the meanings of words with suffixes.

Objectives
- Define *suffix*.
- Recall the meaning of suffixes.
- Use sentence-level context as a clue to the meaning of a word or phrase.

Learn

Questions About Suffixes

Students will learn how to answer questions about words that end with suffixes. They will read and work through several exercises about suffixes.

Objectives

- Identify and use suffixes to determine word meaning.
- Use sentence-level context as a clue to the meaning of a word or phrase.

Try It

Answer Questions About Suffixes

Students will show their comprehension of the skills they have learned by answering several questions about words with suffixes.

Objectives

- Identify and use suffixes to determine word meaning.
- Use sentence-level context as a clue to the meaning of a word or phrase.

Unit Checkpoint

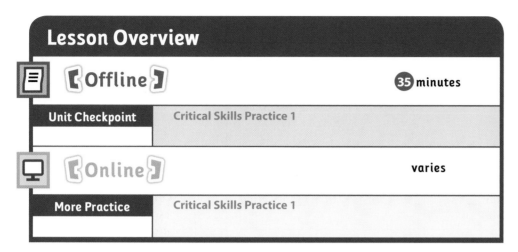

Lesson Overview

〔Offline〕 — 35 minutes

Unit Checkpoint	Critical Skills Practice 1

〔Online〕 — varies

More Practice	Critical Skills Practice 1

〔Materials〕

Supplied

- *K¹² Language Arts Assessments*, pp. WS 1–7

Objectives

- Identify and use prefixes to determine word meaning.
- Identify and use suffixes to determine word meaning.
- Identify a complete sentence.
- Expand sentences by adding details.
- Use a verb that agrees with its subject.
- Spell homophones.
- Spell compound words.

〔Offline〕 35 minutes

Unit Checkpoint

Critical Skills Practice 1

Explain that students are going to show what they have learned about prefixes, suffixes, sentences, subject–verb agreement, homophones, and compound words.

1. Give students the Unit Checkpoint pages.

2. Read the directions together. Have students complete the Checkpoint on their own.

3. Use the Answer Key to score the Checkpoint and then enter the results online.

4. Review each exercise with students. Work with students to correct any exercise that they missed.

Reward: If students score 80 percent or more on the Unit Checkpoint, add a sticker for this unit on the My Accomplishments chart. If students did not score 80 percent or more, work with them to revise their work until they do score 80 percent.

Name _____ Date _____

Unit Checkpoint Learning Coach Instructions
Critical Skills Practice 1

Explain that students are going to show what they have learned about prefixes, suffixes, sentences, subject–verb agreement, homophones, and compound words.

1. Give students the Unit Checkpoint pages.
2. Read the directions together. Have students complete the Checkpoint on their own.
3. Use the Answer Key to score the Checkpoint and then enter the results online.
4. Review each exercise with students. Work with students to correct any exercise they missed.

Name _____ Date _____

Unit Checkpoint Answer Key
Critical Skills Practice 1

Part 1. Prefixes
Read and answer each question.

1. Read this sentence.

   It was unfair for Jen to start running before Rex said, "Go."

   In this sentence, why does the writer uses the word *unfair*?
   A. to show that what Jen did was fair
   B. to show that what Jen did was not fair
   C. to show that what Jen did was fair again
   D. to show that what Jen did was fair earlier

2. Which prefix can be added to the word *believe* to make a word that means "the opposite of believe"?
   A. dis–   B. pre–   C. re–   D. mis–

3. Read this sentence.

   Wally _____ paid for all of the food for the party months ago, so our dinner didn't cost us anything.

   Which prefix should be added to the word *paid* to make the sentence true?
   A. mis–   B. dis–   C. un–   **D.** pre–

---

4. Read this sentence.

   Lola misbehaved when the babysitter was here, and Mom and Dad were angry when they found out.

   What does the prefix *mis*– tell us in this sentence?
   A. Lola behaved in a funny way.
   B. Lola behaved well.
   C. Lola behaved badly.
   D. Lola behaved for most of the night.

5. Which prefix can be added to the word *play* to make a word that means "play again"?
   A. mis–   B. pre–   **C.** re–   D. un–

Part 2. Suffixes
Read and answer each question.

6. Read this sentence.

   As she left for summer camp, Meredith said a tearful good-bye to her parents.

   In this sentence, why does the writer uses the word *tearful*?
   A. to show that Meredith did not cry as she left for summer camp
   B. to show that Meredith did not want to cry as she left for summer camp
   C. to show that Meredith's parents cried as she left for summer camp
   D. to show that Meredith cried a lot as she left for summer camp

---

Name _____ Date _____

7. Which suffix can be added to the word *sing* to make a new word that means "a person who sings"?
   A. –ful   C. –less
   B. –er   D. –ous

8. Read this sentence.

   It was so courage_____ of Lisa to pull Rich from the ocean that the mayor gave her a medal.

   Which suffix should be added to the word *courage* to make the sentence true?
   A. –ous   C. –er
   B. –able   D. –less

9. Read this sentence.

   Luckily, the mug I broke this morning is *replaceable*.

   What does the suffix *–able* tell us in this sentence?
   A. The mug was empty when it broke.
   B. The mug was full when it broke.
   C. The mug cannot be replaced.
   D. The mug can be replaced.

10. Which suffix can be added to the word *luck* to make a word that means "without luck"?
   A. –ous   C. –er
   B. –able   **D.** –less

Name _____ Date _____

Part 3. Sentences and Subject–Verb Agreement
Read and answer each question.

11. Which word group is a complete sentence?
   A. Washed the car on Sunday.
   B. Mom mowed the lawn.
   C. Cleaned her room all morning.
   D. The trash can in the corner.

12. Which words could correctly complete this sentence?

   The gray basement door _____ .

   A. swings open
   B. downstairs here
   C. near the kitchen
   D. with the gold handle

13. Read this sentence.

   The wolf came closer to the campfire, and the campers noticed.

   What is the best place to add the words *even though it was hot* to the sentence?
   A. after *wolf*
   B. after *came*
   C. after *campfire*
   D. after *campers*

Name _____ Date _____

14. Read this sentence.

   The airplane roar over the houses.

   What is the correct way to write the underlined words?
   A. The airplanes roars   C. The airplane roaring
   B. The airplane will roared   **D.** The airplane roars

15. Which sentence is written correctly?
   A. Raindrops falls on our heads.
   B. Runners cross the finish line.
   C. Newspapers piles up on the front step.
   D. Paintings hangs on the walls of the house.

Part 4. Homophones and Compound Words
Read and answer each question.

16. Read this sentence.

   I hear that you know how to play the piano, sew I want to talk to you.

   Which underlined word should be replaced with a word that sounds the same but is spelled differently?
   A. hear   B. know   **C.** sew   D. to

17. Which underlined word is used correctly?
   A. You can have one or the other but not both.
   B. They're is a big bug in the kitchen.
   C. I saw the fluffy tail of a dear disappear into the woods.
   D. Kendra eight lunch with Todd at noon.

Name _____ Date _____

18. Read this sentence.

   As Julia ate some fruitcake, she picked out a blueberry with a teespoon to give to her teammate.

   Which word in the sentence is spelled wrong?
   A. fruitcake   **C.** teespoon
   B. blueberry   D. teammate

19. Read this sentence.

   Phil was on the highway last Sunday when he realized that he left the handbook in the pocket of his raincoat.

   Which word in the sentence is spelled wrong?
   A. highway   C. handbook
   B. Sunday   **D.** raincoat

20. Read this sentence.

   Carla likes to dadream about what it would be like to fly like a bird.

   What is the correct way to spell the underlined word?
   A. daydreem   **C.** daydream
   B. daidream   D. daedreem

 **varies**

Work **together** with students to complete the online More Practice activity.

More Practice

Critical Skills Practice 1

Go over students' results on the Unit Checkpoint. If necessary, have students complete the appropriate review activities listed in the table online. Help students locate the activities and provide support as needed.

 The time students need to complete this activity will vary. Set aside enough time for students to complete all review activities, if they need to do so.

Objectives

• Evaluate Unit Checkpoint results and choose activities for more practice.

Share Information in a Letter

Unit Focus

In the grammar part of the unit, students will learn about capitalization and punctuation in letters. They will

- Learn the proper use of capital letters and commas when writing addresses and dates.
- Learn the parts of a personal letter, including its heading, salutation or greeting, body, closing, and signature, as well as how to write each one correctly.
- Learn how to properly address an envelope by including not only the recipient's name and address, but also the sender's return address.

In the composition part of the unit, students will write a personal letter. They will

- Use their journal to freewrite.
- Brainstorm topics for three different kinds of personal letters and develop plans for all three.
- Write a draft of a friendly letter, a thank-you letter, or an invitation.
- Revise and proofread their personal letter.
- Write a final copy of their personal letter to share.
- Learn the parts of an e-mail, including what information belongs in each field, as well as how to compose a message with a greeting, body, closing, and signature.

Unit Plan		Online	Offline
Lesson 1	Capital Letters & Commas in Days & Dates and Journal Entry	15 minutes	20 minutes
Lesson 2	Model Personal Letter	20 minutes	15 minutes
Lesson 3	Heading of a Letter and Plan a Friendly Letter	20 minutes	15 minutes
Lesson 4	Greeting & Closing of a Letter and Plan a Thank-You Letter	20 minutes	15 minutes
Lesson 5	Addresses and Plan a Letter of Invitation	20 minutes	15 minutes
Lesson 6	Draft Your Personal Letter	10 minutes	25 minutes
Lesson 7	Letters as E-mails	15 minutes	20 minutes
Lesson 8	Revise Your Personal Letter	10 minutes	25 minutes
Lesson 9	Unit Review and Proofread Your Personal Letter	20 minutes	15 minutes
Lesson 10	Unit Checkpoint and Publish Your Personal Letter	15 minutes	20 minutes

Capital Letters & Commas in Days & Dates and Journal Entry

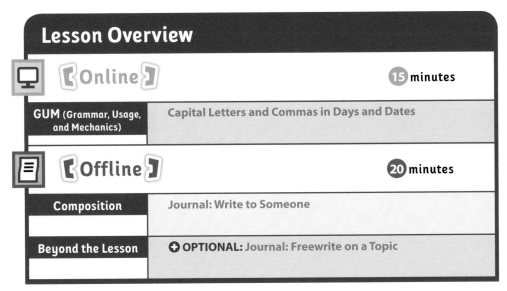

Lesson Overview

Online		**15** minutes
GUM (Grammar, Usage, and Mechanics)	Capital Letters and Commas in Days and Dates	
Offline		**20** minutes
Composition	Journal: Write to Someone	
Beyond the Lesson	⊕ OPTIONAL: Journal: Freewrite on a Topic	

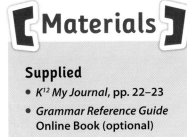

Materials

Supplied
- *K¹² My Journal*, pp. 22–23
- *Grammar Reference Guide* Online Book (optional)

Advance Preparation

To prepare for the GUM portion of this lesson, review Capitalization (Parts of a Letter; Days, Months, and Holidays) and Commas (In the Heading, Greeting, and Closing of a Letter) in the *Grammar Reference Guide* (linked in the online lesson) to familiarize yourself with the topics.

Big Ideas

▸ Journal writing is a form of freewriting. It is an opportunity to get ideas on paper without regard for correctness of the language or the format of a piece of writing.
▸ To improve, writers require frequent practice.

 **Online** **15 minutes**

Students will work online **independently** to complete an activity on using capital letters and commas correctly when writing days and dates. Help students locate the online activity.

GUM (Grammar, Usage, and Mechanics)

Capital Letters and Commas in Days and Dates
Students will learn rules for capitalizing the names of months and days, as well as where to place a comma when writing a date. They will then practice using proper capitalization and punctuation in days and dates.

Objectives
- Use a capital letter to begin the name of a day.
- Use a capital letter to begin the name of a month.
- Use a comma in a date.

 **Offline** **20 minutes**

Work **together** with students to complete the offline Composition and Beyond the Lesson activities.

Composition

 Journal: Write to Someone
Students will respond to a journal prompt by writing about the purpose of letters, some of the people they've written letters to, and their reasons for writing. Gather *K¹² My Journal* and have students turn to pages 22 and 23.

Objectives
- Respond to a journal prompt.
- Freewrite about a topic.

1. Tell students they are going to write in their journal about the reasons that people write letters. To help students think of several reasons for writing letters, ask them to think about their answers to the following questions.

   ▸ Have you ever written a letter to someone? Whom did you write to? What was your reason for writing? Why did you write a letter rather than talk to the person, either in person or over the phone?

   ▸ Have you ever received a letter from someone? Why did this person write to you? What was the letter about? How did receiving the letter make you feel?

   ▸ What are some advantages of putting thoughts, ideas, and feelings in writing rather than simply talking about them? Do you like to keep things that people give you? How are letters more lasting than conversations?

2. Have students respond to the prompt in their journal. Encourage students to write in complete sentences, although it is not a requirement when they are freewriting in their journal.

TIP Students should write for about 20 minutes. Freewriting allows students to use their imagination to write what they want without worrying about being graded, so encourage them to keep writing for the entire time. If students have trouble writing for 20 minutes, use the prompting questions in Step 1 or have them list ideas or words. If they want to keep writing beyond the suggested time limit, praise them for their enthusiasm and offer to let them complete their entry later in the day as a reward.

Beyond the Lesson

OPTIONAL: Journal: Freewrite on a Topic

This activity is OPTIONAL. It is intended for students who have extra time and would benefit from extra practice. Feel free to skip this activity. Gather *K¹² My Journal*.

1. Have students either respond to a prompt in Thoughts and Experiences (pages 50–93) or write about their own topic on the next available page in Ideas (pages 96–139).

2. Encourage students to explore their thoughts and write as much as they want. There are no rules. If students wish, ideas can be fleshed out into a more developed composition at a later time.

TIP Studies show that students who write more frequently become better writers.

Objectives
- Respond to a journal prompt.
- Freewrite about a topic.

Model Personal Letter

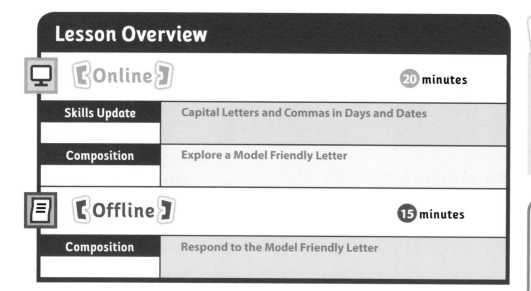

Lesson Overview

🖥 [Online] ⏱20 minutes

Skills Update	Capital Letters and Commas in Days and Dates
Composition	Explore a Model Friendly Letter

📄 [Offline] ⏱15 minutes

Composition	Respond to the Model Friendly Letter

Advance Preparation

To prepare for this lesson, review Resources (Model Personal [Friendly] Letter) in the *Grammar Reference Guide* to familiarize yourself with the topic. In this lesson, students begin to accumulate documents that they will need as they work on their personal letter. You might want to provide students with a folder or large envelope in which to keep these documents.

Big Ideas

- ▸ Friendly letters, also called personal letters, are written to share news, information, ideas, or feelings.
- ▸ When a writer uses the correct format, capitalization, and punctuation in a letter, the reader is better able to focus on the writer's ideas.

[Materials]

Supplied
- *K¹² Language Arts Activity Book*, pp. WS 51–54
- *Grammar Reference Guide* Online Book (optional)

Keywords

audience – a writer's readers

body (of a friendly letter) – the main text of a friendly letter

closing (of a friendly letter) – the part of a friendly letter that follows the body; for example, *Your friend* or *Love*

friendly letter – a kind of letter used to share thoughts, feelings, and news

heading – the first part of a letter that has the writer's address and the date

purpose – the reason for writing

salutation (of a friendly letter) – the greeting of a letter, which usually says, "Dear (name of recipient),"

signature (of a friendly letter) – the end of a letter where the writer writes his or her name

tone – the writer's attitude toward the topic or subject

voice – the way a piece of writing sounds

 **20 minutes**

Students will work online to review capital letters and commas in days and dates and to read and explore a model friendly letter. Help students locate the online activities.

Skills Update

Capital Letters and Commas in Days and Dates

Students will review how to use capital letters and commas correctly when writing days and dates by completing Skills Update exercises. Sit with students as they do this activity and note if they answer correctly.

⊃ **Learning Coach Check-In** How did students do on the Skills Update?

▸ **All answers correct:** Great! Skip the review screen and go on to the next activity.

▸ **Any answers incorrect:** Take a few minutes to review capitalization and punctuation in days and dates now. Use the links on the screen after the Skills Update to take another look at the online activities or review Capitalization (Parts of a Letter; Days, Months, and Holidays) and Commas (In the Heading, Greeting, and Closing of a Letter) in the *Grammar Reference Guide* together.

 This activity will require extra time if students need to review capitalization and punctuation in days and dates. Take the extra 5–10 minutes to review now because new skills build on what students have already learned.

> **Objectives**
> - Use a capital letter to begin the name of a day.
> - Use a capital letter to begin the name of a month.
> - Use a comma in a date.

Composition

Explore a Model Friendly Letter

By reading and exploring a model friendly letter, students will learn what a personal letter is and how it is organized.

 A friendly letter is one kind of personal letter. An invitation and a thank-you letter are also personal letters. If students are not comfortable reading the model friendly letter for this activity online, they may read the model on page WS 51 in *K¹² Language Arts Activity Book*.

> **Objectives**
> - Recognize the parts of a friendly letter.
> - Identify the purpose of a friendly letter.
> - Identify the audience of a friendly letter.
> - Identify voice and tone.

[Offline] ⏱ 15 minutes

Work **together** with students to complete the offline Composition activity.

Composition

Respond to the Model Friendly Letter

Students will review what they learned about the model friendly letter. Turn to pages WS 51–54 in *K¹² Language Arts Activity Book*.

1. Have students reread Ron's letter on page WS 51.

2. Have students complete the Activity Book pages about Ron's letter. Provide support as necessary, encouraging students to write in complete sentences. Students should refer to Ron's personal letter as needed.

TIP Keep Ron's letter in a safe place so students can refer to it later.

Objectives

- Recognize the parts of a friendly letter.
- Describe the elements of a friendly letter.
- Identify the purpose of a friendly letter.
- Identify the audience of a friendly letter.
- Identify voice and tone.

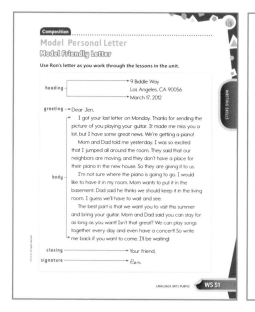

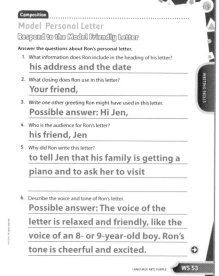

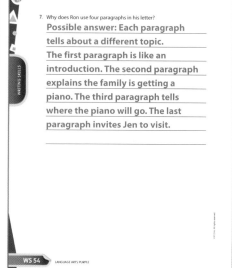

Heading of a Letter and Plan a Friendly Letter

Lesson Overview

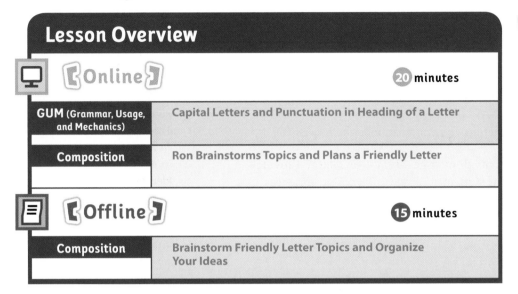

Online		20 minutes
GUM (Grammar, Usage, and Mechanics)	Capital Letters and Punctuation in Heading of a Letter	
Composition	Ron Brainstorms Topics and Plans a Friendly Letter	

Offline		15 minutes
Composition	Brainstorm Friendly Letter Topics and Organize Your Ideas	

Materials

Supplied
- *K¹² Language Arts Activity Book*, pp. WS 55–56
- *Grammar Reference Guide* Online Book (optional)

Keywords
friendly letter – a kind of letter used to share thoughts, feelings, and news

heading – the first part of a letter that has the writer's address and the date

Advance Preparation

To prepare for the GUM portion of this lesson, review Capitalization (Parts of a Letter) and Commas (In the Heading, Greeting, and Closing of a Letter) in the *Grammar Reference Guide* (linked in the online lesson) to familiarize yourself with the topics.

Big Ideas

- Friendly letters, also called personal letters, are written to share news, information, ideas, or feelings.
- When a writer uses the correct format, capitalization, and punctuation in a letter, the reader is better able to focus on the writer's ideas.

 **minutes**

Students will work online **independently** to complete an activity on capital letters and punctuation in the heading of a letter and to learn how to brainstorm topics and plan a friendly letter. Help students locate the online activities.

GUM (Grammar, Usage, and Mechanics)

Capital Letters and Punctuation in Heading of a Letter
Students will learn how to use capital letters and punctuation in the heading of a letter.

 Objectives
- Recognize proper capitalization and punctuation in the heading of a letter.
- Use capital letters and commas correctly in the heading of a letter.

Composition

Ron Brainstorms Topics and Plans a Friendly Letter
By watching Ron brainstorm his topic and plan his friendly letter, students will learn how to brainstorm topics and plan their own friendly letter.

Objectives
- Choose a topic.
- Use a graphic organizer to plan.

 **Offline** ⏱ **15** minutes

Work **together** with students to complete the offline Composition activity.

Composition

Brainstorm Friendly Letter Topics and Organize Your Ideas
Students will brainstorm and choose a topic for their own friendly letter. Then they will organize their ideas. Turn to pages WS 55 and 56 in *K¹² Language Arts Activity Book*.

1. Have students complete Activity Book page WS 55 to brainstorm and choose a topic for their friendly letter. Provide support as necessary, encouraging students to think about what ideas, thoughts, news, or feelings they would like to share, as well as whom they would like to share them with. Remind students that during brainstorming, no idea is a bad idea. The point is to list as many ideas as possible before choosing a topic.

2. Once students choose a topic, have them turn the Activity Book page over to begin to organize their ideas. Have students complete the form on page WS 56 by listing the purpose of their letter before briefly describing who their audience will be and what information they plan to include in the body of their letter. Remind students that they do not need to use complete sentences on the form.

TIP Keep students' completed form in a safe place so they can refer to it later.

 Objectives
- Choose a topic.
- Use a graphic organizer to plan.

Greeting & Closing of a Letter and Plan a Thank-You Letter

Lesson Overview

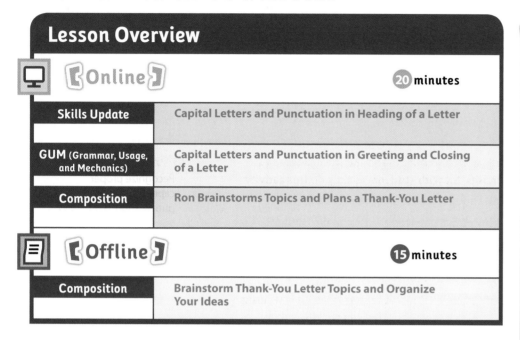

[Online] — 20 minutes

Skills Update	Capital Letters and Punctuation in Heading of a Letter
GUM (Grammar, Usage, and Mechanics)	Capital Letters and Punctuation in Greeting and Closing of a Letter
Composition	Ron Brainstorms Topics and Plans a Thank-You Letter

[Offline] — 15 minutes

Composition	Brainstorm Thank-You Letter Topics and Organize Your Ideas

Materials

Supplied
- *K¹² Language Arts Activity Book*, pp. WS 57–58
- *Grammar Reference Guide* Online Book (optional)

Keywords

closing (of a friendly letter) – the part of a friendly letter that follows the body, for example, *Your friend* or *Love*

salutation (of a friendly letter) – the greeting of a letter, which usually says, "Dear (name of recipient),"

thank-you letter – a kind of friendly letter in which the writer thanks someone for something

Advance Preparation

To prepare for the GUM portion of this lesson, review Capitalization (Parts of a Friendly Letter) and Commas (In the Heading, Greeting, and Closing of a Letter) in the *Grammar Reference Guide* (linked in the online lesson) to familiarize yourself with the topics.

Big Ideas

Thank-you notes and invitations typically follow the format of a friendly letter.

 **20 minutes**

Students will work online to review capitalization and punctuation in the heading of a letter, to complete an activity on capitalization and punctuation in the greeting and closing of a letter, and to learn how to brainstorm topics and plan a thank-you letter. Help students locate the online activities.

Skills Update

Capital Letters and Punctuation in Heading of a Letter
Students will review how to use capitalization and punctuation in the heading of a letter by completing Skills Update exercises. Sit with students as they do this activity and note if they answer correctly.

➲ **Learning Coach Check-In** How did students do on the Skills Update?

▸ **All answers correct:** Great! Skip the review screen and go on to the next activity.

▸ **Any answers incorrect:** Take a few minutes to review the rules about capitalization and punctuation in the heading of a letter now. Use the links on the screen after the Skills Update to take another look at the online activities or review Capitalization (Parts of a Letter) and Commas (In the Heading, Greeting, and Closing of a Letter) in the *Grammar Reference Guide* together.

 TIP This activity will require extra time if students need to review the rules on capitalization and punctuation in the heading of a letter. Take the extra 5–10 minutes to review now because new skills build on what students have already learned.

 Objectives
- Recognize proper capitalization and punctuation in the heading of a letter.
- Use capital letters and commas correctly in the heading of a letter.

GUM (Grammar, Usage, and Mechanics)

Capital Letters and Punctuation in Greeting and Closing of a Letter
Students will learn how to use capitalization and punctuation in the greeting and closing of a letter.

Objectives
- Recognize capital letters and commas in the greeting and closing of a letter.
- Use capital letters and commas in the greeting and closing of a letter.

Composition

Ron Brainstorms Topics and Plans a Thank-You Letter
By watching Ron brainstorm his topic and plan his thank-you letter, students will learn how to brainstorm topics and plan their own thank-you letter.

 Objectives
- Choose a topic.
- Use a graphic organizer to plan.

 **15** minutes

Work **together** with students to complete the offline Composition activity.

Composition

Brainstorm Thank-You Letter Topics and Organize Your Ideas
Students will brainstorm and choose a topic for their own thank-you letter. Then they will organize their ideas. Turn to pages WS 57 and 58 in *K¹² Language Arts Activity Book*.

1. Have students complete Activity Book page WS 57 to brainstorm and choose a topic for their thank-you letter. Provide support as necessary, encouraging students to think about what they have to be thankful for, as well as whom they should express their gratitude to. Remind students that during brainstorming, no idea is a bad idea. The point is to list as many ideas as possible before choosing a topic.

2. Once students choose a topic, have them turn the Activity Book page over to begin to organize their ideas. Have students complete the form on page WS 58 by listing the purpose of their thank-you letter before briefly describing who their audience will be and what information they plan to include in the body of their letter. Remind students that they do not need to use complete sentences on the form.

 Keep students' completed form in a safe place so they can refer to it later.

Objectives
* Choose a topic.
* Use a graphic organizer to plan.

Addresses and Plan a Letter of Invitation

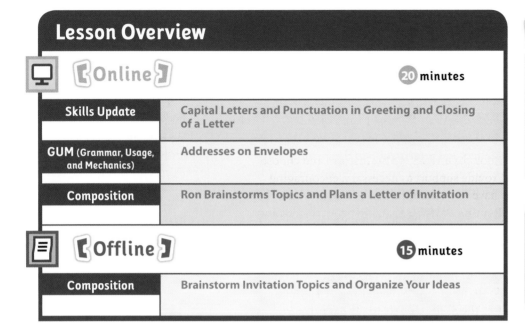

Lesson Overview

💻 Online — 20 minutes

Skills Update	Capital Letters and Punctuation in Greeting and Closing of a Letter
GUM (Grammar, Usage, and Mechanics)	Addresses on Envelopes
Composition	Ron Brainstorms Topics and Plans a Letter of Invitation

📄 Offline — 15 minutes

Composition	Brainstorm Invitation Topics and Organize Your Ideas

Materials

Supplied

- *K¹² Language Arts Activity Book*, pp. WS 59–60
- *Grammar Reference Guide* Online Book (optional)

Keywords

invitation – a kind of personal letter or a form in which the writer invites someone to attend a party or other special occasion

Advance Preparation

To prepare for the GUM portion of this lesson, review Resources (Model Envelope for a Personal Letter) in the *Grammar Reference Guide* (linked in the online lesson) to familiarize yourself with the topic.

Big Ideas

- ▶ Envelopes must be addressed in a precise format in order for the post office to deliver the mail accurately.
- ▶ Thank-you notes and invitations typically follow the format of a friendly letter.

 **minutes**

Students will work online to review capital letters and punctuation in the greeting and closing of a letter, to complete an activity on addresses on envelopes, and to learn how to brainstorm topics and plan a letter of invitation. Help students locate the online activities.

Skills Update

Capital Letters and Punctuation in Greeting and Closing of a Letter
Students will review how to use capital letters and punctuation in the greeting and closing of a letter by completing Skills Update exercises. Sit with students as they do this activity and note if they answer correctly.

⮑ **Learning Coach Check-In** How did students do on the Skills Update?

▸ **All answers correct:** Great! Skip the review screen and go on to the next activity.

▸ **Any answers incorrect:** Take a few minutes to review the rules about capitalization and punctuation in the greeting and closing of a letter now. Use the links on the screen after the Skills Update to take another look at the online activities or review Capitalization (Parts of a Friendly Letter) and Commas (In the Heading, Greeting, and Closing of a Letter) in the *Grammar Reference Guide* together.

TIP This activity will require extra time if students need to review the rules on capitalization and punctuation in the greeting and closing of a letter. Take the extra 5–10 minutes to review now because new skills build on what students have already learned.

> **Objectives**
> * Recognize capital letters and commas in the greeting and closing of a letter.
> * Use capital letters and commas in the greeting and closing of a letter.

GUM (Grammar, Usage, and Mechanics)

Addresses on Envelopes
Students will learn what belongs on the front of an envelope—the recipient's address, the sender's return address, and a stamp—and where to place each element.

> **Objectives**
> * Use capital letters and punctuation correctly in addresses.
> * Address an envelope.

Composition

Ron Brainstorms Topics and Plans a Letter of Invitation
By watching Ron brainstorm his topic and plan his invitation, students will learn how to brainstorm topics and plan their own invitation.

> **Objectives**
> * Choose a topic.
> * Use a graphic organizer to plan.

 **15 minutes**

Work **together** with students to complete the offline Composition activity.

Composition
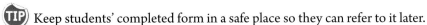

Brainstorm Invitation Topics and Organize Your Ideas

Students will brainstorm and choose a topic for their invitation. Then they will organize their ideas. Turn to pages WS 59 and 60 in *K¹² Language Arts Activity Book*.

1. Have students complete Activity Book page WS 59 to brainstorm and choose a topic for their invitation. Provide support as necessary, encouraging students to think about what events and celebrations will be happening soon, as well as whom they might like to invite to these events and celebrations. Remind students that during brainstorming, no idea is a bad idea. The point is to list as many ideas as possible before choosing a topic.

2. Once students choose a topic, have them turn the Activity Book page over to begin to organize their ideas. Have students complete the form on page WS 60 by listing the purpose of their invitation before briefly describing who their audience will be and what information they plan to include in the body of their letter. Remind students that they do not need to use complete sentences on the form.

TIP Keep students' completed form in a safe place so they can refer to it later.

Objectives
- Choose a topic.
- Use a graphic organizer to plan.

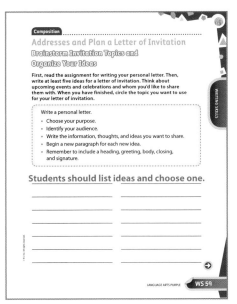

Draft Your Personal Letter

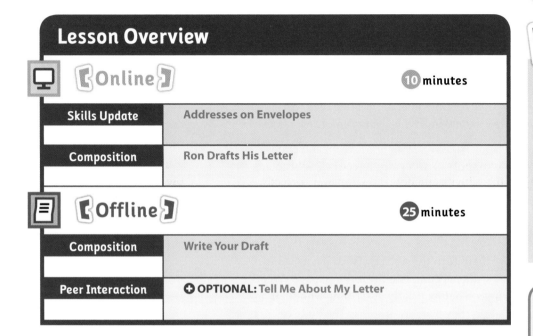

Lesson Overview

💻 [Online] 10 minutes

Skills Update	Addresses on Envelopes
Composition	Ron Drafts His Letter

📄 [Offline] 25 minutes

Composition	Write Your Draft
Peer Interaction	➕ OPTIONAL: Tell Me About My Letter

[Materials]

Supplied
- *K¹² Language Arts Activity Book*, pp. WS 51, 56, 58, 60–66
- *Grammar Reference Guide* Online Book (optional)
- drafting page (optional printout)
- Personal Letter: Feedback Sheet (printout)

Keywords
audience – a writer's readers
purpose – the reason for writing
tone – the writer's attitude toward the topic or subject
voice – the way a piece of writing sounds

Advance Preparation

Gather page WS 51 (Model Friendly Letter) and students' completed forms for brainstorming the friendly letter, thank-you letter, and invitation letter topics on pages WS 56, 58, and 60 in *K¹² Language Arts Activity Book*. Print the Personal Letter: Feedback Sheet from the online lesson.

Big Ideas

- Friendly letters, also called personal letters, are written to share news, information, ideas, or feelings.
- Thank-you notes and invitations typically follow the format of a friendly letter.

 **10** minutes

Students will work online to review how to address an envelope and to learn how to begin drafting a personal letter. Help students locate the online activities. Note that this lesson does not contain any new Grammar, Usage, and Mechanics activities so that students can concentrate on beginning their draft.

Skills Update

Addresses on Envelopes
Students will review how to address an envelope by completing Skills Update exercises. Sit with students as they do this activity and note if they answer correctly.

⊃ **Learning Coach Check-In** How did students do on the Skills Update?

▸ **All answers correct:** Great! Skip the review screen and go on to the next activity.

▸ **Any answers incorrect:** Take a few minutes to review how to address an envelope now. Use the links on the screen after the Skills Update to take another look at the online activities or review Resources (Model Envelope for a Personal Letter) in the *Grammar Reference Guide* together.

 This activity will require extra time if students need to review how to address an envelope. Take the extra 5–10 minutes to review now because new skills build on what students have already learned.

> **Objectives**
> - Use capital letters and punctuation correctly in addresses.
> - Address an envelope.

Composition

Ron Drafts His Letter
By watching how Ron drafts his personal letter, students will learn how to begin drafting their own personal letter.

> **Objectives**
> - Draft a personal letter.
> - Determine the purpose and audience for a piece of writing.
> - Use an appropriate voice and tone.

 **25** minutes

Work **together** with students to complete the offline Composition and Peer Interaction activities.

Composition ....

Write Your Draft

Students brainstormed and organized ideas for three kinds of personal letters. They will choose one kind of letter to write. Students will begin drafting the personal letter they have chosen. Have them gather the model personal letter and their three completed planning forms. Turn to pages WS 61–64 in *K¹² Language Arts Activity Book*.

Objectives
- Draft a personal letter.
- Determine the purpose and audience for a piece of writing.
- Use an appropriate voice and tone.

1. Before students begin to draft a personal letter, have them check the three forms they filled out and decide which kind of letter they want to write: a friendly letter, a thank-you letter, or a letter of invitation.

2. Help students start drafting by reminding them to refer to Ron's model friendly letter and their planning form as necessary. The model will help students remember what elements their letter should include, and their form will help them remember which ideas to include in their writing.

3. Remind students that a draft does not have to be perfect. It's just a first try at putting ideas on paper.

4. Have students use the lined Activity Book pages to begin drafting their personal letter. Students should write only in the white rows, because the purple rows will be used for making revisions to the draft later. If needed, additional drafting pages can be printed from the online lesson.

TIP Keep students' drafting pages in a safe place so they can continue working on them later. If students want to use a reference material such as the *Grammar Reference Guide* or a dictionary while drafting, suggest that they wait until they are revising or proofreading. Looking up information while drafting can interfere with students' flow of ideas.

⮑ **Learning Coach Check-in** When students have finished their draft, read and review it using the Personal Letter: Feedback Sheet, but do not go over the feedback sheet with students now. The notes you take on this sheet will guide your feedback to students as they revise their draft in a later lesson. Keep the feedback sheet in a safe place until students are ready to revise their draft.

Card WS 51

Composition

Model Personal Letter
Model Friendly Letter

Use Ron's letter as you work through the lessons in the unit.

heading → 9 Biddle Way
Los Angeles, CA 90056
→ March 17, 2012

greeting → Dear Jen,

body →
I got your last letter on Monday. Thanks for sending the picture of you playing your guitar. It made me miss you a lot, but I have some great news. We're getting a piano!

Mom and Dad told me yesterday. I was so excited that I jumped all around the room. They said that our neighbors are moving, and they don't have a place for their piano in the new house. So they are giving it to us.

I'm not sure where the piano is going to go. I would like to have it in my room. Mom wants to put it in the basement. Dad said he thinks we should keep it in the living room. I guess we'll have to wait and see.

The best part is that we want you to visit this summer and bring your guitar. Mom and Dad said you can stay for as long as you want! Isn't that great? We can play songs together every day and even have a concert! So write me back if you want to come. I'll be waiting!

closing → Your friend,

signature → Ron

WS 51   LANGUAGE ARTS PURPLE

Card WS 56

Answer the questions about the kind of letter you are planning.

What kind of letter are you planning?

☐ Friendly Letter   ☐ Thank-You Letter   ☐ Invitation

What is your purpose? _____

Who is your audience? _____

What information will you include in the body of your letter? _____

_____

_____

_____

_____

_____

_____

_____

_____

WS 56   LANGUAGE ARTS PURPLE

Card WS 58

Answer the questions about the kind of letter you are planning.

What kind of letter are you planning?

☐ Friendly Letter   ☐ Thank-You Letter   ☐ Invitation

What is your purpose? _____

_____

Who is your audience? _____

What information will you include in the body of your letter? _____

_____

_____

_____

_____

_____

_____

_____

WS 58   LANGUAGE ARTS PURPLE

Card WS 60

Answer the questions about the kind of letter you are planning.

What kind of letter are you planning?

☐ Friendly Letter   ☐ Thank-You Letter   ☐ Invitation

What is your purpose? _____

_____

Who is your audience? _____

_____

What information will you include in the body of your letter? _____

_____

_____

_____

_____

_____

_____

_____

_____

WS 60   LANGUAGE ARTS PURPLE

Card WS 61

Composition

Draft Your Personal Letter
Write Your Draft

Read the assignment. Use your personal letter planning form to help you write the first draft of your personal letter. Write only on the white rows. You will use the purple rows for revisions later.

Write a personal letter.
- Choose your purpose.
- Identify your audience.
- Write the information, thoughts, and ideas you want to share.
- Begin a new paragraph for each new idea.
- Remember to include a heading, greeting, body, closing, and signature.

Start here ▶

LANGUAGE ARTS PURPLE   WS 61

Peer Interaction

✚ OPTIONAL: Tell Me About My Letter

This activity is OPTIONAL. It is intended for students who have extra time and would benefit from extra practice. Feel free to skip this activity.

Students can benefit from exchanging personal letters with another student. Each writer should receive feedback. To complete this optional activity, turn to pages WS 65 and 66 in *K¹² Language Arts Activity Book*. (Additional copies of the Peer Interaction Form can be printed from the online lesson.)

1. Have students exchange drafts with other students.

2. Have students use the Activity Book pages to provide others with feedback about their writing.

TIP In the upcoming revising lesson, students may use the feedback provided from others students to improve their personal letter.

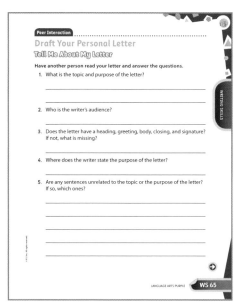

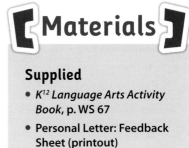

Letters as E-mails

Lesson Overview

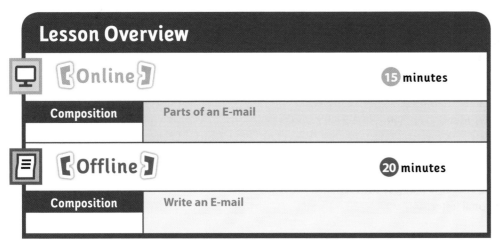

Online	15 minutes
Composition	Parts of an E-mail

Offline	20 minutes
Composition	Write an E-mail

Materials

Supplied
- *K¹² Language Arts Activity Book*, p. WS 67
- Personal Letter: Feedback Sheet (printout)

Advance Preparation

If you have not already completed the Personal Letter: Feedback Sheet, do so during this lesson while students work independently. You will need to share this form with students in the next lesson.

Big Ideas

When writing an e-mail, writers should follow the conventions appropriate for technology, but maintain standard written English.

 **Online** 15 minutes

Students will work online **independently** to complete an activity on the parts of an e-mail. Help students locate the online activity.

Composition

Parts of an E-mail

Students will learn about the parts of an e-mail, including what belongs in each field. They will be instructed how to include the greeting, the body of a message, and the closing and signature in an e-mail.

Objectives
- Write an e-mail.

 **20 minutes**

Work **together** with students to complete the offline Composition activity.

Composition

Write an E-mail

Students will practice creating an e-mail of their own. Turn to page WS 67 in *K¹² Language Arts Activity Book*. Have students complete the Activity Book page.

TIP If you would like students to compose and send a real e-mail, guide them as they fill in the proper fields of an e-mail on the computer and write a short message. Students may write to you or to someone else whose e-mail address you (or they) know.

Objectives
- Write an e-mail.

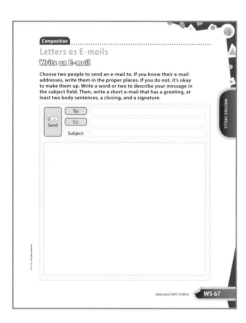

Revise Your Personal Letter

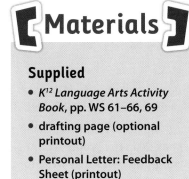
Lesson Overview

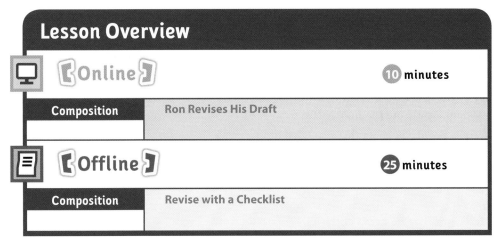

	Online	10 minutes
Composition	Ron Revises His Draft	

	Offline	25 minutes
Composition	Revise with a Checklist	

Materials

Supplied
- *K¹² Language Arts Activity Book*, pp. WS 61–66, 69
- drafting page (optional printout)
- **Personal Letter: Feedback Sheet (printout)**

Advance Preparation

Gather pages WS 61–66 (Write Your Draft, students' draft of their personal letter and Tell Me About My Letter, if completed) in *K¹² Language Arts Activity Book* and the completed Personal Letter: Feedback Sheet. You will review the feedback with students.

 **10 minutes**

Students will work online **independently** to learn how to revise a personal letter. Help students locate the online activity.

Composition

Ron Revises His Draft
By watching how Ron revises his personal letter draft, students will learn how to revise their own draft.

 Objectives
- Revise a personal letter.
- Provide complete information.
- Revise the organization of a letter.

 **25 minutes**

Work **together** with students to complete the offline Composition activity.

Composition

Revise with a Checklist

Students will revise their personal letter. Have them gather their personal letter draft and any completed Peer Interaction forms. Turn to page WS 69 in *K¹² Language Arts Activity Book* and gather the Personal Letter: Feedback Sheet that you filled out.

1. Use the Personal Letter: Feedback Sheet to guide your discussion with students.

   ▸ Tell students the strengths of their letter. Provide positive comments about the ideas, language, details, or other elements of the letter you enjoyed.

   ▸ Walk through the Purpose and Content and Structure and Organization sections of the feedback sheet with students. Do not address your comments in the Grammar and Mechanics section at this time. You can work with students on grammar and mechanics when they proofread. Providing these corrections at this time may distract students from the real work of revising for content and structure.

   ▸ As you go through the feedback sheet with students, encourage them to actively revise their draft based on your feedback. Reassure students that it's okay to remove ideas or sentences from their letter. Doing so may help their letter stay focused on their topic, even if something they cut was included in their planning form.

   ▸ As students revise their draft, have them use the purple rows to mark their revisions.

2. Once you've reviewed your comments on the first two sections of the feedback sheet with students, have them review their draft once more, using the revision checklist on the Activity Book page. Students should check off each box on the checklist as they complete the items.

Objectives

• Revise a personal letter.
• Provide complete information.
• Revise the organization of a letter.

3. If students received feedback from peers, discuss with them how they might use it to improve their letter. Help students decide what peer feedback would be useful to include in their revisions.

4. If students' revised personal letter has many changes that make the letter difficult to read and understand, encourage them to make a clean copy before they proofread in a later lesson. Additional drafting pages can be printed from the online lesson.

TIP Keep students' revised personal letter in a safe place so they can refer to it later.

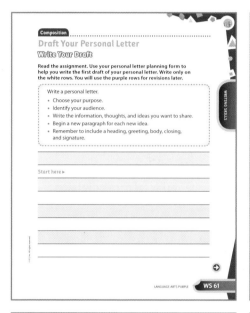

Unit Review and Proofread Your Personal Letter

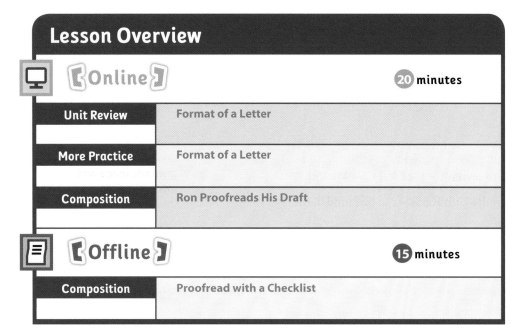

Lesson Overview

🖥 [Online] 20 minutes

Unit Review	Format of a Letter
More Practice	Format of a Letter
Composition	Ron Proofreads His Draft

📄 [Offline] 15 minutes

Composition	Proofread with a Checklist

Materials

Supplied

- *K¹² Language Arts Activity Book*, pp. WS 61–64, 70
- *Grammar Reference Guide* Online Book (optional)
- drafting page (optional printout)
- Personal Letter: Feedback Sheet (printout)

Keywords

audience – a writer's readers

body (of a friendly letter) – the main text of a friendly letter

closing (of a friendly letter) – the part of a friendly letter that follows the body; for example, *Your friend* or *Love*

friendly letter – a kind of letter used to share thoughts, feelings, and news

heading – the first part of a letter that has the writer's address and the date

invitation – a kind of personal letter or a form in which the writer invites someone to attend a party or other special occasion

purpose – the reason for writing

salutation (of a friendly letter) – the greeting of a letter, which usually says, "Dear (name of recipient),"

signature (of a friendly letter) – the end of a letter where the writer writes his or his name

thank-you letter – a kind of friendly letter in which the writer thanks someone for something

tone – the writer's attitude toward the topic or subject

voice – the way a piece of writing sounds

Advance Preparation

Gather pages WS 61–64 (Write Your Draft, students' draft of their personal letter) in *K¹² Language Arts Activity Book* and the completed Personal Letter: Feedback Sheet. If students' revised letter has many changes that make it difficult to read and understand, you may want to encourage them to make a clean copy before they proofread in this lesson. Additional drafting pages can be printed from the online lesson.

Big Ideas

▶ Envelopes must be addressed in a precise format in order for the post office to deliver the mail accurately.

▶ When a writer uses the correct format, capitalization, and punctuation in a letter, the reader is better able to focus on the writer's ideas.

 **minutes**

Students will work online to review the grammar, usage, and mechanics skills learned in the unit and to learn how to proofread a personal letter. Help students locate the online activities.

Unit Review

Format of a Letter

Students will review what they have learned about formatting personal letters, including how to write headings, greetings, body paragraphs, closings, and signatures, as well as how to address an envelope, to review for the Unit Checkpoint.

TIP A full list of objectives covered in the Unit Review can be found in the online lesson.

 Objectives
- Complete a review of grammar, usage, and mechanics skills.

More Practice

Format of a Letter

Go over students' results on the Unit Review and, if necessary, have students complete the appropriate review activities listed in the table online. Help students locate the activities. Provide support as needed.

TIP The time students need to complete this activity will vary. Set aside enough time for students to complete all review activities, if they need to do so.

 Objectives
- Evaluate Unit Review results and choose activities for more practice.

Composition

Ron Proofreads His Draft

By watching how Ron proofreads his personal letter draft, students will learn how to proofread their own draft.

 Objectives
- Proofread a letter.
- Use capital letters in heading, greeting, and closing.
- Use commas in heading, greeting, and closing.
- Indent each paragraph.

 **Offline** 🕐 **minutes**

Work **together** with students to complete the offline Composition activity.

Composition •••

Proofread with a Checklist

Students will proofread their personal letter. Have them gather their personal letter draft. Turn to page WS 70 in *K¹² Language Arts Activity Book* and gather the Personal Letter: Feedback Sheet that you filled out.

1. Review with students your comments in the Grammar and Mechanics section of the feedback sheet. As you go through the feedback sheet with students, encourage them to use the purple rows on their drafting pages to actively mark changes based on your feedback.

2. Once you've reviewed your comments in the Grammar and Mechanics section of the feedback sheet with students, have them review their draft once more using the proofreading checklist. Students should check off each box on the checklist as they complete each item.

TIP Keep students' proofread letter in a safe place so they can refer to it later.

Objectives

• Proofread a letter.

• Use capital letters in heading, greeting, and closing.

• Use commas in heading, greeting, and closing.

• Indent each paragraph.

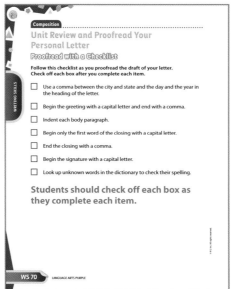

Unit Checkpoint and Publish Your Personal Letter

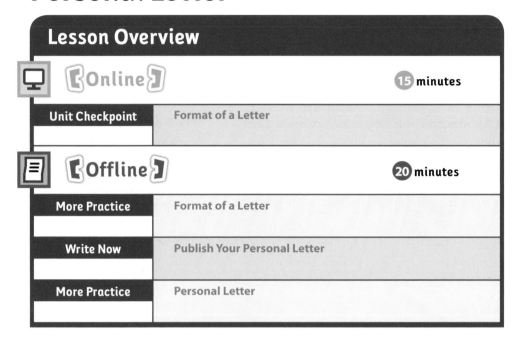

Lesson Overview

🖥 〔Online〕   🕐 15 minutes

Unit Checkpoint	Format of a Letter

📄 〔Offline〕   🕐 20 minutes

More Practice	Format of a Letter
Write Now	Publish Your Personal Letter
More Practice	Personal Letter

Advance Preparation

Gather pages WS 61–64 (Write Your Draft, students' draft of their personal letter) in *K¹² Language Arts Activity Book*, which students should have revised and proofread.

Big Ideas

Envelopes must be addressed in a precise format in order for the post office to deliver the mail accurately.

〔Materials〕

Supplied

- *K¹² Language Arts Activity Book*, pp. WS 61–64, 71–72
- *Grammar Reference Guide* Online Book (optional)
- Capital Letters and Commas in Days and Dates (optional printout)
- Capital Letters and Punctuation in Heading of a Letter (optional printout)
- Capital Letters and Punctuation in Greeting and Closing of a Letter (optional printout)
- Addresses on Envelopes (optional printout)
- Personal Letter: Rubric and Sample Responses (printout)
- lined writing page (optional printout)

Keywords

closing (of a friendly letter) – the part of a friendly letter that follows the body; for example, *Your friend* or *Love*

heading – the first part of a letter that has the writer's address and the date

salutation (of a friendly letter) – the greeting of a letter, which usually says, "Dear (name of recipient),"

tone – the writer's attitude toward the topic or subject

voice – the way a piece of writing sounds

 **15** minutes

Students will work online **independently** to complete the Unit Checkpoint. Help students locate the Unit Checkpoint and provide support as necessary.

Unit Checkpoint

Format of a Letter

Students will complete an online Unit Checkpoint about formatting personal letters, including how to write headings, greetings, body paragraphs, closings, and signatures, as well as how to address an envelope. If necessary, read the directions to students.

TIP A full list of objectives covered in the Unit Checkpoint can be found in the online lesson.

> **Objectives**
> • Complete a Unit Checkpoint on grammar, usage, and mechanics skills.

[Offline] **20** minutes

Work **together** with students to complete the offline More Practice and Write Now activities.

More Practice

Format of a Letter

Go over students' results on the Unit Checkpoint and, if necessary, print out and have them complete the appropriate practice pages listed in the table online. Students can complete all necessary pages now or, if more time is needed, they can spread them out over the next few days. They can also review the appropriate sections of the *Grammar Reference Guide* with you. If students scored less than 80 percent on the Unit Checkpoint, you may want them to retake the Checkpoint after completing the additional activity pages.

TIP The time students need to complete this activity will vary. Set aside enough time for students to complete some or all activity pages and to retake the Unit Checkpoint, if they need to do so. Students may retake the Unit Checkpoint immediately, but having them complete the practice pages and then retake it might be more effective.

> **Objectives**
> • Evaluate Unit Checkpoint results and choose activities for more practice.

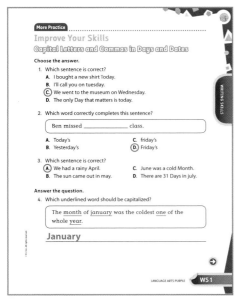

More Practice

Improve Your Skills
Capital Letters and Commas in Days and Dates

Choose the answer.

1. Which sentence is correct?
   A. I bought a new shirt Today.
   B. I'll call you on tuesday.
   C. We went to the museum on Wednesday. *(circled)*
   D. The only Day that matters is today.

2. Which word correctly completes this sentence?

   Ben missed _____ class.

   A. Today's   C. friday's
   B. Yesterday's   D. Friday's *(circled)*

3. Which sentence is correct?
   A. We had a rainy April. *(circled)*   C. June was a cold Month.
   B. The sun came out in may.   D. There are 31 Days in july.

Answer the question.

4. Which underlined word should be capitalized?

   The <u>month</u> of <u>january</u> was the coldest <u>one</u> of the whole <u>year</u>.

   January

5. Which underlined word should be capitalized?

   I told you <u>yesterday</u> that I was going to the movies <u>today</u>, <u>tomorrow</u>, and <u>thursday</u>.

   Thursday

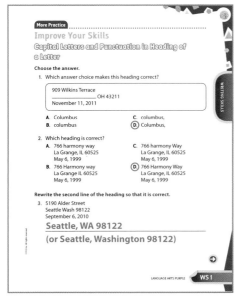

More Practice

Improve Your Skills
Capital Letters and Punctuation in Heading of a Letter

Choose the answer.

1. Which answer choice makes this heading correct?

   909 Wilkins Terrace
   _____ OH 43211
   November 11, 2011

   A. Columbus   C. columbus,
   B. columbus   D. Columbus, *(circled)*

2. Which heading is correct?
   A. 766 harmony way
      La Grange, IL 60525
      May 6, 1999
   B. 766 Harmony way
      La Grange IL 60525
      May 6, 1999
   C. 766 harmony Way
      La Grange, IL 60525
      May 6, 1999
   D. 766 Harmony Way *(circled)*
      La Grange, IL 60525
      May 6, 1999

Rewrite the second line of the heading so that it is correct.

3. 5190 Alder Street
   Seattle Wash 98122
   September 6, 2010

   Seattle, WA 98122

   (or Seattle, Washington 98122)

Place the two missing commas where they belong.

4. 15433 Puritan Street
   Detroit, MI 98122
   February 14, 2012

Rewrite the heading correctly.

5. 828 Riverside drive
   New York Ny 10032
   August 30 2007

   828 Riverside Drive

   New York, NY 10032

   August 30, 2007

More Practice

Improve Your Skills
Capital Letters and Punctuation in Greeting and Closing of a Letter

Answer the question.

1. Write this greeting correctly: Dear Mr. Billups

   Dear Mr. Billups,

Choose the answer.

2. Which greeting is written correctly?
   A. Dear Mrs. Harkin –   C. Dear Mrs. Harkin.
   B. Dear Mrs. Harkin!   D. Dear Mrs. Harkin, *(circled)*

3. Which answer choice correctly completes this greeting?

   Dear _____

   A. Peter   B. peter   C. Peter, *(circled)*   D. peter,

4. Which answer choice correctly completes this closing?

   Your _____

   A. Sister,   B. sister, *(circled)*   C. Sister   D. sister

5. Which closing and signature are correctly written?
   A. Your friend, *(circled)*   C. Your friend Melanie
      Melanie
   B. Your friend –   D. Your Friend
      Melanie   Melanie

More Practice

Improve Your Skills
Addresses on Envelopes

Choose the answer.

1. Which answer choice correctly completes this address?

   Tom Stokes
   298 Cornell Avenue
   _____ NY 12231

   A. albany   C. Albany *(circled)*
   B. Alb'y   D. AL

2. Which answer choice correctly completes this address?

   Rosa Mariposa
   53 Butler Drive
   Albuquerque, _____ 87190

   A. Nm   C. nm
   B. NM *(circled)*   D. nM

3. Which answer choice correctly completes this address?

   _____
   8 Clark Street
   Indianapolis, IN 46250

   A. Bryan Addison *(circled)*   C. Bryan addison
   B. bryan addison   D. bryan Addison

4. Which answer choice correctly completes this address?

   Natasha Reynolds
   612 Pine Avenue
   Bangor, _____ 04401

   A. Me.   C. M.E.
   B. Me   D. ME *(circled)*

5. Which answer choice correctly completes this address?

   Taylor Dussinger
   2910 10th Street
   _____ AR 72217

   A. Little Rock, *(circled)*   C. Little Rock –
   B. Little Rock.   D. Little Rock:

Address the envelope.

6. Write a return address in the left-hand corner. Write the name and address of the person receiving the letter in the correct place.

Write Now •••

 Publish Your Personal Letter

Students will publish their personal letter. Have them gather their proofread draft. Turn to pages WS 71 and 72 in *K[12] Language Arts Activity Book*.

> **Objectives**
> • Make a clean copy of a personal letter.

1. Explain to students that they will finish their personal letter by completing the last stage of the writing process—publishing their work.
   Say: Publishing your writing means making a clean and final copy that is ready for sharing with others.

   ▸ To be ready to publish your personal letter, you should have finished revising and proofreading your draft.

   ▸ The final copy should be your best effort and should not have any errors.

2. Explain that the final copy should be written clearly and neatly on clean sheets of paper. Tell students that they should use good handwriting and leave spaces between words so that others can read what they wrote.

3. Have students use the lined Activity Book pages to write their final copy. If needed, additional lined writing pages can be printed from the online lesson.

4. Use the materials and instructions in the online lesson to evaluate students' finished writing. You will be looking at students' writing to evaluate the following:

   ▸ **Purpose and Content:** Choose the kind of letter student wrote. If a **friendly letter**, it shares news, ideas, thoughts, or feelings. If a **thank-you letter**, it expresses the writer's gratitude to someone. If an **invitation**, it tells of an upcoming event or celebration and invites someone to attend. The purpose is clear, but one or two ideas are not expressed completely or clearly. Fewer than three irrelevant details are in the letter, and the writing is somewhat fluent.

   ▸ **Structure and Organization:** The letter has been revised. With perhaps one exception, the letter contains a heading, a greeting, at least three body paragraphs, and a closing and signature, each of which is written correctly and is in the proper place. Most body paragraphs are indented.

   ▸ **Grammar and Mechanics:** The letter has been proofread using a checklist, and few errors remain.

5. Enter students' scores online for each rubric category.

6. If students' writing scored a 1 in any category, work with them to revise and proofread their work.

7. Suggest that students share their personal letter with their audience—the person they wrote to. Have students address an envelope and mail the letter, if possible.

TIP Tell students that producing a piece of writing that is ready to publish and share with others is a great accomplishment. Let students know that the effort they put in to publish a letter is something to be proud of.

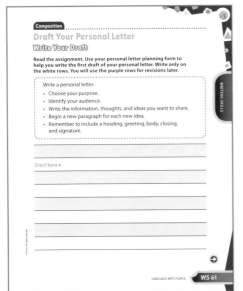

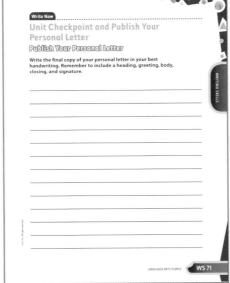

More Practice

Personal Letter

If students' writing did not meet objectives, have them complete the appropriate review activities listed in the table online. Follow the online instructions to help students revise and edit their work. Impress upon students that revising makes their work better. Writing is a process, and each time they revise their letter they are improving their writing. Always begin with something positive to say. If there is one detail, for example, mention it and say how this detail helps you picture what is being written about.

Help students locate the activities and provide support as needed.

Objectives
• Revise a personal letter.

 Reward: When students score 80 percent or above on the Unit Checkpoint and their writing is Level 2 or higher on the Personal Letter grading rubric, add a sticker for this unit on the My Accomplishments chart.

Nouns and Informative Essay

Unit Focus

In the grammar part of the unit, students will learn about nouns. They will

▶ Learn the definitions of *common noun* and *proper noun* and how to identify them in sentences.
▶ Learn the definitions of *collective*, *abstract*, and *compound nouns*, as well as how to identify all three in sentences.
▶ Form regular and irregular plural nouns.
▶ Form singular and plural possessive nouns.
▶ Learn the definition of *simple subject* and how to find the simple subject in a sentence.

In the composition part of the unit, students will write an informative essay. They will

▶ Use their journal to freewrite.
▶ Brainstorm a topic and plan their essay.
▶ Write a draft that has an introduction, a body, and a conclusion.
▶ Draw a picture to accompany their essay and make their points stronger.
▶ Revise and proofread their informative essay.
▶ Write a final copy of their informative essay to share.

Unit Plan

		Online	Offline
Lesson 1	Common & Proper Nouns and Journal Entry	15 minutes	20 minutes
Lesson 2	Collective, Abstract, & Compound Nouns and Model Informative Essay	20 minutes	15 minutes
Lesson 3	Singular & Plural Nouns and Brainstorm Topics	20 minutes	15 minutes
Lesson 4	Plan Your Informative Essay	20 minutes	15 minutes
Lesson 5	Singular Possessive Nouns and Draft Your Informative Essay	15 minutes	20 minutes
Lesson 6	Plural Possessive Nouns and Draft Your Informative Essay	15 minutes	20 minutes
Lesson 7	Simple Subjects	15 minutes	20 minutes
Lesson 8	Revise Your Informative Essay	10 minutes	25 minutes
Lesson 9	Unit Review and Proofread Your Informative Essay	20 minutes	15 minutes
Lesson 10	Unit Checkpoint and Publish Your Informative Essay	15 minutes	20 minutes

Common & Proper Nouns and Journal Entry

Lesson Overview

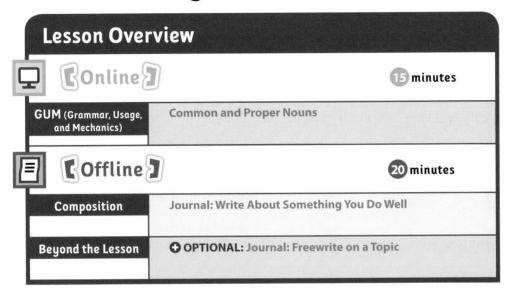

💻	**⟦Online⟧**		🕐 **15** minutes
GUM (Grammar, Usage, and Mechanics)	Common and Proper Nouns		

📄	**⟦Offline⟧**		🕐 **20** minutes
Composition	Journal: Write About Something You Do Well		
Beyond the Lesson	➕ **OPTIONAL:** Journal: Freewrite on a Topic		

⟦Materials⟧

Supplied
- *K¹² My Journal*, pp. 24–25
- *Grammar Reference Guide* Online Book (optional)

Keywords

common noun – a word that names any person, place, thing, or idea

noun – a word that names a person, place, thing, or idea

proper noun – the name of a particular person, place, thing, or idea; proper nouns begin with a capital letter

Advance Preparation

To prepare for the GUM portion of this lesson, review Nouns (Common Nouns; Proper Nouns) in the *Grammar Reference Guide* (linked in the online lesson) to familiarize yourself with the topic.

Big Ideas

▸ A noun is a basic part of speech. Understanding nouns gives one a basic vocabulary for building sentences and grasping how language works.

▸ Journal writing is a form of freewriting. It is an opportunity to get ideas on paper without regard for correctness of the language or for the format of a piece of writing.

▸ To improve, writers require frequent practice.

 **15 minutes**

Students will work online **independently** to complete an activity on common and proper nouns. Help students locate the online activity.

 GUM (Grammar, Usage, and Mechanics)

Common and Proper Nouns
Students will learn what common and proper nouns are and practice identifying both in sentences.

 Objectives
- Identify common and proper nouns.
- Use common and proper nouns.

 **20 minutes**

Work **together** with students to complete the offline Composition and Beyond the Lesson activities.

Composition

 Journal: Write About Something You Do Well
Students will respond to a journal prompt by describing something they do well. Gather *K¹² My Journal* and have students turn to pages 24 and 25.

Objectives
- Respond to a journal prompt.
- Freewrite about a topic.

1. Tell students they are going to write in their journal about something they do well. To help students think of something they do well, ask them to think about their answers to the following questions.

   ▸ What are some activities that you like to do? Why do you like to do these activities? Did anyone teach you how to do these things, or did you teach yourself?

   ▸ Have other people ever told you that you are good at doing some activity or at behaving in some way? What were they talking about? Why do you think others thought you were good at this activity or behavior?

   ▸ What is something that you have done that made you proud? Describe what allowed you to do this.

2. Have students respond to the prompt in their journal. Remind them to include details about what skill or talent they have for a particular activity or behavior, how they developed that skill or talent, and how their abilities make them feel. Encourage students to write in complete sentences, although it is not a requirement when they are freewriting in their journal.

TIP Students should write for about 20 minutes. Freewriting allows students to use their imaginations to write what they want without worrying about being graded, so encourage them to keep writing for the entire time. If students have trouble writing for 20 minutes, use the prompting questions in Step 1 or have them list ideas or words. If they want to keep writing beyond the suggested time limit, praise them for their enthusiasm and offer to let them complete their entry later in the day as a reward.

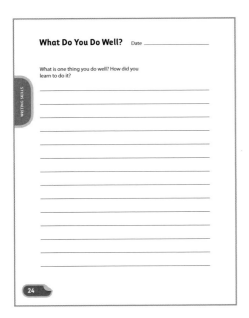

Beyond the Lesson

 **OPTIONAL: Journal: Freewrite on a Topic**

This activity is OPTIONAL. It is intended for students who have extra time and would benefit from extra practice. Feel free to skip this activity. Gather *K¹² My Journal*.

1. Have students either respond to a prompt in Thoughts and Experiences (pages 50–93) or write about their own topic on the next available page in Ideas (pages 96–139).

2. Encourage students to explore their thoughts and write as much as they want. There are no rules. If students wish, ideas can be fleshed out into a more developed composition at a later time.

TIP Studies show that students who write more frequently become better writers.

Objectives
- Respond to a journal prompt.
- Freewrite about a topic.

Collective, Abstract, & Compound Nouns and Model Informative Essay

[Materials]

Supplied

- *K¹² Language Arts Activity Book*, pp. WS 73–76
- *Grammar Reference Guide* Online Book (optional)

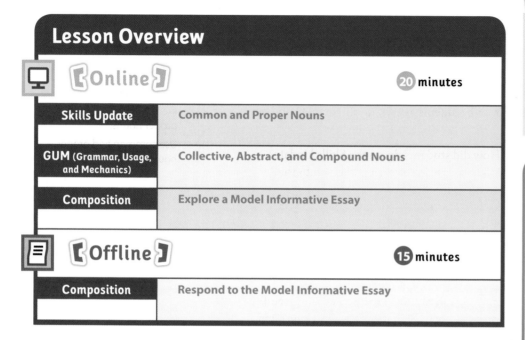

Lesson Overview

[Online]   **20** minutes

Skills Update	Common and Proper Nouns
GUM (Grammar, Usage, and Mechanics)	Collective, Abstract, and Compound Nouns
Composition	Explore a Model Informative Essay

[Offline]   **15** minutes

Composition	Respond to the Model Informative Essay

Keywords

abstract noun – a word that names an idea

body – the main text of a piece of writing

collective noun – a word that means a group of things but is usually singular

compound noun – a noun made up of two or more words

conclusion – the final paragraph of a written work

detail – a fact or description that tells more about a topic

fact – something that can be proven true

informative essay – a kind of writing that informs or explains

introduction – the first paragraph of an essay, identifying the topic and stating the main idea

topic – the subject of a piece of writing

topic sentence – the sentence that expresses the main idea of the paragraph

Advance Preparation

To prepare for the GUM portion of this lesson, review Nouns (Concrete Nouns; Abstract Nouns; Collective Nouns; Compound Nouns) in the *Grammar Reference Guide* to familiarize yourself with the topic. In this lesson, students begin to accumulate documents they will need as they work on their informative essay. You might want to provide students with a folder or large envelope in which to keep these documents.

Big Ideas

- The study of writing models provides students with opportunities to read, analyze, and emulate good models.
- Student writers should be provided with good models for a particular type of writing, and these models become the focus of the instruction.

 **minutes**

Students will work online to review common and proper nouns; to complete an activity on collective, abstract, and compound nouns; and to read and explore a model informative essay. Help students locate the online activities.

Skills Update

Common and Proper Nouns

Students will review how to identify and use common and proper nouns by completing Skills Update exercises. Sit with students as they do this activity and note if they answer correctly.

➲ **Learning Coach Check-In** How did students do on the Skills Update?
  ▸ **All answers correct:** Great! Skip the review screen and go on to the next activity.
  ▸ **Any answers incorrect:** Take a few minutes to review common and proper nouns now. Use the links on the screen after the Skills Update questions to take another look at the online activities or review Nouns (Common Nouns; Proper Nouns) in the *Grammar Reference Guide* together.

 This activity will require extra time if students need to review common and proper nouns. Take the extra 5–10 minutes to review now because new skills build on what students have already learned.

Objectives
• Identify common and proper nouns.
• Use common and proper nouns.

GUM (Grammar, Usage, and Mechanics)

Collective, Abstract, and Compound Nouns

Students will learn what collective, abstract, and compound nouns are and practice identifying and using all three in sentences.

Objectives
• Use collective nouns.
• Use abstract nouns.
• Identify compound nouns.
• Use compound nouns.

Composition

Explore a Model Informative Essay

By reading and exploring a model informative essay, students will learn what an informative essay is and how it is organized.

 If students are not comfortable reading the model informative essay for this activity online, they may read the model on page WS 73 and 74 in *K¹² Language Arts Activity Book*.

Objectives
• Describe the elements of an informative essay.

 Offline **15** minutes

Work **together** with students to complete the offline Composition activity.

Composition

Respond to the Model Informative Essay

Students will review what they learned about the model informative essay. Turn to pages WS 73–76 in *K¹² Language Arts Activity Book*.

1. Have students reread Serena's informative essay on pages WS 73 and 74.

2. Have students complete the Activity Book pages about Serena's informative essay. Provide support as necessary, encouraging students to write in complete sentences. Students should refer to Serena's informative essay as needed.

TIP Keep Serena's informative essay in a safe place, so students can refer to it later.

Objectives
- Describe the elements of an informative essay.

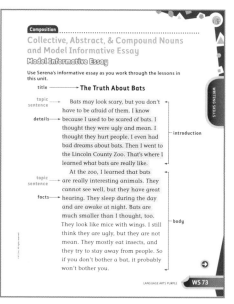

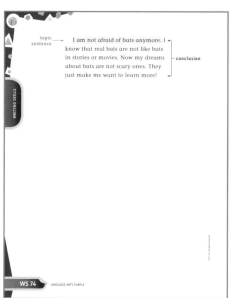

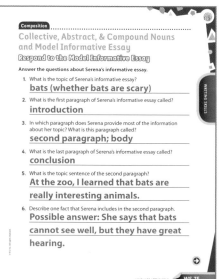

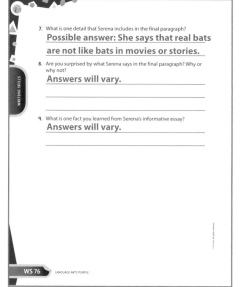

Singular & Plural Nouns and Brainstorm Topics

Lesson Overview

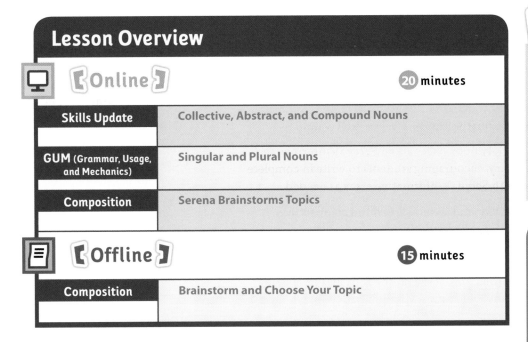

🖥 **Online**		**20 minutes**
Skills Update	Collective, Abstract, and Compound Nouns	
GUM (Grammar, Usage, and Mechanics)	Singular and Plural Nouns	
Composition	Serena Brainstorms Topics	

📄 **Offline**		**15 minutes**
Composition	Brainstorm and Choose Your Topic	

Materials

Supplied
- *K¹² Language Arts Activity Book*, pp. WS 77–78
- *K¹² My Journal*, pp. 24–25 (optional)
- *Grammar Reference Guide* Online Book (optional)

Keywords

brainstorming – before writing, a way for the writer to come up with ideas

plural noun – a word that names more than one person, place, thing, or idea

singular noun – a word that names one person, place, thing, or idea

Advance Preparation

To prepare for the GUM portion of this lesson, review Nouns (Singular and Plural Nouns; Regular Plural Nouns; Irregular Plural Nouns) in the *Grammar Reference Guide* (linked in the online lesson) to familiarize yourself with the topic.

Big Ideas

Speakers tend to use the singular and plural form of nouns correctly. The more challenging aspect of using plural nouns is to spell them correctly.

Online 20 minutes

Students will work online to review collective, abstract, and compound nouns; to complete an activity on singular and plural nouns; and to learn how to brainstorm topics for their informative essay. Help students locate the online activities.

Skills Update

Collective, Abstract, and Compound Nouns

Students will review how to identify and use collective, abstract, and compound nouns by completing Skills Update exercises. Sit with students as they do this activity and note if they answer correctly.

➲ **Learning Coach Check-In** How did students do on the Skills Update?

▸ **All answers correct:** Great! Skip the review screen and go on to the next activity.

▸ **Any answers incorrect:** Take a few minutes to review collective, abstract, and compound nouns now. Use the links on the screen after the Skills Update questions to take another look at the online activities or review Nouns (Collective Nouns; Abstract Nouns; Compound Nouns) in the *Grammar Reference Guide* together.

TIP This activity will require extra time if students need to review collective, abstract, and compound nouns. Take the extra 5–10 minutes to review now because new skills build on what students have already learned.

Objectives
- Use collective nouns.
- Use abstract nouns.
- Identify compound nouns.
- Use compound nouns.

GUM (Grammar, Usage, and Mechanics)

Singular and Plural Nouns

Students will learn what singular and plural nouns are and practice identifying both singular and plural nouns. They will also learn how to form regular and irregular plural nouns.

Objectives
- Identify singular nouns.
- Identify plural nouns.
- Form and use plural nouns.
- Form and use irregular plural nouns.

Composition

Serena Brainstorms Topics

By watching Serena brainstorm topics, students will learn how to brainstorm topics for their own informative essay.

Objectives
- Brainstorm topics for an informative essay.
- Choose a topic.

 **15 minutes**

Work **together** with students to complete the offline Composition activity.

Composition

Brainstorm and Choose Your Topic

Students will brainstorm and choose a topic for their own informative essay. Turn to pages WS 77 and 78 in *K¹² Language Arts Activity Book*.

1. Allow students to use the What Do You Do Well? topic in their journal (pages 24 and 25) for their informative essay, if they wish. If students choose to do so, then no further brainstorming is necessary; they do not need to complete the Activity Book pages. For students needing a topic, continue with Step 2.

2. Have students complete the Activity Book pages to brainstorm and choose an essay topic. Provide support as necessary. Remind students that during brainstorming, no idea is a bad idea. The point is to list as many ideas as possible before choosing a topic.

> **Objectives**
> - Brainstorm topics for an informative essay.
> - Choose a topic.

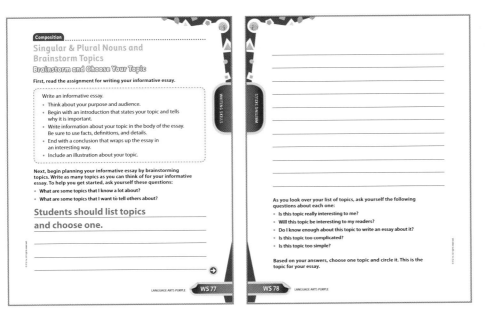

Plan Your Informative Essay

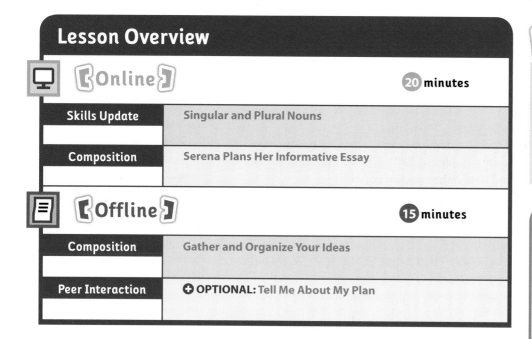

Lesson Overview

Online — 20 minutes

Skills Update	Singular and Plural Nouns
Composition	Serena Plans Her Informative Essay

Offline — 15 minutes

Composition	Gather and Organize Your Ideas
Peer Interaction	⊕ OPTIONAL: Tell Me About My Plan

Materials

Supplied

- *K¹² Language Arts Activity Book*, pp. WS 79–81
- *Grammar Reference Guide* Online Book (optional)

Keywords

audience – a writer's readers

definition – a statement that tells what a word means

detail – a fact or description that tells more about a topic

fact – something that can be proven true

purpose – the reason for writing

Big Ideas

Writing varies by purpose and audience. The specific reason for writing and the writer's intended readers (audience) determine the correct form and language to use.

Online 🕮 20 minutes

Students will work online to review singular and plural nouns and to learn how to use a graphic organizer to organize ideas for their informative essay. Help students locate the online activities.

Skills Update ....

Singular and Plural Nouns

Students will review how to identify singular and plural nouns, as well as how to form both regular and irregular plural nouns, by completing Skills Update exercises. Sit with students as they do this activity and note if they answer correctly.

> ⟳ **Learning Coach Check-In** How did students do on the Skills Update?

> ▸ **All answers correct:** Great! Skip the review screen and go on to the next activity.

> ▸ **Any answers incorrect:** Take a few minutes to review singular and plural nouns now. Use the links on the screen after the Skills Update to take another look at the online activities or review Nouns (Singular and Plural Nouns; Regular Plural Nouns; Irregular Plural Nouns) in the *Grammar Reference Guide* together.

TIP This activity will require extra time if students need to review singular and plural nouns. Take the extra 5–10 minutes to review now because new skills build on what students have already learned.

Objectives
- Identify singular nouns.
- Identify plural nouns.
- Form and use plural nouns.
- Form and use irregular plural nouns.

Composition ....

Serena Plans Her Informative Essay

By watching how Serena uses a graphic organizer, students will learn how to organize ideas for their own informative essay.

Objectives
- Determine purpose and audience.
- Use a graphic organizer to plan.
- Group related information together.
- Develop the topic with facts, definitions, and details.
- Include illustrations when useful.

 **Offline** ⑮ minutes

Work **together** with students to complete the offline Composition and Peer Interaction activities.

Composition ●●

Gather and Organize Your Ideas

Students will use a graphic organizer to gather and organize details about their informative essay. Turn to pages WS 79 and 80 in *K¹² Language Arts Activity Book*.

1. Have students complete the graphic organizer on page WS 79 by filling it in with ideas and details they want to include in their informative essay. Provide support as necessary. Remind students that they do not need to use complete sentences on the graphic organizer.

2. On the reverse side of the graphic organizer, encourage students to draw a picture that somehow relates to the points they intend to make in their informative essay.

TIP Keep students' completed graphic organizer and picture in a safe place so they can refer to them later.

 Objectives
- Determine purpose and audience.
- Use a graphic organizer to plan.
- Group related information together.
- Develop the topic with facts, definitions, and details.
- Include illustrations when useful.

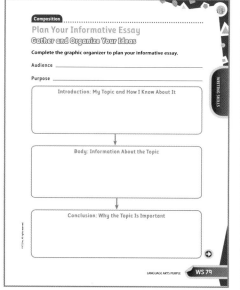

Peer Interaction

⊕ **OPTIONAL:** Tell Me About My Plan

This activity is OPTIONAL. It is intended for students who have extra time and would benefit from extra practice. Feel free to skip this activity.

Students can benefit from exchanging graphic organizers with another student. Each writer should receive feedback. To complete this optional activity, turn to page WS 81 in *K¹² Language Arts Activity Book*. (Additional copies of the Peer Interaction Form can be printed from the online lesson.)

1. Have students exchange graphic organizers with other students.

2. Have students complete the Activity Book page to give others feedback about their plan for the essay and their drawing.

TIP In the upcoming drafting lessons, students may use the feedback provided from other students as they write and seek to improve their essay.

Objectives
- Use feedback from others to plan.

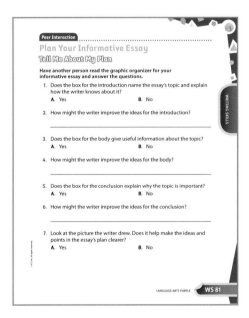

Singular Possessive Nouns and Draft Your Informative Essay

Lesson Overview

🖥 Online — 15 minutes

GUM (Grammar, Usage, and Mechanics)	Singular Possessive Nouns
Composition	Serena Begins Her Draft

📄 Offline — 20 minutes

Composition	Write Your Draft

Materials

Supplied

- *K¹² Language Arts Activity Book*, pp. WS 73–74, 79–81, 83–86
- *Grammar Reference Guide* Online Book (optional)
- drafting page (optional printout)

Keywords

body – the main text of a piece of writing

introduction – the first paragraph of an essay, identifying the topic and stating the main idea

possessive noun – the form of a noun that shows ownership

transition – a word or phrase that connects ideas

Advance Preparation

To prepare for the GUM portion of this lesson, review Nouns (Possessive Nouns) in the *Grammar Reference Guide* (linked in the online lesson) to familiarize yourself with the topic. Gather pages WS 73 and 74 (Model Informative Essay), 79 and 80 (Gather and Organize Your Ideas, students' completed graphic organizer), and 81 (Tell Me About My Plan, if completed) in *K¹² Language Arts Activity Book*. You will review the peer feedback with students.

Big Ideas

▶ Writing varies by purpose and audience. The specific reason for writing and the writer's intended readers (audience) determine the correct form and language to use.

▶ Possessive nouns can be recognized by their use of an apostrophe and the letter *s*, which may come before or after the apostrophe depending on the form of the word. A common error is to use an apostrophe to spell the plural form of a noun. An apostrophe is used only for the possessive form.

 **15 minutes**

Students will work online **independently** to complete activities on singular possessive nouns and to learn how to begin drafting an informative essay. Help students locate the online activities.

GUM (Grammar, Usage, and Mechanics)

Singular Possessive Nouns
Students will learn what a singular possessive noun is and practice identifying and forming singular possessive nouns.

Objectives
- Recognize possessive nouns.
- Form singular possessive nouns.

Composition

Serena Begins Her Draft
By watching how Serena begins to draft her informative essay, students will learn how to begin drafting their own informative essay.

Objectives
- Write an informative essay.
- Introduce a topic.
- Organize ideas in logical order.
- Use transitions to connect ideas.

 **20 minutes**

Work **together** with students to complete the offline Composition activity.

Composition

Write Your Draft
Students will begin drafting their informative essay. Have them gather the model informative essay and their completed graphic organizer, as well as any completed Peer Interaction forms. Turn to pages WS 83–86 in *K¹² Language Arts Activity Book*.

Objectives
- Write an informative essay.
- Introduce a topic.
- Organize ideas in logical order.
- Use transitions to connect ideas.

1. If students received feedback from peers, discuss with them how they might use it to improve their essay plan. Help students decide what peer feedback would be useful to include in their plan and have them revise their plan as appropriate.

2. Help students start drafting by reminding them to refer to Serena's informative essay and their graphic organizer, along with the Peer Interaction form (if applicable), as necessary. The model will help students remember what elements their essay should include, and their graphic organizer and the peer interaction form will help them remember which details to include and where to place them.

3. Remind students that a draft does not have to be perfect. It's just a first try at putting ideas on paper. Tell students that they will start writing their draft in this lesson and they will finish in the next lesson.

4. Have students use the lined Activity Book pages to begin drafting their informative essay. Students should write only in the white rows because the purple rows will be used for making revisions to the draft later. If needed, additional drafting pages can be printed from the online lesson.

TIP Keep students' drafting pages in a safe place, so they can continue working on them later. If students want to use a reference material such as the *Grammar Reference Guide* or a dictionary while drafting, suggest that they wait until they are revising or proofreading. Looking up information while drafting can interfere with students' flow of ideas.

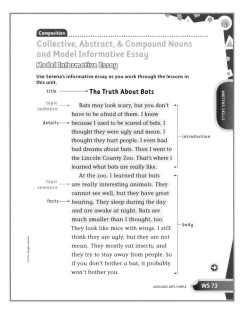

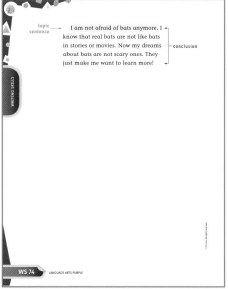

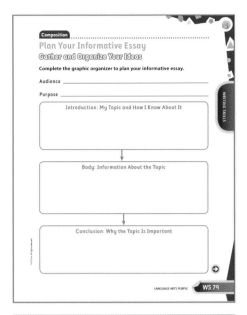

Plan Your Informative Essay
Gather and Organize Your Ideas

Complete the graphic organizer to plan your informative essay.

Audience _____

Purpose _____

> **Introduction: My Topic and How I Know About It**

↓

> **Body: Information About the Topic**

↓

> **Conclusion: Why the Topic Is Important**

WRITING SKILLS

Plan Your Informative Essay
Tell Me About My Plan

Have another person read the graphic organizer for your informative essay and answer the questions.

1. Does the box for the introduction name the essay's topic and explain how the writer knows about it?
   A. Yes   **B.** No

2. How might the writer improve the ideas for the introduction?
   _____

3. Does the box for the body give useful information about the topic?
   A. Yes   **B.** No

4. How might the writer improve the ideas for the body?
   _____

5. Does the box for the conclusion explain why the topic is important?
   A. Yes   **B.** No

6. How might the writer improve the ideas for the conclusion?
   _____

7. Look at the picture the writer drew. Does it help make the ideas and points in the essay's plan clearer?
   A. Yes   **B.** No

WRITING SKILLS

Singular Possessive Nouns and Draft Your Informative Essay
Write Your Draft

Read the assignment. Use your graphic organizer to help you write the first draft of your informative essay. Write only on the white rows. You will use the purple rows for revisions later.

> Write an informative essay.
> - Think about your purpose and audience.
> - Begin with an introduction that states your topic and tells why it is important.
> - Write information about your topic in the body of the essay. Be sure to use facts, definitions, and details.
> - End with a conclusion that wraps up the essay in an interesting way.
> - Include an illustration about your topic.

Start here ►

WRITING SKILLS

Plural Possessive Nouns and Draft Your Informative Essay

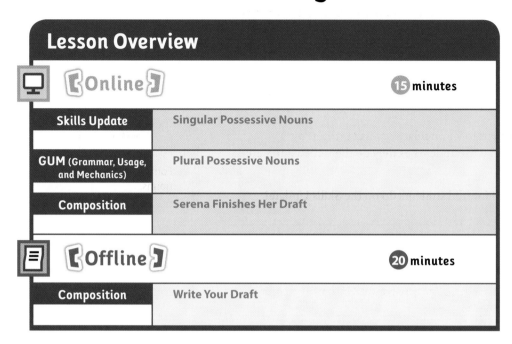

Lesson Overview

Online — 15 minutes

Skills Update	Singular Possessive Nouns
GUM (Grammar, Usage, and Mechanics)	Plural Possessive Nouns
Composition	Serena Finishes Her Draft

Offline — 20 minutes

Composition	Write Your Draft

Materials

Supplied

- *K¹² Language Arts Activity Book*, pp. WS 73–74, 79–80, 83–86
- *Grammar Reference Guide* Online Book (optional)
- drafting page (optional printout)
- Informative Essay: Feedback Sheet (printout)

Keywords

conclusion – the final paragraph of a written work

possessive noun – the form of a noun that shows ownership

transition – a word or phrase that connects ideas

Advance Preparation

To prepare for the GUM portion of this lesson, review Nouns (Possessive Nouns) in the *Grammar Reference Guide* (linked in the online lesson) to familiarize yourself with the topic. Gather pages WS 73 and 74 (Model Informative Essay), 79 and 80 (Gather and Organize Your Ideas, students' completed graphic organizer), and 83–86 (Write Your Draft, students' partially completed draft of their informative essay) in *K¹² Language Arts Activity Book*. Print the Informative Essay: Feedback Sheet from the online lesson.

Big Ideas

▸ Writing varies by purpose and audience. The specific reason for writing and the writer's intended readers (audience) determine the correct form and language to use.

▸ Possessive nouns can be recognized by their use of an apostrophe and the letter *s*, which may come before or after the apostrophe depending on the form of the word. A common error is to use an apostrophe to spell the plural form of a noun. An apostrophe is used only for the possessive form.

 ⏱ **minutes**

Students will work online to review singular possessive nouns, to complete an activity on plural possessive nouns, and to learn how to finish drafting an informative essay. Help students locate the online activities.

Skills Update

Singular Possessive Nouns

Students will review how to identify and form singular possessive nouns by completing Skills Update exercises. Sit with students as they do this activity and note if they answer correctly.

> ➲ **Learning Coach Check-In** How did students do on the Skills Update?

> ▸ **All answers correct:** Great! Skip the review screen and go on to the next activity.

> ▸ **Any answers incorrect:** Take a few minutes to review singular possessive nouns now. Use the links on the screen after the Skills Update to take another look at the online activities or review Nouns (Possessive Nouns) in the *Grammar Reference Guide* together.

TIP This activity will require extra time if students need to review singular possessive nouns. Take the extra 5–10 minutes to review now because new skills build on what students have already learned.

Objectives
- Recognize possessive nouns.
- Form singular possessive nouns.

GUM (Grammar, Usage, and Mechanics)

Plural Possessive Nouns

Students will learn what a plural possessive noun is and practice identifying and forming plural possessive nouns.

Objectives
- Recognize possessive nouns.
- Form plural possessive nouns.

Composition

Serena Finishes Her Draft

By watching how Serena finishes drafting her informative essay, students will learn how to finish drafting their own informative essay.

Objectives
- Write an informative essay.
- Introduce a topic.
- Organize ideas in logical order.
- Use transitions to connect ideas.
- Provide a concluding statement or section.

 **Offline** 20 minutes

Work **together** with students to complete the offline Composition activity.

Composition

Write Your Draft

Students will finish drafting their informative essay, and you will review it. Have them gather the model informative essay, their completed graphic organizer page, and their informative essay draft. You will also need the Informative Essay: Feedback Sheet, printable from the online lesson.

1. Have students finish drafting their informative essay, continuing to write only in the white rows. If needed, additional drafting pages can be printed from the online lesson.

2. As students write, remind them to refer to Serena's informative essay and their Gather and Organize Your Ideas page as necessary. Continue to emphasize that drafts are not meant to be perfect. They are a work in progress.

TIP Keep students' informative essay in a safe place so they can continue working on it later. If students want to use a reference material such as the *Grammar Reference Guide* or a dictionary while drafting, suggest that they wait until they are revising or proofreading. Looking up information while drafting can interfere with students' flow of ideas.

⮌ **Learning Coach Check-In** When students have finished their draft, read and review it using the Informative Essay: Feedback Sheet, but do not go over the feedback sheet with students now. The notes you take on this sheet will guide your feedback to students as they revise their draft in a later lesson. Keep the feedback sheet in a safe place until students are ready to revise their draft.

> **Objectives**
> - Write an informative essay.
> - Introduce a topic.
> - Organize ideas in logical order.
> - Use transitions to connect ideas.
> - Provide a concluding statement or section.

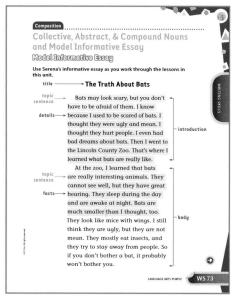
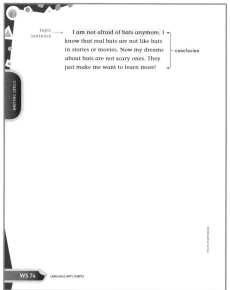

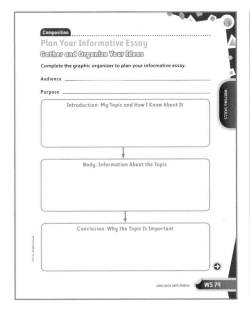

Composition

Plan Your Informative Essay
Gather and Organize Your Ideas

Complete the graphic organizer to plan your informative essay.

Audience _____

Purpose _____

> Introduction: My Topic and How I Know About It

> Body: Information About the Topic

> Conclusion: Why the Topic Is Important

Composition

Singular Possessive Nouns and Draft Your Informative Essay
Write Your Draft

Read the assignment. Use your graphic organizer to help you write the first draft of your informative essay. Write only on the white rows. You will use the purple rows for revisions later.

> Write an informative essay.
> - Think about your purpose and audience.
> - Begin with an introduction that states your topic and tells why it is important.
> - Write information about your topic in the body of the essay. Be sure to use facts, definitions, and details.
> - End with a conclusion that wraps up the essay in an interesting way.
> - Include an illustration about your topic.

Start here ►

Simple Subjects

Lesson Overview

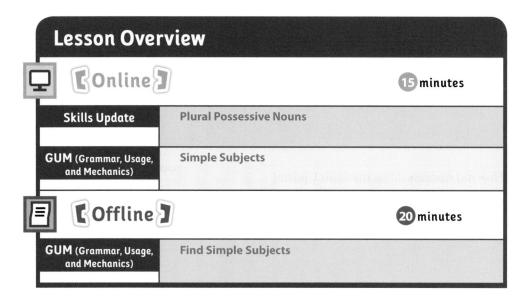

🖥 **Online**		15 minutes
Skills Update	Plural Possessive Nouns	
GUM (Grammar, Usage, and Mechanics)	Simple Subjects	

📄 **Offline**		20 minutes
GUM (Grammar, Usage, and Mechanics)	Find Simple Subjects	

Materials

Supplied

- *K¹² Language Arts Activity Book*, p. WS 87
- *Grammar Reference Guide* Online Book (optional)
- Informative Essay: Feedback Sheet (printout)

Keywords

simple subject – the subject noun or pronoun without any of its modifiers

Advance Preparation

To prepare for this lesson, review Parts of a Sentence (Simple Subject) in the *Grammar Reference Guide* (linked in the online lesson) to familiarize yourself with the topic. If you have not already completed the Informative Essay: Feedback Sheet, do so during this lesson while students work independently. You will need to share this form with students in the next lesson.

Big Ideas

A noun is a basic part of speech. Understanding nouns gives one a basic vocabulary for building sentences and grasping how language works.

 **15 minutes**

Students will work online to review plural possessive nouns and to complete an activity on simple subjects. Help students locate the online activities.

Skills Update

Plural Possessive Nouns

Students will review how to identify and form plural possessive nouns by completing Skills Update exercises. Sit with students as they do this activity and note if they answer correctly.

 Learning Coach Check-In How did students do on the Skills Update?

▸ **All answers correct:** Great! Skip the review screen and go on to the next activity.

▸ **Any answers incorrect:** Take a few minutes to review plural possessive nouns now. Use the links on the screen after the Skills Update to take another look at the online activities or review Nouns (Possessive Nouns) in the *Grammar Reference Guide* together.

TIP This activity will require extra time if students need to review plural possessive nouns. Take the extra 5–10 minutes to review now because new skills build on what students have already learned.

Objectives
- Recognize possessive nouns.
- Form plural possessive nouns.

GUM (Grammar, Usage, and Mechanics)

Simple Subjects

Students will learn how to identify the simple subject of a sentence.

Objectives
- Identify the simple subject.

 **Offline** **20** minutes

Work **together** with students to complete the offline GUM activity.

GUM (Grammar, Usage, and Mechanics) ·

Find Simple Subjects

Students will practice identifying simple subjects. Turn to page WS 87 in
K¹² Language Arts Activity Book. Have students complete the Activity Book page.

Objectives
• Identify the simple subject.

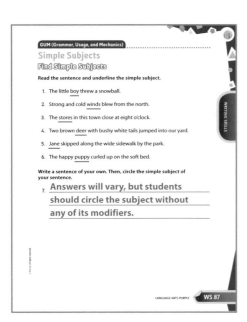

GUM (Grammar, Usage, and Mechanics)
Simple Subjects
Find Simple Subjects

Read the sentence and underline the simple subject.

1. The little boy threw a snowball.
2. Strong and cold winds blew from the north.
3. The stores in this town close at eight o'clock.
4. Two brown deer with bushy white tails jumped into our yard.
5. Jane skipped along the wide sidewalk by the park.
6. The happy puppy curled up on the soft bed.

Write a sentence of your own. Then, circle the simple subject of your sentence.

7. **Answers will vary, but students should circle the subject without any of its modifiers.**

LANGUAGE ARTS PURPLE   **WS 87**

Revise Your Informative Essay

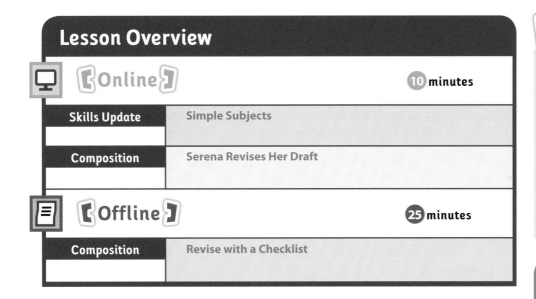

Lesson Overview

Online		**10** minutes
Skills Update	Simple Subjects	
Composition	Serena Revises Her Draft	

Offline		**25** minutes
Composition	Revise with a Checklist	

Materials

Supplied

- *K¹² Language Arts Activity Book*, pp. WS 83–86, 89
- *Grammar Reference Guide* Online Book (optional)
- drafting page (optional printout)
- Informative Essay: Feedback Sheet (printout)

Keywords

transition – a word or phrase that connects ideas

Advance Preparation

Gather pages WS 83–86 (Write Your Draft, students' draft of their informative essay) in *K¹² Language Arts Activity Book* and the completed Informative Essay: Feedback Sheet. You will review the feedback with students.

 **Online** ⑩ **minutes**

Students will work online to review simple subjects and to learn how to revise an informative essay. Help students locate the online activities.

Skills Update

Simple Subjects

Students will review how to identify simple subjects by completing Skills Update exercises. Sit with students as they do this activity and note if they answer correctly.

 Learning Coach Check-In How did students do on the Skills Update?

- ▸ **All answers correct:** Great! Skip the review screen and go on to the next activity.
- ▸ **Any answers incorrect:** Take a few minutes to review simple subjects now. Use the links on the screen after the Skills Update to take another look at the online activities or review Parts of a Sentence (Simple Subject) in the *Grammar Reference Guide* together.

TIP This activity will require extra time if students need to review simple subjects. Take the extra 5–10 minutes to review now because new skills build on what students have already learned.

> **Objectives**
> - Identify the simple subject.

Composition

Serena Revises Her Draft

By watching how Serena revises her informative essay draft, students will learn how to revise their own draft.

> **Objectives**
> - Revise an informative essay.
> - Use transitions to connect ideas.
> - Provide complete information.
> - Organize ideas in a logical order.

 **25 minutes**

Work **together** with students to complete the offline Composition activity.

Composition

Revise with a Checklist

Students will revise their informative essay. Have them gather their informative essay draft. Turn to page WS 89 in *K¹² Language Arts Activity Book* and gather the Informative Essay: Feedback Sheet that you filled out.

1. Use the Informative Essay: Feedback Sheet to guide your discussion with students.

   ▸ Tell students the strengths of their essay. Provide positive comments about the ideas, language, details, or other elements of the essay you enjoyed.

   ▸ Walk through the Purpose and Content and Structure and Organization sections of the feedback sheet with students. Do not address your comments in the Grammar and Mechanics section at this time. You can work with students on grammar and mechanics when they proofread. Providing these corrections at this time may distract students from the real work of revising for content and structure.

   ▸ As you go through the feedback sheet with students, encourage them to actively revise their draft based on your feedback. Reassure students that it's okay to remove ideas or sentences from their essay. Doing so may help their essay stay focused on their topic, even if something they cut was included in their graphic organizer.

   ▸ As students revise their draft, have them use the purple rows to mark their revisions.

2. Once you've reviewed your comments on the first two sections of the feedback sheet with students, have them review their draft once more, using the revision checklist on the Activity Book page. Students should check off each box on the checklist as they complete each item.

Objectives

- Revise an informative essay.
- Use transitions to connect ideas.
- Provide complete information.
- Organize ideas in a logical order.

3. If the revised informative essay has many changes that make the essay difficult to understand, encourage students to make a clean copy before they proofread in a later lesson. Additional drafting pages can be printed from the online lesson.

TIP Keep students' revised informative essay in a safe place so they can refer to it later.

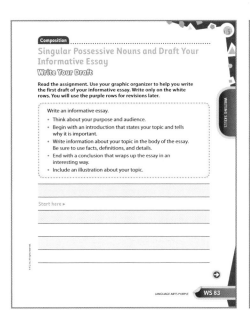

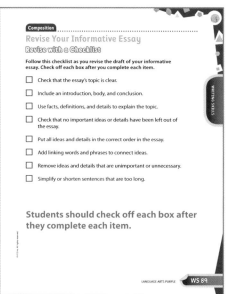

Unit Review and Proofread Your Informative Essay

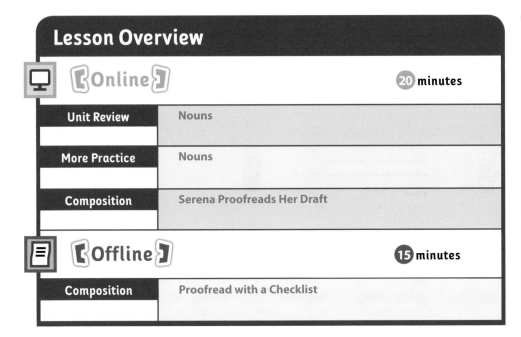

Lesson Overview

🖥 Online — 20 minutes

Unit Review	Nouns
More Practice	Nouns
Composition	Serena Proofreads Her Draft

≣ Offline — 15 minutes

Composition	Proofread with a Checklist

Advance Preparation

Gather pages WS 83–86 (Write Your Draft, students' draft of their informative essay) in *K¹² Language Arts Activity Book* and the completed Informative Essay: Feedback Sheet. If the revised essay has many changes that make it difficult to read and understand, you may want to encourage students to make a clean copy before they proofread in this lesson. Additional drafting pages can be printed from the online lesson.

〖 Materials 〗

Supplied

- *K¹² Language Arts Activity Book*, pp. WS 83–86, 89
- *Grammar Reference Guide* Online Book (optional)
- drafting page (optional printout)
- Informative Essay: Feedback Sheet (printout)

Keywords

abstract noun – a word that names an idea

collective noun – a word that means a group of things but is usually singular

common noun – a word that names any person, place, thing, or idea

compound noun – a noun made up of two or more words

compound sentence – a sentence that has at least two independent parts

conjunction – a word used to join parts of a sentence

plural noun – a word that names more than one person, place, thing, or idea

possessive noun – the form of a noun that shows ownership

proper noun – the name of a particular person, place, thing, or idea; proper nouns begin with a capital letter

simple subject – the subject noun or pronoun without any of its modifiers

singular noun – a word that names one person, place, thing, or idea

 **20 minutes**

Students will work online to review the grammar, usage, and mechanics skills learned in the unit and to learn how to proofread an informative essay. Help students locate the online activities.

Unit Review

Nouns

Students will review what they have learned about nouns to review for the Unit Checkpoint.

 TIP A full list of objectives covered in the Unit Review can be found in the online lesson.

> ⭐ **Objectives**
> - Complete a review of grammar, usage, and mechanics skills.

More Practice

Nouns

Go over students' results on the Unit Review and, if necessary, have them complete the appropriate review activities listed in the table online. Help students locate the activities and provide support as needed.

 TIP The time students need to complete this activity will vary. Set aside enough time for students to complete all review activities, if they need to do so.

> ⭐ **Objectives**
> - Evaluate Unit Review results and choose activities for more practice.

Composition

Serena Proofreads Her Draft

By watching how Serena proofreads her informative essay draft, students will learn how to proofread their own draft.

> **Objectives**
> - Proofread an informative essay.
> - Capitalize proper nouns.
> - Spell plural nouns correctly.
> - Use a comma before the conjunction in a compound sentence.

 **15 minutes**

Work **together** with students to complete the offline Composition activity.

Composition

Proofread with a Checklist

Students will proofread their informative essay. Have them gather their informative essay draft. Turn to page WS 90 in *K¹² Language Arts Activity Book* and gather the Informative Essay: Feedback Sheet that you filled out.

1. Review with students your comments in the Grammar and Mechanics section of the feedback sheet. As you go through the feedback sheet with them, encourage students to use the purple rows on their drafting pages to actively mark changes based on your feedback.

2. Once you've reviewed your comments in the Grammar and Mechanics section of the feedback sheet with students, have them review their draft once more using the proofreading checklist. Students should check off each box on the checklist as they complete each item.

3. If the revised informative essay has many changes that make the essay difficult to understand, encourage students to make a clean copy before they proofread.

TIP Keep students' proofread essay in a safe place so they can refer to it later.

Objectives
- Proofread an informative essay.
- Capitalize proper nouns.
- Spell plural nouns correctly.
- Use a comma before the conjunction in a compound sentence.

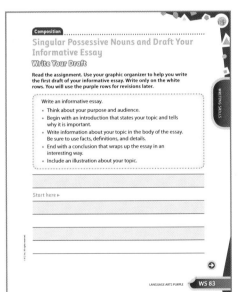

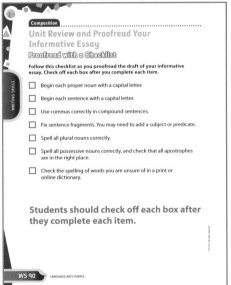

Unit Checkpoint and Publish Your Informative Essay

Lesson Overview

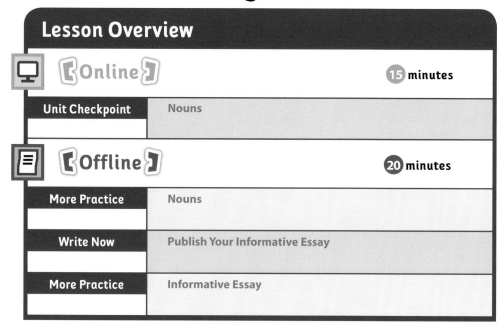

Online		15 minutes
Unit Checkpoint	Nouns	

Offline		20 minutes
More Practice	Nouns	
Write Now	Publish Your Informative Essay	
More Practice	Informative Essay	

Advance Preparation

Gather pages WS 83–86 (Write Your Draft, students' draft of their informative essay) in *K¹² Language Arts Activity Book,* which students should have already revised and proofread.

Materials

Supplied

- *K¹² Language Arts Activity Book,* pp. WS 83–86, 91–94
- *Grammar Reference Guide* Online Book (optional)
- Common and Proper Nouns (optional printout)
- Collective, Abstract, and Compound Nouns (optional printout)
- Singular and Plural Nouns (optional printout)
- Singular and Plural Possessive Nouns (optional printout)
- Simple Subjects (optional printout)
- Informative Essay: Rubric and Sample Responses (printout)
- lined writing page (optional printout)

 **15** minutes

Students will work online **independently** to complete the Unit Checkpoint. Help students locate the Unit Checkpoint and provide support as necessary.

Unit Checkpoint

Nouns

Students will complete an online Unit Checkpoint about nouns. If necessary, read the directions to students.

 A full list of objectives covered in the Unit Checkpoint can be found in the online lesson.

Objectives
- Complete a Unit Checkpoint on grammar, usage, and mechanics skills.

Offline **20** minutes

Work **together** with students to complete the offline More Practice and Write Now activities.

More Practice

Nouns

Go over students' results on the Unit Checkpoint and, if necessary, print out and have them complete the appropriate practice pages listed in the table online. Students can complete all necessary pages now or, if more time is needed, they can spread them out over the next few days. They can also review the appropriate sections of the *Grammar Reference Guide* with you. If students scored less than 80 percent on the Unit Checkpoint, you may want them to retake the checkpoint after completing the additional activity pages.

 The time students need to complete this activity will vary. Set aside enough time for students to complete some or all activity pages and to retake the Unit Checkpoint if they need to do so. Students may retake the Unit Checkpoint immediately, but having them complete the practice pages and then retake it might be more effective.

Objectives
- Evaluate Unit Checkpoint results and choose activities for more practice.

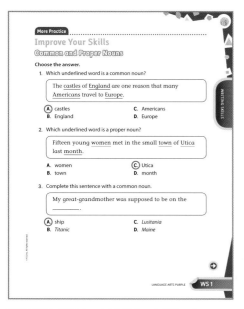

More Practice

Improve Your Skills
Common and Proper Nouns

Choose the answer.

1. Which underlined word is a common noun?

   The castles of England are one reason that many Americans travel to Europe.

   (A) castles   C. Americans
   B. England   D. Europe

2. Which underlined word is a proper noun?

   Fifteen young women met in the small town of Utica last month.

   A. women   (C) Utica
   B. town   D. month

3. Complete this sentence with a common noun.

   My great-grandmother was supposed to be on the _____.

   (A) ship   C. Lusitania
   B. Titanic   D. Maine

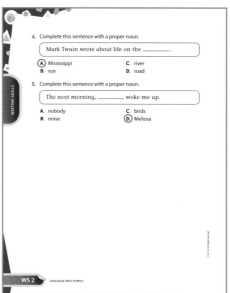

4. Complete this sentence with a proper noun.

   Mark Twain wrote about life on the _____.

   (A) Mississippi   C. river
   B. run   D. road

5. Complete this sentence with a proper noun.

   The next morning, _____ woke me up.

   A. nobody   C. birds
   B. noise   (D) Melissa

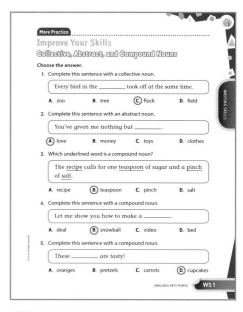

More Practice

Improve Your Skills
Collective, Abstract, and Compound Nouns

Choose the answer.

1. Complete this sentence with a collective noun.

   Every bird in the _____ took off at the same time.

   A. zoo   B. tree   (C) flock   D. field

2. Complete this sentence with an abstract noun.

   You've given me nothing but _____.

   (A) love   B. money   C. toys   D. clothes

3. Which underlined word is a compound noun?

   The recipe calls for one teaspoon of sugar and a pinch of salt.

   A. recipe   (B) teaspoon   C. pinch   D. salt

4. Complete this sentence with a compound noun.

   Let me show you how to make a _____.

   A. deal   (B) snowball   C. video   D. bed

5. Complete this sentence with a compound noun.

   These _____ are tasty!

   A. oranges   B. pretzels   C. carrots   (D) cupcakes

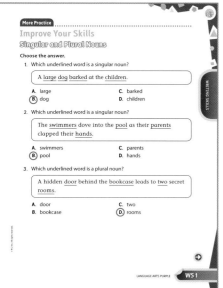

More Practice

Improve Your Skills
Singular and Plural Nouns

Choose the answer.

1. Which underlined word is a singular noun?

   A large dog barked at the children.

   A. large   C. barked
   (B) dog   D. children

2. Which underlined word is a singular noun?

   The swimmers dove into the pool as their parents clapped their hands.

   A. swimmers   C. parents
   (B) pool   D. hands

3. Which underlined word is a plural noun?

   A hidden door behind the bookcase leads to two secret rooms.

   A. door   C. two
   B. bookcase   (D) rooms

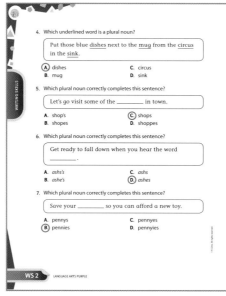

4. Which underlined word is a plural noun?

   Put those blue dishes next to the mug from the circus in the sink.

   (A) dishes   C. circus
   B. mug   D. sink

5. Which plural noun correctly completes this sentence?

   Let's go visit some of the _____ in town.

   A. shop's   (C) shops
   B. shopes   D. shoppes

6. Which plural noun correctly completes this sentence?

   Get ready to fall down when you hear the word _____.

   A. ashs's   C. ashs
   B. ashe's   (D) ashes

7. Which plural noun correctly completes this sentence?

   Save your _____ so you can afford a new toy.

   A. pennys   C. pennyes
   (B) pennies   D. pennyies

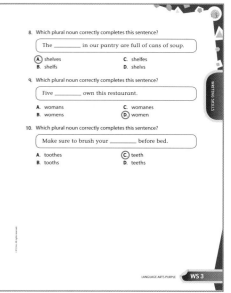

8. Which plural noun correctly completes this sentence?

   The _____ in our pantry are full of cans of soup.

   (A) shelves   C. shelfes
   B. shelfs   D. shelvs

9. Which plural noun correctly completes this sentence?

   Five _____ own this restaurant.

   A. womans   C. womanes
   B. womens   (D) women

10. Which plural noun correctly completes this sentence?

    Make sure to brush your _____ before bed.

    A. toothes   (C) teeth
    B. tooths   D. teeths

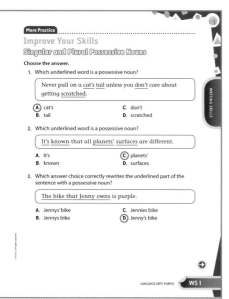

More Practice

Improve Your Skills
Singular and Plural Possessive Nouns

Choose the answer.

1. Which underlined word is a possessive noun?

   Never pull on a cat's tail unless you don't care about getting scratched.

   (A) cat's   C. don't
   B. tail   D. scratched

2. Which underlined word is a possessive noun?

   It's known that all planets' surfaces are different.

   A. It's   (C) planets'
   B. known   D. surfaces

3. Which answer choice correctly rewrites the underlined part of the sentence with a possessive noun?

   The bike that Jenny owns is purple.

   A. Jennys' bike   C. Jennies bike
   B. Jennys bike   (D) Jenny's bike

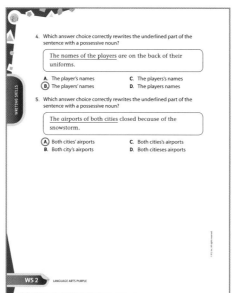

4. Which answer choice correctly rewrites the underlined part of the sentence with a possessive noun?

   The names of the players are on the back of their uniforms.

   A. The player's names   C. The players's names
   (B) The players' names   D. The players names

5. Which answer choice correctly rewrites the underlined part of the sentence with a possessive noun?

   The airports of both cities closed because of the snowstorm.

   (A) Both cities' airports   C. Both cities's airports
   B. Both city's airports   D. Both citieses airports

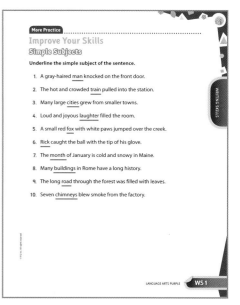

More Practice

Improve Your Skills
Simple Subjects

Underline the simple subject of the sentence.

1. A gray-haired man knocked on the front door.

2. The hot and crowded train pulled into the station.

3. Many large cities grew from smaller towns.

4. Loud and joyous laughter filled the room.

5. A small red fox with white paws jumped over the creek.

6. Rick caught the ball with the tip of his glove.

7. The month of January is cold and snowy in Maine.

8. Many buildings in Rome have a long history.

9. The long road through the forest was filled with leaves.

10. Seven chimneys blew smoke from the factory.

Write Now

Publish Your Informative Essay

Students will publish their informative essay. Have them gather their proofread draft. Turn to pages WS 91–94 in *K¹² Language Arts Activity Book*.

> **Objectives**
> * Make a clean copy of the essay.
> * Include illustrations when useful.

1. Explain to students that they will finish their informative essay by completing the last step in the writing process—publishing their work.
   Say: Publishing your writing means making a clean and final copy that is ready for sharing with others.

   ▸ To be ready to publish your informative essay, you should have finished revising and proofreading your draft.

   ▸ The final copy should be your best effort and should not have any errors.

2. Explain that the final copy should be written clearly and neatly on clean sheets of paper. Tell students that they should use good handwriting and leave spaces between words so that others can read what they wrote.

3. Have students use the lined Activity Book pages to write their final copy. If needed, additional writing pages can be printed from the online lesson.

4. Remind students that an illustration can be helpful to readers of an informative essay. Encourage students to draw a picture that relates to the topic of their essay now. They may use the picture they drew when they filled in their graphic organizer. If they want to use a different picture, they may draw in the space provided on the clean copy of their essay or on a separate blank sheet of paper. If students have trouble deciding what to draw, ask the following questions.

   ▸ What is your essay about? Who or what is the most important person, place, or thing in your essay?

   ▸ What are the most important points of your essay? Is there anything that you can draw to make readers better understand one of those points?

   ▸ What picture did you draw when you were planning your essay? Can you improve that drawing or redraw the same thing?

5. Use the materials and instructions in the online lesson to evaluate students' finished writing. You will be looking at students' writing to evaluate the following:

   ▸ **Purpose and Content:** The essay focuses on a single topic. Only a few of the facts and details are irrelevant to the topic, and the essay's purpose is to inform readers. The writing has some sentence fluency.

   ▸ **Structure and Organization:** The essay has been revised. It has an introduction, a body, and a conclusion. The piece is mostly organized.

   ▸ **Grammar and Mechanics:** The essay has been proofread using a checklist, and few errors remain. Most sentences are complete, and most nouns are spelled correctly.

6. Enter students' scores online for each rubric category.

7. If students' writing scored a 1 in any category, work with them to revise and proofread their work.

8. Suggest that, if possible, students share their informative essay with anyone who is a part of the audience they identified for their work. In addition, people special to students, such as grandparents, would likely enjoy hearing the essay read to them or having a copy of the essay to keep.

TIP Tell students that producing a piece of writing that is ready to publish and share with others is a great accomplishment. Let students know that the effort they put in to publish an essay is something to be proud of.

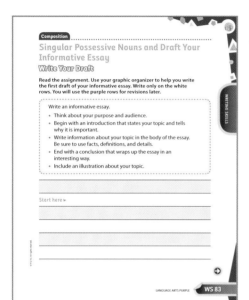

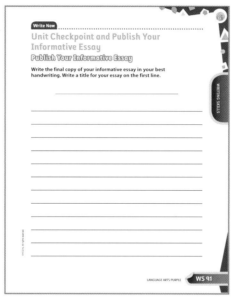

More Practice

Informative Essay

If students' writing did not meet objectives, have them complete the appropriate review activities listed in the table online. Follow the online instructions to help them edit and revise their work. Impress upon students that revising makes their work better. Writing is a process, and each time they revise their essay they are making their writing stronger and better. Always begin with something positive to say. If there is one detail, for example, mention it and say how this helps you picture what is being written about.

Help students locate the activities and provide support as needed.

Reward: When students score 80 percent or above on the Unit Checkpoint and their writing is Level 2 or higher on the Informative Essay grading rubric, add a sticker for this unit on the My Accomplishments chart.

Objectives
- Revise an informative essay.

Critical Skills Practice 2

Unit Focus

In this unit, students will practice answering questions about skills associated with language, vocabulary, and spelling. They will

- Review the present, past, and future tenses of verbs and practice answering questions about them.
- Recall what synonyms and antonyms are and apply that knowledge to answering questions about them.
- Identify the subject and verb in a sentence and practice recognizing correct agreement of a verb with its subject.
- Review vowel suffixes and practice spelling verbs with vowel suffixes.

Unit Plan		**〔Offline〕**	**〔Online〕**
Lesson 1	Language Skills (B)		35 minutes
Lesson 2	Vocabulary Skills (C)		35 minutes
Lesson 3	Language Skills (C)		35 minutes
Lesson 4	Spelling Skills (B)		35 minutes
Lesson 5	Unit Checkpoint	35 minutes	varies

Language Skills (B)

Lesson Overview

Materials

There are no materials to gather for this lesson.

Online — 35 minutes

Get Ready	Verbs
Learn	Questions About Verb Tense
Try It	Answer Questions About Verb Tense

Keywords

future tense – a form of a verb that names an action that will happen later

past tense – the form of the verb that tells what has already happened

present tense – the verb form that tells what is happening now

verb – a word that shows action or a state of being

Big Ideas

Practice answering the kinds of questions often found on standardized tests can make taking the tests less stressful for students.

Online — 35 minutes

Students will work online **independently** to complete Get Ready, Learn, and Try It activities. Help students locate the online activities.

Get Ready

Verbs

Students will review what verbs are and how to identify a verb in a sentence.

Objectives
● Identify verbs in sentences.

Learn

Questions About Verb Tense

Students will learn how to answer questions about verb tenses by reading and working through several exercises.

Objectives
- Identify and use verbs in simple present, simple past, and simple future tenses.

Try It

Answer Questions About Verb Tense

Students will show their comprehension and ability to respond to questions about verb tenses.

Objectives
- Identify and use verbs in simple present, simple past, and simple future tenses.

Vocabulary Skills (C)

Lesson Overview

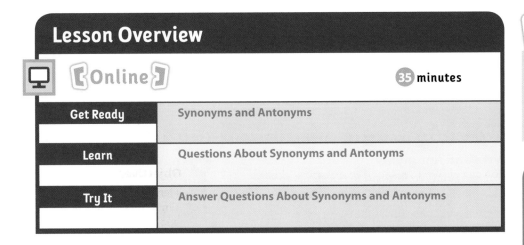

 Online · 35 minutes

Get Ready	Synonyms and Antonyms
Learn	Questions About Synonyms and Antonyms
Try It	Answer Questions About Synonyms and Antonyms

Materials

There are no materials to gather for this lesson.

Keywords

antonym – a word that means the opposite of another word

synonym – a word that means the same, or almost the same, as another word

Big Ideas

Practice answering the kinds of questions often found on standardized tests can make taking the tests less stressful for students.

 **35 minutes**

Students will work online **independently** to complete Get Ready, Learn, and Try It activities. Help students locate the online activities.

Get Ready ·

Synonyms and Antonyms
Students will review what synonyms and antonyms are.

 Objectives
• Recall what synonyms and antonyms are.

Learn

Questions About Synonyms and Antonyms
Students will learn how to answer questions about synonyms and antonyms by reading and working through several exercises.

Objectives
- Identify synonyms.
- Identify antonyms.

Try It

Answer Questions About Synonyms and Antonyms
Students will show their comprehension and ability to respond to questions about synonyms and antonyms.

Objectives
- Identify synonyms.
- Identify antonyms.

Language Skills (C)

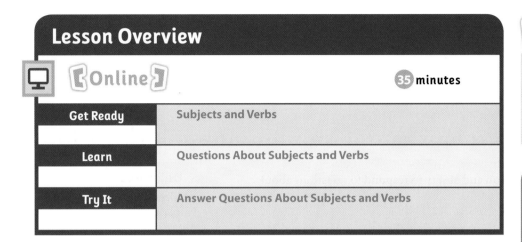

Lesson Overview

🖥️ 【Online】 ⏱ 35 minutes

Get Ready	Subjects and Verbs
Learn	Questions About Subjects and Verbs
Try It	Answer Questions About Subjects and Verbs

【Materials】

There are no materials to gather for this lesson.

Keywords

compound subject – two or more subjects that have the same predicate

pronoun – a word that takes the place of one or more nouns

subject – a word or words that tell whom or what the sentence is about

subject–verb agreement – the way a subject and verb match when both are singular or both are plural

verb – a word that shows action or a state of being

Big Ideas

Practice answering the kinds of questions often found on standardized tests can make taking the tests less stressful for students.

【Online】 ⏱ 35 minutes

Students will work online **independently** to complete Get Ready, Learn, and Try It activities. Help students locate the online activities.

Get Ready ....

Subjects and Verbs
Students will review what subjects and verbs are before identifying subjects and verbs in sentences.

Objectives
• Identify the subject and verb of a sentence.

Learn

Questions About Subjects and Verbs
Students will learn how to answer questions about subject–verb agreement by reading and working through several exercises.

Objectives
- Identify the subject and verb of a sentence.
- Use a verb that agrees with its subject.

Try It

Answer Questions About Subjects and Verbs
Students will show their comprehension and ability to respond to questions about subject–verb agreement.

Objectives
- Identify the subject and verb of a sentence.
- Use a verb that agrees with its subject.

Spelling Skills (B)

Lesson Overview

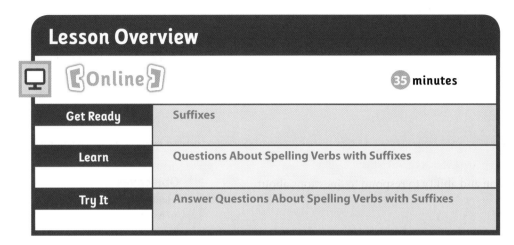

Online		35 minutes
Get Ready	Suffixes	
Learn	Questions About Spelling Verbs with Suffixes	
Try It	Answer Questions About Spelling Verbs with Suffixes	

[Materials]

There are no materials to gather for this lesson.

Keywords

suffix – a word part added to the end of a base word or root that changes the meaning or part of speech of a word

Big Ideas

Practice answering the kinds of questions often found on standardized tests can make taking the tests less stressful for students.

Online 35 minutes

Students will work online **independently** to complete Get Ready, Learn, and Try It activities. Help students locate the online activities.

Get Ready ....

Suffixes
Students will review what suffixes are and recall that the suffixes –*ed* and –*ing* are used with verbs.

Objectives
* Recall the meaning of suffixes.

Learn

Questions About Spelling Verbs with Suffixes

Students will learn how to answer questions about spelling verbs with the
suffixes –*ed* and –*ing*.

Objectives

- Spell words ending in the vowel suffix –*ed*.
- Spell words ending in the vowel suffix –*ing*.

Try It

Answer Questions About Spelling Verbs with Suffixes

Students will show their comprehension and ability to respond to questions about
spelling verbs with the suffixes –*ed* and –*ing*.

Objectives

- Spell words ending in the vowel suffix –*ed*.
- Spell words ending in the vowel suffix –*ing*.

Unit Checkpoint

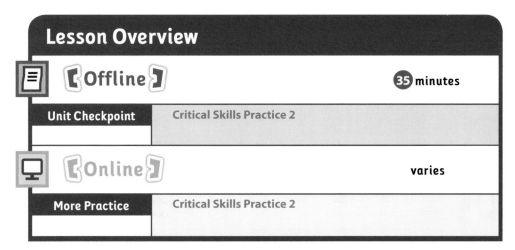

Lesson Overview

Offline — 35 minutes

Unit Checkpoint	Critical Skills Practice 2

Online — varies

More Practice	Critical Skills Practice 2

Materials

Supplied

- *K¹² Language Arts Assessments*, pp. WS 9–15

Objectives

- Identify and use verbs in simple present, simple past, and simple future tenses.
- Identify synonyms.
- Identify antonyms.

- Identify the subject and verb of a sentence.
- Use a verb that agrees with its subject.
- Spell words ending in the vowel suffix –ed.
- Spell words ending in the vowel suffix –ing.

Offline — 35 minutes

Unit Checkpoint

Critical Skills Practice 2

Explain that students are going to show what they have learned about verb tenses, synonyms and antonyms, subject–verb agreement, and the suffixes –ed and –ing.

1. Give students the Unit Checkpoint pages.

2. Read the directions together. Have students complete the Checkpoint on their own.

3. Use the Answer Key to score the Checkpoint and then enter the results online.

4. Review each exercise with students. Work with students to correct any exercise that they missed.

Reward: If students score 80 percent or more on the Unit Checkpoint, add a sticker for this unit on the My Accomplishments chart. If students did not score 80 percent or more, work with them to revise their work until they do score 80 percent.

Panel 1 (WS 9)

Name _____ Date _____

Unit Checkpoint Learning Coach
Instructions
Critical Skills Practice 2

Explain that students are going to show what they have learned about verb tenses, synonyms and antonyms, subject–verb agreement, and the suffixes –ed and –ing.

1. Give students the Unit Checkpoint pages.
2. Read the directions together. Have students complete the Checkpoint on their own.
3. Use the Answer Key to score the Checkpoint and then enter the results online.
4. Review each exercise with students. Work with students to correct any exercise that they missed.

Panel 2 (WS 10)

Name _____ Date _____

Unit Checkpoint Answer Key
Critical Skills Practice 2

Part 1. Verb Tenses
Read and answer each question.

1. Read this paragraph.

   The lion roared. Gorillas sat up in the trees. A snake hissed as it <u>moves</u> over a rock.

   What is the correct way to rewrite the underlined verb to match the tense of the rest of the verbs in the paragraph?
   A. move   C. will move
   (B) moved   D. moving

2. Read this sentence.

   Later tonight, Dan will close the door, but he <u>opened</u> the windows.

   Which choice shows the correct tense for the underlined verb?
   (A) will open   C. opens
   B. open   D. opening

3. Which underlined verb needs to be changed?
   A. <u>Pour</u> me a glass of water, please.
   B. Someday Ginny <u>will visit</u> Alaska.
   C. Jim <u>raked</u> leaves yesterday afternoon.
   (D) Rome <u>hosts</u> the Olympics in 1960.

Panel 3 (WS 11)

Name _____ Date _____

4. Read this sentence.

   Before Harriet was born, her parents <u>live</u> in a house near the river.

   Which choice shows the correct tense for the underlined verb?
   A. living   C. will live
   B. lives   (D) lived

5. Which underlined verb needs to be changed?
   A. Holly <u>cleaned</u> her room last Sunday.
   B. The cat <u>purrs</u> in the den.
   (C) <u>Finished</u> your peas, please.
   D. The sun <u>will shine</u> tomorrow.

Part 2. Synonyms and Antonyms
Read and answer each question.

6. Read this sentence.

   The old house was dark and spooky, but Gina never showed that she was <u>afraid</u>.

   Which word is an antonym for *afraid*?
   A. happy   (C) brave
   B. scared   D. sad

7. Which word is a synonym for *shiny*?
   A. dull   C. dark
   (B) bright   D. new

Panel 4 (WS 12)

Name _____ Date _____

8. Which two words are antonyms?
   (A) smooth, rough   C. fix, repair
   B. straight, long   D. hold, carry

9. Read this paragraph.

   Not many girls my age like to knit. That doesn't matter to me, though. I love to knit. It <u>relaxes</u> me and makes me feel creative. I have knitted blankets, scarves, and hats. This winter, I'm going to knit a sweater for my grandmother. She is the one who taught me to knit in the first place. It has been her favorite hobby since she was a little girl, too.

   Which word means almost the same thing as *relaxes*?
   A. bores   B. interests   C. excites   (D) calms

10. Read this paragraph.

    The squirrel jumped onto a thick branch and looked up. Farther up the tree, a few skinny branches blew in the wind. Jumping on them would not be safe. So the squirrel turned its head and made a decision. It left the tree and leaped onto the roof of a nearby house. Moments later, the squirrel's bushy tail disappeared as the animal scurried out of sight.

    Which two words from the paragraph have almost the same meaning?
    A. head, tail   (C) jumped, leaped
    B. thick, skinny   D. farther, nearby

Panel 5 (WS 13)

Name _____ Date _____

Part 3. Subject–Verb Agreement
Read and answer each question.

11. Read this sentence.

    Tom <u>fill</u> the bucket with water.

    What is the correct way to write the underlined words?
    A. Tom filling   C. Tom fill's
    (B) Tom fills   D. Tom are filling

12. Read this sentence.

    Bees _____ as hard as any animal.

    What is the correct way to complete this sentence?
    A. work's   C. works
    B. working   (D) work

13. Read this sentence.

    <u>Everyone want</u> a puppy.

    What is the correct way to write the underlined words?
    (A) Everyone wants
    B. Everyones wants
    C. Everyone wanting
    D. Everyones want

Panel 6 (WS 14)

Name _____ Date _____

14. Read this sentence.

    <u>Several people lives</u> on farms.

    What is the correct way to write the underlined words?
    A. Several people will lives
    B. Several people is living
    (C) Several people live
    D. Several people live's

15. Read this sentence.

    The <u>knife and spoon belongs</u> next to the plate.

    What is the correct way to write the underlined words?
    A. The knife and spoons are belonging
    B. The knife and spoon belonging
    C. The knife and spoons belongs
    (D) The knife and spoon belong

Part 4. Vowels Ending in –ed and –ing
Read and answer each question.

16. Read this sentence.

    I <u>work</u> very hard.

    If the suffix –ed is added to the word *work*, what is the correct way to spell the new word?
    A. workeed   (B) worked   C. workied   D. workd

Panel 7 (WS 15)

Name _____ Date _____

17. Read this sentence.

    Jess's sister was <u>push</u> the cart.

    If the suffix –ing is added to the word *push*, what is the correct way to spell the new word?
    A. pushiing   (C) pushing
    B. pushying   D. pushhing

18. Read this sentence.

    Two balls <u>slam</u> into the wall.

    If the suffix –ed is added to the word *slam*, what is the correct way to spell the new word?
    (A) slammed   C. slammeed
    B. slamed   D. slamd

19. Read this sentence.

    I was <u>hopeing</u> you would be here.

    How should the underlined word be spelled?
    A. hopping   C. hopiing
    (B) hoping   D. hopeng

20. Read this sentence.

    Alana <u>wipeed</u> her dirty hands on a towel after she put away her shovel.

    How should the underlined word be spelled?
    A. wipped   C. wippeed
    B. wipd   (D) wiped

 **varies**

Work **together** with students to complete the online More Practice activity.

More Practice ....

Critical Skills Practice 2

Go over students' results on the Unit Checkpoint. If necessary, have students complete the appropriate review activities listed in the table online. Help students locate the activities and provide support as needed.

 The time students need to complete this activity will vary. Set aside enough time for students to complete all review activities, if they need to do so.

Objectives
- Evaluate Unit Checkpoint results and choose activities for more practice.

UNIT OVERVIEW   Verbs and Persuasive Essay

Unit Focus

In the grammar part of the unit, students will learn about verbs. They will learn how to

- ▶ Identify and use action verbs.
- ▶ Identify and use being verbs.
- ▶ Identify and use helping verbs.
- ▶ Identify and use verb phrases.
- ▶ Identify the simple predicate in a sentence.

In the composition part of the unit, students will write a persuasive essay. They will

- ▶ Use their journal to freewrite.
- ▶ Explore a model persuasive essay.
- ▶ Brainstorm and choose a topic for their essay.
- ▶ Decide on an opinion and reasons that support the opinion.
- ▶ Write a draft of a persuasive essay.

Unit Plan		〖Online〗	〖Offline〗
Lesson 1	Action Verbs and Journal Entry	15 minutes	20 minutes
Lesson 2	Being Verbs and Model Persuasive Essay	20 minutes	15 minutes
Lesson 3	Helping Verbs & Verb Phrases and Brainstorm Topics	20 minutes	15 minutes
Lesson 4	Simple Predicates and Choose a Topic	20 minutes	15 minutes
Lesson 5	Verb Phrases and Fact or Opinion	20 minutes	15 minutes
Lesson 6	Inverted Sentence Order and Support Your Opinion	20 minutes	15 minutes
Lesson 7	Draft Your Persuasive Essay	15 minutes	20 minutes
Lesson 8	Unit Review and Draft Your Persuasive Essay	20 minutes	15 minutes
Lesson 9	Unit Checkpoint and Draft Your Persuasive Essay	20 minutes	15 minutes

Action Verbs and Journal Entry

Lesson Overview

〔Online〕   15 minutes

GUM (Grammar, Usage, and Mechanics)	Action Verbs

〔Offline〕   20 minutes

Composition	Journal: Write About Something You Feel Strongly About
Beyond the Lesson	➕ OPTIONAL: Journal: Freewrite on a Topic

〔Materials〕

Supplied
- *K¹² My Journal* pp. 26–27
- *Grammar Reference Guide* Online Book (optional)

Keywords
action verb – a word that shows action

Advance Preparation

To prepare for the GUM portion of this lesson, review Verbs (Action Verbs) in the *Grammar Reference Guide* (linked in the online lesson) to familiarize yourself with the topic. Students will be writing a persuasive essay in this unit about a community issue that interests them. In the Turn a Persuasive Essay into a Business Letter unit, they will learn the conventions of a business letter and turn their persuasive essay into a business letter. Guide students as they choose their topic, purpose, and audience for the persuasive essay so that they can make a smooth and logical transition to a business letter.

Big Ideas

- ► Journal writing is a form of freewriting. It is an opportunity to get ideas on paper without regard for correctness of the language or the format of a piece of writing.
- ► To improve, writers require frequent practice.
- ► By recognizing and using action verbs, writers help their writing come alive.

 **15 minutes**

Students will work online **independently** to complete an activity on identifying and using action verbs. They will also learn to choose strong verbs to replace weak ones. Help students locate the online activity.

GUM (Grammar, Usage, and Mechanics)

Action Verbs

Students will learn how to find and use action verbs in sentences. They will learn that they should use strong verbs whenever possible. Then they will practice indentifying and using action verbs in sentences.

Objectives
- Identify action verbs.
- Replace weak verbs with strong action verbs.
- Use action verbs in sentences.

 **20 minutes**

Work **together** with students to complete the offline Composition and Beyond the Lesson activities.

Composition

 **Journal: Write About Something You Feel Strongly About**

Students will respond to a journal prompt by writing on two things they feel strongly about. They will write about their strong opinion and why they feel that way. Gather *K¹² My Journal* and have students turn to pages 26 and 27.

Objectives
- Respond to a journal prompt.
- Freewrite about a topic.

1. Tell students they are going to write in their journal about something they feel strongly about. To help students think of strong opinions they have, tell them to think about their answers to the following questions.

   ‣ Do you have any favorite activities, places, or things? If you could spend time in only one place, or do only one thing, what would it be?
   ‣ Is there something that you always want to share with your friends or family members? Why do you want to share it?
   ‣ Is there something in your home, neighborhood, or town that you want to change? Do you think about how something could be different or better? Why do you care so much about it?

2. Have students respond to the prompt in their journal. Encourage them to write in complete sentences, although it is not a requirement when they are freewriting in their journal.

TIP Students should write for about 20 minutes. Freewriting allows students to use their imagination to write what they want without worrying about being graded, so encourage them to keep writing for the entire time. If students have trouble writing for 20 minutes, use the prompting questions in Step 1 or have them list ideas or words. If they want to keep writing beyond the suggested time limit, praise them for their enthusiasm and offer to let them complete their entry later in the day as a reward.

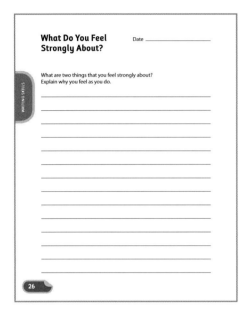

What Do You Feel Strongly About?   Date _____

What are two things that you feel strongly about? Explain why you feel as you do.

26

Beyond the Lesson

OPTIONAL: Journal: Freewrite on a Topic

This activity is OPTIONAL. It is intended for students who have extra time and would benefit from extra practice. Feel free to skip this activity. Gather *K¹² My Journal*.

1. Have students either respond to a prompt in Thoughts and Experiences (pages 50–93) or write about their own topic on the next available page in Ideas (pages 96–139).

2. Encourage students to explore their thoughts and write as much as they want. There are no rules. If students wish, ideas can be fleshed out into a more developed composition at a later time.

TIP Sometimes, students can get stuck trying to come up with a subject to write about. Freewriting can help students avoid getting stuck by having them jump right in without planning what they will write about. Studies show that students who write more frequently become better writers.

Objectives

- Respond to a journal prompt.
- Freewrite about a topic.

Being Verbs and Model Persuasive Essay

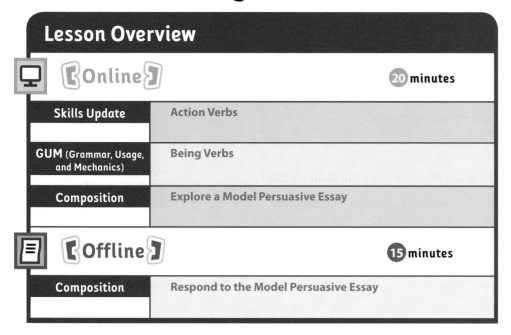

Lesson Overview

🖥 Online — 20 minutes

Skills Update	Action Verbs
GUM (Grammar, Usage, and Mechanics)	Being Verbs
Composition	Explore a Model Persuasive Essay

☰ Offline — 15 minutes

Composition	Respond to the Model Persuasive Essay

Materials

Supplied
- *K¹² Language Arts Activity Book*, pp. WS 95–98
- *Grammar Reference Guide* Online Book (optional)

Keywords

being verb – a verb that does not express action; for example, *am*, *is*, *are*, *was*, *were*

fact – something that can be proven true

opinion – something that a person thinks or believes, but which cannot be proven to be true

persuasive essay – an essay in which the writer tries to convince readers to agree with a stand on an issue

tone – the writer's attitude toward the topic or subject

Advance Preparation

To prepare for the GUM portion of this lesson, review Verbs (Being Verbs) in the *Grammar Reference Guide* (linked in the online lesson) to familiarize yourself with the topic. In this lesson, students begin to accumulate documents that they will need as they work on their persuasive essay. You might want to provide students with a folder or large envelope in which to keep these documents.

Big Ideas

► Persuasive writing begins with the writer's opinion on a topic. In order to convince the audience of the correctness of the position, the writer supports the opinion with facts, statistics, and expert testimony.

► Writing is the communication of ideas in a structured, orderly form.

 **Online** 20 minutes

Students will work online to review action verbs, to learn how to identify and use being verbs, and to explore a model persuasive essay. Help students locate the online activities.

Skills Update

Action Verbs

Students will review how to use action verbs correctly by completing Skills Update exercises. Sit with students as they do this activity and note if they answer correctly.

⟳ **Learning Coach Check-In** How did students do on the Skills Update?

▸ **All answers correct:** Great! Skip the review screen and go on to the next activity.

▸ **Any answers incorrect:** Take a few minutes to review action verbs now. Use the links on the screen after the Skills Update to take another look at the online activities or review Verbs (Action Verbs) in the *Grammar Reference Guide* together.

 TIP This activity will require extra time if students need to review action verbs. Take the extra 5–10 minutes to review now because new skills build on what students have already learned.

> **Objectives**
> - Identify action verbs.
> - Replace weak verbs with strong action verbs.
> - Use action verbs in sentences.

GUM (Grammar, Usage, and Mechanics)

Being Verbs

Students will learn what being verbs are and how to identify them in a sentence. They will then practice using being verbs in sentences.

> **Objectives**
> - Identify being verbs.
> - Use being verbs in sentences.

Composition

Explore a Model Persuasive Essay

By reading and exploring a model persuasive essay, students will learn what a persuasive essay is and how it is organized.

 TIP Seeing a final version of a persuasive essay helps students see the goal of this unit. It will be easier for them to understand each step in the process if they know how the steps result in a finished product. If students are not comfortable reading the model persuasive essay for this activity online, they may read the model on page WS 95 and 96 in *K¹² Language Arts Activity Book*.

> **Objectives**
> - Describe the elements of a persuasive essay.
> - Identify an opinion.
> - Identify reasons that support an opinion.
> - Recognize the tone of the essay.
> - Recognize the structure of the essay.
> - Use linking words and phrases to connect opinions and reasons.

Offline 15 minutes

Work **together** with students to complete the offline Composition activity.

Composition

Respond to the Model Persuasive Essay

Students will review what they learned about the model persuasive essay. Turn to pages WS 97 and 98 in *K¹² Language Arts Activity Book*.

1. Have students reread Johnny's persuasive essay on pages WS 95 and 96.

2. Have students complete the Activity Book pages about Johnny's essay. Provide support as necessary, encouraging students to write in complete sentences. Students should refer to Johnny's persuasive essay as needed.

TIP Keep Johnny's persuasive essay in a safe place so students can refer to it later.

Objectives

- Describe the elements of a persuasive essay.
- Identify an opinion.
- Identify reasons that support an opinion.
- Recognize the tone of the essay.
- Recognize the structure of the essay.
- Use linking words and phrases to connect opinions and reasons.

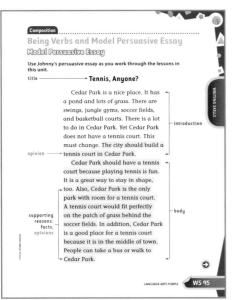

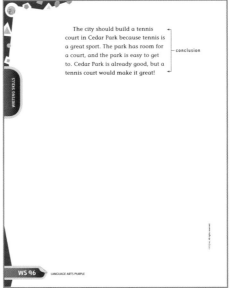

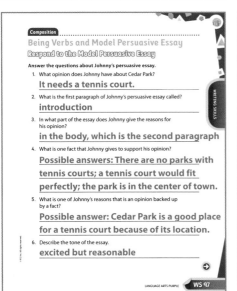

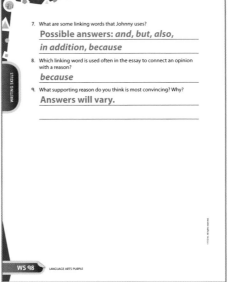

Helping Verbs & Verb Phrases and Brainstorm Topics

Lesson Overview

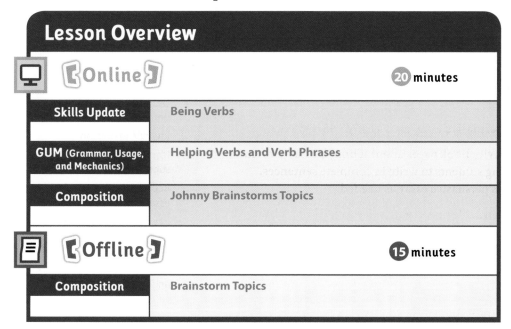

🖥 **〚Online〛**		**20** minutes
Skills Update	Being Verbs	
GUM (Grammar, Usage, and Mechanics)	Helping Verbs and Verb Phrases	
Composition	Johnny Brainstorms Topics	

▤ **〚Offline〛**		**15** minutes
Composition	Brainstorm Topics	

Advance Preparation

To prepare for the GUM portion of this lesson, review Verbs (Helping Verbs and Verb Phrases) in the *Grammar Reference Guide* (linked in the online lesson) to familiarize yourself with the topic.

Big Ideas

By recognizing and using action verbs, writers help their writing come alive.

〚Materials〛

Supplied

- *K¹² Language Arts Activity Book*, pp. WS 99
- *K¹² My Journal*, pp. 26–27 (optional)
- *Grammar Reference Guide* Online Book (optional)

Keywords

audience – a writer's readers

brainstorming – before writing, a way for the writer to come up with ideas

helping verb – a word that works with the main verb to show action; for example, *has, have, will, do, did, can*

purpose – the reason for writing

verb phrase – a main verb and one or more helping verbs

 **20 minutes**

Students will work online to review being verbs, to learn how to identify and use helping verbs in verb phrases, and to learn how Johnny brainstorms topics for his persuasive essay. Help students locate the online activities.

Skills Update

Being Verbs

Students will review how to use being verbs correctly by completing Skills Update exercises. Sit with students as they do this activity and note if they answer correctly.

⊃ **Learning Coach Check-In** How did students do on the Skills Update?

▸ **All answers correct:** Great! Skip the review screen and go on to the next activity.

▸ **Any answers incorrect:** Take a few minutes to review being verbs now. Use the links on the screen after the Skills Update to take another look at the online activities or review Verbs (Being Verbs) in the *Grammar Reference Guide* together.

TIP This activity will require extra time if students need to review being verbs. Take the extra 5–10 minutes to review now because new skills build on what students have already learned.

Objectives
- Identify being verbs.
- Use being verbs in sentences.

GUM (Grammar, Usage, and Mechanics)

Helping Verbs and Verb Phrases

Students will learn what helping verbs are and how to identify them in a sentence. They will then practice using helping verbs and verb phrases in sentences.

Objectives
- Identify and use verb phrases.
- Identify helping verbs.
- Identify verbs in sentences.

Composition

Johnny Brainstorms Topics

By learning how Johnny brainstorms topics for his persuasive essay, students will learn strategies for brainstorming and prepare to plan their own persuasive essay.

Objectives
- Brainstorm topics for a persuasive essay.

 **15 minutes**

Work **together** with students to complete the offline Composition activity.

Composition

Brainstorm Topics

Students will brainstorm topics for their own persuasive essay. Turn to page WS 99 in *K¹² Language Arts Activity Book*.

> **Objectives**
> • Brainstorm topics for a persuasive essay.

1. Allow students to use the What Do You Feel Strongly About? topic in their journal (pages 26 and 27) for their persuasive essay, but only if they wrote about a community topic. If students have their topic, then no further brainstorming is necessary; they do not need to complete the Activity Book page. For students needing a topic, continue with Step 2.

2. Have students complete the Activity Book page to brainstorm essay topics about their town, city, or neighborhood.

3. Have students ask themselves the following questions to help them brainstorm.

   ▸ What are things that I care about?
   ▸ What will make a good topic?
   ▸ Who am I trying to convince?

4. Provide support as necessary. Remind students that during brainstorming, no idea is a bad idea. The point is to list as many ideas as possible before choosing a topic.

TIP Keep students' brainstorming page in a safe place so they can refer to it later.

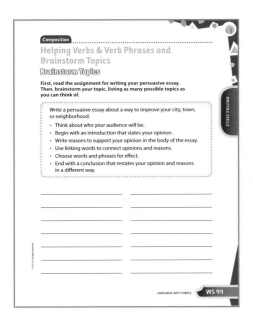

Simple Predicates and Choose a Topic

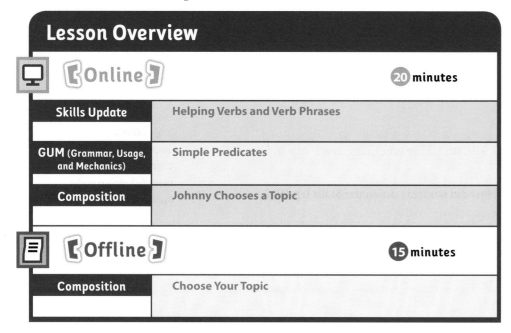

Lesson Overview

Online — 20 minutes

Skills Update	Helping Verbs and Verb Phrases
GUM (Grammar, Usage, and Mechanics)	Simple Predicates
Composition	Johnny Chooses a Topic

Offline — 15 minutes

Composition	Choose Your Topic

Materials

Supplied
- *K¹² Language Arts Activity Book*, pp. WS 99–100, 102
- *Grammar Reference Guide* Online Book (optional)

Keywords
fact – something that can be proven true

opinion – something that a person thinks or believes, but which cannot be proven to be true

predicate – the verb or verb phrase in a sentence

Advance Preparation

To prepare for the GUM portion of this lesson, review Parts of a Sentence (Simple Predicate, or Verb) in the *Grammar Reference Guide* (linked in the online lesson) to familiarize yourself with the topic. Gather page WS 99 (Brainstorm Topics, students' completed brainstorming page) in *K¹² Language Arts Activity Book*.

Big Ideas

- ▶ Writing is the communication of ideas in a structured, orderly form.
- ▶ By recognizing and using action verbs, writers help their writing come alive.

 **minutes**

Students will work online to review helping verbs and verb phrases, to learn how to identify the simple predicate, and to learn how Johnny chooses a topic for his persuasive essay. Help students locate the online activities.

Skills Update

Helping Verbs and Verb Phrases

Students will review how to use helping verbs and verb phrases correctly by completing Skills Update exercises. Sit with students as they do this activity and note if they answer correctly.

➲ **Learning Coach Check-In** How did students do on the Skills Update?

- ▶ **All answers correct:** Great! Skip the review screen and go on to the next activity.
- ▶ **Any answers incorrect:** Take a few minutes to review verb phrases now. Use the links on the screen after the Skills Update to take another look at the online activities or review Verbs (Helping Verbs and Verb Phrases) in the *Grammar Reference Guide* together.

 This activity will require extra time if students need to review helping verbs and verb phrases. Take the extra 5–10 minutes to review now because new skills build on what students have already learned.

Objectives
- Identify and use verb phrases.
- Identify helping verbs.
- Identify verbs in sentences.

GUM (Grammar, Usage, and Mechanics)

Simple Predicates

Students will learn how to identify the simple predicate in a sentence. The simple predicate is the same as the verb in the sentence.

Objectives
- Identify the simple predicate, or verb, in a sentence.

Composition

Johnny Chooses a Topic

By seeing how Johnny chooses a topic for his persuasive essay, students will learn how to select their own topic.

Objectives
- Choose a topic for a persuasive essay.
- State an opinion.
- Write an opinion statement.
- Use a graphic organizer to plan.

 **Offline** ⏱ **15** minutes

Work **together** with students to complete the offline Composition activity.

Composition

Choose Your Topic

Students will choose a topic for their persuasive essay and state their opinion about the topic. Have them gather their brainstorming page. Turn to page WS 100 in *K¹² Language Arts Activity Book*.

1. Have students complete the Activity Book page. Help them choose a topic by having them think about the answers to these questions.

   ▸ Are any of your possible topics not that interesting to you?

   ▸ Which topics do you think other people will be interested in?

   ▸ Are there any topics you don't have a strong opinion about?

   ▸ Who are you writing this essay for? Who will your audience be?

2. Once they have chosen a topic, have students write their topic on the line and fill in the My Opinion About the Topic box in the graphic organizer on page WS 102 (Gather and Organize Your Ideas).

TIP Keep students' graphic organizer in a safe place so they can add to it later.

> ### Objectives
> - Choose a topic for a persuasive essay.
> - State an opinion.
> - Write an opinion statement.
> - Use a graphic organizer to plan.

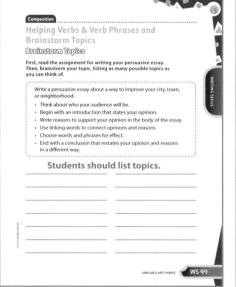

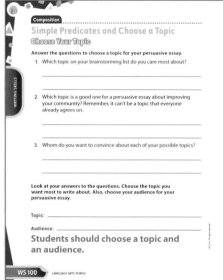

Verb Phrases and Fact or Opinion

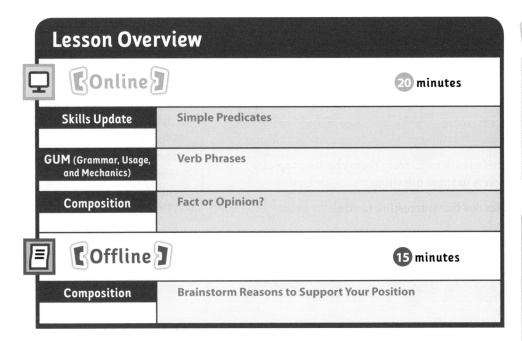

Lesson Overview

Online — 20 minutes

Skills Update	Simple Predicates
GUM (Grammar, Usage, and Mechanics)	Verb Phrases
Composition	Fact or Opinion?

Offline — 15 minutes

Composition	Brainstorm Reasons to Support Your Position

Materials

Supplied

- *K12 Language Arts Activity Book*, pp. WS 101
- *Grammar Reference Guide* Online Book (optional)

Keywords

fact – something that can be proven true

opinion – something that a person thinks or believes, but which cannot be proven to be true

verb phrase – a main verb and one or more helping verbs

Advance Preparation

To prepare for the GUM portion of this lesson, review Verbs (Verb Phrases) in the *Grammar Reference Guide* (linked in the online lesson) to familiarize yourself with the topic.

Big Ideas

- Persuasive writing begins with the writer's opinion on a topic. In order to convince the audience of the correctness of the position, the writer supports the opinion with facts, statistics, and expert testimony.
- Writing is the communication of ideas in a structured, orderly form.
- By recognizing and using action verbs, writers help their writing come alive.

 **20 minutes**

Students will work online to review simple predicates, to learn how to identify and use verb phrases, and to explore how Johnny supports his position with facts and opinions. Help students locate the online activities.

Skills Update

Simple Predicates

Students will review how to identify simple predicates by completing Skills Update exercises. Sit with students as they do this activity and note if they answer correctly.

⊃ **Learning Coach Check-In** How did students do on the Skills Update?

▸ **All answers correct:** Great! Skip the review screen and go on to the next activity.

▸ **Any answers incorrect:** Take a few minutes to review simple predicates now. Use the links on the screen after the Skills Update to take another look at the online activities or review Parts of a Sentence (Simple Predicate, or Verb) in the *Grammar Reference Guide* together.

TIP This activity will require extra time if students need to review simple predicates Take the extra 5–10 minutes to review now because new skills build on what students have already learned.

Objectives
- Identify the simple predicate, or verb, in a sentence.

GUM (Grammar, Usage, and Mechanics)

Verb Phrases

Students will learn that either a verb or a verb phrase can be the simple predicate of a sentence.

Objectives
- Identify the simple predicate, or verb, in a sentence.

Composition

Fact or Opinion?

Students will learn how Johnny brainstorms reasons to support his position for his persuasive essay. He also determines which reasons are facts and which are opinions.

Objectives
- Distinguish between fact and opinion.
- List reasons for an opinion.

 **minutes**

Work **together** with students to complete the offline Composition activity.

Composition

Brainstorm Reasons to Support Your Position
Students will brainstorm reasons to support their topic and opinion in their persuasive essay. They will then classify the reasons as facts or opinions. Turn to page WS 101 in *K¹² Language Arts Activity Book*.

Objectives
- Distinguish between fact and opinion.
- List reasons for an opinion.

1. Have students complete the Activity Book page. Help students brainstorm reasons supporting their opinion by asking them to think about answers to the following questions.

   ▶ What do you think is most important about your topic?
   ▶ If you wanted to convince me that your opinion is correct, what are the first three things you would say?
   ▶ Imagine you were trying to convince a stranger that your opinion is correct. What would you say to the stranger?

 Keep students' brainstorming list in a safe place so they can refer to it later.

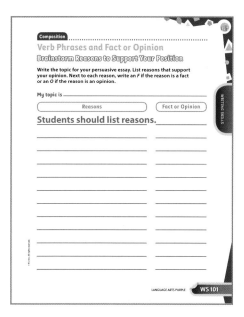

Inverted Sentence Order and Support Your Opinion

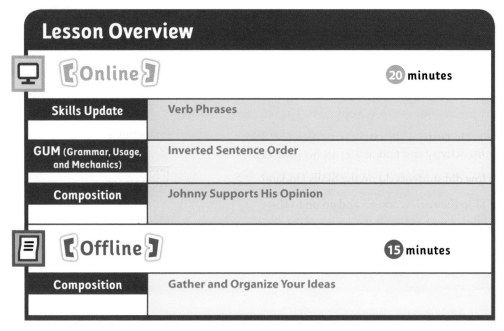

Lesson Overview

Online — 20 minutes

Skills Update	Verb Phrases
GUM (Grammar, Usage, and Mechanics)	Inverted Sentence Order
Composition	Johnny Supports His Opinion

Offline — 15 minutes

| Composition | Gather and Organize Your Ideas |

Materials

Supplied
- *K¹² Language Arts Activity Book*, pp. WS 101–102
- *Grammar Reference Guide* Online Book (optional)

Keywords
fact – something that can be proven true
inverted order – of a sentence, order in which the verb comes before the subject
opinion – something that a person thinks or believes, but which cannot be proven to be true

Advance Preparation

To prepare for the GUM portion of this lesson, review Verbs (Verb Phrases) in the *Grammar Reference Guide* (linked in the online lesson) to familiarize yourself with the topic. Gather pages WS 101 (Brainstorm Reasons to Support Your Position, students completed list of reasons) and 102 (Gather and Organize Your Ideas, students' partially completed graphic organizer) in *K¹² Language Arts Activity Book*.

Big Ideas

▸ Persuasive writing begins with the writer's opinion on a topic. In order to convince the audience of the correctness of the position, the writer supports the opinion with facts, statistics, and expert testimony.
▸ Writing is the communication of ideas in a structured, orderly form.
▸ By recognizing and using action verbs, writers help their writing come alive.

 **minutes**

Students will work online to review verb phrases, to learn how to identify verbs when a sentence is in inverted order, and to explore how Johnny chooses reasons to support his opinion in his persuasive essay. Help students locate the online activities.

Skills Update

Verb Phrases

Students will review how to use verb phrases correctly by completing Skills Update exercises. Sit with students as they do this activity and note if they answer correctly.

➲ **Learning Coach Check-In** How did students do on the Skills Update?

▸ **All answers correct:** Great! Skip the review screen and go on to the next activity.

▸ **Any answers incorrect:** Take a few minutes to review verb phrases now. Use the links on the screen after the Skills Update to take another look at the online activities or review Verbs (Verb Phrases) in the *Grammar Reference Guide* together.

 This activity will require extra time if students need to review verb phrases. Take the extra 5–10 minutes to review now because new skills build on what students have already learned.

> **Objectives**
> • Identify the simple predicate, or verb, in a sentence.

GUM (Grammar, Usage, and Mechanics)

Inverted Sentence Order

Students will learn how to identify the verb in a sentence that is in an inverted order.

> **Objectives**
> • Identify the verb in a sentence in inverted order.

Composition

Johnny Supports His Opinion

Students will explore how Johnny chooses reasons to support his opinion in his persuasive essay and writes them on his graphic organizer. They will learn how to choose the best reasons to include in their own persuasive essay.

> **Objectives**
> • Provide reasons that support an opinion.
> • Use a graphic organizer to plan.

 **15 minutes**

Work **together** with students to complete the offline Composition activity.

Composition

Gather and Organize Your Ideas

Students will look over their list of reasons to support their opinion and pick three to include in their persuasive essay. They will also add a final statement to convince readers to agree with them. Have students gather their brainstorming list of reasons and partially completed graphic organizer.

 Objectives
- Provide reasons that support an opinion.
- Use a graphic organizer to plan.

1. Have students read their brainstorming list of reasons. Help them choose three reasons to support their opinion by having them think about the answers to the following questions.

   ▶ What are the three strongest facts that support your opinion?
   ▶ Are all of your facts connected to your topic?
   ▶ What are three reasons that readers should agree with your opinion?

2. Have students finish their partially completed graphic organizer. Provide support as necessary.

TIP Keep students' graphic organizer in a safe place so they can refer to it later.

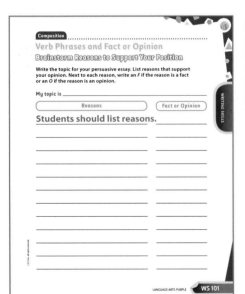

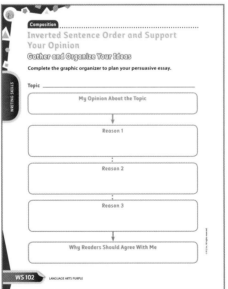

Draft Your Persuasive Essay

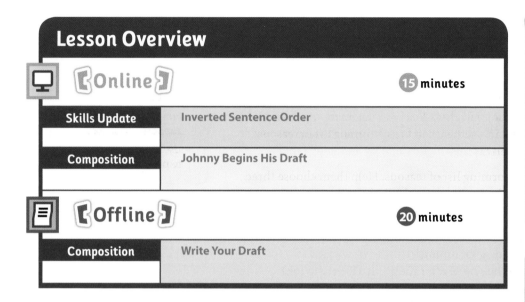

Lesson Overview

Online — 15 minutes

Skills Update	Inverted Sentence Order
Composition	Johnny Begins His Draft

Offline — 20 minutes

Composition	Write Your Draft

Materials

Supplied

- *K¹² Language Arts Activity Book*, pp. WS 95–96, 102–108
- *Grammar Reference Guide* Online Book (optional)
- drafting page (optional printout)

Keywords

body – the main text of a piece of writing

fact – something that can be proven true

introduction – the first paragraph of an essay, identifying the topic and stating the main idea

opinion – something that a person thinks or believes, but which cannot be proven to be true

Advance Preparation

Gather pages WS 95 and 96 (Model Persuasive Essay) and 102 (Gather and Organize Your Ideas, students' completed graphic organizer) in *K¹² Language Arts Activity Book*.

Big Ideas

- ▸ Persuasive writing begins with the writer's opinion on a topic. In order to convince the audience of the correctness of the position, the writer supports the opinion with facts, statistics, and expert testimony.
- ▸ Writing is the communication of ideas in a structured, orderly form.

 **15 minutes**

Students will work online to review identifying verbs when a sentence is in inverted order and to learn about writing the introduction and body of a persuasive essay. Help students locate the online activities.

Skills Update

Inverted Sentence Order

Students will review how to find verbs in a sentence in inverted order by completing Skills Update exercises. Sit with students as they do this activity and note if they answer correctly.

⮑ **Learning Coach Check-In** How did students do on the Skills Update?

▸ **All answers correct:** Great! Skip the review screen and go on to the next activity.

▸ **Any answers incorrect:** Take a few minutes to review inverted sentence order now. Use the links on the screen after the Skills Update to take another look at the online activities or review Verbs (Verb Phrases) in the *Grammar Reference Guide* together.

TIP This activity will require extra time if students need to review inverted sentence order. Take the extra 5–10 minutes to review now because new skills build on what students have already learned.

Objectives
- Identify the verb in a sentence in inverted order.

Composition

Johnny Begins His Draft

By exploring how Johnny begins his draft, students will learn how to write the introduction and body of a persuasive essay.

Objectives
- Write a persuasive essay.
- State an opinion.
- Introduce a topic.
- Provide reasons that support an opinion.
- Use linking words and phrases to connect opinions and reasons.
- Choose words and phrases for effect.

 **20 minutes**

Work **together** with students to complete the offline Composition activity.

Composition

Write Your Draft

Students will begin drafting their persuasive essay. Have them gather the model persuasive essay and their completed graphic organizer. Turn to pages WS 103–108 in *K¹² Language Arts Activity Book*.

1. Help students start drafting by reminding them to refer to Johnny's persuasive essay and the information on their completed graphic organizer as necessary. The model will help students remember what elements their introduction and body should include, and the information on their graphic organizer will help them remember which reasons to include and where to place them in the body.

2. Remind students that a draft does not have to be perfect. It's just a first try at putting ideas on paper. Tell students that they will start writing their draft in this lesson and finish it over the next two lessons.

3. Have students use the lined Activity Book pages to begin drafting their persuasive essay. Students should write only in the white rows, because the purple rows will be used for revising the draft later. If needed, additional drafting pages can be printed from the online lesson.

TIP Keep students' draft in a safe place so they can continue working on it later. The most important part of an introduction is a clearly stated opinion on the topic. If students are struggling, have them begin by writing the opinion, and then ask them to write more before or after that opinion. If students want to use a reference material such as the *Grammar Reference Guide* or a dictionary while drafting, suggest that they wait until they are revising or proofreading. Looking up information while drafting can interfere with students' flow of ideas.

Objectives
- Write a persuasive essay.
- State an opinion.
- Introduce a topic.
- Provide reasons that support an opinion.
- Use linking words and phrases to connect opinions and reasons.
- Choose words and phrases for effect.

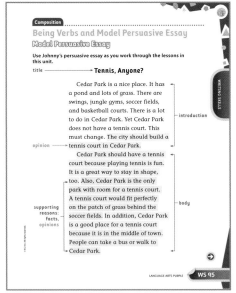

Composition

Being Verbs and Model Persuasive Essay
Model Persuasive Essay

Use Johnny's persuasive essay as you work through the lessons in this unit.

title —————→ **Tennis, Anyone?**

Cedar Park is a nice place. It has a pond and lots of grass. There are swings, jungle gyms, soccer fields, and basketball courts. There is a lot to do in Cedar Park. Yet Cedar Park does not have a tennis court. This must change. The city should build a tennis court in Cedar Park. ⟵ introduction

opinion —————→ tennis court in Cedar Park.

Cedar Park should have a tennis court because playing tennis is fun. It is a great way to stay in shape, too. Also, Cedar Park is the only park with room for a tennis court. A tennis court would fit perfectly on the patch of grass behind the soccer fields. In addition, Cedar Park is a good place for a tennis court because it is in the middle of town. People can take a bus or walk to Cedar Park. ⟵ body

supporting reasons: facts, opinions

LANGUAGE ARTS PURPLE **WS 95**

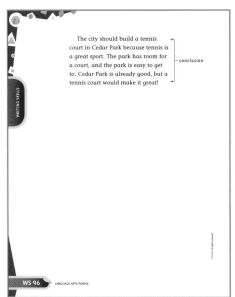

The city should build a tennis court in Cedar Park because tennis is a great sport. The park has room for a court, and the park is easy to get to. Cedar Park is already good, but a tennis court would make it great! ⟵ conclusion

WS 96 LANGUAGE ARTS PURPLE

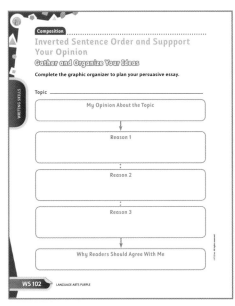

Composition

Inverted Sentence Order and Suppport Your Opinion
Gather and Organize Your Ideas

Complete the graphic organizer to plan your persuasive essay.

Topic _____

| My Opinion About the Topic |
| Reason 1 |
| Reason 2 |
| Reason 3 |
| Why Readers Should Agree With Me |

WS 102 LANGUAGE ARTS PURPLE

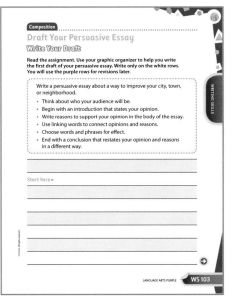

Composition

Draft Your Persuasive Essay
Write Your Draft

Read the assignment. Use your graphic organizer to help you write the first draft of your persuasive essay. Write only on the white rows. You will use the purple rows for revisions later.

Write a persuasive essay about a way to improve your city, town, or neighborhood.
- Think about who your audience will be.
- Begin with an introduction that states your opinion.
- Write reasons to support your opinion in the body of the essay.
- Use linking words to connect opinions and reasons.
- Choose words and phrases for effect.
- End with a conclusion that restates your opinion and reasons in a different way.

Start here ▸

LANGUAGE ARTS PURPLE **WS 103**

Unit Review and Draft Your Persuasive Essay

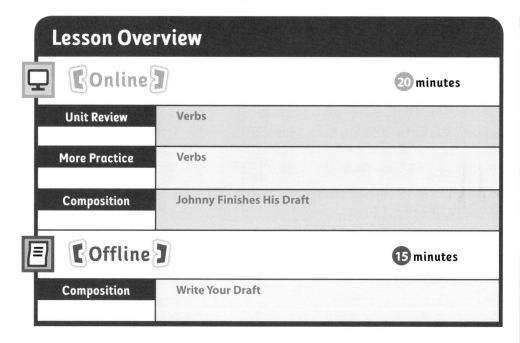

Lesson Overview

🖥 〔Online〕 20 minutes

Unit Review	Verbs
More Practice	Verbs
Composition	Johnny Finishes His Draft

📄 〔Offline〕 15 minutes

Composition	Write Your Draft

Materials

Supplied

- *K¹² Language Arts Activity Book*, pp. WS 95–96, 102–108
- *Grammar Reference Guide* Online Book (optional)
- drafting page (optional printout)

Keywords

action verb – a word that shows action

being verb – a verb that does not express action; for example, *am, is, are, was, were*

body – the main text of a piece of writing

conclusion – the final paragraph of a written work

fact – something that can be proven true

helping verb – a word that works with the main verb to show action; for example, *has, have, will, do, did, can*

inverted order – of a sentence, order in which the verb comes before the subject

opinion – something that a person thinks or believes, but which cannot be proven to be true

predicate – the verb or verb phrase in a sentence

verb phrase – a main verb and one or more helping verbs

Advance Preparation

Gather pages WS 95–96 (Model Persuasive Essay), 102 (Gather and Organize Your Ideas, students' completed graphic organizer), and 103–108 (Write Your Draft, students' partially completed draft of their persuasive essay) in *K¹² Language Arts Activity Book.*

Big Ideas

- ▶ Persuasive writing begins with the writer's opinion on a topic. In order to convince the audience of the correctness of the position, the writer supports the opinion with facts, statistics, and expert testimony.
- ▶ Writing is the communication of ideas in a structured, orderly form.

 **20** **minutes**

Students will work online to review the grammar, usage, and mechanics skills learned in the unit and to learn how to write the conclusion of a persuasive essay. Help students locate the online activities.

Unit Review

Verbs

Students will review what they have learned about verbs, including how to identify and use action verbs, being verbs, helping verbs, verb phrases, the simple predicate, and verbs in inverted sentences, to review for the Unit Checkpoint.

TIP A full list of objectives covered in the Unit Review can be found in the online lesson.

 Objectives
- Complete a review of grammar, usage, and mechanics skills.

More Practice

Verbs

Go over students' results on the Unit Review and, if necessary, have them complete the appropriate review activities listed in the table online. Help students locate the activities and provide support as needed.

TIP The time students need to complete this activity will vary. Set aside enough time for students to complete all review activities, if they need to do so.

 Objectives
- Evaluate Unit Review results and choose activities for more practice.

Composition

Johnny Finishes His Draft

By exploring how Johnny finishes his draft, students will learn how to write the conclusion of a persuasive essay.

 Objectives
- Write a persuasive essay.
- Introduce a topic.
- State an opinion.
- Provide reasons that support an opinion.
- List reasons for an opinion.
- Choose words and phrases for effect.
- Use linking words and phrases to connect opinions and reasons.
- Provide a concluding section or statement.

 **15 minutes**

Work **together** with students to complete the offline Composition activity.

Composition

Write Your Draft

Students will continue drafting their persuasive essay. Have them gather the model persuasive essay, their completed graphic organizer, and their persuasive essay draft.

1. Help students continue drafting their persuasive essay by reminding them to refer to Johnny's persuasive essay and the information on their completed graphic organizer as necessary. Students' introduction and at least part of the body, if not all, should be complete by the end of this lesson. If students have time, they should begin writing the conclusion.

2. Remind students that they have one more drafting lesson in this unit.

 TIP Keep students' draft in a safe place so they can continue working on it later. An author can use opinions to support a position in a persuasive essay, as long as those opinions can be justified with facts or strong reasoning. Some students may have trouble understanding the difference between opinions that are well supported and opinions that just state a feeling. Remind them to use words like *because* when using opinions in a persuasive essay.

> **Objectives**
> - Write a persuasive essay.
> - Introduce a topic.
> - State an opinion.
> - Provide reasons that support an opinion.
> - List reasons for an opinion.
> - Choose words and phrases for effect.
> - Use linking words and phrases to connect opinions and reasons.
> - Provide a concluding section or statement.

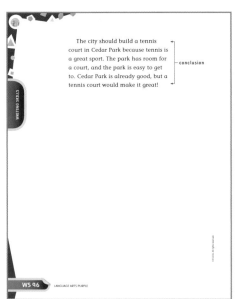

Composition

Being Verbs and Model Persuasive Essay
Model Persuasive Essay

Use Johnny's persuasive essay as you work through the lessons in this unit.

title ⟶ **Tennis, Anyone?**

Cedar Park is a nice place. It has a pond and lots of grass. There are swings, jungle gyms, soccer fields, and basketball courts. There is a lot to do in Cedar Park. Yet Cedar Park does not have a tennis court. This must change. The city should build a tennis court in Cedar Park.

introduction

opinion ⟶

Cedar Park should have a tennis court because playing tennis is fun. It is a great way to stay in shape, too. Also, Cedar Park is the only park with room for a tennis court. A tennis court would fit perfectly on the patch of grass behind the soccer fields. In addition, Cedar Park is a good place for a tennis court because it is in the middle of town. People can take a bus or walk to Cedar Park.

supporting reasons: facts, opinions

body

The city should build a tennis court in Cedar Park because tennis is a great sport. The park has room for a court, and the park is easy to get to. Cedar Park is already good, but a tennis court would make it great!

conclusion

WS 95 LANGUAGE ARTS PURPLE

LANGUAGE ARTS PURPLE WS 96

Composition

Inverted Sentence Order and Suppport Your Opinion
Gather and Organize Your Ideas

Complete the graphic organizer to plan your persuasive essay.

Topic _____

| My Opinion About the Topic |

| Reason 1 |

| Reason 2 |

| Reason 3 |

| Why Readers Should Agree With Me |

WS 102 LANGUAGE ARTS PURPLE

Composition

Draft Your Persuasive Essay
Write Your Draft

Read the assignment. Use your graphic organizer to help you write the first draft of your persuasive essay. Write only on the white rows. You will use the purple rows for revisions later.

Write a persuasive essay about a way to improve your city, town, or neighborhood.
- Think about who your audience will be.
- Begin with an introduction that states your opinion.
- Write reasons to support your opinion in the body of the essay.
- Use linking words to connect opinions and reasons.
- Choose words and phrases for effect.
- End with a conclusion that restates your opinion and reasons in a different way.

Start here ▸

LANGUAGE ARTS PURPLE WS 103

Unit Checkpoint and Draft Your Persuasive Essay

Lesson Overview

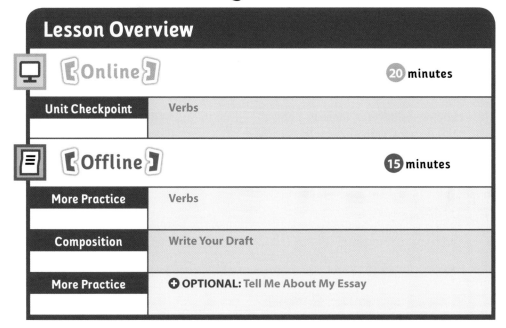

💻 **[Online]**		**20** minutes
Unit Checkpoint	Verbs	
📄 **[Offline]**		**15** minutes
More Practice	Verbs	
Composition	Write Your Draft	
More Practice	⊕ OPTIONAL: Tell Me About My Essay	

[Materials]

Supplied

- *K¹² Language Arts Activity Book*, pp. WS 95–96, 102–109
- *Grammar Reference Guide* Online Book (optional)
- Action Verbs and Being Verbs (optional printout)
- Helping Verbs and Verb Phrases (optional printout)
- Simple Predicate (optional printout)
- Inverted Sentence Order (optional printout)
- Persuasive Essay: Feedback Sheet (printout)
- drafting page (optional printout)

Advance Preparation

Gather pages WS 95–96 (Model Persuasive Essay), 102 (Gather and Organize Your Ideas, students' completed graphic organizer), and 103–108 (Write Your Draft, students' partially completed draft of their persuasive essay) in *K¹² Language Arts Activity Book*. Print the Persuasive Essay: Feedback Sheet from the online lesson.

Big Ideas

- ▸ Persuasive writing begins with the writer's opinion on a topic. In order to convince the audience of the correctness of the position, the writer supports the opinion with facts, statistics, and expert testimony.
- ▸ Writing is the communication of ideas in a structured, orderly form.
- ▸ By recognizing and using action verbs, writers help their writing come alive.

 **20 minutes**

Students will work online **independently** to complete the Unit Checkpoint. Help students locate the online checkpoint.

Unit Checkpoint

Verbs

Students will complete an online Unit Checkpoint about verbs, including how to identify and use action verbs, being verbs, helping verbs, verb phrases, the simple predicate, and verbs in inverted sentences. If necessary, read the directions to students.

 TIP A full list of objectives covered in the Unit Checkpoint can be found in the online lesson.

> **Objectives**
> • Complete a Unit Checkpoint on grammar, usage, and mechanics skills.

 **15 minutes**

Work **together** with students to complete the offline More Practice, Composition, and Peer Interaction activities.

More Practice

Verbs

Go over students' results on the Unit Checkpoint and, if necessary, print out and have them complete the appropriate practice pages listed in the table online. Students can complete all necessary pages now, or if more time is needed, they can spread them out over the next few days. They can also review the appropriate sections of the *Grammar Reference Guide* with you. If students scored less than 80 percent on the Unit Checkpoint, you may want them to retake the Checkpoint after completing the additional activity pages.

 TIP The time students need to complete this activity will vary. Set aside enough time for students to complete some or all activity pages and to retake the Unit Checkpoint, if they need to do so. Students may retake the Unit Checkpoint immediately, but having them complete the practice pages and then retake it might be more effective.

> **Objectives**
> • Evaluate Unit Checkpoint results and choose activities for more practice.

 Reward: When students score 80 percent or above on the Unit Checkpoint, add a sticker for this unit on the My Accomplishments chart.

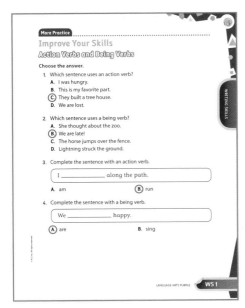

More Practice

Improve Your Skills
Action Verbs and Being Verbs

Choose the answer.

1. Which sentence uses an action verb?
   A. I was hungry.
   B. This is my favorite part.
   C. They built a tree house.
   D. We are lost.

2. Which sentence uses a being verb?
   A. She thought about the zoo.
   B. We are late!
   C. The horse jumps over the fence.
   D. Lightning struck the ground.

3. Complete the sentence with an action verb.

   I _____ along the path.

   A. am   B. run

4. Complete the sentence with a being verb.

   We _____ happy.

   A. are   B. sing

LANGUAGE ARTS PURPLE   **WS 1**

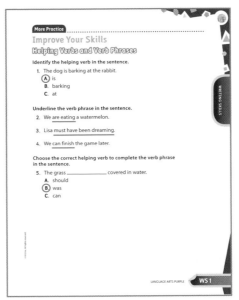

More Practice

Improve Your Skills
Helping Verbs and Verb Phrases

Identify the helping verb in the sentence.

1. The dog is barking at the rabbit.
   A. is
   B. barking
   C. at

Underline the verb phrase in the sentence.

2. We are eating a watermelon.

3. Lisa must have been dreaming.

4. We can finish the game later.

Choose the correct helping verb to complete the verb phrase in the sentence.

5. The grass _____ covered in water.
   A. should
   B. was
   C. can

LANGUAGE ARTS PURPLE   **WS 1**

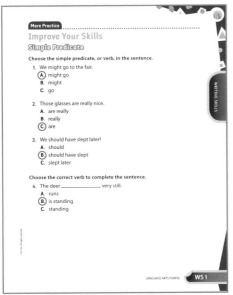

More Practice

Improve Your Skills
Simple Predicate

Choose the simple predicate, or verb, in the sentence.

1. We might go to the fair.
   A. might go
   B. might
   C. go

2. Those glasses are really nice.
   A. are really
   B. really
   C. are

3. We should have slept later!
   A. should
   B. should have slept
   C. slept later

Choose the correct verb to complete the sentence.

4. The deer _____ very still.
   A. runs
   B. is standing
   C. standing

LANGUAGE ARTS PURPLE   **WS 1**

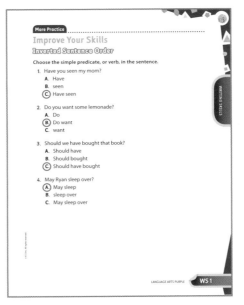

More Practice

Improve Your Skills
Inverted Sentence Order

Choose the simple predicate, or verb, in the sentence.

1. Have you seen my mom?
   A. Have
   B. seen
   C. Have seen

2. Do you want some lemonade?
   A. Do
   B. Do want
   C. want

3. Should we have bought that book?
   A. Should have
   B. Should bought
   C. Should have bought

4. May Ryan sleep over?
   A. May sleep
   B. sleep over
   C. May sleep over

LANGUAGE ARTS PURPLE   **WS 1**

Composition

Write Your Draft

Students will finish drafting their persuasive essay, and you will review it. Have them gather the model persuasive essay, their completed graphic organizer, and their persuasive essay draft. You will also need the Persuasive Essay: Feedback Sheet, printable from the online lesson.

1. Have students finish drafting their persuasive essay, continuing to write only in the white rows. If needed, additional drafting pages can be printed from the online lesson.

2. As students write, remind them to refer to Johnny's persuasive essay and their graphic organizer as necessary. Continue to emphasize that drafts are not meant to be perfect. They are a work in progress.

   ⮌ **Learning Coach Check-In** When students have finished their draft, read and review it using the Persuasive Essay: Feedback Sheet, but do not go over the feedback sheet with students now. The notes you take on this sheet will guide your feedback to students as they revise their draft in a later lesson. Keep the feedback sheet in a safe place until students are ready to revise their draft.

TIP Keep students' persuasive essay draft in a safe place so they can use it later. In the Turn a Persuasive Essay into a Business Letter unit, students will revise and proofread their persuasive essay and turn it into a business letter.

Objectives
- Write a persuasive essay.
- Introduce a topic.
- State an opinion.
- Provide reasons that support an opinion.
- Choose words and phrases for effect.
- Use linking words and phrases to connect opinions and reasons.
- Provide a concluding section or statement.

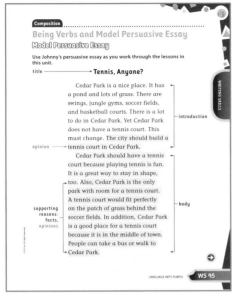

Composition

Being Verbs and Model Persuasive Essay
Model Persuasive Essay

Use Johnny's persuasive essay as you work through the lessons in this unit.

title ⟶ **Tennis, Anyone?**

Cedar Park is a nice place. It has a pond and lots of grass. There are swings, jungle gyms, soccer fields, and basketball courts. There is a lot to do in Cedar Park. Yet Cedar Park does not have a tennis court. This must change. The city should build a tennis court in Cedar Park. ⟵ introduction

opinion ⟶

Cedar Park should have a tennis court because playing tennis is fun. It is a great way to stay in shape, too. Also, Cedar Park is the only park with room for a tennis court. A tennis court would fit perfectly on the patch of grass behind the soccer fields. In addition, Cedar Park is a good place for a tennis court because it is in the middle of town. People can take a bus or walk to Cedar Park. ⟵ body

supporting reasons: facts, opinions

WS 95 · LANGUAGE ARTS PURPLE

The city should build a tennis court in Cedar Park because tennis is a great sport. The park has room for a court, and the park is easy to get to. Cedar Park is already good, but a tennis court would make it great! ⟵ conclusion

WS 96 · LANGUAGE ARTS PURPLE

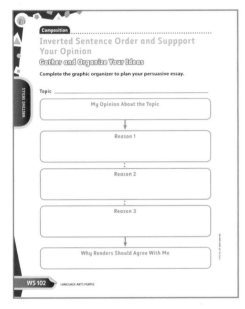

Composition

Inverted Sentence Order and Support Your Opinion
Gather and Organize Your Ideas

Complete the graphic organizer to plan your persuasive essay.

Topic _____

My Opinion About the Topic

↓

Reason 1

↓

Reason 2

↓

Reason 3

↓

Why Readers Should Agree With Me

WS 102 · LANGUAGE ARTS PURPLE

Composition

Draft Your Persuasive Essay
Write Your Draft

Read the assignment. Use your graphic organizer to help you write the first draft of your persuasive essay. Write only on the white rows. You will use the purple rows for revisions later.

Write a persuasive essay about a way to improve your city, town, or neighborhood.
- Think about who your audience will be.
- Begin with an introduction that states your opinion.
- Write reasons to support your opinion in the body of the essay.
- Use linking words to connect opinions and reasons.
- Choose words and phrases for effect.
- End with a conclusion that restates your opinion and reasons in a different way.

Start here ▸

LANGUAGE ARTS PURPLE · WS 103

Peer Interaction

⊕ OPTIONAL: Tell Me About My Essay

This activity is OPTIONAL. It is intended for students who have extra time and would benefit from extra practice. Feel free to skip this activity.

Students can benefit from exchanging their persuasive essay with another student. Each writer should receive feedback. To complete this optional activity, turn to page WS 109 in *K¹² Language Arts Activity Book*. (Additional copies of the Peer Interaction Form can be printed from the online lesson.)

1. Have students exchange drafts with other students.

2. Have students use the Activity Book page to provide others with feedback about their writing.

TIP In the upcoming revising lesson, students may use the feedback provided from others students to improve their essay.

> ### Objectives
> - Use guidance from adults and peers to revise writing.
> - Collaborate with peers on writing projects.

UNIT OVERVIEW — Turn a Persuasive Essay into a Business Letter

Unit Focus

In the grammar part of the unit, students will learn about the format of a business letter. They will

- Learn how to format a business letter.
- Learn how to write an inside address.
- Learn how to write the salutation and closing of a business letter.
- Learn how to address a business envelope.

In the composition part of the unit, students will turn a persuasive essay into a business letter. They will

- Use their journal to freewrite.
- Revise their persuasive essay using a checklist.
- Address a business envelope.
- Turn their persuasive essay into a business letter.
- Proofread and publish their business letter.

Unit Plan		Online	Offline
Lesson 1	Parts of a Business Letter and Journal Entry	15 minutes	20 minutes
Lesson 2	Inside Address and Revise Your Persuasive Essay	20 minutes	15 minutes
Lesson 3	Salutation & Closing and Revise Your Persuasive Essay	20 minutes	15 minutes
Lesson 4	Address an Envelope to a Business	15 minutes	20 minutes
Lesson 5	Unit Review and Turn Your Essay into a Business Letter	20 minutes	15 minutes
Lesson 6	Unit Checkpoint and Proofread Your Letter & Envelope	20 minutes	15 minutes
Lesson 7	Publish Your Business Letter	15 minutes	20 minutes

Parts of a Business Letter and Journal Entry

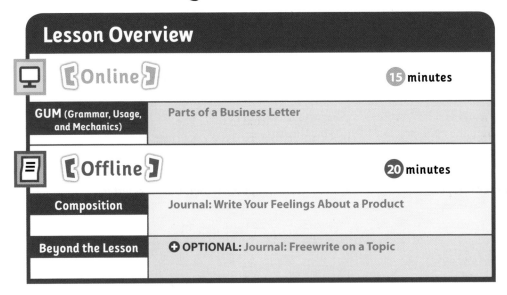

Lesson Overview

Online		15 minutes
GUM (Grammar, Usage, and Mechanics)	Parts of a Business Letter	

Offline		20 minutes
Composition	Journal: Write Your Feelings About a Product	
Beyond the Lesson	✚ OPTIONAL: Journal: Freewrite on a Topic	

Materials

Supplied
- *K¹² My Journal*, pp. 28–29
- *Grammar Reference Guide* Online Book (optional)

Keywords

business letter – a letter written to an organization or a person at a business

closing (of a business letter) – the part of a business letter that follows the body text, containing a phrase such as "Sincerely" or "Yours truly"

heading – the first part of a letter that has the writer's address and the date

inside address – the part of a business or formal letter that comes after the heading and before the greeting, made up of the name and address of the person to whom the letter is written

return address – the name and address of the sender, written in the upper left corner of an envelope

salutation (of a business letter) – the greeting of a business letter, which usually says, "Dear (name of recipient)"; it is followed by a colon

signature (of a business letter) – the part of a business letter following the closing, consisting of the writer's signature above the writer's typed name

Advance Preparation

To prepare for the GUM portion of this lesson, review Resources (Model Business [Formal] Letter) in the *Grammar Reference Guide* (linked in the online lesson) to familiarize yourself with the topic.

Big Ideas

▸ Journal writing is a form of freewriting. It is an opportunity to get ideas on paper without regard for correctness of the language or the format of a piece of writing.

▸ To improve, writers require frequent practice.

▸ Business letters, or formal letters, may be written to express an opinion, to order a product, to complain about a purchase or service, to make an inquiry, or to congratulate a person or group. The format of a business letter is different from the format of a friendly letter.

▸ When a writer uses the correct format, the reader is better able to focus on the writer's ideas.

 **Online** **15 minutes**

Students will work online **independently** to complete an activity on formatting and identifying the parts of a business letter. Help students locate the online activity.

GUM (Grammar, Usage, and Mechanics)

Parts of a Business Letter
Students will learn about the different parts of a business letter. They will learn how to properly format a business letter. Then they will practice identifying the parts of a business letter.

 Objectives
- Recognize the parts of a formal, or business, letter.

Offline **20 minutes**

Work **together** with students to complete the offline Composition and Beyond the Lesson activities.

Composition

 Journal: Write Your Feelings About a Product
Students will respond to a journal prompt by writing about a product. They will write about whether they are happy or unhappy with the product and why. Gather *K¹² My Journal* and have students turn to pages 28 and 29.

 Objectives
- Respond to a journal prompt.
- Freewrite about a topic.

1. Tell students they are going to write in their journal about a product—for example, toothpaste, sunscreen, shampoo, soap, backpack, or pet food—they are either happy or unhappy with. To help students think of a product, ask the following questions.

   ▸ What is a product you use all the time? Why do you use it so often?
   ▸ Are there any products that you like to tell others to use? Are there any products that you tell your friends to stay away from?
   ▸ If you had to choose your favorite product, what would it be?

2. Have students respond to the prompt in their journal. Encourage them to write in complete sentences, although it is not a requirement when they are freewriting in their journal.

TIP Students should write for about 20 minutes. Freewriting allows students to use their imaginations to write what they want without worrying about being graded, so encourage them to keep writing for the entire time. If students have trouble writing for 20 minutes, use the prompting questions in Step 1or have them list ideas or words. If they want to keep writing beyond the suggested time limit, praise them for their enthusiasm and offer to let them complete their entry later in the day as a reward.

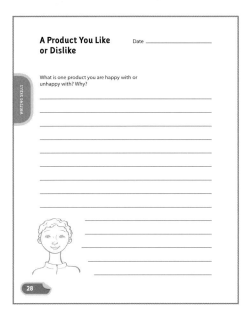

Beyond the Lesson

○ OPTIONAL: Journal: Freewrite on a Topic

This activity is OPTIONAL. It is intended for students who have extra time and would benefit from extra practice. Feel free to skip this activity. Gather *K¹² My Journal*.

1. Have students either respond to a prompt in Thoughts and Experiences (pages 50–93) or write about their own topic on the next available page in Ideas (pages 96–139).

2. Encourage students to explore their thoughts and write as much as they want. There are no rules. If students wish, ideas can be fleshed out into a more developed composition at a later time.

TIP Freewriting gives students a chance to write without worrying about grammar and rules. It is purely creative and can help even the most reluctant writers get comfortable creating words on the page.

Objectives
- Respond to a journal prompt.
- Freewrite about a topic.

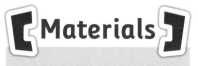

Inside Address and Revise Your Persuasive Essay

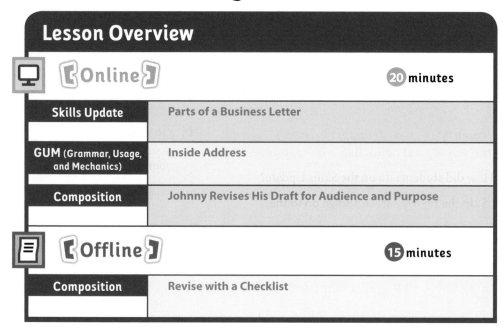

Lesson Overview

Online — 20 minutes

Skills Update	Parts of a Business Letter
GUM (Grammar, Usage, and Mechanics)	Inside Address
Composition	Johnny Revises His Draft for Audience and Purpose

Offline — 15 minutes

Composition	Revise with a Checklist

Materials

Supplied

- *K¹² Language Arts Activity Book*, pp. WS 103–109, 111
- *Grammar Reference Guide* Online Book (optional)
- Persuasive Essay: Feedback Sheet (printout)
- drafting page (optional printout)

Keywords

audience – a writer's readers

inside address – the part of a business or formal letter that comes after the heading and before the greeting, made up of the name and address of the person to whom the letter is written

purpose – the reason for writing

Advance Preparation

To prepare for the GUM portion of this lesson, review Resources (Model Business [Formal] Letter) in the *Grammar Reference Guide* (linked in the online lesson) to familiarize yourself with the topic. Gather pages WS 103–108 (Write Your Draft, students' draft of their persuasive essay) and 109 (Tell Me About My Essay, if completed) in *K¹² Language Arts Activity Book* and the completed Persuasive Essay: Feedback Sheet. You will review the feedback with students.

Big Ideas

- Business letters, or formal letters, may be written to express an opinion, to order a product, to complain about a purchase or service, to make an inquiry, or to congratulate a person or group. The format of a business letter is different from the format of a friendly letter.
- When a writer uses the correct format, capitalization, and punctuation in a letter, the reader is better able to focus on the writer's ideas.

 **20 minutes**

Students will work online to review the parts of a business letter, to learn how to write the inside address of a business letter, and to learn how to revise a persuasive essay for audience and purpose. Help students locate the online activities.

Skills Update

Parts of a Business Letter
Students will review the parts of a business letter by completing Skills Update exercises. Sit with students as they do this activity and note if they answer correctly.

⊃ **Learning Coach Check-In** How did students do on the Skills Update?

- ▶ **All answers correct:** Great! Skip the review screen and go on to the next activity.
- ▶ **Any answers incorrect:** Take a few minutes to review the parts of a business letter now. Use the links on the screen after the Skills Update to take another look at the online activities or review Resources (Model Business [Formal] Letter) in the *Grammar Reference Guide* together.

TIP This activity will require extra time if students need to review the parts of a business letter. Take the extra 5–10 minutes to review now because new skills build on what students have already learned.

 Objectives
- Recognize the parts of a formal, or business, letter.

GUM (Grammar, Usage, and Mechanics)

Inside Address
Students will learn how to write the inside address of a business letter and where it is located in the letter. They will then practice identifying and using the different parts of an inside address.

 Objectives
- Recognize the parts of a formal, or business, letter.
- Recognize the parts of an inside address.

Composition

Johnny Revises His Draft for Audience and Purpose
By watching how Johnny revises his persuasive essay draft for audience and purpose, students will be ready to begin revising their own draft.

 Objectives
- Revise a persuasive essay.
- Revise language based on purpose and audience.

 **15** minutes

Work **together** with students to complete the offline Composition activity.

Composition

Revise with a Checklist

This lesson is the first of two lessons for revising the persuasive essay. Have students gather their persuasive essay draft and any completed Peer Interaction Forms. Turn to page WS 111 in *K¹² Language Arts Activity Book* and gather the Persuasive Essay: Feedback Sheet that you filled out.

 Objectives
- Revise a persuasive essay.
- Revise language based on purpose and audience.

1. Use the Persuasive Essay: Feedback Sheet to guide your discussion with students.

   ‣ Tell students the strengths of their essay. Provide positive comments about the ideas, language, details, or other elements of the essay you enjoyed.

   ‣ Walk through the Purpose and Content and Structure and Organization sections of the feedback sheet with students. Do not address your comments in the Grammar and Mechanics section at this time. You can work with students on grammar and mechanics when they proofread. Offering these corrections now may distract students from the real work of revising for content and structure.

   ‣ As you go through the feedback sheet with students, encourage them to actively revise their draft based on your feedback. Reassure students that it's okay to remove ideas or sentences from their essay. Doing so may help their essay stay focused on their topic, even if something they cut was included in their graphic organizer.

   ‣ As students revise their draft, have them use the purple rows to mark their revisions.

2. Once you've reviewed your comments on the first two sections of the feedback sheet with students, have them review their draft once more, using the revising checklist on the Activity Book page. Students should check off each box on the checklist as they complete each item. Remind students that they can continue revising their essay in the next lesson.

3. If students received feedback from peers, discuss with them how they might use it to improve their essay. Help them decide what peer feedback would be useful to include in their revisions.

4. If students' revised persuasive essay has many changes that make the essay difficult to read and understand, encourage them to make a clean copy before the next lesson. Additional drafting pages can be printed from the online lesson.

TIP Keep students' revised persuasive essay and checklist in a safe place so they can refer to them later.

Composition

Draft Your Persuasive Essay

Write Your Draft

Read the assignment. Use your graphic organizer to help you write the first draft of your persuasive essay. Write only on the white rows. You will use the purple rows for revisions later.

> Write a persuasive essay about a way to improve your city, town, or neighborhood.
> • Think about who your audience will be.
> • Begin with an introduction that states your opinion.
> • Write reasons to support your opinion in the body of the essay.
> • Use linking words to connect opinions and reasons.
> • Choose words and phrases for effect.
> • End with a conclusion that restates your opinion and reasons in a different way.

Start here ▸

LANGUAGE ARTS PURPLE **WS 103**

Peer Interaction

Unit Checkpoint and Draft Your Persuasive Essay

Tell Me About My Essay

Have another person read your persuasive essay and answer the questions.

1. What is the opinion in the essay?

2. What supporting reason makes you **most** likely to agree?

3. What supporting reason makes you **least** likely to agree?

4. Does the conclusion clearly restate the opinion?

5. Does the writer convince you that his or her opinion is correct? If so, how?

LANGUAGE ARTS PURPLE **WS 109**

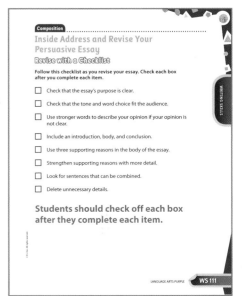

Composition

Inside Address and Revise Your Persuasive Essay

Revise with a Checklist

Follow this checklist as you revise your essay. Check each box after you complete each item.

☐ Check that the essay's purpose is clear.

☐ Check that the tone and word choice fit the audience.

☐ Use stronger words to describe your opinion if your opinion is not clear.

☐ Include an introduction, body, and conclusion.

☐ Use three supporting reasons in the body of the essay.

☐ Strengthen supporting reasons with more detail.

☐ Look for sentences that can be combined.

☐ Delete unnecessary details.

Students should check off each box after they complete each item.

LANGUAGE ARTS PURPLE **WS 111**

Salutation & Closing and Revise Your Persuasive Essay

Lesson Overview

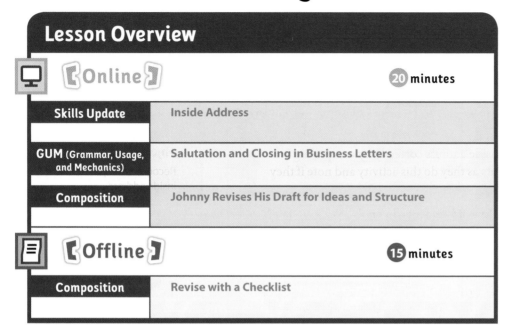

Online — 20 minutes

Skills Update	Inside Address
GUM (Grammar, Usage, and Mechanics)	Salutation and Closing in Business Letters
Composition	Johnny Revises His Draft for Ideas and Structure

Offline — 15 minutes

Composition	Revise with a Checklist

Materials

Supplied
- *K¹² Language Arts Activity Book*, p. WS 103–108, 111
- *Grammar Reference Guide* Online Book (optional)
- drafting page (optional printout)

Keywords

closing (of a business letter) – the part of a business letter that follows the body text, containing a phrase such as "Sincerely" or "Yours truly"

reason – a statement that explains why something is or why it should be

salutation (of a business letter) – the greeting of a business letter, which usually says, "Dear (name of recipient)"; it is followed by a colon

Advance Preparation

To prepare for the GUM portion of this lesson, review Resources (Model Business [Formal] Letter) in the *Grammar Reference Guide* (linked in the online lesson) to familiarize yourself with the topic. Gather pages WS 103–108 (Write Your Draft, students' draft of their persuasive essay), which students should have begun revising, and 111 (Revise with a Checklist) in *K¹² Language Arts Activity Book*.

Big Ideas

- Business letters, or formal letters, may be written to express an opinion, to order a product, to complain about a purchase or service, to make an inquiry, or to congratulate a person or group. The format of a business letter is different from the format of a friendly letter.
- Persuasive writing begins with the writer's opinion on a topic. In order to convince the audience of the correctness of the position, the writer supports the opinion with facts, statistics, and expert testimony.
- When a writer uses the correct format, capitalization, and punctuation in a letter, the reader is better able to focus on the writer's ideas.

 **20 minutes**

Students will work online to review the inside address of a business letter, to learn how to identify and write the salutation and closing of a business letter, and to learn how to revise a persuasive essay for ideas and structure. Help students locate the online activities.

Skills Update

Inside Address

Students will review how to write an inside address correctly by completing Skills Update exercises. Sit with students as they do this activity and note if they answer correctly.

> ⤺ **Learning Coach Check-In** How did students do on the Skills Update?

> ▸ **All answers correct:** Great! Skip the review screen and go on to the next activity.

> ▸ **Any answers incorrect:** Take a few minutes to review inside address now. Use the links on the screen after the Skills Update to take another look at the online activities or review Resources (Model Business [Formal] Letter) in the *Grammar Reference Guide* together.

 This activity will require extra time if students need to review the inside address of a business letter. Take the extra 5–10 minutes to review now because new skills build on what students have already learned.

GUM (Grammar, Usage, and Mechanics)

Salutation and Closing in Business Letters

Students will learn how to properly write the salutation and closing of a business letter. They will then practice identifying and using salutations and closings.

> **Objectives**
> • Recognize the parts of an inside address.

> **Objectives**
> • Recognize how a salutation begins and ends in a business letter.
> • Recognize how a closing begins and ends in a business letter.

Composition

Johnny Revises His Draft for Ideas and Structure

By watching how Johnny revises his persuasive essay draft for ideas and structure, students will be ready to continue revising their own draft.

Objectives
- Revise a persuasive essay.
- Check that the essay has an introduction, body, and conclusion.
- Check that the body of the essay has three reasons.
- Strengthen reasons that support a stand.
- Delete unnecessary details.

 **minutes**

Work **together** with students to complete the offline Composition activity.

Composition

Revise with a Checklist

Students will use a checklist to continue revising their persuasive essays. Have students gather their persuasive essay draft and revising checklist.

1. Have students reread their persuasive essay and continue using the checklist to revise their essay.

2. Have students revise their essay, focusing on making sure the essay is properly structured and the ideas are clear.

Objectives
- Revise a persuasive essay.
- Check that the essay has an introduction, body, and conclusion.
- Check that the body of the essay has three reasons.
- Strengthen reasons that support a stand.
- Delete unnecessary details.

3. If students' revised persuasive essay has many changes that make the essay difficult to read and understand, encourage them to make a clean copy before the next lesson. Additional drafting pages can be printed from the online lesson.

TIP Keep students' revised persuasive essay in a safe place so they can refer to it later.

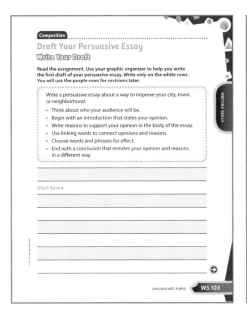

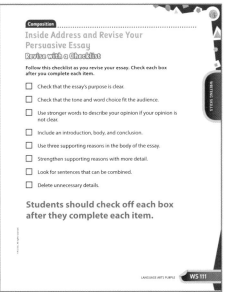

Address an Envelope to a Business

Lesson Overview

Online   15 minutes

Skills Update	Salutation and Closing in Business Letters
GUM (Grammar, Usage, and Mechanics)	Addresses on Business Envelopes

Offline   20 minutes

| GUM (Grammar, Usage, and Mechanics) | Address a Business Envelope |

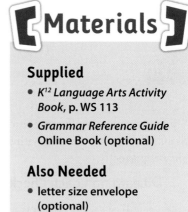

Materials

Supplied
- *K¹² Language Arts Activity Book*, p. WS 113
- *Grammar Reference Guide* Online Book (optional)

Also Needed
- letter size envelope (optional)

Advance Preparation

To prepare for this lesson, review Resources (Model Envelope for a Business Letter) in the *Grammar Reference Guide* (linked in the online lesson) to familiarize yourself with the topic. Beginning in the next lesson, students will be turning their persuasive essay into a business letter. In this lesson, they will learn how to address an envelope that is going to a business. Find a name and address that students can use for addressing the envelope. Ideally this name and address should be of the audience for the essay. In the publishing lesson, students will type their business letter and print it. They will then have the option to mail their business letter, with your permission.

 **minutes**

Students will work online to review the salutation and closing of a business letter and to learn how to address an envelope for a business letter. Help students locate the online activities.

Skills Update

Salutation and Closing in Business Letters

Students will review the salutation and closing of a business letter by completing Skills Update exercises. Sit with students as they do this activity and note if they answer correctly.

➲ **Learning Coach Check-In** How did students do on the Skills Update?

▸ **All answers correct:** Great! Skip the review screen and go on to the next activity.

▸ **Any answers incorrect:** Take a few minutes to review the salutation and closing of a business letter now. Use the links on the screen after the Skills Update to take another look at the online activities or review Resources (Model Business [Formal] Letter) in the *Grammar Reference Guide* together.

TIP This activity will require extra time if students need to review the salutation and closing of a business letter. Take the extra 5–10 minutes to review now because new skills build on what students have already learned.

Objectives
- Recognize how a salutation begins and ends in a business letter.
- Recognize how a closing begins and ends in a business letter.

GUM (Grammar, Usage, and Mechanics)

Addresses on Business Envelopes

Students will learn how to properly address an envelope for a business letter. They will then practice identifying correctly written business envelopes.

Objectives
- Recognize the parts of a business envelope.
- Address a business envelope.

 **20 minutes**

Work **together** with students to complete the offline Grammar, Usage, and Mechanics activity.

GUM (Grammar, Usage, and Mechanics)

Address a Business Envelope

Students will practice addressing a business envelope. Turn to page WS 113 in *K¹² Language Arts Activity Book*.

1. Show students the name and address of the person and company to whom they may send their business letter.

2. If students want, allow them to also address an actual envelope with the name and address of the person to whom they are writing.

TIP If students address an actual envelope, put it in a safe place so they can use it later.

Objectives

• Address a business envelope.

Unit Review and Turn Your Essay into a Business Letter

Lesson Overview

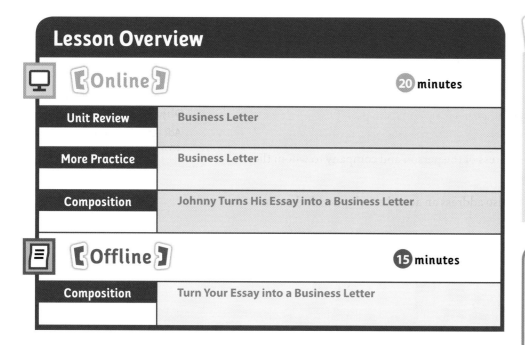

Online — 20 minutes

Unit Review	Business Letter
More Practice	Business Letter
Composition	Johnny Turns His Essay into a Business Letter

Offline — 15 minutes

| Composition | Turn Your Essay into a Business Letter |

Advance Preparation

Gather pages WS 103–108 (Write Your Draft, students' draft of their persuasive essay), which students should have revised.

Big Ideas

▶ Business letters, or formal letters, may be written to express an opinion, to order a product, to complain about a purchase or service, to make an inquiry, or to congratulate a person or group. The format of a business letter is different from the format of a friendly letter.

▶ Persuasive writing begins with the writer's opinion on a topic. In order to convince the audience of the correctness of the position, the writer supports the opinion with facts, statistics, and expert testimony.

▶ When a writer uses the correct format, capitalization, and punctuation in a letter, the reader is better able to focus on the writer's ideas.

Materials

Supplied

- *K¹² Language Arts Activity Book*, pp. WS 103–108, 115–116
- *Grammar Reference Guide* Online Book (optional)
- drafting Page (optional printout)

Keywords

audience – a writer's readers

closing (of a business letter) – the part of a business letter that follows the body text, containing a phrase such as "Sincerely" or "Yours truly"

heading – the first part of a letter that has the writer's address and the date

inside address – the part of a business or formal letter that comes after the heading and before the greeting, made up of the name and address of the person to whom the letter is written

purpose – the reason for writing

return address – the name and address of the sender, written in the upper left corner of an envelope

salutation (of a business letter) – the greeting of a business letter, which usually says, "Dear (name of recipient)"; it is followed by a colon

signature (of a business letter) – the part of a business letter following the closing, consisting of the writer's signature above the writer's typed name

 **minutes**

Students will work online to review the grammar, usage, and mechanics skills learned in the unit and to learn how to turn a persuasive essay into a business letter. Help students locate the online activities.

Unit Review

Business Letter

Students will review what they have learned about the parts of a business letter, including the inside address, the salutation and closing, the signature, and the address on a business envelope, to review for the Unit Checkpoint.

TIP A full list of objectives covered in the Unit Review can be found in the online lesson.

Objectives
- Complete a review of grammar, usage, and mechanics skills.

More Practice

Business Letter

Go over students' results on the Unit Review and, if necessary, have them complete the appropriate review activities listed in the table online. Help students locate the activities and provide support as needed.

TIP The time students need to complete this activity will vary. Set aside enough time for students to complete all review activities, if they need to do so.

Objectives
- Evaluate Unit Review results and choose activities for more practice.

Composition

Johnny Turns His Essay into a Business Letter

By exploring how Johnny turns his revised persuasive essay into a business letter, students will prepare to create their own business letter.

Objectives
- Implement the parts of a business letter.

 **Offline** ⏱ **15** minutes

Work **together** with students to complete the offline Composition activity.

Composition

Turn Your Essay into a Business Letter

Students will add the elements of a business letter to their persuasive essay. Have students gather their revised persuasive essay and turn to page WS 115 and 116 in *K¹² Language Arts Activity Book.*

1. Have students reread their essay and look at the model business letter on the Activity Book pages.

2. Have students add the elements of a business letter to their draft. They will add a heading, inside address, salutation, closing, and signature. Remind students that the parts they are adding should begin at the left edge, or margin, of their paper, and that they should include both their first and last names in the signature, even though the model uses only a first name. Provide support as necessary.

TIP Students may write the heading, inside address, and salutation on a clean sheet of drafting paper and attach it to the beginning of their essay draft. In the publishing lesson, students will have an opportunity to make a clean copy of the entire letter by typing it. At that time, you can assist them in formatting the letter correctly. Keep students' draft in a safe place so they can refer to it later.

> **Objectives**
> • Implement the parts of a business letter.

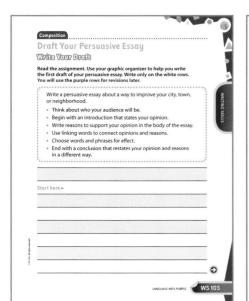

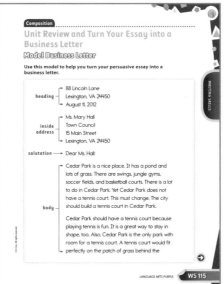

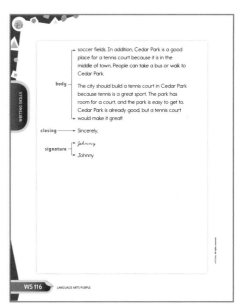

Unit Checkpoint and Proofread Your Letter & Envelope

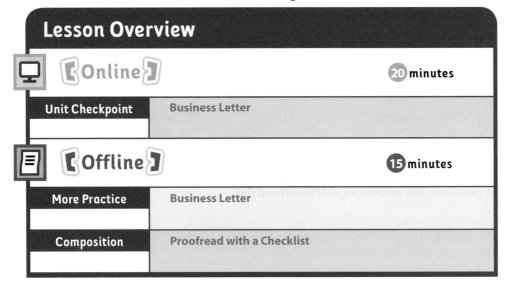

Lesson Overview

Online — 20 minutes

Unit Checkpoint	Business Letter

Offline — 15 minutes

More Practice	Business Letter
Composition	Proofread with a Checklist

Materials

Supplied

- *K¹² Language Arts Activity Book*, pp. WS 103–108, 117
- *Grammar Reference Guide* Online Book (optional)
- Parts of a Business Letter (optional printout)
- Inside Address (optional printout)
- Salutation and Closing in Business Letters (optional printout)
- Addresses on a Business Envelope (optional printout)
- Persuasive Essay: Feedback Sheet (printout)
- drafting page (optional printout)

Advance Preparation

Gather pages WS 103–108 (Write Your Draft, students' draft of their business letter) in *K¹² Language Arts Activity Book* and the completed Persuasive Essay: Feedback Sheet. If students' revised letter has many changes that make it difficult to read and understand, you may want to encourage them to make a clean copy before they proofread in this lesson. Additional drafting pages can be printed from the online lesson.

Big Ideas

- Business letters, or formal letters, may be written to express an opinion, to order a product, to complain about a purchase or service, to make an inquiry, or to congratulate a person or group. The format of a business letter is different from the format of a friendly letter.
- Persuasive writing begins with the writer's opinion on a topic. In order to convince the audience of the correctness of the position, the writer supports the opinion with facts, statistics, and expert testimony.
- When a writer uses the correct format, capitalization, and punctuation in a letter, the reader is better able to focus on the writer's ideas.

 **20** minutes

Students will work online **independently** to complete the Unit Checkpoint. Help students locate the online checkpoint.

Unit Checkpoint

Business Letter

Students will complete an online Unit Checkpoint about the parts of a business letter, including the inside address, the salutation and closing, the signature, and the address on a business envelope. If necessary, read the directions to students.

 Although students are taking the GUM Checkpoint in this lesson, they will continue to work on the Composition portion of this unit during this lesson and the next one.

Objectives
- Complete a Unit Checkpoint on grammar, usage, and mechanics skills.

 **15** minutes

Work **together** with students to complete the offline More Practice and Composition activities.

More Practice

Business Letter

Go over students' results on the Unit Checkpoint and, if necessary, print out and have them complete the appropriate practice pages listed in the table online. Students can complete all necessary pages now or, if more time is needed, they can spread them out over the next few days. They can also review the appropriate sections of the *Grammar Reference Guide* with you. If students scored less than 80 percent on the Unit Checkpoint, you may want them to retake the Checkpoint after completing the additional activity pages.

 The time students need to complete this activity will vary. Set aside enough time for students to complete some or all activity pages and to retake the Unit Checkpoint, if they need to do so. Students may retake the Unit Checkpoint immediately, but having them complete the practice pages and then retake it might be more effective.

Objectives
- Evaluate Unit Checkpoint results and choose activities for more practice.

More Practice

Improve Your Skills
Parts of a Business Letter

Label each part of the business letter.

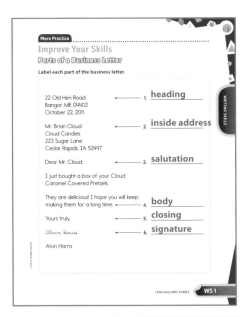

22 Old Hen Road
Bangor, ME 04402
October 22, 2011 ————→ 1. **heading**

Mr. Brian Cloud
Cloud Candies
223 Sugar Lane
Cedar Rapids, IA 52497 ————→ 2. **inside address**

Dear Mr. Cloud: ————→ 3. **salutation**

I just bought a box of your Cloud
Caramel Covered Pretzels.

They are delicious! I hope you will keep
making them for a long time. ————→ 4. **body**

Yours truly, ————→ 5. **closing**

Alvin Harris ————→ 6. **signature**

Alvin Harris

More Practice

Improve Your Skills
Inside Address

Practice identifying parts of an inside address.

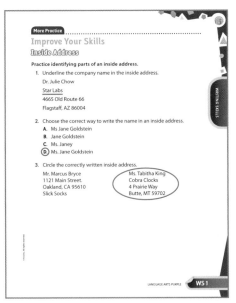

1. Underline the company name in the inside address.
   Dr. Julie Chow
   <u>Star Labs</u>
   4665 Old Route 66
   Flagstaff, AZ 86004

2. Choose the correct way to write the name in an inside address.
   A. Ms Jane Goldstein
   B. Jane Goldstein
   C. Ms. Janey
   (D) Ms. Jane Goldstein

3. Circle the correctly written inside address.
   Mr. Marcus Bryce
   1121 Main Street.
   Oakland, CA 95610
   Slick Socks

   (Ms. Tabitha King
   Cobra Clocks
   4 Prairie Way
   Butte, MT 59702)

More Practice

Improve Your Skills
Salutation and Closing in Business Letters

Choose the answer.

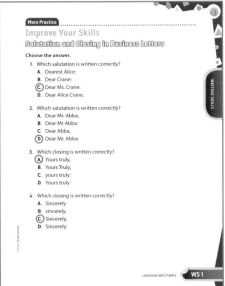

1. Which salutation is written correctly?
   A. Dearest Alice:
   B. Dear Crane:
   (C) Dear Ms. Crane:
   D. Dear Alice Crane,

2. Which salutation is written correctly?
   A. Dear Mr. Abba.
   B. Dear Mr Abba:
   C. Dear Abba,
   (D) Dear Mr. Abba,

3. Which closing is written correctly?
   (A) Yours truly,
   B. Yours Truly,
   C. yours truly:
   D. Yours truly

4. Which closing is written correctly?
   A. Sincerely
   B. sincerely,
   (C) Sincerely,
   D. Sincerely:

More Practice

Improve Your Skills
Addresses on a Business Envelope

Practice addressing a business envelope. Write the return address and the reader's address in the correct place.

Return Address:	Reader's Address:
Maria Sanchez	Mr. Silva Marks
13 Abdo Road	Elm Pictures
Dayton, OH 45408	3323 Greene Street
	Queens, NY 11355

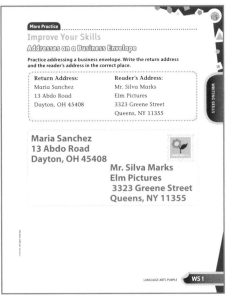

**Maria Sanchez
13 Abdo Road
Dayton, OH 45408**

**Mr. Silva Marks
Elm Pictures
3323 Greene Street
Queens, NY 11355**

Composition

Proofread with a Checklist

Students will proofread their business letter. Have them gather their business letter draft. Turn to page WS 117 in *K¹² Language Arts Activity Book* and gather the Persuasive Essay: Feedback Sheet that you filled out.

Objectives
- Proofread a business letter.

1. If students did not do so in advance, have them make a clean copy of their draft, if necessary, before proceeding to proofread. Additional drafting pages can be printed from the online lesson.

2. Review with students your comments in the Grammar and Mechanics section of the feedback sheet. As you go through the feedback sheet with students, encourage them to use the purple rows on their drafting pages to actively mark changes based on your feedback.

3. Once you've reviewed your comments in the Grammar and Mechanics section of the feedback sheet with students, have them review their draft once more using the proofreading checklist. Students should check the boxes on the checklist as they complete the items.

4. If you wish, go over the proofreading checklist with students to help them find errors in capitalization and punctuation in the format of their business letter.

TIP Keep students' proofread letter in a safe place so they can refer to it later.

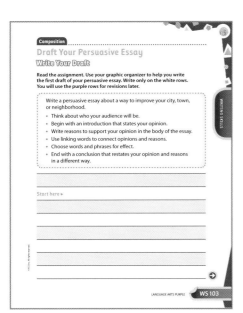

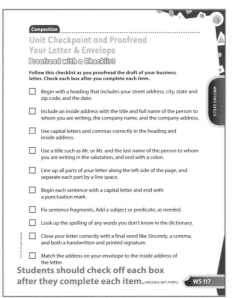

Publish Your Business Letter

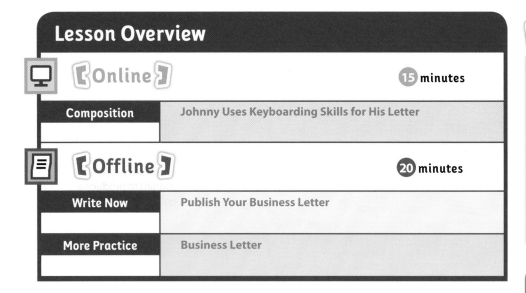

Lesson Overview

🖥️ **[Online]**		**15 minutes**
Composition	Johnny Uses Keyboarding Skills for His Letter	

📄 **[Offline]**		**20 minutes**
Write Now	Publish Your Business Letter	
More Practice	Business Letter	

Materials

Supplied
- *K¹² Language Arts Activity Book*, pp. WS 103–108, 115–116
- Business Letter: Rubric and Sample Responses (printout)
- lined writing page (optional printout)

Keywords

keyboarding – using a word processing program to produce a piece of writing

Advance Preparation

Gather pages WS 103–108 (Write Your Draft, students' draft of their business letter), which students should have revised and proofread, and 115–116 (Model Business Letter) in *K¹² Language Arts Activity Book*. If students' revised and proofread letter has many changes that make it difficult to read and understand, you may want to encourage them to make a clean copy before they type their letter. Lined writing pages can be printed from the online lesson. Students should use a word processing program to publish their business letter. They may need your help with keyboarding skills, and you are encouraged to give them guidance and support in producing the typed letter.

Big Ideas

- ▸ Business letters, or formal letters, may be written to express an opinion, to order a product, to complain about a purchase or service, to make an inquiry, or to congratulate a person or group. The format of a business letter is different from the format of a friendly letter.
- ▸ Persuasive writing begins with the writer's opinion on a topic. In order to convince the audience of the correctness of the position, the writer supports the opinion with facts, statistics, and expert testimony.
- ▸ When a writer uses the correct format, capitalization, and punctuation in a letter, the reader is better able to focus on the writer's ideas.

 **15 minutes**

Students will work online **independently** to learn about typing a business letter. Help students locate the online activity.

 **Composition** ....

Johnny Uses Keyboarding Skills for His Letter

By exploring how Johnny types his business letter, students will prepare to use a word processing program to publish their own letter.

 Objectives
- Make a clean copy of a business letter.
- Use a word processing program to produce a final draft.

 20 minutes

Work **together** with students to complete the offline Write Now and More Practice activities.

Write Now ....

Publish Your Business Letter

Students will publish their business letter. Have them gather their proofread draft and the model business letter.

 Objectives
- Make a clean copy of a business letter.
- Use a word processing program to produce a final draft.

1. Explain to students that they will finish their business letter by completing the last stage of the writing process—publishing their work.
   Say: Publishing your writing means making a clean and final copy that is ready for sharing with others.

   ▸ To be ready to publish your personal letter, you should have finished revising and proofreading your draft.
   ▸ The final copy should be your best effort and should not have any errors.

2. Explain that the final copy will be typed using word processing software. Tell students that when they have finished typing their letter, they will print it so it is ready to send.

3. Have students type their letter using word processing software. Remind them to make sure all parts of the letter line up on the left, and that there is a space between each section of the letter and each paragraph in the body. Because all parts of a business letter begin at the left side of the paper, students will not have to indent any text. However, you may help them with their typing skills, if necessary.

4. If you wish, allow students to mail their letter to their audience. Have them address an envelope or use the one they addressed in the Address an Envelope to a Business lesson.

5. Use the materials and instructions in the online lesson to evaluate students' finished writing. You will be looking at students' writing to evaluate the following:

   ▶ **Purpose and Content:** The business letter has a purpose and audience and uses mostly appropriate language. The letter has a stated opinion and at least three supporting reasons, although all reasons may not be explained well and there may be an unnecessary detail.

   ▶ **Structure and Organization:** The letter has been revised. It contains at least four parts of a business letter: a heading, inside address, salutation, body paragraphs, closing, and signature. All parts of the letter begin along the left side of the page, but some of the spacing is inconsistent.

   ▶ **Grammar and Mechanics:** The letter has been proofread using a checklist, and only a few errors remain. Most sentences are complete, and the capitalization and punctuation of the parts of a letter are mostly correct.

6. Enter students' scores online for each rubric category.

7. If students' writing scored a 1 in any category, work with them to revise and proofread their work.

TIP Tell students that producing a piece of writing that is ready to publish and share with others is a great accomplishment. Let students know that the effort they put in to publish a letter is something to be proud of.

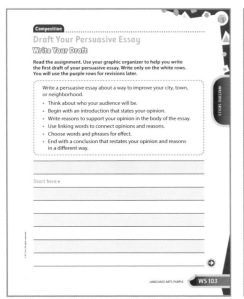

More Practice

Business Letter

If students' writing did not meet objectives, have them complete the appropriate review activities listed in the table online. Follow the online instructions to help students revise and edit their work. Impress upon students that revising makes their work better. Writing is a process, and each time they revise their letter they are improving their writing. Always begin with something positive to say. If there is one detail, for example, mention it and say how this detail helps you picture what is being written about.

Help students locate the activities and provide support as needed.

Reward: When students score 80 percent or above on the Unit Checkpoint and their writing is Level 2 or higher on the Business Letter grading rubric, add a sticker for this unit on the My Accomplishments chart.

Critical Skills Practice 3

Unit Focus

In this unit, students will practice answering questions about skills associated with spelling, vocabulary, and language. They will learn how to answer multiple choice questions about

- ► Alphabetizing words
- ► Distinguishing between the literal and nonliteral meanings of words
- ► Parts of speech
- ► Shades of meaning of closely related words

Unit Plan		**[Offline]**	**[Online]**
Lesson 1	Spelling Skills (C)		35 minutes
Lesson 2	Vocabulary Skills (D)		35 minutes
Lesson 3	Language Skills (D)		35 minutes
Lesson 4	Vocabulary Skills (E)		35 minutes
Lesson 5	Unit Checkpoint	35 minutes	varies

Spelling Skills (C)

Lesson Overview

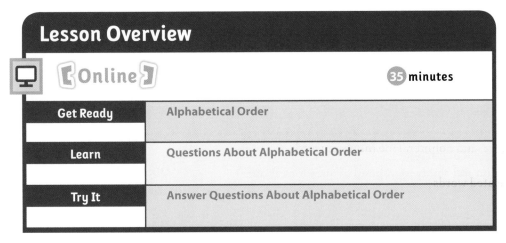

Online		35 minutes
Get Ready	Alphabetical Order	
Learn	Questions About Alphabetical Order	
Try It	Answer Questions About Alphabetical Order	

Materials

There are no materials to gather for this lesson.

Keywords

alphabetical order – a sequence according to position in the alphabet; for example, in alphabetical order, *at* comes before *bat*, which comes before *cat*

Big Ideas

Practice answering the kinds of questions often found on standardized tests can make taking the tests less stressful for students.

Online 35 minutes

Students will work online **independently** to complete Get Ready, Learn, and Try It activities. Help students locate the online activities.

Get Ready

Alphabetical Order
Students will review what alphabetical order is and how to alphabetize words.

Objectives
• Alphabetize words.

Learn

Questions About Alphabetical Order
Students will learn how to answer questions about alphabetizing words by working through several exercises.

Objectives
- Alphabetize words.
- Alphabetize words to the third letter.

Try It

Answer Questions About Alphabetical Order
Students will show their comprehension and ability to respond to questions about alphabetizing words.

Objectives
- Alphabetize words.
- Alphabetize words to the third letter.

Vocabulary Skills (D)

Lesson Overview

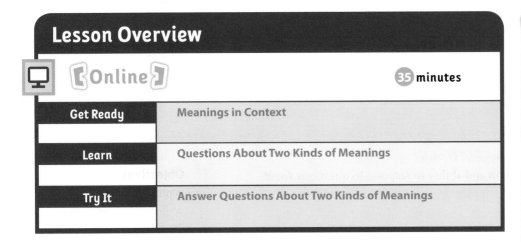

Online		35 minutes
Get Ready	Meanings in Context	
Learn	Questions About Two Kinds of Meanings	
Try It	Answer Questions About Two Kinds of Meanings	

Materials

There are no materials to gather for this lesson.

Keywords

context clue – a word or phrase in a text that helps you figure out the meaning of an unknown word

literal meaning – following the usual, or exact, meaning of words

nonliteral meaning – a figure of speech; a word or phrase that exaggerates or changes the usual meaning of the word or words in the phrase

Big Ideas

Practice answering the kinds of questions often found on standardized tests can make taking the tests less stressful for students.

 **Online** 35 minutes

Students will work online **independently** to complete Get Ready, Learn, and Try It activities. Help students locate the online activities.

Get Ready

Meanings in Context
Students will review the idea that words and phrases can have both literal and nonliteral meanings, and they will focus on the role that context clues can play in helping readers determine which meaning of a word or phrase an author intended.

Objectives
- Distinguish the literal and nonliteral meaning of words and phrases in context.

Learn •••

Questions About Two Kinds of Meanings

Students will learn how to answer questions about words and phrases that have both literal and nonliteral meanings by reading and working through several exercises.

Objectives
- Distinguish the literal and nonliteral meaning of words and phrases in context.

Try It •••

Answer Questions About Two Kinds of Meanings

Students will show their comprehension and ability to respond to questions about words and phrases that have both literal and nonliteral meanings.

Objectives
- Distinguish the literal and nonliteral meaning of words and phrases in context.

Language Skills (D)

Lesson Overview

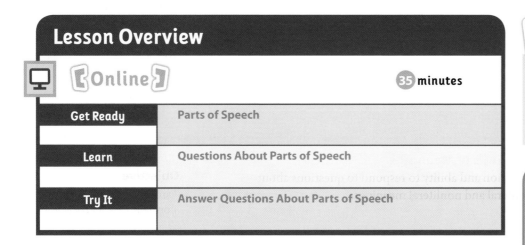

		35 minutes
Get Ready	Parts of Speech	
Learn	Questions About Parts of Speech	
Try It	Answer Questions About Parts of Speech	

Keywords

noun – a word that names a person, place, thing, or idea

part of speech – the category that words belong to according to how they are used in a sentence, such as *noun*, *verb*, and *adjective*

verb – a word that shows action or a state of being

Big Ideas

Practice answering the kinds of questions often found on standardized tests can make taking the tests less stressful for students.

Online 35 minutes

Students will work online **independently** to complete Get Ready, Learn, and Try It activities. Help students locate the online activities.

Get Ready •

Parts of Speech
Students will review what is meant by the term *parts of speech*. Then they will go over what nouns and verbs are and how nouns and verbs function in a sentence.

Objectives
• Identify parts of speech.

Learn

Questions About Parts of Speech
Students will learn how to answer questions about nouns and verbs and how each
one functions in a sentence by reading and working through several exercises.

Objectives
- Identify parts of speech.
- Identify how a part of speech is used in a sentence.

Try It

Answer Questions About Parts of Speech
Students will show their comprehension and ability to respond to questions about
nouns and verbs and how each one functions in sentences.

Objectives
- Identify parts of speech.
- Identify how a part of speech is used in a sentence.

Vocabulary Skills (E)

Lesson Overview

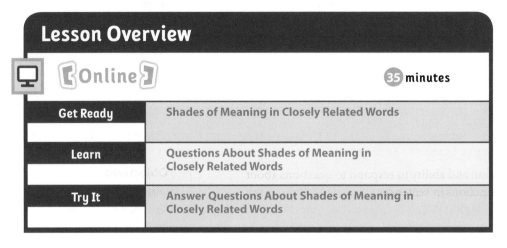

 Online		35 minutes
Get Ready	Shades of Meaning in Closely Related Words	
Learn	Questions About Shades of Meaning in Closely Related Words	
Try It	Answer Questions About Shades of Meaning in Closely Related Words	

Materials

There are no materials to gather for this lesson.

Keywords

shades of meaning – small differences in meaning between similar words or phrases

Big Ideas

Practice answering the kinds of questions often found on standardized tests can make taking the tests less stressful for students.

 Online 35 minutes

Students will work online **independently** to complete Get Ready, Learn, and Try It activities. Help students locate the online activities.

Get Ready

Shades of Meaning in Closely Related Words

Students will review the term *shades of meaning* and recall that some words have meanings that are similar but slightly different from one another. They will focus on the importance of being able to recognize shades of meaning and on how using words whose meanings are similar but slightly different can impact the meaning of a sentence.

Objectives

- Define *shades of meaning*.

Learn

Questions About Shades of Meaning in Closely Related Words
By working through several exercises, students will learn how to answer questions about how words whose meanings are similar but slightly different from one another can affect sentences.

Objectives
- Distinguish shades of meaning among related words.

Try It

Answer Questions About Shades of Meaning in Closely Related Words
Students will show their comprehension and ability to respond to questions about words whose meanings are similar but slightly different from one another and the effect such words can have on sentences.

Objectives
- Distinguish shades of meaning among related words.

Unit Checkpoint

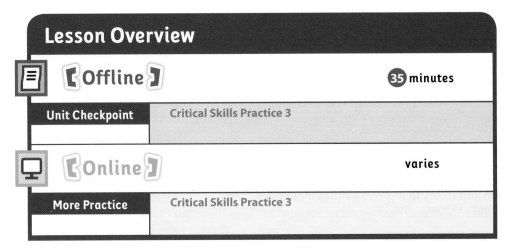

Lesson Overview

 【Offline】 ... **35** minutes

Unit Checkpoint	Critical Skills Practice 3

【Online】 ... varies

More Practice	Critical Skills Practice 3

Objectives
- Alphabetize words.
- Alphabetize words to the third letter.
- Distinguish the literal and nonliteral meaning of words and phrases in context.
- Identify parts of speech.
- Identify how a part of speech is used in a sentence.
- Distinguish shades of meaning among related words.

【Materials】

Supplied
- *K¹² Language Arts Assessments*, pp. WS 17–23

 **【Offline】** **35** minutes

Unit Checkpoint ....

Critical Skills Practice 3
Explain that students are going to show what they have learned about alphabetical order, literal and nonliteral word meanings, parts of speech, and shades of meaning in related words.

1. Give students the Unit Checkpoint pages.

2. Read the directions together. Have students complete the Checkpoint on their own.

3. Use the Answer Key to score the Checkpoint and then enter the results online.

4. Review each exercise with students. Work with students to correct any exercise that they missed.

 Reward: If students score 80 percent or more on the Unit Checkpoint, add a sticker for this unit on the My Accomplishments chart. If students did not score 80 percent or more, work with them to revise their work until they do score 80 percent.

Name _____ Date _____

Unit Checkpoint Learning Coach Instructions
Critical Skills Practice 3

Explain that students are going to show what they have learned about alphabetical order, literal and nonliteral word meanings, parts of speech, and shades of meaning in related words.

1. Give students the Unit Checkpoint pages.
2. Read the directions together. Have students complete the Checkpoint on their own.
3. Use the Answer Key to score the Checkpoint and then enter the results online.
4. Review each exercise with students. Work with students to correct any exercise they missed.

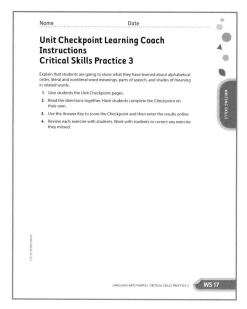

LANGUAGE ARTS PURPLE | CRITICAL SKILLS PRACTICE 3   WS 17

Name _____ Date _____

Unit Checkpoint Answer Key
Critical Skills Practice 3

Part 1. Alphabetical Order
Read and answer each question.

1. Which group of words is in alphabetical order?
   - **(A) moose, private, thorn, wheel**
   - B. drift, heal, opinion, jury
   - C. instant, last, hurry, shell
   - D. able, cures, friend, enemy

2. Read this list of words.

   | since | seek | start | spoon |

   If this list were in ABC order, which word would be first?
   - A. since
   - **(B) seek**
   - C. start
   - D. spoon

3. Which group of words is in alphabetical order?
   - A. illness, ivory, irritate, industry
   - **(B) vast, very, villain, vote**
   - C. reap, rate, rope, rust
   - D. ceiling, cork, creepy, city

4. Read this list of words.

   | joy | joke | job | jogger |

   If this list were in ABC order, which word would be last?
   - **(A) joy**
   - B. joke
   - C. job
   - D. jogger

WS 18   LANGUAGE ARTS PURPLE | CRITICAL SKILLS PRACTICE 3

Name _____ Date _____

5. Which group of words is in alphabetical order?
   - A. neat, nest, nets, neon
   - B. alarm, alert, album, alter
   - C. crib, crops, creak, crust
   - **(D) trade, tropical, trust, try**

Part 2. Literal and Nonliteral Word Meanings
Read and answer each question.

6. Read this paragraph.

   > Nora tried everything she could think of to get Avery to tell her the secret. First, she asked. Then, she begged. She tried to bully Avery into telling her, and she asked Avery as nicely as she could. But Avery would not tell Nora the secret. Finally, Nora dropped the subject.

   What does the word dropped mean in this paragraph?
   - A. let fall from one's hands
   - **(C) stopped talking about**
   - B. put down
   - D. lowered the price of

7. Read this sentence.

   > Mary was grateful for the ocean breeze, which kept her cool.

   What does the phrase kept her cool mean in this sentence?
   - A. remained calm
   - **(B) stopped her from feeling hot**
   - C. made others admire her
   - D. angered her

LANGUAGE ARTS PURPLE | CRITICAL SKILLS PRACTICE 3   WS 19

---

8. Read this paragraph.

   > Minutes passed, and Pat grew more and more angry. He was trying to read in his bedroom, and his sisters knew that. Yet they kept playing their favorite song over and over as loud as they could downstairs. Pat knew that he could not take it much longer. If they weren't quiet soon, he was going to snap.

   Which sentence uses snap in the same way it is used in the paragraph?
   - A. You can have anything you want with just a snap of your fingers.
   - B. I'll snap your gloves to your coat so you don't lose them.
   - **(C) I did not mean to snap at you for being late.**
   - D. Gretchen thought that it would be hard to juggle, but Anderson told her it was a snap.

9. Read this sentence.

   > Did Evelyn rattle Dennis when she crept up behind him and shouted in his ear?

   Which sentence uses rattle in the same way it is used in the sentence?
   - A. Yvonne can rattle off the names of every American president in under a minute.
   - B. I heard it rattle before I saw the scary snake at the zoo.
   - C. When Vickie was a baby, she loved to play with her rattle.
   - **(D) Everyone talking at once might rattle and upset the little boy.**

WS 20   LANGUAGE ARTS PURPLE | CRITICAL SKILLS PRACTICE 3

---

10. Read this sentence.

    > Roger always tries to tackle the toughest problems first.

    What does the word tackle mean?
    - **(A) work on**
    - B. drag to the ground
    - C. fish with
    - D. avoid

Part 3. Parts of Speech
Read and answer each question.

11. Read this sentence.

    > Two mice crept quietly through the kitchen.

    Which underlined word is a noun?
    - A. Two
    - **(B) mice**
    - C. crept
    - D. quietly

12. Read this sentence.

    > The blond woman spoke slowly.

    What does the noun do in this sentence?
    - A. The noun describes the color of a person's hair.
    - **(B) The noun names the subject.**
    - C. The noun shows an action.
    - D. The noun describes how fast a person talks.

LANGUAGE ARTS PURPLE | CRITICAL SKILLS PRACTICE 3   WS 21

---

13. Read this sentence.

    > Five hands slowly rose.

    Which underlined word is a verb?
    - A. Five
    - C. slowly
    - B. hands
    - **(D) rose**

14. Read this sentence.

    > An excited dog barks at the worried mail carrier.

    What does the verb do in this sentence?
    - A. The verb describes an animal.
    - B. The verb names the subject.
    - **(C) The verb shows action.**
    - D. The verb describes a person.

15. Read this sentence.

    > The big blue bus drove slowly down the street.

    Which underlined word is a noun?
    - A. big
    - C. drove
    - B. blue
    - **(D) street**

WS 22   LANGUAGE ARTS PURPLE | CRITICAL SKILLS PRACTICE 3

Part 4. Shades of Meaning in Related Words
Read and answer each question.

16. Which sentence expresses the most certainty?
    - **(A) I knew that you would like it.**
    - B. I thought that you would like it.
    - C. I hoped that you would like it.
    - D. I wondered if you would like it.

17. Which sentence tells Danielle's opinion about Kyle's singing?
    - A. Danielle wondered if Kyle's singing was beautiful.
    - **(B) Danielle thought that Kyle's singing was beautiful.**
    - C. Danielle hoped that Kyle's singing was beautiful.
    - D. Danielle heard that Kyle's singing was beautiful.

18. Which sentence tells that Joy secretly thought Michael was planning a surprise party?
    - A. Joy heard that Michael was planning a surprise party.
    - B. Joy hoped that Michael was planning a surprise party.
    - **(C) Joy suspected that Michael was planning a surprise party.**
    - D. Joy knew that Michael was planning a surprise party.

19. Which sentence expresses the strongest feeling?
    - A. Derrick is worried.
    - C. Derrick is scared.
    - **(B) Derrick is terrified.**
    - D. Derrick is afraid.

20. Which sentence describes the worst weather?
    - A. It drizzled last night.
    - C. It rained last night.
    - B. It showered last night.
    - **(D) It poured last night.**

LANGUAGE ARTS PURPLE | CRITICAL SKILLS PRACTICE 3   WS 23

 **varies**

Work **together** with students to complete the online More Practice activity.

More Practice

Critical Skills Practice 3

Go over students' results on the Unit Checkpoint. If necessary, have students complete the appropriate review activities listed in the table online. Help students locate the activities and provide support as needed.

TIP The time students need to complete this activity will vary. Set aside enough time for students to complete all review activities, if they need to do so.

 Objectives
- Evaluate Unit Checkpoint results and choose activities for more practice.

Semester Review and Checkpoint

Unit Focus

In this unit, students will review what they have learned about sentences; sentence combining; capital letters and commas in a letter; nouns; verbs; the parts of a business letter; and other language, vocabulary, and spelling skills. They will

▶ Complete two review activities containing multiple choice questions about the skills taught this semester.

▶ Return to activities from different units, as necessary, to do more practice on these skills.

▶ Complete two checkpoints that test their ability to answer questions on the grammar, usage, mechanics, and critical skills taught during this semester.

Unit Plan [Online]

Lesson 1	Semester Review: Sentences, Sentence Combining, Capital Letters & Commas in a Letter, and Critical Skills	35 minutes
Lesson 2	Semester Checkpoint: Sentences, Sentence Combining, Capital Letters & Commas in a Letter, and Critical Skills	35 minutes
Lesson 3	Semester Review: Nouns, Verbs, Parts of a Business Letter, and Critical Skills	35 minutes
Lesson 4	Semester Checkpoint: Nouns, Verbs, Parts of a Business Letter, and Critical Skills	35 minutes

Semester Review: Sentences, Sentence Combining, Capital Letters & Commas in a Letter, and Critical Skills

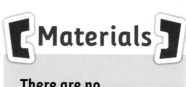

Lesson Overview

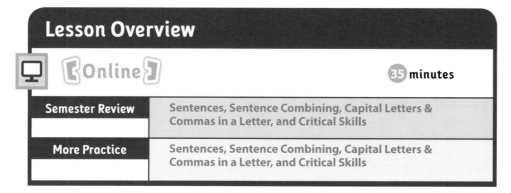

Online   35 minutes

Semester Review	Sentences, Sentence Combining, Capital Letters & Commas in a Letter, and Critical Skills
More Practice	Sentences, Sentence Combining, Capital Letters & Commas in a Letter, and Critical Skills

   35 minutes

Students will work online **independently** to review the grammar, usage, mechanics, and critical skills from this semester. Help students locate the online activities.

Semester Review

Sentences, Sentence Combining, Capital Letters & Commas in a Letter, and Critical Skills
Students will review what they have learned about sentences; sentence combining; using capital letters and commas in a letter; and other language, spelling, and vocabulary skills to review for the Semester Checkpoint.

 A full list of objectives covered in the Semester Review can be found in the online lesson.

Objectives
- Complete a Semester Review of grammar, usage, mechanics, and critical skills.

More Practice

Sentences, Sentence Combining, Capital Letters & Commas in a Letter, and Critical Skills
Go over students' results on the Semester Review and, if necessary, have them complete the appropriate review activities listed in the table online. Help students locate the activities and provide support as needed.

 The time students need to complete this activity will vary. Set aside enough time for students to complete all review activities, if they need to do so.

Objectives
- Evaluate Semester Review results and choose activities for more practice.

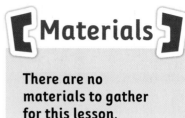

Semester Checkpoint: Sentences, Sentence Combining, Capital Letters & Commas in a Letter, and Critical Skills

Materials

There are no materials to gather for this lesson.

Lesson Overview

 **35 minutes**

Semester Checkpoint	Sentences, Sentence Combining, Capital Letters & Commas in a Letter, and Critical Skills
More Practice	Sentences, Sentence Combining, Capital Letters & Commas in a Letter, and Critical Skills

Online   35 minutes

Students will work online to complete the Semester Checkpoint and More Practice activities. Help students locate the activities and provide support as necessary.

Semester Checkpoint

Sentences, Sentence Combining, Capital Letters & Commas in a Letter, and Critical Skills

Students will complete an online Semester Checkpoint about sentences, sentence combining, using capital letters and commas in a letter, and critical skills. If necessary, read the directions to students.

TIP A full list of objectives covered in the Semester Checkpoint can be found in the online lesson.

Objectives
• Complete a Semester Checkpoint on grammar, usage, mechanics, and critical skills.

More Practice

Sentences, Sentence Combining, Capital Letters & Commas in a Letter, and Critical Skills

Go over students' results on the Semester Checkpoint and, if necessary, have them complete the appropriate review activities listed in the table online. If students scored less than 80 percent on the Semester Checkpoint, you may want them to retake the checkpoint after completing the review activities.

TIP The time students need to complete this activity will vary. Set aside enough time for students to review and to retake the Semester Checkpoint, if they need to do so. Students may retake the Semester Checkpoint immediately, but having them review and then retake it might be more effective.

Objectives
• Evaluate Semester Checkpoint results and choose activities for more practice.

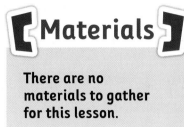

Semester Review: Nouns, Verbs, Parts of a Business Letter, and Critical Skills

Materials

There are no materials to gather for this lesson.

Lesson Overview

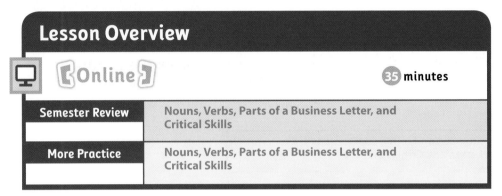

Online (35) minutes

Semester Review	Nouns, Verbs, Parts of a Business Letter, and Critical Skills
More Practice	Nouns, Verbs, Parts of a Business Letter, and Critical Skills

Online (35) minutes

Students will work online **independently** to review the grammar, usage, mechanics, and critical skills from this semester. Help students locate the online activities.

Semester Review

Nouns, Verbs, Parts of a Business Letter, and Critical Skills
Students will review what they have learned about nouns; verbs; the parts of a business letter; and other language, spelling, and vocabulary skills to review for the Semester Checkpoint.

TIP A full list of objectives covered in the Semester Review can be found in the online lesson.

Objectives
• Complete a Semester Review of grammar, usage, mechanics, and critical skills.

More Practice

Nouns, Verbs, Parts of a Business Letter, and Critical Skills
Go over students' results on the Semester Review and, if necessary, have them complete the appropriate review activities listed in the table online. Help students locate the activities and provide support as needed.

TIP The time students need to complete this activity will vary. Set aside enough time for students to complete all review activities, if they need to do so.

Objectives
• Evaluate Semester Review results and choose activities for more practice.

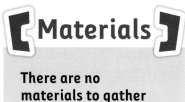
Semester Checkpoint: Nouns, Verbs, Parts of a Business Letter, and Critical Skills

[Materials]

There are no materials to gather for this lesson.

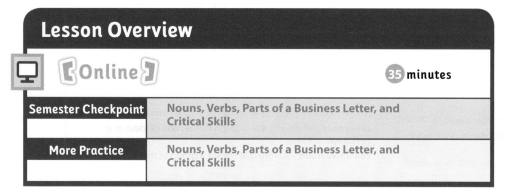

Lesson Overview

[Online]   **35** minutes

Semester Checkpoint	Nouns, Verbs, Parts of a Business Letter, and Critical Skills
More Practice	Nouns, Verbs, Parts of a Business Letter, and Critical Skills

 **[Online]** **35** minutes

Students will work online to complete the Semester Checkpoint and More Practice activities. Help students locate the activities and provide support as necessary.

Semester Checkpoint

Nouns, Verbs, Parts of a Business Letter, and Critical Skills
Students will complete an online Semester Checkpoint about nouns; verbs; parts of a business letter; and other language, spelling, and vocabulary skills. If necessary, read the directions to students.

TIP A full list of objectives covered in the Semester Checkpoint can be found in the online lesson.

 Objectives
• Complete a Semester Checkpoint on grammar, usage, mechanics, and critical skills.

More Practice

Nouns, Verbs, Parts of a Business Letter, and Critical Skills
Go over students' results on the Semester Checkpoint and, if necessary, have them complete the appropriate review activities listed in the table online. If students scored less than 80 percent on the Semester Checkpoint, you may want them to retake the checkpoint after completing the review activities.

TIP The time students need to complete this activity will vary. Set aside enough time for students to review and to retake the Semester Checkpoint, if they need to do so. Students may retake the Semester Checkpoint immediately, but having them review and then retake it might be more effective.

 Objectives
• Evaluate Semester Checkpoint results and choose activities for more practice.

 Reward: When students score 80 percent or above on both Semester Checkpoints, add a sticker for this unit on the My Accomplishments chart.

K¹² Language Arts Purple Keywords

abbreviation – the shortened form of a word or phrase

abstract noun – a word that names an idea

action verb – a word that shows action

adjective – a word that describes a noun or a pronoun

adverb – a word that describes a verb, an adjective, or another adverb

adverb of manner – an adverb that answers the question, "How?"

adverb of place – an adverb that answers the question, "Where?"

adverb of time – an adverb that answers the question, "When?"

alliteration – the use of words with the same or close to the same beginning sounds

almanac – a book that comes out each year with facts about many topics

alphabetical order – a sequence according to position in the alphabet; for example, in alphabetical order, *at* comes before *bat*, which comes before *cat*

antecedent – the noun or pronoun that a pronoun points back to

antonym – a word that means the opposite of another word

article – the adjective *a*, *an*, or *the*

atlas – a book of maps

audience – a writer's readers

author – a writer

author's purpose – the reason the author wrote a text: to entertain, to inform, to express an opinion, or to persuade

autobiography – the story of a person's life written by that person

being verb – a verb that does not express action; for example, *am, is, are, was, were*

bibliography card – a note card on which one writes the source of a fact

biography – the story of someone's life written by another person

body – the main text of a piece of writing

body (of a friendly letter) – the main text of a friendly letter

book review – a piece of writing that gives an opinion about a book and tells about it

brainstorming – before writing, a way for the writer to come up with ideas

business letter – a letter written to an organization or a person at a business

call number – a number given to each item held by a library

caption – writing printed with a picture that describes or explains the picture

card catalog – usually offered online, a record of a library's holdings in alphabetical order by title, author, and subject

case – the form of a noun or pronoun based on its use in a sentence

cause – the reason something happens

character – a person or animal in a story

chronological order – a way to organize that puts details in time order

citation – a note that says where the author found a specific piece of information

clarity – of writing, the quality of being clear and easy to understand

clause – a group of words that has a subject and a verb

climax – the turning point in a story

closing (of a business letter) – the part of a business letter that follows the body text, containing a phrase such as "Sincerely" or "Yours truly"

closing (of a friendly letter) – the part of a friendly letter that follows the body; for example, *Your friend* or *Love*

cluster – a type of graphic organizer in which words and phrases about a topic are jotted down and connected

coherence – of writing, the smooth connection of ideas in a paragraph or essay

collective noun – a word that means a group of things but is usually singular

comma mistake – a mistake that occurs when two sentences are joined only with a comma

command – a kind of sentence that gives an order or makes a request

common noun – a word that names any person, place, thing, or idea

comparative form – the form of an adjective or adverb used to compare two things

compare – to explain how two or more things are alike

comparison – a look at how two things are alike

complement – a word that completes the meaning of a verb

complete predicate – the verb in a sentence and all the words that belong with and describe the verb

complete sentence – a group of words that tells a complete thought

complete subject – the part of the sentence that tells whom or what the sentence is about

complex sentence – a sentence that has one independent part and at least one dependent part

compound antecedent – two or more words a pronoun points back to

compound noun – a noun made up of two or more words

compound predicate – two or more predicates that have the same subject

compound sentence – a sentence that has at least two independent parts

compound subject – two or more subjects that have the same predicate

compound verb – two or more verbs with the same subject

compound word – a word made from two smaller words

comprehension – understanding

computer catalog – an online record of a library's holdings; also *card catalog*

concluding sentence – the last sentence of a paragraph; often summarizes the paragraph

conclusion – a decision made about something not stated, using information provided and what is already known (Literature & Comprehension)

conclusion – the final paragraph of a written work (Writing Skills: Composition)

concrete noun – a word that names a physical person, place, or thing

conflict – a problem or issue that a character faces in a story

conjunction – a word used to join parts of a sentence, such as *and*, *but*, and *or*

consequence – what happens because of an action or event

content – the information or ideas in a piece of writing

context clue – a word or phrase in a text that helps you figure out the meaning of an unknown word

contraction – a shortened word or words where an apostrophe replaces missing letters

contrast – to explain how two or more things are different

coordinating conjunction – one of seven words—*and, but, for, nor, or, so, yet*—that connect two independent clauses

couplet – two successive lines of poetry that work together and often rhyme

declarative sentence – a group of words that makes a statement

definition – a statement that tells what a word means

demonstrative adjective – one of four describing words—*this, that, these, those*—that point out an object or objects

dependent clause – a group of words that has a subject and a verb but cannot stand alone as a sentence

dependent part – about a sentence, a group of words that has a subject and verb but cannot stand on its own as a sentence

description – writing that uses words that show how something looks, sounds, feels, tastes, or smells.
Example: The sky is a soft, powdery blue, and the golden sun feels warm on my face.

descriptive adjective – a word that describes a noun or a pronoun

detail – a fact or description that tells more about a topic

diagram – a drawing or design that shows how pieces of information are related

dialect – a way of speaking that is particular to a certain group of people, place, or time

dialogue – the words that characters say in a written work

dictionary – a reference work made up of words with their definitions, in alphabetical order

direct quotation – the exact words of a speaker or writer

domain name – the part of an Internet address stating the site's general type, such as .com, .org, .edu, or .gov.

draft – an early effort at a piece of writing, not the finished work

drafting – of writing, the stage or step of the process in which the writer first writes the piece

drama – another word for *play*

effect – the result of a cause

encyclopedia – a reference work made up of articles on many topics, usually in alphabetical order

evidence – a specific detail, such as a fact or expert opinion, that supports a reason

example – a specific instance of something, used to illustrate an idea

exclamation – a kind of sentence that shows strong feeling

exclamatory sentence – a group of words that shows strong feeling

fable – a story that teaches a lesson and may contain animal characters

fact – something that can be proven true

fairy tale – a folktale with magical elements

fantasy – a story with characters, settings, or other elements that could not really exist

feedback – information given to help improve a piece of writing

fiction – make-believe stories

fictional narrative – a term often used for *short story*

figurative language – words that describe something by comparing it to something completely different
Example: Rain fell in buckets and the streets looked like rivers.

first-person narrator – a narrator who tells a story from the first-person point of view

first-person point of view – the telling of a story by a character in that story, using pronouns such as *I, me*, and *we*

focus – the direction or emphasis of a piece of writing; writing with a focus sticks to the main idea and does not include lots of ideas that are unrelated

folktale – a story, which usually teaches a lesson important to a culture, that is passed down through many generations

foreshadowing – hints inside a piece of writing about what will happen later in the story

fragment – an incomplete sentence that begins with a capital letter and ends with a punctuation mark

freewriting – a way for a writer to pick a topic and write as much as possible about it within a set time limit

friendly letter – a kind of letter used to share thoughts, feeling, and news

future tense – a form of a verb that names an action that will happen later

gender – the masculine, feminine, or neuter form of a noun or pronoun

generalization – a statement meant to describe a whole group
Example: Everyone loves a parade.

glossary – a list of important terms and their meanings that is usually found in the back of a book

graphic – a picture, photograph, map, diagram, or other image

graphic organizer – a visual device, such as a diagram or chart, that helps a writer plan a piece of writing

greeting – the part of a letter that begins with the word *Dear* followed by a person's name; also called the *salutation*

heading – a title within the body of a text that tells the reader something important about a section of the text (Literature & Comprehension)

heading – the first part of a letter that has the writer's address and the date (Writing Skills: Composition)

helping verb – a word that works with the main verb to show action; for example, *has, have, will, do, did, can*

hero – a character who must struggle to overcome problems in a story and whose actions and traits are admired by others

historical fiction – a story set in a historical time period that includes facts about real people, places, and events, but also contains fictional elements that add dramatic interest to the story

homophone – a word that sounds the same as another word but has a different spelling and meaning

hook – a surprising idea or group of words used to grab the reader's attention, usually at the beginning of a work

how-to paper – a paragraph or essay that explains how to do or make something

hyperbole – exaggeration
Example: Steve was so hungry he could've eaten 50 steak dinners.

idiom – a group of words that does not actually mean what it says; for example, *raining cats and dogs, a month of Sundays*

illustration – a drawing

illustrator – the person who draws the pictures that go with a story

imagery – language that helps readers imagine how something looks, sounds, smells, feels, or tastes

imperative sentence – a group of words that gives a command or makes a request

independent clause – a group of words that has a subject and a verb and can stand alone as a sentence

independent part – about a sentence, a group of words that has a subject and a verb and can stand on its own as a sentence

index – an alphabetical list at the end of a book or magazine that tells the pages where a subject or name can be found

infer – to use clues to make a guess

inference – a guess that readers make using the clues that authors give them in a piece of writing

informative essay – a kind of writing that informs or explains

inside address – the part of a business or formal letter that comes after the heading and before the greeting, made up of the name and address of the person to whom the letter is written

intensive pronoun – a pronoun used for emphasis, but not necessary to the meaning of the sentence
Example: I *myself* don't agree with that statement.

interjection – a word (or words) that expresses strong feeling

Internet – a global communications system of linked computer networks

interrogative sentence – a group of words that asks a question

introduction – the first paragraph of an essay, identifying the topic and stating the main idea

introductory element – a word, phrase, or clause that begins a sentence

introductory sentence – the first sentence in a piece of writing

inverted order – of a sentence, order in which the verb comes before the subject

invitation – a kind of personal letter or a form in which the writer invites someone to attend a party or other special occasion

irregular verb – a verb that does not add –d or –ed to the present form to make the past and the past participle

journal – a notebook where a writer regularly records experiences and ideas

journal entry – a response to a specific prompt or an instance of recording one's thoughts and experiences

keyboarding – using a word processing program to produce a piece of writing

legend – a story that is passed down for many years to teach the values of a culture; a legend may or may not contain some true events or people

limiting adjective – an adjective that is a number or an amount; for example, *seven, two, few, several*

line – a row of words in a poem

literal meaning – following the usual, or exact, meaning of words

literature – made-up stories, true stories, poems, and plays

logical order – a way to organize that groups details in a way that makes sense

main character – an important person, animal, or other being who is central to the plot

main clause – another name for an independent clause

main idea – the most important point the author makes; it may be stated or unstated

map key – a guide to what the symbols on a map mean

media – all the ways by which something can be shown, shared, or expressed

metaphor – a figure of speech that compares two unlike things, without using the word *like* or *as*
Example: The cat's eyes were emeralds shining in the night.

modifier – a word or phrase that describes another word

monologue – lines spoken in a play to show that a character is thinking or talking to himself

mood – the emotions or feelings conveyed in a literary work

moral – the lesson of a story, particularly a fable

myth – a story that explains how something came to be and that usually contains magical figures as characters

mythology – all the myths of one group of people

narrative – a kind of writing that tells a story

narrator – the teller of a story

nominative case – the form of a noun or a pronoun used as a subject or a predicate nominative

nonfiction – writings about true things

nonliteral meaning – a figure of speech; a word or phrase that exaggerates or changes the usual meaning of the word or words in the phrase

noun – a word that names a person, place, thing, or idea

novel – a fictional story of length

number – the form of a word that shows if it is singular or plural

object – a noun or pronoun that follows a preposition or an action verb

objective case – the form of a noun or pronoun used as a direct object, indirect object, or object of a preposition

object of a preposition – a noun or a pronoun that follows a preposition and completes its meaning

object pronoun – a pronoun in the objective case; for example, *me, him, her, us, them*

onomatopoeia – the use of words that show sounds; for example, *moo, woof, quack, squash*

opinion – something that a person thinks or believes, but which cannot be proven to be true

order of importance – a way to organize that presents details from least to most important, or from most to least important

order words – words that connect ideas or a series of steps, or create a sequence, such as *first, next, later, finally*

organization – of a piece of writing, the way the ideas are arranged

outline – an organized list of topics in an essay

pace – the speed, and the change of speeds, of a speaker's delivery

paired passages – a set of passages that are related in some way

paragraph – a group of sentences about one topic

paragraph outline – a list of paragraph topics in an essay

paraphrase – to restate information in one's own words

part of speech – the category that words belong to according to how they are used in a sentence, such as *noun, verb,* and *adjective*

past participle – the principal part of the verb used to form the perfect tenses

past tense – the form of the verb that tells what has already happened

pattern of organization – the order by which details are arranged

period fiction – a fictional story set in a historical time period that depicts how people lived and acted during the time

personal narrative – an essay about a personal experience of the writer

personal pronoun – a word that takes the place of one of more nouns; the personal pronouns are *I, me, you, he, him, she, her, it, we, us, they,* and *them*

personification – giving human qualities to something that is not human
Example: The thunder shouted from the clouds.

perspective – the way someone sees the world

persuasive essay – an essay in which the writer tries to convince readers to agree with a stand on an issue

phrase – a word group that acts as one part of speech; for example, an adjective phrase or an adverb phrase

plagiarism – use of another person's words without giving that person credit as a source

plot – what happens in a story; the sequence of events

plural noun – a word that names more than one person, place, thing, or idea

poem – a piece of poetry

poet – one who writes poetry

poetry – writing that uses language, sound, and rhythm to make readers feel, experience, or imagine something

point of view – the perspective a story is told from

positive form – the form of an adjective or adverb without any special ending

possessive case – the form of a noun or a pronoun that shows ownership

possessive noun – the form of a noun that shows ownership

possessive pronoun – the form of a pronoun that shows ownership

predicate – the verb or verb phrase in a sentence

prediction – a guess about what might happen that is based on information in a story and what you already know

prefix – a word part with its own meaning that can be added to the beginning of a base word or root to make a new word with a different meaning

preposition – a word that begins a phrase that ends with a noun or pronoun
Examples: In the phrases "over the bridge" and "to me," the words *over* and *to* are prepositions.

prepositional phrase – a group of words that begins with a preposition and usually ends with the noun or a pronoun that is the object of the preposition

presentation – an oral report, usually with visuals

present tense – the verb form that tells what is happening now

prewriting – the stage or step of writing in which a writer chooses a topic, gathers ideas, and plans what to write

principal part – one of four basic verb forms—present, present participle, past, past participle

problem – an issue a character must solve in a story

process – a series of steps that explains how to do something

process paper – a paragraph or essay that explains how to do something

pronoun – a word that takes the place of one or more nouns

pronoun–antecedent agreement – the way a pronoun and its antecedent match in number and gender

proofreading – the stage or step of the writing process in which the writer checks for errors in grammar, punctuation, capitalization, and spelling

proper noun – the name of a particular person, place, thing, or idea; proper nouns begin with a capital letter

publishing – the stage or step of the writing process in which the writer makes a clean copy of the piece and shares it

purpose – the reason for writing

question – a kind of sentence that asks something

quotation – a report of exact words spoken or written, usually placed within quotation marks

quotation marks – punctuation that encloses a quotation, or the exact words of a speaker or writer

realistic fiction – a made-up story that has no magical elements

reason – a statement that explains why something is or why it should be

reference – a work that contains useful information for a writer such as an encyclopedia, a dictionary, or a website

reflexive pronoun – a word that refers back to another noun or pronoun in the sentence and is necessary to the meaning of the sentence
Example: The politicians voted *themselves* a pay raise.

regular verb – a verb that adds –*d* or –*ed* to the present form to make the past and the past participle

research – to find information through study rather than through personal experience

research report – a type of essay based mainly on the author's research

return address – the name and address of the sender, written in the upper left corner of an envelope

revising – the stage or step of the writing process in which the writer rereads and edits the draft, correcting errors and making changes in content or organization that improve the piece

rhyme – the use of words that end with the same sounds; for example, *cat* and *hat* rhyme

rhyme scheme – the pattern of rhymes made by the last sounds in the lines of a poem, shown by a different letter of the alphabet to represent each rhyme

rubric – the criteria used to evaluate a piece of writing

run-on – two or more sentences that have been joined without a conjunction or proper punctuation

salutation (of a business letter) – the greeting of a business letter, which usually says, "Dear (name of recipient)"; it is followed by a colon

salutation (of a friendly letter) – the greeting of a letter, which usually says, "Dear (name of recipient),"

search engine – software that searches for websites, usually by keywords

second-person point of view – the telling of a story, or addressing a piece of writing, directly to the audience, using the second-person pronoun *you*

sensory detail – descriptive detail that appeals to any of the five senses—sight, hearing, touch, smell, or taste

sensory language – language that appeals to the five senses

sentence – a group of words that tells a complete thought

sentence combining – joining two sentences that have similar parts into one sentence

sentence expanding – adding details, such as descriptive words and phrases, to sentences

sequence – the order in which things happen

setting – when and where a story takes place

shades of meaning – small differences in meaning between similar words or phrases

showing language – words used to create pictures in the reader's mind, rather than words that merely tell what happened
Example: The sun blazed on the street, and my bare feet sizzled like a frying egg each time I took a step.
[as opposed to] The sun was hot, and my bare feet burned each time I took a step.

sidebar – a short text within a larger text that tells something related but not necessary to the main story

signature (of a business letter) – the part of a business letter following the closing, consisting of the writer's signature above the writer's typed name

signature (of a friendly letter) – the end of a letter where the writer writes his or her name

simile – a comparison between two things using the word *like* or *as*
Example: I didn't hear him come in because he was as quiet as a mouse.

simple predicate – the verb of a sentence without any of its modifiers, objects, or complements

simple sentence – a sentence that is one independent part, a group of words with one subject and one verb that express a complete thought

simple subject – the subject noun or pronoun without any of its modifiers

singular noun – a word that names one person, place, thing, or idea

solution – how a character solves a problem in a story

source – a provider of information; a book, a historical document, online materials, and an interviewee are all sources

spatial order – a way to organize that arranges details by their location

speaker – the narrator of a poem

speaker tag – the part of a dialogue that identifies who is speaking

stanza – a group of lines in a poem

statement – a kind of sentence that tells something

story map – a kind of a graphic organizer that helps a writer plan a story

structure – the way a piece of writing is organized

style – the words the writer chooses and the way the writer arranges the words into sentences

subject – a word or words that tell whom or what the sentence is about

subject pronoun – a pronoun used as a subject or predicate nominative

subject–verb agreement – the way a subject and verb match when both are singular or both are plural

subordinate clause – a group of words that has a subject and a verb but cannot stand alone as a sentence; also called a *dependent clause*

subordinating conjunction – a word that is used to introduce a dependent clause

suffix – a word part added to the end of a base word or root that changes the meaning or part of speech of a word

summarize – to tell in order the most important ideas or events of a text (Literature & Comprehension)

summarize – to restate briefly the main points of a text (Writing Skills: Composition)

summary – a short retelling that includes only the most important ideas or events of a text

superlative form – the form of an adjective or adverb that compares more than two things

supporting details – the sentences that give information about the main idea or topic sentence

supporting paragraphs (body) – a series of paragraphs that give information to support the thesis of an essay

suspense – uncertainty about what will happen

symbol – an object that stands for or represents something else; for example, a heart is a symbol of love

symbolism – the use of symbols in writing

synonym – a word that means the same, or almost the same, as another word

table of contents – a list at the start of a book that gives the titles of the book's stories, poems, articles, chapters, or nonfiction pieces and the pages where they can be found

tense – the time that verbs show, such as present, future, or past

text feature – part of a text that helps a reader locate information and determine what is most important; some examples are the title, table of contents, headings, pictures, and glossary

thank-you letter – a kind of friendly letter in which the writer thanks someone for something

theme – the author's message or big idea

thesaurus – a reference work that gives synonyms and antonyms for words

thesis – the most important point, or main idea, of an essay

thesis statement – the sentence that states the main idea of an essay

third-person point of view – the telling of a story by someone outside of the action, using the third-person pronouns *he*, *she*, and *they*

time line – a line showing dates and events in the order that they happened

time order – the arrangement of ideas according to when they happened

tone – the author's feelings toward the subject and characters of a text (Literature & Comprehension)

tone – a speaker's attitude as shown by his or her voice (Writing Skills: Composition)

tone – the writer's attitude toward the topic or subject (Writing Skills: Composition)

topic – the subject of a text (Literature & Comprehension)

topic – the subject of a piece of writing (Writing Skills: Composition)

topic sentence – the sentence that expresses the main idea of the paragraph

trait – a quality of a person or character

transition – a word or phrase that connects ideas

unity – when all sentences in a paragraph or all paragraphs in an essay support the main idea

URL – the Internet address of a website; stands for *uniform resource locator*

verb – a word that shows action or a state of being

verb phrase – a main verb and one or more helping verbs

villain – a bad or evil character who often works against the hero of a story

visual – a graphic, picture, or photograph

visualization – a picture of something in one's mind

voice – the way a piece of writing sounds

volume – how loud or soft a speaker's voice is

website – a place on the Internet devoted to a specific organization, group, or individual

Works Cited page – a list of sources cited in the text of a research report

writer's craft – the techniques a writer uses and the decisions a writer makes to develop an essay

writing prompt – a sentence or sentences that ask for a particular kind of writing